The Pre-K Debates

The Pre-K Debates

Current Controversies and Issues

edited by

Edward Zigler, Ph.D.
Yale University
New Haven, Connecticut

Walter S. Gilliam, Ph.D.
Yale School of Medicine
New Haven, Connecticut

and

W. Steven Barnett, Ph.D.
National Institute for Early Education Research
Rutgers, The State University of New Jersey
New Brunswick

·PAUL·H·
BROOKES
PUBLISHING Co.®

Baltimore • London • Sydney

Paul H. Brookes Publishing Co.
Post Office Box 10624
Baltimore, Maryland 21285-0624
USA

www.brookespublishing.com

Copyright © 2011 by Paul H. Brookes Publishing Co., Inc.
All rights reserved.

"Paul H. Brookes Publishing Co." is a registered trademark of
Paul H. Brookes Publishing Co., Inc.

Classroom Assessment Scoring System and CLASS are trademarks of Robert C. Pianta.

Typeset by Aptara, Inc., Falls Church, Virginia.
Manufactured in the United States of America by
Sheridan Books, Inc., Chelsea, Michigan.

Library of Congress Cataloging-in-Publication Data

The pre-K debates : current controversies and issues / edited by Edward Zigler, Walter S. Gilliam, and W. Steven
    Barnett.
        p.   cm.
    Includes bibliographical references and index.
    ISBN-13: 978-1-59857-183-7 (pbk.)
    ISBN-10: 1-59857-183-4 (pbk.)
    1. Education, Preschool—Curricula—Standards—United States.   2. Curriculum planning—Standards—United
States.   3. Head Start programs—United States.   I. Zigler, Edward, 1930-   II. Gilliam, Walter S.   III. Barnett,
W. Steven.
LB1140.4.P73 2011
372.210973—dc23   2011017969

British Library Cataloguing in Publication data are available from the British Library.

2015   2014   2013   2012   2011

10   9   8   7   6   5   4   3   2   1

Contents

DMACC ECE
964 6502

About the Editors

Edward Zigler, Ph.D., Sterling Professor of Psychology, Emeritus, Yale University, and Director Emeritus of the Edward Zigler Center in Child Development and Social Policy. Dr. Zigler was a member of the National Planning and Steering Committee of Project Head Start. In 1970, he was named by President Nixon to become the first Director of the Office of Child Development (now the Administration on Children, Youth and Families) and Chief of the U.S. Children's Bureau. While in Washington, D.C., Dr. Zigler was responsible for administering the nation's Head Start program and led efforts to conceptualize and mount other innovative programs such as Home Start, Education for Parenthood, the Child Development Associate, and the Child and Family Resource Program.

Walter S. Gilliam, Ph.D., Associate Professor of Child Psychiatry and Psychology, Yale School of Medicine, 230 South Frontage Road, Post Office Box 207900, New Haven, Connecticut 06520. Dr. Gilliam is the Director of Yale's Edward Zigler Center in Child Development and Social Policy. His research involves policies regarding early childhood education and child care, ways to improve the quality of early childhood services, the impact of early childhood education programs on children's school readiness, and effective methods for reducing classroom behavior problems and the incidence of preschool expulsion.

W. Steven Barnett, Ph.D., Board of Governors Professor and Co-director of the National Institute for Early Education Research, Rutgers, The State University of New Jersey, 120 Albany Street, Suite 500, New Brunswick, New Jersey 08901. Dr. Barnett's research includes studies of the economics of early care and education, including costs and benefits, the long-term effects of preschool programs on children's learning and development, and the distribution of educational opportunities. He earned his Ph.D. in economics at the University of Michigan and got his start in the early childhood field working on the Perry Preschool Study at the HighScope Educational Research Foundation.

About the Contributors

Debra J. Ackerman, Ph.D., Associate Director, Understanding Teaching Quality Center, Rosedale Road, MS 02-T, Princeton, New Jersey 08541. Dr. Ackerman is an education policy researcher. Her work focuses on the effects of policies and program elements on teachers' practice and students' learning outcomes.

Sandra J. Bishop-Josef, Ph.D., Assistant Director, the Edward Zigler Center in Child Development and Social Policy, Child Study Center, Yale School of Medicine, 310 Prospect Street, New Haven, Connecticut 06511. Dr. Bishop-Josef's research interests include child maltreatment, child and family services, and the application of research to social policy.

Barbara T. Bowman, M.A., Irving B. Harris Professor of Child Development, Erikson Institute, 451 North LaSalle Street, Chicago, Illinois 60654. Dr. Bowman is one of the founders of the Erikson Institute and served as its president from 1994 to 2001. In addition, Professor Bowman is Chief Officer in the Office of Early Childhood Education, Chicago Public Schools, where she administers a program for 30,000 preschool children, including 24,000 3- and 4-year-olds in an educational program and 5,000 infants and toddlers in a prevention program.

of the Infant Language Laboratory at Temple University and Cofounder of The Ultimate Block Party. Among her awards are the Urie Bronfenbrenner Award for Lifetime Contribution to Developmental Psychology. Her research in the areas of early language development, literacy, and infant cognition resulted in 11 books and more than 100 publications.

Marilou Hyson, Ph.D., Consultant, Early Childhood Development and Education, Box 592, Stockbridge, Massachusetts 01262. Dr. Hyson is Affiliate Faculty Member in Applied Developmental Psychology at George Mason University. Formerly Editor-in-Chief of *Early Childhood Research Quarterly* and Associate Executive Director for Professional Development with the National Association for the Education of Young Children, Dr. Hyson has consulted in Vietnam, Indonesia, Bangladesh, and Bhutan through the World Bank and Save the Children.

Sharon Lynn Kagan, Ed.D., Virginia and Leonard Marx Professor of Early Childhood and Family Policy and Co-director of the National Center for Children and Families, Teachers College, Columbia University, 525 West 120th Street, Box 226, New York, New York 10027. Dr. Kagan is Professor Adjunct at Yale University's Child Study Center. Through her leadership in the field and her 15 books and 250 articles, Dr. Kagan has helped shape early childhood practice and policies in the United States and in countries throughout the world.

J. Ronald Lally, Ed.D., Co-director, WestEd Center for Child & Family Studies, 180 Harbor Drive, Suite 112, Sausalito, California 94965. An expert on early development, Dr. Lally has directed the work of WestEd's Program for Infant/Toddler Care (PITC) since 1985. He is one of the founders and a board member of ZERO TO THREE: National Center for Infants, Toddlers, and Families. For 40 years, working with state and federal governments, he has charted the direction of quality infant-toddler child care in the United States and abroad.

David Lawrence, Jr., President, The Early Childhood Initiative Foundation, 3250 SW Third Avenue, Miami, Florida 33129. Mr. Lawrence is University Scholar for Early Childhood Development and Readiness at the University of Florida. He is a nationally known journalist who retired in 1999 as publisher of *The Miami Herald* to devote his energies toward building a movement on behalf of high-quality early childhood development, care, and education.

John M. Love, Ph.D., President, Ashland Institute for Early Childhood Science and Policy, 1016 Canyon Park Drive, Ashland, Oregon 97520. Dr. Love received his Ph.D. in child behavior and development from the University of Iowa and retired in 2010 after 18 years with Mathematica Policy Research, Inc., in Princeton, New Jersey, where he directed the national evaluation of the Early Head Start program. He currently consults with various agencies on early childhood program evaluation issues and is developing a program of research with the Ashland Institute.

Alison Lutton, M.Ed., Senior Director of Higher Education Accreditation and Program Support, National Association for the Education of Young Children, 1313 L Street NW, Suite 500, Washington, DC 20005. Ms. Lutton's 30-year career in early childhood education includes direct work with children and families, consulting, community college faculty, and administrative positions. She has 20 years of experience in the development of early childhood professional standards and accreditation systems.

Kathleen McCartney, Ph.D., Dean, Harvard Graduate School of Education, 13 Appian Way, Longfellow Hall Room 101, Cambridge, Massachusetts 02138. Dr. McCartney's research program concerns early experience and development, particularly with respect to child care, early childhood education, and poverty. In 2009, she received the Distinguished Contribution Award for the Society for Research in Child Development.

Genevieve Okada, M.A., Doctoral Student of Anthropology, University of California, San Diego, 9500 Gilman Drive, La Jolla, California 92093. Ms. Okada received her bachelor of arts degree in psychology from the University of California, Berkeley, and her master's degree in the psychology of parenthood from New York University, where she worked closely with Dr. C. Cybele Raver and Dr. J. Lawrence Aber. As a doctoral student in anthropology at the University of California, San Diego, she is specializing in psychological anthropology, and her primary research interests include parenting, child development, race, ethnicity, religion, and identity.

Robert C. Pianta, Ph.D., Dean, Curry School of Education, University of Virginia, 417 Emmet Street South, Post Office Box 400260, Charlottesville, Virginia 22904. Dr. Pianta is the Novartis Professor of Education and Director of University of Virginia's Center for Advanced Study of Teaching and Learning. With his research team, he has developed the Classroom Assessment Scoring System™ (CLASS™; Paul H. Brookes Publishing Co., 2008), a system to measure classroom quality in preschool through 12th grade that has been tested and proven effective in several national studies and is being utilized by every Head Start program in the country.

Helen Raikes, Ph.D., Willa Cather Professor and Professor, Child, Youth and Family Studies, University of Nebraska–Lincoln, 247 Mabel Lee Hall, Lincoln, Nebraska 68588. Dr. Raikes served as Society for Research in Child Development Executive Policy Fellow at the Administration for Children and Families, providing team leadership for initiating the Early Head Start Research and Evaluation Project. Her research emphasis is on children at risk, particularly infants and toddlers.

C. Cybele Raver, Ph.D., Professor, Department of Applied Psychology, The Steinhardt School of Culture, Education and Human Development, New York University, Kimball Hall, 246 Greene Street, Room 403W, New York, New York 10003. Dr. Raver directs New York University's Institute of Human Development and Social Change. Her research focuses on self-regulation and school readiness among young children facing economic hardship, and she examines the mechanisms that support children's positive outcomes in the policy contexts of welfare reform and early educational intervention.

Arthur J. Reynolds, Ph.D., Professor, Institute of Child Development, University of Minnesota, Twin Cities, 51 East River Parkway, Minneapolis, Minnesota, 55455. Dr. Reynolds is Director of the Chicago Longitudinal Study, one of the largest and most extensive studies of the effects of early childhood intervention. He also studies the effects of early childhood intervention on children's development from school entry to early adulthood and the family and school's influences on children's educational success.

Art Rolnick, Ph.D., Senior Fellow, Humphrey School of Public Affairs, 301 19th Avenue South, Minneapolis, Minnesota 55455. Dr. Rolnick is Co-director of the Human Capital Research Collaborative at the Humphrey School of Public Affairs, the University of Minnesota, and is working to advance multidisciplinary research on child development and social policy. He previously served at the Federal Reserve Bank of Minneapolis as Senior Vice President and Director of Research and as Associate Economist with the Federal Open Market Committee—the monetary policy-making body for the Federal Reserve System.

Elizabeth Rose, Ph.D., Library Director, Fairfield Museum and History Center, 370 Beach Road, Fairfield, Connecticut 06824. Dr. Rose is a historian with interests in family history, education, and social policy. She is the author of *The Promise of Preschool: From Head Start to Universal Pre-kindergarten* (Oxford University Press, 2010) and *A Mother's Job: The History of Day Care, 1890–1960* (Oxford University Press, 1999).

Lawrence J. Schweinhart, Ph.D., President, HighScope Educational Research Foundation, 600 North River Street, Ypsilanti, Michigan 48198. Dr. Schweinhart has been President of HighScope Educational Research Foundation since 2003 and a researcher there since 1975. His research has focused on evaluative research on the practices and effects of early childhood programs, especially the HighScope Perry Preschool Study.

Deborah Stipek, Ph.D., James Quillen Dean and Professor of Education, Stanford School of Education, 485 Lasuen Mall, Stanford University, Stanford, California 94305. Dr. Stipek received her doctorate in developmental psychology from Yale University. She served 10 of her 23 years at the University of California, Los Angeles, as Director of the Corinne Seeds University Elementary School and the Urban Education Studies Center and joined the Stanford School of Education as Dean and Professor of Education in January 2001.

Ruby Takanishi, Ph.D., President and CEO, Foundation for Child Development, 295 Madison Avenue, 40th Floor, New York, New York 10017. Dr. Takanishi works at the Foundation for Child Development, which initiated a 10-year commitment to promoting the integration of early learning programs with K–12 education reform in 2003. Her interest in how research on children's development can inform public policy and programs is a lifelong concern.

Judy A. Temple, Ph.D., Associate Professor of Public Affairs and Applied Economics, University of Minnesota, Twin Cities, Humphrey Institute of Public Affairs, 149 Humphrey Center, 301 19th Avenue S, Minneapolis, Minnesota 55455. Dr. Temple's research focuses on economic evaluations (including cost–benefit analyses) of education interventions. She is a co-principal investigator with the Chicago Longitudinal Study, which has followed more than 1,200 students from low-income neighborhoods from kindergarten into adulthood.

Sara D. Watson, Ph.D., Senior Officer, The Pew Charitable Trusts, 901 E Street NW, 10th Floor, Washington, DC 20004. Dr. Watson is Director of the Partnership for America's Economic Success. From 2001 to 2008, she managed Pew's Pre-K for All campaign. She has a master of public policy degree and a Ph.D. from Harvard University's John F. Kennedy School of Government.

Barry A.B. White, M.P.P., Research Fellow, Institute of Child Development, University of Minnesota, Twin Cities, 51 East River Parkway, Minneapolis, Minnesota, 55455. Mr. White is a research fellow at the Institute of Child Development, University of Minnesota. In general, his research involves calculating the costs and benefits of the Chicago Child-Parent Centers, one of the most extensive studies of the effects of early childhood intervention. Mr. White specializes in the use of benefit–cost analysis and related techniques to investigate the economic returns to early intervention for at-risk children. He is also interested in estimating the effects of early intervention on social and economic well-being throughout adulthood. Mr. White received his M.P.P. from the Humphrey School of Public Affairs, University of Minnesota.

Barbara A. Willer, Ph.D., Deputy Executive Director, National Association for the Education of Young Children (NAEYC), 1313 L Street NW, Suite 500, Washington, DC 20005. Dr. Willer oversees the Program Recognition and Support Division of NAEYC, which sets and monitors standards of quality for programs in early childhood education. NAEYC accredits and/or recognizes programs serving young children as well as professional preparation programs in institutions of higher education that meet its standards.

Daniel E. Witte, J.D., Director, Sutherland Institute's Center for Educational Progress, Crane Building, 307 West 200 South, Suite 5005, Salt Lake City, Utah 84101. Mr. Witte has a master's degree in organizational behavior, as well as an extensive background in issues related to parental liberty and educational choice. He has worked with the Utah Supreme Court; the U.S. Attorney's Office in the District of Utah; the Tenth and Seventh Federal Circuit Courts of Appeal; law firms in Korea and Puerto Rico; Senator Robert Bennett (Senate Banking Committee) in Washington, D.C.; the

Honorable Judge Alan E. Norris of the United States Circuit Court of Appeals for the Sixth Circuit; and various financial institutions as a commercial litigator and associate general counsel.

Martha Zaslow, Ph.D., Director, Office for Policy and Communications of the Society for Research in Child Development, 1313 L Street NW, Suite 140, Washington, DC 20005. Dr. Zaslow, a developmental psychologist, is Senior Scholar at Child Trends in Washington, D.C. Her research focuses on the utilization of early care and education and approaches to measuring and strengthening quality in these settings.

provided across a wide array of provider organizations (e.g., public schools, private schools, Head Start grantees, child care providers, other nonprofit agencies). Which programs are best equipped to provide a quality preschool experience to young children, and how can a system of early education best be created from the programmatic building blocks that currently exist?

Parts II and III include issues that do not fit neatly into debates, but they are important nonetheless. These topics address questions such as the following:

- How do we ensure quality and accountability in preschool programs? (Chapters 25–28)
- What should come before and after preschool? (Chapters 29–34)
- What lessons can be learned from state efforts to implement prekindergarten systems? (Chapters 35 and 36)
- What might be the dangers in overselling preschool as a magical elixir to cure all of the ails in our educational system? (Chapters 37 and 38)

The purpose of this book is not to settle these debates. Rather, it is to allow the interested reader an opportunity to better appreciate the differing perspectives and opinions, understand the reach and limits of the existing evidence in favor of each position, and form his or her own conclusion. As the French essayist Joseph Joubert (1754–1824) opined, "It is better to debate a question without settling it than to settle a question without debating it" (Lyttelton, 1899). With this in mind, this book is not intended to close any debates, but rather to open them up for greater illumination and wider participation. Enter the debaters.

An Overview of Preschool

STUDY QUESTIONS

- What types of programs have the most positive effects on later outcomes for children?

- To what degree are the following aspects of families—income, environment, genetics, quality of parenting—responsible for producing ability gaps?

- What are the three main arguments for Pew's campaign for universal pre-K?

CHAPTER 1
Effective Child Development Strategies

James J. Heckman

This chapter makes four points about designing effective child development strategies. The first point is that early intervention is effective, and the earlier it comes, the better. The second point is that a major channel through which early intervention programs operate is by producing noncognitive or "soft" skills. Soft skills are often neglected in economic and social policy forums. Policy makers need to rethink the way they evaluate the success and failure of child development programs. Focusing only on cognitive skills misses an important part of the story. The third point is that subsidies for early childhood programs should be targeted toward disadvantaged families. In light of stringency in budgets, programs should be subsidized only for the most disadvantaged families, where the measure of disadvantage is the quality of parenting. It is for children from such families that economic returns are the highest. Social efficiency is enhanced and inequality is reduced by targeting the most disadvantaged. The fourth point is that early childhood intervention efforts should not be conceived of as exclusively governmental programs. Engagement of nongovernmental entities and competition among providers at an assured level of quality will promote diversity and quality and enlarge the funding base to support such programs.

AMERICAN SOCIETY IS BECOMING POLARIZED AND LESS PRODUCTIVE

Since the 1980s, American society has polarized. A greater percentage of children is attending and graduating college. At the same time, a greater percentage is dropping out of secondary school, producing a growing underclass, neither working nor going to school (Heckman & LaFontaine, 2010). Seventy-five percent of American youth who apply to the military are ineligible to serve because of low cognitive capacities, criminal records, or obesity. Twenty percent of the U.S. work force has such a low rate of literacy that it cannot understand the instructions on a vial of pills (Heckman & Masterov, 2007). This chapter summarizes a body of literature that articulates a coherent approach to addressing these and related problems. That literature is rooted in the economics, psychology, and biology of human development (see Cunha & Heckman, 2007, 2008, 2009; Heckman, 2008; Heckman & Masterov, 2007).

A COHERENT APPROACH TO SKILL POLICY

My argument can be summarized by 18 points:

1. Many major economic and social problems such as crime, teenage pregnancy, obesity, high school dropout rates, and adverse health conditions can be traced to low levels of skill and ability in society.
2. In analyzing ability, society needs to recognize its multiple facets.
3. Current public policy discussions focus on promoting and measuring cognitive ability through IQ and achievement tests. For example, in the United States, the accountability standards in the No Child Left Behind Act of 2001 (PL 107-110) concentrate attention on achievement test scores, not evaluating a range of other factors that promote success in school and life.
4. Cognitive abilities are important determinants of socioeconomic success.
5. Socioemotional abilities, physical and mental health, perseverance, attention, motivation, and self-confidence are, too.
6. They contribute to performance in society at large and even help determine scores on the very tests that are used to monitor cognitive achievement.
7. Ability gaps between the advantaged and disadvantaged open up early in the lives of children.
8. Family environments of young children are major predictors of cognitive and socioemotional abilities, as well as crime, health, and obesity.
9. More than genetics is at work.
10. The evidence that documents the powerful role of early family influence on adult outcomes is a source of concern because family environments in the United States and many other countries around the world have deteriorated since the 1970s.

Chapter 1 draws on the author's joint work with Flavio Cunha, Seong Moon, Rodrigo Pinto, Peter Savelyev, and Sergio Urzua. This research was supported by the Committee for Economic Development through grants from the Pew Charitable Trusts and the Partnership for America's Economic Success, the JB & MK Pritzker Family Foundation, the Susan Thompson Buffett Foundation, and the Eunice Kennedy Shriver National Institute of Child Health and Human Development (Grant R01HD043411). The views expressed in this chapter are those of the author and not necessarily those of the funders listed here.

11. Experimental evidence on the effectiveness of early interventions in disadvantaged families is consistent with a large body of nonexperimental evidence that adverse family environments, especially adverse parenting, substantially impair child outcomes.

12. If society intervenes early enough, it can raise the cognitive and socioemotional abilities and the health of disadvantaged children.

13. Early interventions reduce inequality by promoting schooling, reducing crime, and reducing teenage pregnancy.

14. They also foster work-force productivity.

15. These interventions have high benefit–cost ratios and rates of return.

16. Early interventions have much higher economic returns than later interventions such as reduced pupil–teacher ratios, public job training, convict rehabilitation programs, adult literacy programs, tuition subsidies, expenditure on police, or a variety of other programs.

17. Life cycle skill formation is dynamic in nature. Skill begets skill; motivation begets motivation. If a child is not motivated and stimulated to learn and engage early on in life, the more likely it is that, when the child becomes an adult, he or she will fail in social and economic life. The longer society waits to intervene in the life cycle of a disadvantaged child, the more costly it is to remediate disadvantage. Similar dynamics appear to be at work in shaping child health and mental health.

18. A major refocus of policy is required to understand the life cycle of skill and health formation and the importance of the early years in creating inequality and opportunity, and in producing skills for the work force.

I now document some of the major points. Cunha and Heckman (2007, 2009) and Heckman (2008) present more comprehensive discussions.

THE IMPORTANCE OF COGNITIVE AND NONCOGNITIVE SKILLS

Recent research has shown that earnings, employment, labor force participation, college attendance, teenage pregnancy, participation in risky activities, compliance with health protocols, and participation in crime strongly depend on cognitive and noncognitive abilities. By noncognitive abilities I mean socioemotional regulation, delay of gratification, personality factors, and the ability to work with others.

Much public policy discussion focuses on cognitive test scores or "smarts." The No Child Left Behind Act in the United States focuses on achievement on a test administered at certain grades to measure the success or failure of schools. Yet, the body of evidence surveyed in Borghans, Duckworth, Heckman, and ter Weel (2008) showed that, as is intuitively obvious and commonsensical, much more than smarts is required for success in a number of domains of life. They documented the predictive power of motivation, sociability, the ability to work with others, attention, self-control, self-esteem, delay of gratification, and health in a variety of life outcomes.

The importance of noncognitive skills tends to be underrated in current policy discussions because these skills are thought to be hard to measure. In fact, they have been measured, and they predict success (see Heckman, Humphries, & Mader, 2011). Recent evidence shows that the workplace is increasingly oriented toward a greater valuation of social interaction and sociability (Borghans et al., 2008).

Cognitive and noncognitive ability are important determinants of schooling and socioeconomic success. In the United States and many countries around the world, schooling gaps across ethnic and income groups have more to do with ability deficits than family finances in the school-age years. (See the evidence in Cunha & Heckman, 2007, 2008.) Those with higher cognitive and noncognitive abilities are more likely to take postschool job training and to participate in civic life. They are less likely to be obese and are more likely to have greater physical and mental health. Cognitive and noncognitive skills are equally predictive of success in many aspects of life. (See Heckman, Stixrud, & Urzua, 2006.)

ABILITY GAPS ARE THE MAJOR REASON FOR THE SCHOOLING ACHIEVEMENT GAP

Controlling for ability measured at school age, in the United States minorities are more likely to attend college than others despite their lower family incomes. Deficits in college going between minority and majority groups are not caused by high tuition costs or family income at the age children decide to go to college (see Cameron & Heckman, 2001).

ABILITY GAPS OPEN UP AT EARLY AGES

Gaps in the abilities that play such an important role in determining diverse adult labor market and health outcomes open up at early ages across socioeconomic groups (Cunha, Heckman, Lochner, & Masterov, 2006). Schooling after the second grade plays only a minor role in alleviating these gaps. Schooling quality and school resources have relatively small effects on ability deficits and only marginally account for any divergence by age in test scores across children from different socioeconomic groups.

The evidence on the early emergence of gaps leaves open the question of which aspects of families are responsible for producing ability gaps. Are the gaps due to genes? To family environments? Family investment decisions? The evidence from the intervention studies suggests an important role for investments and family environments in determining adult capacities above and beyond genes and also in conjunction with genes (Cunha & Heckman, 2009; Heckman, 2008).

FAMILY ENVIRONMENTS

The evidence that family environments matter greatly in producing abilities is a source of concern because a greater fraction of American children is being born into disadvantaged families. This trend is occurring in many countries around the world. (See, e.g., Arias, Azuara, Bernal, Heckman, & Villarreal, 2009, for evidence on Mexico.) Measured by the quality of its parenting, American family life is under challenge. A divide is opening up in early family environments. Those born into disadvantaged environments receive relatively less stimulation and child development resources than those from advantaged families (see McLanahan, 2004). A main source of child disadvantage is the quality of parenting.

More educated women work more than in the past, but, at the same time, are spending more time in child development. Less educated women also work more but are not increasing their child investments. Children born into disadvantaged environments receive relatively less stimulation and child development resources than those from advantaged families, and the gap is growing over time. This creates persistence of inequality across generations through the mechanism of differentials in parenting. It raises an environmental version of concerns similar to those raised by the eugenics movement a century ago.

CRITICAL AND SENSITIVE PERIODS

Knudsen, Heckman, Cameron, and Shonkoff (2006) discussed the large body of evidence on sensitive and critical periods in human development. Different types of abilities appear to be manipulable at different ages. IQ scores become stable by approximately age 10, suggesting a sensitive period for their formation in children younger than 10 years (Schuerger & Witt, 1989). On average, the later that remediation is given to a disadvantaged child, the less effective it is. A lot of evidence suggests that the returns to adolescent education for the most disadvantaged and less able are lower than the returns for the more advantaged (Carneiro & Heckman, 2003). The available evidence suggests that for many skills and human capacities, later intervention for disadvantage may be possible, but it is much more costly than early remediation to achieve a given level of adult performance (Cunha, Heckman, & Schennach, 2010).

KEY POLICY ISSUES

From the point of view of social policy, the key question is how easy is it to remediate the effect of early disadvantage? How costly is it to delay addressing the problems raised by early disadvantage? How critical is investment in the early years and for what traits? What is the optimal timing for intervention to improve abilities?

What Programs Should Be Used?

Programs that target the early years seem to have the greatest promise. The Nurse-Family Partnership Program (Olds, 2002), the Abecedarian Program (Campbell, et al., 2002), and the HighScope Perry preschool program (Schweinhart et al., 2005) have been evaluated and show high returns. Programs with home visits affect the lives of the parents and create permanent changes in home environments that support the child after center-based interventions end. Programs that build self-control, character, and motivation and do not focus exclusively on cognition appear to be the most effective.

Who Should Provide the Programs?

In designing any early childhood program that aims to improve the cognitive and socioemotional skills of disadvantaged children, it is important to respect the sanctity of early family life and to respect cultural diversity. The goal of early childhood programs should be to create a base of productive skills and traits for disadvantaged children living in culturally diverse settings. By engaging private industry and other groups that draw in private resources, create community support, and represent diverse points of view, effective and culturally sensitive programs will be created.

Who Should Pay for Them?

One could make early childhood programs universal to avoid stigmatization. Universal programs would be much more expensive and create the possibility of deadweight losses whereby public programs displace private investments by families. One solution is to make the programs universal but to offer a sliding fee schedule to avoid deadweight losses.

Will the Programs Achieve High Levels of Compliance?

It is important to recognize potential problems with program compliance. Many successful programs change the values and motivation of the child. Some of these changes may run counter to the values of parents. There may be serious tensions between the needs of the child and the acceptance of interventions by the parent. Developing culturally diverse programs will help avoid such tensions. One cannot assume that there will be no conflict between the values of society as it seeks to develop the potential of a child and the values of the family, although the extent of such conflicts is not yet known.

SUMMARY

Many current social problems have their roots in ability deficits. Such deficits open up early in life and persist. They produce lifetime inequality and reduce productivity. Evidence from a variety of studies has shown that there are critical and sensitive periods for development. Sensitive periods come earlier in life for cognitive traits. They come later for noncognitive traits. This pattern is associated with slower development of the prefrontal cortex. Noncognitive traits stimulate production of cognitive traits and are major contributors to human performance. The powerful role of noncognitive traits and the possibilities of interventions to improve these traits are currently neglected in most public policy discussions.

Later-life investment is less effective if an adequate base has not been created in early life. A portfolio of investment weighted toward the early years is optimal. Society ignores this knowledge, devoting relatively more resources to adolescent remediation than to childhood prevention for children born into disadvantaged environments (Cunha & Heckman, 2009; Moon, 2010). Children from advantaged environments by and large receive substantial early investment, whereas children from disadvantaged environments typically do not. There is a strong case for public support for funding interventions in early childhood for disadvantaged children.

The appropriate measure of disadvantage is the quality of parenting, not income per se. Schools and tuition do not matter as much as is often thought. Interventions should be directed toward the malleable early years if society is to succeed in reducing inequality and promoting productivity in American society.

CHAPTER 2

The Right Policy at the Right Time

The Pew Prekindergarten Campaign

Sara D. Watson

In 2001, The Pew Charitable Trusts learned of an important strategy that could dramatically improve children's success but had been largely overlooked by policy makers: high-quality early education programs in the years just before kindergarten. Pew launched a new campaign to highlight the evidence and advance policies at the state and federal levels to provide voluntary, high-quality prekindergarten (pre-K) for every 3- and 4-year-old child.

Seven years later, the *Wall Street Journal* would call the pre-K movement "one of the most significant expansions in public education in the 90 years since World War I" (Solomon, 2007). With the help of hundreds of partners across the country building on decades of work by children's advocates, this movement is propelling the nation toward a future in which pre-K is no longer a luxury for the rich or a social service for the poor, but an essential part of a high-quality education for America's children. This chapter will answer two questions: How did this happen, and—even more important—how can we use the lessons learned to inform public debates on other policies essential to help children thrive? The momentum and experience from the pre-K campaign can inform new public debates on key issues facing states and the nation.

PEW'S APPROACH TO POLICY CHANGE

After 40 years of efforts to reform education at the local, state, and national levels, Pew wanted to see greater improvements in the system and in children's achievement. In 2000, Susan Urahn, then Director of Education, began to survey the field to identify a new course of action whereby Pew could inform substantial and lasting policy change. At the suggestion of Steven Barnett, an economist at Rutgers University, she examined the data on pre-K and realized that it could have a profound impact on children's school and life success. She also learned that despite decades of hard work by advocates, both foundation funding and policy makers' interest had not caught up to the research evidence on the benefits of high-quality early education.

Pre-K fit Pew's criteria for selecting issues around which it would build policy campaigns: rigorous, objective evidence of impact; bipartisan support; important yet manageable in scope and ripe for serious public debate. When these criteria align, Pew believes that an issue is most ready for serious consideration by policy makers and the public.

Although any major policy area will have myriad important aspects, policy making tends to be incremental. Pew's experience has shown that, when faced with a long list of legislative demands, most policy makers will throw up their hands and tell advocates to come back when they have narrowed their list. So, Pew's philosophy is to examine all the factors that affect an important goal and then select a sharp focus. The approach is to identify which specific policy within a given agenda—whether the environment, the economy, or consumer health—is most ripe for movement at a given time, push it as far as it will go, and when that window closes, carefully choose the next issue. This approach does not mean that other policies related to the larger goal are less important, only less ready. They should not be ignored, just prioritized over time based on what the nation is prepared to tackle.

At any one time, hundreds of important policy issues deserve attention, but only a few are ready for serious action. This generally requires a combination of enthusiastic leaders, compelling new data or events, and some deep shift in public sentiment. With respect to pre-K, several factors contributed to the "ripeness" of the policy: the growing body of research showing the importance of early brain development (e.g., Shonkoff & Phillips, 2000); decades of advocacy for child care funding; interest

Chapter 2 was previously published as Watson, S. (2010). *The right policy at the right time: The Pew pre-kindergarten campaign.* Washington, DC: Pew Center on the States. Reprinted by permission. Copyright © 2010 by Pew Charitable Trusts.

among some long-standing funders in the field; and the increasing understanding that many of the seeds of educational success (or failure) are sown in the earliest years. Pew's deliberations also were informed by the experiences of the three states (Georgia, New York, and Oklahoma) that had already made commitments to providing pre-K for all 4-year-olds. Among these, Georgia's program was particularly well known in the early childhood community.

On the other hand, the nation was still deeply ambivalent about public investment in out-of-home care for 3- and 4-year-old children, with opposition increasing with regard to even younger children. Policy makers and the public did not yet recognize pre-K as a powerful education reform rather than the last 2 years of child care before kindergarten.

Weighing all the risks, in the end, the combination of strong evidence of impact and the chance for Pew to make a difference convinced the organization in September 2001 to commit to a 7- to 10-year effort, assuming progress along the way indicated continued opportunity for success.

A NEW CAMPAIGN DESIGN

The Pew pre-K campaign was designed from the outset to work mainly at the state level, with attention to federal policy as opportunities arose. This approach reflected the dominant role states play in education, and it provided 50 different chances to make progress, rather than the single instance afforded by a focus on federal policy. In addition, Pew concentrated its initial efforts on states where a commitment to this new idea could provide a model for the rest of the country. Then, Pew served as the hub of a multifaceted campaign, designed at its simplest level to bring together both traditional and unlikely allies, fund good research, and make the data available and accessible to policy makers (Bushouse, 2009). The campaign infrastructure consists of three main elements: advocacy, research, and engaging a broad national constituency (see Figure 2.1).

Pre-K Now's State Campaigns & Selected Pew Initiative Results: 2002–2010

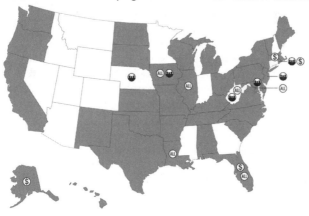

■ Pre-K Now Campaigns
□ No Pre-K Now Presence
ⓐ Enacted Pre-K for All Legislation[a]
◉ Added Pre-K to School Funding Formula
Ⓢ Provided First-Time State Pre-K Investments

Pre-K Now's work and Pew's national leadership paid dividends across the country in the form of increased investments in and access to state pre-k, improved overall program quality and smarter policy-making with respect to planning, funding, governance and implementation. Importantly, the momentum created by Pew and its partners yielded significant gains not only in states with direct Pre-K Now campaign efforts, but in several other states as well.

The key partners in this effort have been the advocates leading the state campaigns, most of whom were working on behalf of young children for decades before Pew arrived and will continue that fight long after this initiative has ended. Those campaigns were run by a variety of organizations, which Pre-K Now recognized as the most capable of realizing policy change in their states. These advocacy groups either focus on pre-k or cover a range of issues and include independent nonprofits, coalitions, sate government entities and research institutes. As Libby Doggett, then-executive director of Pre-K Now, put it, "we have worked with the very best advocates in the country – ones who have a track record of policy victories, who never lose focus on the goal and who work skillfully across both sides of the aisle."

[a] Pre-k for all refers to all four year olds. IL and DC also include three year olds.

Figure 2.1. Pre-K Now's state campaigns and selected Pew initiative results: 2002–2010. (From Watson, S. [2010]. *The right policy at the right time: The Pew pre-kindergarten campaign* [p. 4]. Washington, DC: Pew Center on the States; reprinted by permission.)

Focused Advocacy

As one of its first actions in the pre-K initiative, Pew funded the creation of a new project to run the advocacy effort at the national level; this choice was made because no other group was in a position to make pre-K its top issue. Originally called the Trust for Early Education and later changed to Pre-K Now, it is now a part of Pew. This decision enabled the campaign to shine a much-needed spotlight on the topic. At Pew, Sara D. Watson directed the campaign, and Pre-K Now's leaders have included Libby Doggett, Stephanie Rubin, Danielle Gonzales, and now Marci Young. Pre-K Now has been supported by leading early childhood foundations: the David and Lucile Packard, RGK, McCormick, CityBridge, and Picower Foundations; the Schumann Fund for New Jersey; and the Foundation for Child Development. All of these funders, and others, have also made significant contributions to the pre-K movement in their own right.

The bedrock of Pre-K Now's work is financial and technical support for public education and advocacy efforts in more than 30 states. Pre-K Now's technical assistance includes advice on policy options, peer-to-peer networking, responses to questions, communications expertise, and sharing of effective materials and strategy. The support is tailored to every state's different history, political environment, and advocacy capacity. For example, when Texas was seeking a way to make even incremental progress, the campaign worked with state leaders to identify specific populations of children with critical needs, including those in military families and in foster care, and focused advocacy efforts on serving these groups. The Texas legislature agreed to provide pre-K to the first group in 2006 and the second in 2007 (Guthrow, 2007).

Strategic Communications

A critical reason for Pre-K Now's success has been its ability both to directly use and to assist state campaigns in using effective communications tools to get data in front of decision makers. These tools include generation of extensive media coverage of pre-K; placement of op-ed articles in newspapers; fast response to critical coverage; very targeted use of paid media (see Figure 2.2); dissemination of key data through timely, accessible publications; an effective outreach strategy around those publications; and use of new social networking tools and the latest e-advocacy technology.

Federal Policy

Pre-K Now also supports efforts to educate federal policy makers. Federal policy plays two crucial roles: 1) funding services, mostly for at-risk children, that establish a foundation on which states can build to reach a broader population; and 2) offering incentives to improve the quality of services, including teacher training, data collection, and program monitoring. Although Head Start and Early Head Start are early learning programs for the nation's poorest children and funding under Title I of the Elementary and Secondary Education Act of 1965 (PL 89-10) can be used to support pre-K (Gayl, Young, & Patterson, 2009, 2010), no federal funding source is dedicated to leverage state early education investments. A top priority of the campaign has been securing such a federal funding stream for state pre-K. Pre-K Now participated in drafting three bills during the 110th Congress: the Providing Resources Early for Kids Act (or PRE-K Act), sponsored by Rep. Mazie Hirono (D-HI); the Prepare All Kids Act of 2007, sponsored by Sen. Robert Casey (D-PA) and Rep. Carolyn Maloney (D-NY); and the Ready to Learn Act, sponsored by Sens. Hillary Rodham Clinton (D-NY) and Kit Bond (R-MO). The House Education and Labor Committee approved the Providing Resources Early for Kids Act (PRE-K Act) with bipartisan support, but the legislation did not come up for a vote in the full body. In 2009, the Obama administration proposed the new Early Learning Challenge Fund to support competitive grants to help states improve coordination and quality in serving children from birth to age 5 years (U.S. Department of Education, 2009b).

Other federal advocacy goals have included improving and increasing Head Start, expanding the Higher Education Opportunity Act of 2008 (PL 110-315) to provide professional development to pre-K teachers, and increasing funding for the Child Care and Development Block Grant and incentives to improve services, including teacher training, data collection, and quality assurance (U.S. Department of Education, 2008b; U.S. Department of Health and Human Services, 2010a). Pre-K

THE BEST ECONOMIC RECOVERY PLAN

BUILDS OUR NATION'S HUMAN CAPITAL, STARTING WITH THE YOUNGEST AMERICANS

As Congress continues the critical work of economic recovery, we call for our limited resources to be invested wisely in building human capital from the ground up, starting with our youngest citizens.

The time is now. We cannot afford to wait until budgets are back "in the black" to invest in proven programs that help infants, toddlers, and young children begin school healthy and ready to succeed.

Few investments these days offer a guaranteed investment return. This is one of them. The evidence demonstrating the benefits of quality early care and education programs includes studies that show returns ranging from 2:1 to as high as 17:1.

While the choices are not easy, we are convinced that the wisest road to recovery involves research-based programs that bring short- and long-term benefits; early education and preventive health care for children are prime examples. When we help infants, toddlers, and young children develop optimally, we simultaneously:

- provide families with needed financial relief;
- create jobs;
- grow a capable, team-ready workforce for the future; and
- save states money.

As you weigh which investments will best rebuild our economy, we urge you to ask: *"Does it save dollars in the long term? Improve the workforce? Make us more competitive? Or not?"*

Please choose wisely. Our nation's economic future depends on it.

THE PEW
CENTER ON THE STATES

The Honorable Phil Bredesen
Governor of Tennessee

The Honorable Timothy M. Kaine
Governor of Virginia

The Honorable Ed Rendell
Governor of Pennsylvania

The Honorable Diane Denish
Lieutenant Governor of New Mexico

Sheriff Drew Alexander
Summit County, Ohio

Steve Bartlett
President and Chief Executive Officer,
The Financial Services Roundtable;
former U.S. Representative

Major General Buford "Buff" Blount
(U.S. Army-Retired)

Dana Connors
CEO, Maine Chamber of Commerce

Rob Dugger
Managing Director, Tudor Investment Corp;
Advisory Board Chair, Partnership for
America's Economic Success

David Fleming
President, Los Angeles County
Business Federation

Jamie Galbraith
Lloyd M. Bentsen Jr. Chair in Government/
Business Relations, LBJ School of Public
Affairs, The University of Texas at Austin

Stephen Goldsmith
Professor of Government, Harvard's
Kennedy School of Government;
former mayor of Indianapolis

James J. Heckman
Nobel Laureate in Economics and Professor
of Economics at the University of Chicago

Benjamin K. Homan
President and Chief Executive Officer,
Food for the Hungry, Inc

Sheriff Mark Luttrell, Jr.
Shelby County, Tennessee

Ray Marshall
former Secretary of Labor

Rob McKenna
Attorney General, State of Washington

Lenny Mendonca
Chairman, McKinsey Global Institute

Susan Neuman
former Assistant Secretary of Education

The Honorable Michael A. Ramos
District Attorney, San Bernardino County

John Rathgeber
President and CEO, Connecticut
Business and Industry Association

Richard Riley
former Secretary of Education

Jim Wunderman
CEO, Bay Area Council

Sheriff John Zaruba
DuPage County, Illinois

Organizations listed for
identification purposes only

Figure 2.2. Pew advertisement, published in *Roll Call*, February 3, 2009. (From Watson, S. [2010]. *The right policy at the right time: The Pew pre-kindergarten campaign* [p. 5]. Washington, DC: Pew Center on the States; reprinted by permission.)

Dear Kristen,

Meet Sam's newest ally: U.S. military leaders!

Millions of young Americans of military age are unprepared to serve, and a nonpartisan group of retired generals and admirals is saying that investing in early education is the best strategy to improve military readiness.

But, right now, **a critical early education bill is stalled in the Senate.**

It's been two months since the House passed the Early Learning Challenge Fund. Will you join these retired military leaders in reminding the Senate that now is the time to invest in our nation's three and four year olds—the future generation who will preserve our nation's security, freedom and opportunity?

Click here to urge your senators to get moving for Sam and act now on this historic early education funding!

We expected pre-k opponents in the Senate to try to strip this funding from the bill, but we had no idea that even the best pre-k supporters would be dragging their feet!

You and I know that talk alone won't do anything to address the fact that **more than 70 percent of our nation's three and four year olds are just like Sam, without access to publicly funded early learning programs.** The Early Learning Challenge Fund represents a critical opportunity to change that.

Tell your senators that Sam can't wait any longer—pass the Early Learning Challenge Fund, now!

Thanks for being a leader on such an important issue for kids across the country. I'll be in touch soon with more updates on the

> The military wants to make sure Sam can go to pre-k.
>
> But right now, 70% of kids simply don't have access.
>
> The Senate has yet to move on the Early Learning Challenge Fund, billions in early education funding for kids like Sam.
>
> **Urge your senators to stop dragging their feet on pre-k!**

Figure 2.3. No School for Sam e-alert. (From Watson, S. [2010]. *The right policy at the right time: The Pew pre-kindergarten campaign* [p. 6]. Washington, DC: Pew Center on the States; reprinted by permission.)

Now's federal work builds on the expertise of state pre-K leaders. The frequent policy alerts from the Washington, D.C., office help state advocates stay up to date on federal activity so that they can be effective in communicating with their members of Congress. In 2007, Pre-K Now created an e-advocacy campaign entitled No School for Sam (see Figure 2.3) with its own web site and e-mail list, which reaches more than 50,000 people. Over one weekend in early 2009, an alert from this campaign within a campaign led to 7,600 letters urging Congress to include early education funding in the federal stimulus package, the American Recovery and Reinvestment Act (ARRA) of 2009 (PL 111-5). Ultimately, after efforts by many groups, federal lawmakers included $2.1 billion for Head Start and Early Head Start in the ARRA, as well as substantial funds for several other vital early childhood and education programs (Pew Center on the States, 2009).

Engaging New Constituencies

Another part of the Pew pre-K strategy was to provide information and support to 30 national groups from across the political spectrum to develop their own voices on early childhood education (see Table 2.1). Most of these were membership organizations that engaged key constituencies, many from outside the child advocacy field, at the state and national levels. Business leaders, older adults, law enforcement officers, K–12 educators, physicians, and many others came to realize they each had their own unique reasons to support pre-K and were willing to provide their own distinct and compelling messages on pre-K's benefits for children and their communities.

Table 2.1. Strategic partnerships with 30 national organizations

Research experts: National Institute for Early Education Research, MDRC

Policy makers: National Governors Association, National Conference of State Legislatures, National Lieutenant Governors Association, National League of Cities

Law enforcement: Fight Crime: Invest in Kids

Business: Partnership for America's Economic Success, National Association of Manufacturers, U.S. Chamber of Commerce, America's Edge, Committee for Economic Development

K–12 education: Council of Chief State School Officers, National Association of State Boards of Education, National School Boards Association, National Association of Elementary School Principals

African American and Latino leaders: United Negro College Fund, National Association of Latino Elected and Appointed Officials, National Council of La Raza, Latinos United

Early childhood: T.E.A.C.H. Early Childhood Project, Every Child Matters, American Montessori Society

Seniors: Generations United

Physicians: Docs for Tots

Military: Mission: Readiness, Military Child Education Coalition

Journalists: Hechinger Institute for Education and the Media, Education Writers Association

Legal: Education Law Center

Faith community: Shepherding the Next Generation

From Watson, S. (2010). *The right policy at the right time: The Pew pre-kindergarten campaign* (p. 7). Washington, DC: Pew Center on the States; reprinted by permission.

The strategy combined supporting unusual voices, which could capture policy makers' attention in new ways, with traditional children's organizations on the ground in states, who knew the issues and how to mobilize their base. Pew's role was to help all these national partners and state campaigns coordinate their efforts so that national groups' members in the states worked closely with the local leaders, messages were aligned, and all the organizations were using the best research. The president and chief executive officer of Illinois Action for Children, Maria Whelan, observed, "Mobilizing new messengers as well as grassroots children's organizations was key to our success" (personal communication, Fall 2009).

For example, Fight Crime: Invest in Kids engaged law enforcement using evidence of pre-K's benefits for crime reduction, Generations United helped seniors to step forward, and an array of education organizations engaged everyone from elementary school principals to school board members to chief state school officers. Pew also collaborated with other funders and hedge fund manager Robert Dugger to create a new project, called the Partnership for America's Economic Success, to mobilize the critical constituency of business leaders around a range of proven interventions for young children. Finally, a separate but related strategy was to engage organizations that provide information to the media—not as advocates, but to help them understand the research and the role that pre-K plays in education reform.

By cultivating the knowledge and participation of both familiar and new allies and providing them with the data necessary to support their unique perspectives on the importance of early learning, Pew built a nationwide coalition that reflected the breadth of pre-K's potential benefits and effectively communicated that wide-ranging value to policy makers.

National Outreach

Pre-K Now also worked to raise the visibility of pre-K nationally. Although many foundations have supported general public-awareness campaigns, Pew's approach is distinct in that public outreach is tightly aligned with focused advocacy. For example, Pre-K Now hosted several live, interactive, national satellite conferences. Advocates around the country organized local viewing sites, with the 2008 event attracting 4,000 viewers in 185 locations. At these conference sites, people gathered together to hear and speak with national leaders and then discuss their own advocacy plans without having to travel outside the state. Pre-K Now also produced a steady stream of reports that generated significant media coverage, with the report on state progress in fiscal year 2010 covered in more than 3,000 broadcast and print stories.

Independent Research

Ongoing objective research is critical to answering key policy questions, including assessing the impact of current pre-K programs. To provide that data, Pew funded economist Steven Barnett to form an independent research entity, the National Institute for Early Education Research (NIEER) at Rutgers University. The Institute, led by Barnett and child development expert Ellen Frede, independently assesses the costs, benefits, and status of modern pre-K programs. Its research strives to increase transparency and accountability for early childhood policies, conduct and translate research that will provide a basis for more effective early education, and answer the questions that policy makers have about what works before they invest significant additional resources in this new policy. NIEER leaders have testified before or provided formal assistance and information to policy makers in every state and 25 foreign countries (C. Shipp, personal communication, October 21, 2009).

One product that has become an essential tool for advocates and policy makers alike is NIEER's annual yearbook of state pre-K programs, which is now the standard reference on progress in the field (Barnett, Epstein, Friedman, Sansanelli, & Hustedt, 2009). The report has also become a key motivator, with states watching closely to see if policy changes will improve their status (W.S. Barnett, personal communication, October 17, 2009). Other NIEER studies have addressed key questions of how much pre-K and what level of quality will provide what level of impact. Another major effort to which NIEER contributed was a comprehensive meta-analysis summarizing decades of research on the short- and long-term effects of early care and education (Camilli, Vargas, Ryan, & Barnett, 2010). NIEER also provides quick-response data for advocates and decision makers in the midst of pressing policy debates.

Although Pew collaborates with NIEER in identifying which questions are most crucial to answer, NIEER has complete autonomy in conducting its research, translating research from the field for policy makers and the public, and releasing its findings. With a board of advisors consisting of many top scholars, a peer-reviewed policy report series, and a long list of publications in peer-reviewed journals, NIEER has extensive credibility in the field.

STRATEGIC DESIGN CHOICES

Beginning in 2001, Pew made a number of strategic choices both in the initial design and ongoing implementation of the campaign—some widely supported, others more controversial. Collectively, these choices represent a distinctive approach to advocacy that has helped propel this issue forward.

Focus

Advocates agree that every state should have a broad vision of what children need for a good start in life. Less consensus exists on the question of how to achieve that vision. Although many states may be able to make small progress on multiple children's issues at the same time, big victories require a relentless focus on specific priorities. The key is not ignoring other issues, but rather having a plan to bring them to the forefront when the public is ready to tackle them.

When Pew's effort started, pre-K was not widely known as a distinct education program; the focused attention of this campaign has dramatically increased its visibility among policy makers and has solidified its place within the comprehensive set of family, education, health, and other supports that prepares children for success. As Jason Sabo, senior vice president of public policy at the United Ways of Texas, noted, "The focus on pre-K allowed us to win incremental victories for kids, session after session, when little else would have moved in our state. Combined, these incremental victories equal a significant step forward for the children of Texas" (personal communication, Fall 2009).

States have also found that the popularity of pre-K has heightened awareness of the need to support high-quality programs for even younger children. For example, in Oklahoma, according to Assistant State Superintendent of Education Ramona Paul, the attention on pre-K has helped encourage partnerships to establish high-quality infant and toddler programs. With this in mind, Pew has added two campaigns, on home visiting and children's dental health, so that states where those issues are coming to the fore can also capitalize on that momentum.

Pre-K for All

In the debate over using public funds to serve all children versus limiting eligibility, the disagreement in the field is not where pre-K policy should start, only where it should end. Virtually everyone agrees with serving the most at-risk children first. Likewise, there is agreement that, overall, poor children need more extensive help than children from middle-income and affluent families. In short, *universal services* does not mean "identical" services. Pew has supported targeting federal funds at low-income children, with states building on that foundation.

The difference arises between those whose policy approach would go no further than the poorest children and those, including Pew, who focus on the importance of every child having an early learning opportunity. Three main arguments support a "pre-K for all" policy. First, although there is very little doubt that pre-K has the greatest impact on low-income children, data show that middle-class children benefit as well. Many of these children start kindergarten unprepared, and studies of state pre-K in Oklahoma showed significant benefits for children whose family income was too high to qualify for free or reduced-price lunch programs. Children in families just above the poverty line often have the least access to high-quality pre-K (Schulman & Barnett, 2005). Further, although the return on investment per child is greatest for targeted programs, broader ones will generate a greater total benefit.

Second, although programs that target only poor children have historically struggled to serve all their eligible children, policies that strive to eventually provide pre-K for all children are much more likely to reach both the most at-risk children and those who have the least access to early education: children from working class families (Ackerman, Barnett, Hawkinson, Brown, & McGonigle, 2009; Barnett et al., 2009). Third, in some states, such as New York, Oklahoma, and Tennessee, widespread coverage can also contribute to a larger base of support, which can lead to more stable, higher quality programs (K. Schimke, personal communication, Fall 2009; R. Paul, personal communication, Fall 2009). So Pew's focus on making pre-K available to every 3- and 4-year-old child is research based and strategic.

For example, even in the 21st century, the federal Head Start program still only serves half of eligible children (B. Allen, personal communication, May 5, 2010) and many states, including Texas and Delaware, have had the same modest level of pre-K for poor children for years (Barnett et al., 2009). As Diane Neighbors, a leading child advocate and Vice-Mayor of Nashville, Tennessee, said, "By declaring a goal of pre-K for all children, we are able to keep pushing for funding increases over time, instead of stopping when we've covered only the most at-risk children" (personal communication, Fall 2009). Indeed, Pew has supported campaigns that achieved pre-K expansion to serve a substantial majority of children, even if covering every child is a far-off goal. For example, according to Rich Huddleston, Executive Director of Arkansas Advocates for Children and Families, "The Arkansas initiative uses a variety of pre-K services that now reaches almost half of 4-year-olds and one third of 3-year-olds in a high-quality program and aims to reach 70% of both—far more than would be the case if we simply stopped at all poor children" (personal communication, Fall 2009).

One interesting note is that the "for all" philosophy is identical to the approach in Australia and the United Kingdom. The vision outlined in a Commonwealth of Australia report includes "a core universal provision linked to a range of targeted and intensive services" with the specific goal of "universal access to quality early childhood education for all children in the year before school by 2013" (2009, p. 9). The report noted:

> There is also longitudinal evidence from the United Kingdom, based on a sample of over 3,000 children, that quality early childhood education benefit[s] all children and that disadvantaged children benefit more if they attend centres with a mix of children from different social backgrounds… [W]hile the return from some early childhood programs provided to all children would be lower than for targeted programs, it would still be positive overall. This is because all children and families require some support at different times and the largest group of vulnerable children, in terms of actual numbers, is in the middle of the social gradient. Other advantages of universal programs may include greater accessibility, reduced stigma, and a role in assessing and referring those children in need of additional support. (2009, p. 9)

Capturing Evidence of Impact: Education and Economic Development

Pre-K was not always associated with education. So, early on, the campaign made a point to emphasize the benefits of pre-K for children's educational success. This helped build a broad base of public support and gain new allies—particularly the educational community, which has been under increasing pressure to show improved student performance on third-grade tests. According to Robert Sexton, Executive Director of the Prichard Committee for Academic Excellence in Kentucky, "This message enabled us to effectively move the issue as part of our education reform agenda" (personal communication, Fall 2009). The educational focus also allowed campaigns to avoid divisive debates and distracting side issues and helped make the case for high-quality services rather than a maximum number of minimal quality hours.

In addition, as the public has come to better understand pre-K for 3- and 4-year-olds as education, it has set the stage for acceptance of the idea that programs for even younger children should also create an environment that promotes early learning. Richard C. Alexander, a business leader in Oregon and Chair of the Ready for School Campaign, noted,

> The successful and focused first step—reaching 3,000 at-risk preschoolers through Oregon Head Start Prekindergarten Programs—is an important stake in the ground in building a case for reaching children even earlier in their development. It is helping us move to Early Head Start as the next step in establishing a continuum of proven early childhood interventions in Oregon for our most vulnerable children prenatal to five. (personal communication, Fall 2009)

Linda Smith, Executive Director of the National Association for Child Care Resource and Referral Agencies, observed that, "The attention generated by the pre-K movement has helped elevate the recognition that all care for young children should be considered educational as well as nurturing. It will help us make new progress in improving the entire child care system" (personal communication, Fall 2009). Voices for America's Children President and Chief Executive Officer Bill Bentley agreed: "Moving the pre-K agenda throughout the country…was extremely important to advancing broader early childhood efforts nationally" (personal communication, Fall 2009).

Although this focus has been effective, it has also raised some concerns. One is that certain states offer a half-day program with no connection to the additional hours of care working parents need. To address this, Pew supports a diverse delivery system, with pre-K offered not only in schools, but in a variety of community-based settings, such as child care and Head Start centers. This arrangement provides parents with more options, builds on the many good providers already operating, and helps improve the overall system, including the quality of services for infants and toddlers.

Two years into the campaign, a major development occurred: Economists began analyzing the economic development benefits of high-quality pre-K. The new field of study was mainly spurred by the publication of an article by Rolnick and Grunewald (2003) from the Federal Reserve Bank of Minneapolis, which presented data showing pre-K for poor children to be an economic development strategy with a 16% rate of return, better than most stock portfolios (see also Chapter 3). Their article resonated with previous research showing a positive cost–benefit ratio for early care and education, but it also captured the public attention in a new way that heavily influenced the policy debate (Rose, 2010).

This new recognition of the wide-ranging economic impact of pre-K revolutionized the outreach to business leaders and prompted even more policy makers to champion early education. It is also helping to lift the debate out of the quagmire of pitting children's programs against one another. It is not a victory for children if pre-K is funded at the expense of other effective programs. Rather than children's programs competing over which has the highest cost–benefit ratio, all government expenditures become open to scrutiny for their benefits to the economy. Data show that many programs for young children, especially pre-K, are supported by far more evidence of both efficacy and return on investment than other programs that claim to support economic vitality (Wat, 2007).

Selecting States

Rather than picking one set of states for the duration of the 10-year campaign, Pew looked for states that presented opportunities to move the issue and reevaluated those choices each year. Policy change takes a long-term investment, so the campaign did not move in and out of states rapidly. Instead, every year, staff and local advocates reexamined states' leadership and the political context to determine if the environment continued to provide opportunities for victories or had become so unfavorable that forward progress seemed impossible. As a result, new states were added as their campaigns became viable, while others facing obstacles decreased their direct advocacy or pursued planning activities until conditions changed. Even partners without active campaigns were welcomed at networking meetings and had access to other Pre-K Now supports.

Pushing for Quality

Preparing children for success requires, at a minimum, well-trained teachers, small classes, and a good environment—none of which is cheap. Virtually every state has wrestled with whether to start with a program that reaches many children and all corners of the state but features only modest standards or a high-quality one with limited availability. Pew staff recommend the latter—the risk is simply too great that a low-quality program will fail kids, hurting both the children and the opportunity for expansion. Alabama Governor Bob Riley also took a quality-first approach, noting, "Starting with a small, high-quality program allowed us to learn how to make it work in our state and to show it is a wise investment of taxpayer dollars" (personal communication, Fall 2009).

Promoting Accountability

As part of the efforts to ensure that current pre-K programs are working well, Pew, with funding from the Foundation for Child Development and the Joyce Foundation, created the National Task Force on Early Childhood Accountability. This effort, chaired by Sharon Lynn Kagan and staffed by Thomas Schultz, used a national advisory committee to develop recommendations for states on creating systems to evaluate the success of their pre-K programs (Pew Center on the States, 2007).

Several states, including Connecticut, Louisiana, Massachusetts, and Pennsylvania, have used information from the report to establish or improve accountability systems for documenting children's early learning and school readiness. In addition, the report influenced two major initiatives, undertaken by national organizations, to develop better data collection and research-based learning standards for early childhood (T. Schultz, personal communication, June 8, 2010).

Leading with Services to Build Systems

Simply funding new classrooms is not enough. To be effective, services need support systems that prepare well-trained teachers, build facilities, monitor quality, and keep the books, among other things. Efforts to design and create these infrastructure systems are important, and a key question is how to secure public resources to support them. It is difficult to convince the public to pay for systems directly because the connection to children's success is difficult to demonstrate. So, Pew chose a strategy of asking the public to support funding for services that is robust enough to include the infrastructure that enables them to work effectively and ensures quality and accountability.

The strategy is helping: One indicator, the number of programs meeting at least 8 of NIEER's 10 quality benchmarks, has risen from 5 in 2002 to 18 in 2008 (Barnett, Robin, Hustedt, & Schulman, 2003; Barnett et al., 2009). Ceil Zalkind, Executive Director of the Association for Children of New Jersey, noted that "the high quality standards and accompanying financing of our pre-k program enabled us to build professional development systems that have helped almost all our teachers gain a bachelor's degree" (personal communication, Fall 2009). New Mexico Lieutenant Governor Diane Denish stated that the "pre-K campaign for New Mexico's children has also helped generate funds for both professional development and new facilities—critical parts of our whole early education system" (personal communication, Fall 2009).

Building on the Best of Early Childhood and K–12 Education

The theme of school readiness has proven to be powerful and unifying. In addition, linking pre-K to the K–12 system is helpful because of the latter's higher expectations for quality and more stable funding. At the same time, simply adapting general education programs to younger children has drawbacks and risks compromising the nurturing quality of infant programs that is also important for pre-K children (as well as older children). So, the campaign has tried to promote an ideal pre-K system that would borrow from both. From the services for the youngest children, advocates have urged developmentally appropriate practice that uses play to help children learn and accommodates different learning styles and paces. From the K–12 system, advocates fought for credentialed teachers, good pay, quality assurance, and carefully chosen curricula. A good example of this is in Oklahoma, where according to Ramona Paul, "the pre-K program has the strong credential requirements and quality assurance procedures associated with K–12 while also providing a nurturing program that reflects the particular needs of very young children" (personal communication, Fall 2009).

SEEING RESULTS

Although there can be endless debates about individual strategy questions, the ultimate test of any policy is the results. Progress in the states indicates that the pre-K movement has taken hold. In the media, it has risen from the occasional human interest story about parents camping out to secure a coveted classroom slot to a regular part of the education beat, with almost 4,900 print articles on pre-K, preschool, or early education in 2008. (Print stories mentioning the term *pre-K* grew from 155 in 2000 to almost 900 in 2008.) It has transformed from a soft social policy topic to a key economic development strategy and has moved from relative obscurity to a leading election issue. Pre-K was a major element of former Virginia Governor Tim Kaine's education platform when he ran for office in 2005; Governor Bob Riley of Alabama was a consistent champion for pre-K; and in 2008, Democratic and Republican presidential candidates included pre-K in their policy positions

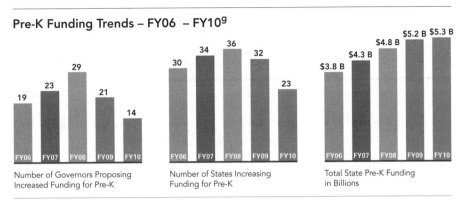

Pre-K Funding Trends – FY06 – FY10[g]

Number of Governors Proposing Increased Funding for Pre-K

Number of States Increasing Funding for Pre-K

Total State Pre-K Funding in Billions

g   Pre-K Now, "Votes Count: Legislative Action on Pre-K Fiscal Year 2010."2.

Figure 2.4.   Pre-K funding trends. (From Watson, S. [2010]. *The right policy at the right time: The Pew prekindergarten campaign* [p. 17]. Washington, DC: Pew Center on the States; reprinted by permission.)

(Wargo, 2008). Pennsylvania Governor Edward Rendell protected early education when battles over the state budget reached historic proportions in 2009 (Pew Center on the States, 2009). Overall, state funding of pre-K rose from $2.4 billion in FY 2002 to $5.3 billion in FY 2010, with enrollment growing from approximately 700,000 children in FY 2002 to 1.2 million in FY 2009 (Barnett et al., 2003; Pre-K Now, 2009). (See Figure 2.4.)

And the programs are working. Studies by NIEER and others showed that pre-K programs in California, New Jersey, New Mexico, and Oklahoma produced significant gains in children's early math and literacy skills (Barnett, Lamy, & Jung, 2005; Wat, 2010). While states must wait for the long-term gains, they are already seeing immediate benefits. In New Jersey, schools with pre-K programs saw retention in first grade drop by as much as 50% (Frede, Jung, Barnett, & Figueras, 2009).

But there is still much work to do. In the 2008–2009 school year, 61% of 4-year-olds and 86% of 3-year-olds did not have access to state or federally funded pre-K (Barnett et al., 2009). Ten states provide no pre-K programs at all (Pew Center on the States, 2009), and many of the available programs are not yet high quality. For instance, seven state programs still meet less than 6 of the 10 NIEER benchmarks (Barnett et al., 2009). Budget battles show that early education remains vulnerable: 10 states decreased their funding for 2010, and in FY09, per-child expenditures declined for the first time in 2 years (Pew Center on the States, 2010). Organizations, publications, and events designed to improve American education still do not always include pre-K as part of the solution. The United States has a long way to go to match the national commitments of competitor nations, especially France, Australia, and the United Kingdom, to provide every child with a core educational experience before kindergarten.

WHAT'S NEXT

While Pew has played a critical role in advancing pre-K policy, keeping the momentum going will require the efforts of many other groups. Fortunately, many established K–12 education organizations are expanding their agendas to include preschool through postsecondary education (P–16), and Pew staff will work with them to incorporate pre-K as part of their ongoing missions. For example, the Data Quality Campaign was created to improve longitudinal data systems across the traditional educational spectrum, but with funding and support from Pew and the David and Lucile Packard Foundation, it will extend its reach to include programs for younger children. Pew also hopes to work collaboratively alongside other new foundation efforts, such as the Kellogg Foundation's initiative for children birth to age 8, the Birth to Five Policy Alliance and First Five Years Fund, and the Annie E. Casey Foundation's new project on reading success, to promote smart advocacy on key early childhood issues.

The success of the pre-K campaign has shown that this formula of a focused, evidence-based, bipartisan agenda, good research, and smart advocacy can be used to win new victories for kids. In 2008, Pew added two campaigns to support proven, voluntary home visiting programs for at-risk new and expectant families and children's dental health. Other funders, including the Doris Duke Charitable Foundation and the Kellogg Foundation, have joined these efforts. Many of the pre-K states have taken on home visiting in particular as a logical next step in building a comprehensive system for young children. This trio of policy goals provides a foothold in the three major areas of young children's development—family, education, and health—and enables Pew's partners to lead with the issues that are most ripe for movement in their states. The key to success is continuing to learn, constantly honing strategies and always presenting the strongest data on the best policies for children, their families, states, and the nation.

The national movement for high-quality, voluntary pre-K for all 3- and 4-year-olds has made great gains over the past decade. Going forward, the partnerships built among foundations, advocates, policy makers, business leaders, law enforcement, educators, and families across the country will be the catalyst for continued work to ensure that states invest taxpayer dollars in proven programs that help all children enter kindergarten prepared to succeed.

PART I

The Debates

DEBATE 1

Targeted versus Universal Preschool

STUDY QUESTIONS

- What are the three main criticisms of targeted preschool? What are the authors' rebuttals?

- How does a universal program generate benefits that a targeted program does not? Do these outcomes outweigh the added expense?

- Do you agree or disagree with the tactic of implementing universal pre-K and then working to make it high quality? Conversely, what are the benefits of starting with a high-quality, targeted pre-K program and then expanding it to a universal program? (See examples in Chapter 6.)

CHAPTER 3

The Economic Case for Targeted Preschool Programs

Art Rolnick and Rob Grunewald

As stewards of the public purse, policy makers are charged with allocating scarce resources to investments that provide the greatest benefits relative to costs. Early childhood education (ECE) targeted for at-risk children is such an investment. Economic research has made the case that investment in ECE for at-risk children provides extraordinary returns. Some of the benefits are private gains for individuals in the form of higher wages later in life, but a majority of the benefits accrue to society as a whole through reduced remedial education and crime costs and higher tax revenue.

However, returns to ECE investments are not all equal. The returns to universal programs (i.e., preschool programs available for all children) are much lower than returns to targeted programs. Indeed, the returns to universal programs appear low even relative to other public investments. Consequently, based on the principle that resources should be invested in the highest return projects, ECE investments should be aimed at our most at-risk children.

In this chapter, we first show that investments in at-risk children achieve substantially higher returns than universal investments. We then respond to several criticisms of targeted preschool programs. We conclude with a discussion of the key features for successfully investing in targeted ECE programs and advocate for a market-based approach.

ECONOMIC RESEARCH FAVORS TARGETED APPROACHES TO EARLY CHILDHOOD EDUCATION

The high return to early childhood investments targeted to at-risk children is well researched. Analyses of the Perry preschool program (Schweinhart et al., 2005), the Abecedarian project (Masse & Barnett, 2002), the Chicago Child-Parent Centers (Reynolds, Temple, Robertson, & Mann, 2002), and the

---

The views expressed in Chapter 3 are the authors' and not those of the Federal Reserve.

Elmira Prenatal/Early Infancy Project (Karoly et al., 1998) show annual rates of return, adjusted for inflation, ranging from 7% to just over 20% and benefit–cost ratios ranging from 4:1 to more than 10:1 (Heckman, Grunewald, & Reynolds, 2006). Researchers followed effects of these ECE programs through adolescence and well into adulthood (Heckman et al., 2006).

These four longitudinal studies form the primary cost–benefit evidence in support of ECE investments targeted to at-risk children (i.e., from low-income households) and their families. Research also suggests that early childhood investments targeted to at-risk children should start well before preschool. Neuroscience shows that the first few years of life are crucial to healthy brain development. Programs that begin early are particularly important to children exposed to toxic stress (National Scientific Council on the Developing Child, 2009).

RETURNS TO TARGETED PROGRAMS ARE HIGHER THAN UNIVERSAL

In this section, we show that returns to targeted preschool programs are higher than universal programs through a critique of the case for universal preschool. Proponents for universal preschool claim that the rate of return to middle-income children on a per-child basis is substantial—even though it is smaller than the return to low-income children. They demonstrate the rate of return to middle-income children in part by extrapolating from the longitudinal studies focused on low-income children. In addition, proponents note that the total return to universal preschool is much larger than the total return to targeted preschool because there are a large number of middle-income children relative to low-income children.

In our response to the case for universal preschool, we begin by discussing three shortcomings in universal proponents' claim that per-child returns to universal preschool are substantial. First, extrapolating evidence from the longitudinal targeted studies to middle-income children is subject to a fair degree of uncertainty. Second, benefits to low-income children from attending universal preschool tend to drive the universal rate of return. Third, universal preschool supplants funds middle- and high-income families would spend on preschool regardless of the availability of universal preschool.

In addition to these shortcomings, we argue that the per-child rate of return is a better criterion for making funding decisions than the total rate of return. Moreover, we contend that the higher overall cost of universal preschool relative to targeted preschool could crowd out investment in potentially higher return investments.

A targeted approach achieves a higher rate of return than a universal approach because low-income children begin at a lower baseline than children from higher-income families. (Children from higher-income families are more likely to start preschool closer to the developmental mean.) Hart and Risley (1995) observed that by the age of 3 years, children who grew up in homes with parents on welfare had only half the number of vocabulary words as children who grew up in homes with college-educated parents. The gap observed by the researchers translates to high costs to society. We argue that a preschool investment in the former child produces a high public return, whereas a preschool investment in the latter produces a modest public return. The longitudinal studies cited previously show that high-quality targeted ECE programs can reduce costs for special education, grade retention, and the criminal justice system and can increase tax revenue (Heckman et al., 2006).

Universal proponents point to studies of universal preschool programs to make the case that children from all income levels benefit from attending. For example, a study of Oklahoma's universal preschool program in Tulsa showed that children from higher income families posted test score gains. However, children who qualified for free lunch and reduced-price lunch had higher test score gains in letter-word identification, spelling, and applied problems than children who paid full price for lunch (Gromley, 2007).

Some researchers have used the cost–benefit study results of the longitudinal studies to help estimate economic returns to universal programs. Examples of applying the results from studies of targeted preschool programs to universal preschool are found in Belfield (2004), Karoly and Bigelow (2005), and Lynch (2007). However, attempts to adjust the economic impact for middle-income and high-income children are subject to a fair degree of uncertainty. For example, the Karoly and Bigelow study of California universal preschool reported that preschool benefit–cost estimates range from roughly 2:1

to more than 4:1. Differences between the estimates are based on different assumptions regarding how much middle-risk and low-risk children benefit from universal preschool relative to high-risk children.

If the per-child rate of return of middle-risk and low-risk children is relatively modest, the participation of high-risk children in universal programs would primarily drive the economic return. In the Karoly and Bigelow study (2005), the most conservative estimate of 2:1 assumed that all benefits to the universal program accrue to high-risk children, who comprise 25% of California's 4-year-old population. The baseline benefit–cost ratio reported in the study was 2.6:1, in which middle-risk children and low-risk children received 50% and 25% of benefits, respectively, relative to high-risk children. (In the simulation, these impacts referred to children who would not have attended preschool without the implementation of the universal program.) The baseline benefit–cost ratio is driven largely by benefits to high-risk children. Furthermore, if the California preschool program was limited to the high-risk children and not offered to all children, overall costs would drop by 75% (the proportion of middle- and low-risk children in the simulation), thus increasing the benefit–cost ratio to closer to 8:1.

Although Karoly and Bigelow (2005) accounted for differences in preschool attendance by risk level, their return to middle-income children may be overstated when existing parental investments are fully taken into account. Offering free preschool to middle- and high-income families only marginally increases the number of these children who enroll in preschool because many are already enrolled in a tuition-based program. In 2005, approximately 47% of children ages 3–5 living below the poverty line were enrolled in a center-based preschool nationally compared with 60% of children ages 3–5 living above the poverty line (National Center for Education Statistics, 2007). This disparity exists despite the availability of Head Start, which is free for children living below the poverty line as defined by the Office of Management and Budget (Improving Head Start for School Readiness Act of 2007, PL 110-134). In 2011, the poverty line for a family of four was $22,350 (U.S. Department of Health and Human Services, 2011). Parents with higher levels of education, which is consistent with higher levels of income, spend more resources on their children for child care than parents with lower levels of education (Rosenbaum & Ruhm, 2007). For example, caregivers with education attainment levels beyond high school spend twice as much per hour on child care as caregivers who did not graduate high school. In addition, children in higher income families on average have a more enriched home environment than children in low-income families. All of this evidence demonstrates that universal preschool tends to supplant resources that higher income families already spend on supporting their children's educational experience.

Universal proponents also point out that because there are a large number of middle-income children relative to low-income children, the total net return to a universal program is substantially higher than targeted programs (Barnett, Brown, & Shore, 2004). However, total net return is not the best criterion for deciding whether to invest; a better criterion is the per-child rate of return. The question should be, how should the next dollar be invested in ECE? The correct answer comes from looking at marginal net benefits, not the total. On the margin, the next dollar spent on at-risk children will produce a bigger bang for the buck than if the next dollar were spent on middle-income children.

However, even when a universal program demonstrates positive marginal net benefits, it is not a sufficient condition for funding. The rate of return or benefit–cost ratio must be compared with other potential investments, including investments to develop human capital, particularly prenatal-to-age-3 programs for at-risk children. For example, the Nurse Family Partnership, which is modeled on the nurse-based home visiting model studied in Elmira, New York, has demonstrated strong public rates of return (Heckman et al., 2006). Other human capital investments may also prove to have higher rates of return than universal preschool, such as after-school programs, teacher compensation reform, classroom size, and summer transition programs. Universal proponents must show that returns to universal preschool trump these other investments.

To illustrate this issue, consider Georgia's universal preschool program and Michigan's targeted program. The overall cost of universal preschool is generally more expensive than a targeted program simply because it encompasses more children. For example, Georgia's universal preschool program reaches 78,310 four-year-olds at an annual cost of $332 million. In contrast, Michigan's preschool program is targeted to 4-year-old children who have educational disadvantages; it reaches 24,091 children for an annual cost of $103 million (Barnett, Epstein, et al., 2009). Compared with Georgia, Michigan has more funds to spend on potentially higher return projects, such as prenatal-to-age-3 programs for at-risk children.

RESPONSE TO THE CRITICS OF A TARGETED APPROACH

In this section, we respond to several criticisms of targeted preschool programs.

Targeted Approach Will Not Garner Political Support

Proponents for universal preschool claim that programs with broad eligibility build a stronger base of political support than targeted preschool. They point to the lack of political backing for programs that support low-income families, including Head Start. However, Americans generally accept and support targeting college scholarships and other financial aid to students from low-income families. The public understands that targeting college financial aid helps support the country's work force and democracy. Similarly, we argue that the public will back targeted preschool as a pillar of human capital development.

Business leaders recognize the high rate of return to targeting at-risk children. For example, the Minnesota Early Learning Foundation (2009), with a board of directors that includes key state business leaders, funds research to learn what works best and is cost effective to promote learning readiness among at-risk children. Furthermore, universal preschool is not a silver bullet to gain political support. The defeat of California's Proposition 82 in 2006 was an indication that voters are not necessarily swayed by arguments for universal preschool (Institute of Government Studies, n.d.).

Targeted Approach Precludes Integrated Classrooms

Targeted approaches can provide integrated programs where children from diverse socioeconomic backgrounds attend. A targeted program can be integrated into the existing system of public and private preschools and child care programs. For example, a scholarship program gives low-income families the opportunity to enroll their children free or at a reduced rate with children from higher income families who pay up to full price.

Targeted Approach Requires Means Testing, Which Is Difficult to Administer

Although there is a cost to means testing preschool applicants, the application process can be simplified to make it easier for families to navigate. Qualification for the preschool program can be linked to eligibility for other means-tested programs, such as temporary financial assistance for families or child care subsidies. We argue that the cost of means-testing families is small relative to the benefits achieved from a targeted program.

Targeted Approach Creates Stigma

Universal advocates claim that targeted preschool stigmatizes low-income families who qualify for the program. Stigma is affected by how targeted programs are presented to the public and eligible families. Stigma is not generally associated with scholarships and financial aid for lower income children to attend college. Instead, college scholarships and financial aid are viewed as a key opportunity both by the public and eligible students. Therefore, targeted preschool should be portrayed primarily as an opportunity to invest in young children, not as a support to low-income families.

Targeted Approach Is Difficult to Bring to Scale and Reach All Eligible Children

Finally, we agree with universal proponents that reaching low-income families is a challenge, but we disagree that means testing is the primary deterrent. A number of low-income families face several challenges, including housing and employment. Reaching these families takes focused resources, including

FOCUSING ON CHILDREN'S OR THE STATE'S INTERESTS?

Conservatives long argued that the upbringing of young children should be the exclusive province of parents, at times infused with a dose of religious guidance. Yes, the state must build common schools for all children, advancing a shared culture, human capital for employers, and greater equity based on the merit of graduates. But government held no legitimate role when it came to advancing the growth and well-being of young children prior to starting school, according to family-first proponents.

This view lost ground and was undercut by a variety of forces beginning in the 1960s. First, the steady rise of mothers seeking jobs outside the home spurred the child care movement. Second, early research inside homes began to estimate the huge influence that parents continued to exercise on children's early development. Psychologists and social scientists, going back to the 1950s, had detailed stark differences in the home environments and practices of poor parents in Chicago, compared with middle-class families, long before children entered school (Hess & Shipman, 1965). The architects of Head Start argued that preschool would help compensate for (or improve) the home practices of low-income families. Scholars then contributed to a lively civic debate, ultimately revealing few negative effects of nonparental child care or preschool, with some concern for a small and short-lived decrement in children's social development (for a review, see Loeb, Bridges, Bassok, Fuller, & Rumberger, 2007).

The current issue is not whether child care and preschool undercut development, but rather how to equalize access to and boost the quality of care to yield stronger gains in early learning. When it comes to preschool, the favored option for parents of 3- and 4-year-olds, two additional questions arise: What collective actors (e.g., government, the mixed market, local nonprofits) will most likely raise the benefits of preschool? And what is the outer limit of cognitive or social returns for children within affordable ways of boosting quality?

Before turning to the evidence, one should consider the philosophical heart of the question. Whether collective actors, especially advocacy groups and policy makers, should focus public resources on poor children or advance a universal entitlement is not a question resolved through science. This is a question of ideology, of how one weighs competing ideals about the state's role in civil society. The idea of making preschool a shared entitlement prompts contention over three sets of ideals—ethical commitments relating to how government should best serve families and voters: 1) Should public resources be used to extend free schooling to all families for children of all ages, independent of parents' ability to pay; 2) should entitlements be awarded to all families when certain children do not benefit, wastefully drawing resources away from other public projects; and 3) should government expand preschool by building out from the public schools or rely on a mix of nonprofit organizations, thickening civil society?

One rendition of these ideals has powered the expansion of public schools since the mid-19th century. Education is viewed as a public good, a shared institution that nurtures engaged citizens, builds from a shared cultural framework and language, and prepares children for our capitalist labor market. But institutional histories matter, as these ideals are weighed differently among neighboring sectors. Take higher education, for example. Affluent and many middle-class parents pay more for their children's college education than do low-income parents. Most states set tuition levels and financial aid in progressive fashion, ensuring that higher income families are charged more.

The advent of preschool centers—going back to the settlement-house movement of the early 20th century—has long reflected a progressive finance structure as well. No state except Oklahoma has regressively opted to subsidize preschool for upper middle-income and wealthy families. Washington, D.C., has shown little interest in departing from its historical focus on poor families. In concert, community activists have sought to thicken civil society, advancing public projects independent of central government, ranging from evangelical Christian groups to urban activists pushing for affordable housing. More than 120,000 nonprofit organizations now operate preschools nationwide (Fuller & Strath, 2001). So, differentiated institutions have arisen in American society, weighing core political ideals quite differently.

Ignorance of institutional history can be costly. Hollywood activist Rob Reiner began his crusade in 2004 to make preschool a free entitlement for all California families, designing a $2.4 billion ballot initiative. To add heft to this cause, Reiner and fellow universal pre-K proponents were eager to pull in the California Teachers Association (CTA), among the top three contributors to state Democrats. Yet the union wanted something in return: legal assurances that most growth would occur within the public schools. The CTA had built little organizing capacity within community nonprofits, but this deal created angst across the nonprofit sector and some Latino organizations. The bulk of new tax resources would have gone to families who already enrolled their 4-year-olds in preschool. The ballot initiative went down by a three-to-two margin.

One major fissure dividing universal pre-K advocates and the older child care lobby is defined by the former's strong trust in education bureaucracies and the virtues of standardizing (or aligning) curricula with the schools to guide early learning. In contrast, the earlier generation of child care activists and early childhood associations favored developmentally appropriate practices and separation from more didactic forms of instruction found in the public schools. As universal pre-K leaders fused themselves to unions and state education departments, President George W. Bush's reform—the No Child Left Behind Act of 2001 (PL 107-110)—kicked in. This accountability effort jammed local educators to show stronger test scores, and universal pre-K advocates jumped on board, arguing that preschool would boost children's early performance in school.

Universal pre-K enthusiasts could not have forecast the fierce backlash that roared back, as local educators and parents worried over No Child Left Behind's emphasis on testing and the narrowing of curriculum to align with an equally thin view of official knowledge. By 2009, just one in four Americans believed that the law had buoyed their local school (Bushaw & McNee, 2009). For many early childhood advocates who had long favored classrooms that nurture children's curiosity and intrinsic motivation, the No Child episode confirmed their fears that awarding preschool to education bureaucrats would encourage didactic teaching and pallid conceptions of child development.

President Barack Obama showed no sign of departing from Washington's historical focus on helping poor children. The expansion of Head Start and Early Head Start, spurred by economic stimulus spending, reinforced the federal emphasis on serving low-income families through a mixed market of providers. The Obama administration shared with Congress an interest in consolidating state preschool efforts, often divorced from Head Start and sustained through a maze of state and federal funding streams.

Against this backdrop of competing political ideals and institutional histories, the universal pre-K movement remains founded on rickety assumptions, backed by shaky evidence. The movement itself is flagging. A portion of its national benefactors are moving on. So, the time is right to reflect on where the universal pre-K movement got it right and where its proponents turned down costly cul-de-sacs. Lessons abound in four arenas:

1. Access to preschool is not a problem for the vast majority of middle-class and affluent families with young children. The pressing problem is uneven quality.

2. No consistent evidence shows that children from middle-class or affluent families benefit from preschool in sustained ways.

3. Awarding schools the authority to run preschools when public education is under intense pressure to raise test scores results in standardized preschools and impoverished conceptions of child development.

4. Preschool quality is often quite high in poor communities. Government has shown promising, though at times uneven, success in raising quality.

The remaining sections of this chapter examine each of these arguments in turn. I set aside a fifth worry about publicly financed entitlements in general, from reducing class size in public schools to providing price subsidies to farmers: all citizens are taxed for services or cash transfers that often serve well-off beneficiaries. Little evidence backs the argument that entitlements narrow disparities in education or family policy, as opposed to progressively targeted programs (Ceci & Papierno, 2005). For example, when Rob Reiner's previously described universal pre-K initiative was put forward, about 60% of new tax revenue would have gone to families whose children were already enrolled (Fuller & Livas, 2006).

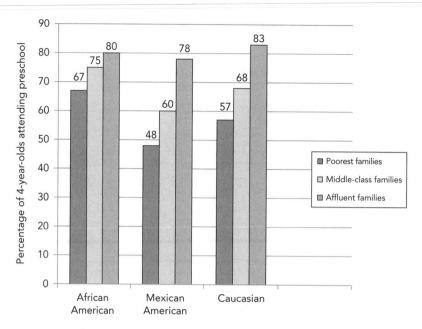

Figure 4.1. Percentage of 4-year-olds attending preschool by ethnicity for the lowest, middle, and highest quintiles of socioeconomic status in 2005. (*Source:* Park, 2007. Analysis by Ed Bein, University of California, Berkeley.)

PRESCHOOL ACCESS REMAINS A PROBLEM

The share of 4-year-olds attending preschool has climbed steadily since the 1970s. In 1970, about 28% of 4-year-olds and 12% of 3-year-olds were enrolled in a preschool center of any type. These rates climbed to 66% and 42%, respectively, by 2002 (Karoly & Bigelow, 2005). Despite rising participation in preschool overall, access remains a problem for specific types of families.

Figure 4.1 displays enrollment rates in 2005 by ethnic group for different socioeconomic groups. This index of the family's socioeconomic status combines school attainment and occupational status of pertinent mothers and fathers, calculated by analysts at the National Center for Education Statistics (Park, 2007). African American children had the highest enrollment rates, independent of the family's socioeconomic status. This is a sign of government's success in narrowing disparities for African American families, stemming from Head Start and state efforts since the 1960s, along with historically high levels of maternal employment in African American communities. Large shares of 4-year-olds from middle-class and affluent homes are also enrolled in preschool. Access is not a problem for them.

About one quarter of mothers with a preschool-age child do not work outside the home. This does not mean that their children would not benefit from attending preschool. However, current enrollment rates may approach the upper limit of the share of middle-class 4-year-olds who will attend preschool. Even in states with entitlements, like Georgia and Oklahoma, enrollments do not range any higher.

Expressed demand for preschool remains low for children from low- and middle-income Latino families. My research team has detailed even lower enrollment rates for immigrant children of Mexican descent, who often live in communities with few preschools. Many Latina mothers continue to stay at home to raise their children or report rather uninviting preschools in their neighborhood (Fuller & Huang, 2003; Liang, Fuller, & Singer, 2002).

Overall, legislating a universal entitlement to preschool (unless attendance was made compulsory) would not markedly increase access for 4-year-olds from middle-class and affluent homes. They already enroll at high rates. Attendance of 3-year-olds is lower for certain groups of children. Yet the universal pre-K movement has focused on 4-year-olds in most states, which is perhaps not the optimal focus. The state's efforts to serve poor families has yet to yield the results for Latino children that we see for African American children. More inventive organizations, diverse staff, and outreach activities may be required. Efforts to first widen access for poor families, then ratchet up eligibility to working class families, may offer a middle ground. In Tulsa, as universal pre-K based in the schools got underway, Head Start leaders shifted their focus to serving toddlers and expanding prenatal care for expectant mothers (Fuller, 2007).

PRESCHOOL YIELDS STRONG BENEFITS FOR AT-RISK CHILDREN

Quality preschool lifts the early development of poor children. This line of research has matured in two ways since the second half of the 20th century. First, scholars have moved from studying small experiments examining large programs, yielding findings that are widely generalizable. The Perry preschool and Abecedarian projects continue to be cited (especially in the media) for their effects among the small numbers of African American children who participated (Campbell et al., 2002; Schweinhart et al., 2005). The Perry preschool project was a true experiment but also included a parent-training component. The Perry preschool cost about $7,581 per child each year; the Abecedarian Project cost $34,476 per child annually, which is 3–5 times the cost of contemporary publicly funded centers (each in 2000 dollars; Schweinhart et al., 2005).

Evaluations of large-scale programs also showed persisting effects for children from poor families on early school achievement and into young adulthood. Reynolds et al. (2002), for instance, drew a sample of 1,539 kindergartners in the mid-1980s, assessing the benefits associated with attending one of 25 child-parent centers operated by the Chicago schools. Even children receiving the most limited treatment displayed cognitive gains that persisted to age 14, with effect sizes ranging from 0.21 of a standard deviation (SD) in kindergarten to 0.16 SD in ninth grade.

Oklahoma's universal preschool effort displays positive benefits, at least in Tulsa, which largely serves poor and working-class families. Gormley, Gayer, Phillips, and Dawson (2005), drawing on a sample of 3,149 kindergartners (two thirds of whom qualified for lunch subsidies), compared children of similar ages who fell on either side of Tulsa's cutoff date for starting kindergarten, allowing for a regression-discontinuity analysis. Attending preschool yielded gains in children's letter-word recognition (0.79 SD) and solving applied problems (0.38 SD).

A second scientific advance, which again revealed distinct benefits for at-risk children, stemmed from national samples of young children who attended preschool centers for varying lengths of time. This resulted from concern over whether earlier results can be generalized to the range of "garden-variety" preschools that operate across the nation. The NICHD Study of Early Care and Youth Development sampled a cohort of infants born to English-speaking parents. This team detailed how the cognitive benefits of longer exposure to child care settings (of variable quality, not only preschools) can still be detected at the end of third grade. Yet assessment scores in reading, math, and memory were just 0.07–0.09 SD higher when youngsters attended preschool, compared with children attending other care arrangements (NICHD, 2005). Eight years after entering the study, less than 10% of the children came from low-income families.

Another study drew from the Early Childhood Longitudinal Study of 14,162 children. Researchers found that children from low-income homes who attended a preschool center the year before entering kindergarten had gained 0.20 SD in language and prereading skills and 0.22 SD in math concepts by the fall of the kindergarten year, compared with similarly low-income children in another form of care (Loeb et al., 2007). Yet effect sizes were even more modest, about half the magnitude, for children from middle-class homes. Benefits appear to persist into first grade for poor children and for the middle-class child attending a primary school in which teachers reported more intensive instructional activities (Magnuson, Ruhm, & Waldfogel, 2004). Garces, Thomas, and Currie (2002) also found higher levels of school achievement for Head Start attendees, especially for Latino and Caucasian children with more highly educated mothers, even after matching siblings who received differing levels of exposure.

Overall, preschool holds consistent benefits for children from low-income families but weak or no effects for those from middle-class and affluent homes. This is not surprising. The small remaining slice of middle-class children who stay at home with a parent or attend another kind of child care arrangement are likely to be in healthy settings. The failure to attend a formal preschool may slow learning of classroom-specific skills, but middle-class children appear to easily catch up. So, this line of research prompts the key policy question: Why would society allocate scarce public funds to subsidize a service for children that yields no consistent benefits?

CENTRAL REGULATION IN A COLORFUL CIVIL SOCIETY

As government has widened access to preschool, policy makers struggle with the question of which local organizations best advance high-quality programs. The bulk of preschoolers are served by nonprofits, with remaining programs situated in public schools (Fuller, 2007). In this context, the decision by universal pre-K advocates to align with teacher unions and education interests and then attempt to fuse preschools to public schools may have been a tactical mistake. The closely related empirical question is whether regulation of preschool quality and curricula via school bureaucracies yields stronger outcomes for kids or narrowing conceptions of child development compared with advancing programs run by nonprofits.

I certainly agree with many advocates that state regulation is required to ensure minimal health and safety standards. But the regulatory habits of government—bolstered by political pressure to show crisp results—now push early educators to shrink their conception of young children's developmental capacities. The second Bush administration, worried over the average quality of Head Start preschools, tried to quickly push an assessment system that solely focused on children's preliteracy and numeracy skills, ignoring the program's holistic approach to child development. The result was a bit nutty. Some assessment items pressed from Washington asked 3- and 4-year-olds—who were often being raised in low-income urban environments—to identify which adults were playing tennis or to count the number of cows roaming about a pasture.

In addition, consider the well-intentioned drive by state education departments to raise children's preliteracy and numeracy skills in hopes of later boosting their standardized test scores. Young children are no longer seen by government agents as developing along cognitive, emotional, and social dimensions. Instead, they are simply creatures that must learn to digest and express phonemes or efficiently count to 20. When I studied Oklahoma's implementation of universal pre-K, I talked to several teachers who, after being trained in bachelor's degree programs where they came to enjoy and nurture the multifaceted nature of young children, were now being pressed by their school principal to line up 4-year-olds in rows of desks and drill them with letters and numbers (Fuller, 2007). The Tulsa school board even capped the amount of time that preschoolers could spend in activity centers. How would this raise test scores?

This push to standardize how young children are to perform cognitively arrives during a period of enormous cultural and linguistic diversity. More than half of all births in several American cities are now to Latino parents. Just under one third of all children in the United States will be of Latino heritage by 2025 (Fry & Passel, 2009). Some grow up speaking English at home, but many others do not. So, now state officials are telling early educators to judge the growth of their preschoolers in terms of progress in reciting elements of a language they do not speak at home. Whether these children are building social skills, learning how to work with peers, or growing more eager to learn does not really interest government. Even otherwise progressive policy makers now back this impoverished concept of how young children learn and grow. It is a remarkable reversal of how Western societies came to understand the natural curiosity and robust potentials of young children, going back to the Enlightenment.

I am not arguing that the preferences or cultural habits of parents should be taken as sacred. What young children learn, and through what kinds of social relationships, must be sensitive to the multiple contexts in which they are growing up, from culturally bound practices to the economic social demands they will later face. But respectful dialogue is required as government or foundation officials press their particular concepts of child development or standardized preschool. Policy makers make all sorts of assumptions about what young children should be learning, rarely slowing down to talk with parents. This likely slows the extent to which certain groups of parents see preschool as an inviting organization (Fuller, Holloway, Rambaud, & Eggers-Piérola, 1996). I also am not arguing against stronger government activism to raise the quality of preschool, but policy makers must be mindful of whether their regulatory measures hold discernible benefits for children, and for which children and families.

IMPROVING QUALITY IN MIXED MARKETS

Universal pre-K advocates rightly emphasize that preschool quality is starkly variable across sectors and individual programs. When I tracked young children in three states through their child care and preschool arrangements with Sharon Lynn Kagan and Susanna Loeb in the wake of welfare reform, we visited preschools in Florida that were crammed with young children and staffed by young women who had only a high school education. The developmental benefits of these centers for children were small to nil, in sharp contrast to strong and persisting benefits for their counterparts attending preschool in California and Connecticut (Bassok, French, Fuller, & Kagan, 2008; Loeb, Fuller, Kagan, & Carroll, 2004).

At first, universal pre-K advocates argued that state governments, after legislating a universal entitlement, would be best positioned to advance quality. As teacher unions and K–12 interest groups joined the cause, the management of preschools by school bureaucracies would further boost quality. However, no sound empirical study has concluded that children attending school-based preschools outperform their counterparts in preschools run by nonprofits (Fuller, 2007). Evidence from Georgia's universal pre-K system shows that children in nonprofit programs may display stronger growth than those in school-based programs. This may be due to nonprofits' greater agility in hiring younger, more energetic teachers, compared with the cobwebs of personnel practices that hamper teacher hiring in the public schools (Henry & Gordon, 2006). Georgia's "universal" preschool program serves a disproportionately large share of children from lower income families than the comparison group that was employed in this study. The authors did include a variety of prior socioeconomic status controls, but differences could still be an artifact of unobserved differences in the child or teacher groups.

So, the mixed-market character of the field does not appear to constrain government's capacity to raise preschool quality. After all, school reformers—from President Obama to urban activists—now argue that the K–12 system is hogtied by the state's monopolizing, hyperregulated control of local schools; instead, it should look more like a mixed market, spurred by the growth of charter and magnet schools, as well as more liberal parental choice.

Government has often succeeded at raising preschool quality, especially in low-income neighborhoods that receive sufficient subsidies. In some states, like California, public preschools must operate under tougher quality standards than programs financed by parental fees. Indeed, we observed corresponding levels of quality among such communities, based on a sample of 166 preschools situated in three states (Fuller, Kagan, Loeb, & Chang, 2004). Policy makers are right to worry about the average quality of certain programs. One evaluation revealed that Head Start does advance children's cognitive growth when measured in kindergarten, but these benefits fade out by first grade (Puma et al., 2010). Importantly, state-funded preschools generally show more robust effects for poor children, compared with Head Start (Barnett et al., 2005; Loeb et al., 2004).

Overall, government can succeed in boosting preschool quality in mixed markets when it carefully targets resources on this policy goal. The returns to quality investments remain mixed, with the disappointingly low benefits of Head Start being the most troubling case in point. But no evidence suggests that handing over preschool organizations to the public schools would yield stronger quality gains, affordable costs, or greater responsiveness to America's diverse communities.

CONCLUSION

State and federal governments should play a forceful role in extending access to high-quality preschools, especially for those children who clearly benefit from this human-scale institution. The idea of a universal preschool entitlement has been a long and costly diversion from the pressing project to narrow disparities in young children's early learning. Government should sustain an enlightened recognition of the robust ways in which young children potentially grow, from their cognitive agility to their emotional well-being and intrinsic curiosity. As central governments falter economically and face stiff pressure to show unambiguous results, they have drifted toward simplistic and efficiently measured forms of learning. This will conflict with the broader ways in which parents see and nurture their children's growth. It will predictably undercut children's own engagement in stultifying classrooms.

Advocates and policy makers can mindfully widen family access to quality preschools by first becoming clear on their underlying ethical position, their bedrock philosophy about the state's role in a democratic and grossly unequal society. It is tempting to advance universal entitlements. However, universal preschool would squander scarce public dollars and likely widen gaps in early learning, as well-heeled communities top up private investment in preschool with public funds, then recruit the most skilled teachers.

Preschool advocates must honestly study the empirical research. Across a variety of programs, populations, and settings, preschools show remarkable benefits for children from low-income families. No national study has yet to show that children from middle-class or affluent families experience sustained benefits from attending preschool (although Bassok, 2010, suggested that some children from middle-class subgroups may benefit from preschool). A preschool entitlement would free up a small slice of parents to enter the labor market and aid the household budget, but the benefits for children would be tiny to nil. Politicians can build stronger trust among voters by funding programs that yield consistent effects, rather than making false promises that simply result in wasting public resources.

CHAPTER 5

Four Reasons the United States Should Offer Every Child a Preschool Education

W. Steven Barnett

Few questions about preschool education spur more spirited debate than whether the program should be targeted or universal. Although there are many ways that public preschool programs could be targeted, what is generally meant in the academic debates is that access should be means tested, limited to children from families below the poverty line or some other income threshold. For several decades, I was an advocate for providing high-quality public preschool education at no cost only to poor children. My view was based on benefit–cost calculations showing that relatively intensive programs for these children produced returns far exceeding their costs and the expectation that returns would be considerably lower for more advantaged children. In more recent years, I have discovered that my former view was based on faulty assumptions (more often implicit than explicit), and new evidence has been developed that expands the knowledge for choosing between targeted and universal policies.

This chapter explains the following four reasons that government should offer every child a high-quality preschool education rather than offer such programs only to poor children:

1. Universal preschool programs will reach a significantly greater percentage of poor children.

2. Universal preschool programs will produce larger educational gains for disadvantaged populations.

3. Children from middle-income families account for most of the nation's problems with inadequate readiness, school failure, and dropout. Universal prekindergarten (pre-K) can increase their readiness to succeed in school.

4. Universal pre-K is likely to yield a larger net economic benefit to the nation.

UNIVERSAL PRE-K WILL REACH MORE DISADVANTAGED CHILDREN

For more than 40 years, the United States has publicly funded programs to provide preschool programs to poor children. The best known of these is Head Start, but other federal, state, and local public preschool programs target low-income families, while preschool special education is available for all children with disabilities. Detailed data from the 2005 National Household Education Survey (NHES) provide the strongest foundation for a policy analysis as they provided estimates of participation in specific types of preschool programs by family income levels. However, the NHES data focus on children who are not yet in kindergarten. Some 4-year-olds attend kindergarten, whereas about 12% of 5-year-olds attend pre-K. To take this into account, adjustments have been made to produce estimates of enrollment for each age cohort (i.e., children who will enter kindergarten in 1 year, children who will enter kindergarten in 2 years).

Updating the NHES figures has little effect on the estimates of total enrollment or on the public-private split. A less detailed national school readiness survey for 2007 that is similar to the NHES indicated no increase in enrollment (Hagedorn, Brock Roth, O'Donnell, Smith, & Mulligan, 2008). The Current Population Survey (CPS) provided another source of data through 2008, although with less detail, and possible differences because of its focus on school enrollment (U.S. Census Bureau, 2008a). The CPS data also indicated no increase in enrollment as a percentage of the population. How can this be squared with the increase in state pre-K enrollment since 2005 (from 20% to 25% at age 4)? The most likely explanation is that many state pre-K programs funded private pre-K to serve children who would have enrolled in those programs anyway. The CPS showed no change in the public-private split in enrollment. If state pre-K raised the quality of the private programs (e.g., as in New Jersey), this would have been the primary benefit of the change. Also, some children enroll in multiple programs, particularly when state pre-K is a part-day program. So children formerly only in Head Start or pre-school special education may be getting more preschool education. Given these results, I rely on the more detailed 2005 NHES data through the remainder of this chapter.

By 2005, Head Start was funded at nearly $7 billion per year and enrolled about 900,000 children, primarily at ages 3 and 4. Head Start received substantial additional funding for 2009 and 2010 for the first time in many years, but little (if any) of this increase was devoted to increasing enrollment at ages 3 and 4 (Haskins & Barnett, 2010). Local schools can use federal Title I funds to provide preschool education for children from low-income families. Unfortunately, there are no hard numbers on the extent to which this is done, nor is it known how many children are provided preschool education with local education funds. The vast majority of states fund preschool education programs, and most of these are means tested. In 2005, only Oklahoma and Georgia could truly be said to be pursuing preschool education for all children. In 2009, Florida surpassed Georgia with a new universal pre-K program. However, Florida mostly served children by paying private child care $2,500 per child for 2.5 hours per day during the school year while setting very low standards. Preschool special education served about 400,000 children at age 3 and 4 years, but this is not an entirely separate enrollment (Barnett et al., 2009).

Government subsidies for child care also provide a substantial source of means-tested public support for preschool program participation. Under welfare reform, federal subsidies for child care have grown to exceed spending on Head Start; by 2005, federal Child Care and Development (CCDF) and Temporary Assistance to Needy Families (TANF) funds spent on child care subsidies exceeded $8 billion. States added more than $3 billion to these subsidies. Other federal subsidies include tax credits (more than $3.5 billion, mostly to middle-income families), and the Child and Adult Care Food Program (more than $2 billion); again, not all of this is for children ages 3 and 4. These child care subsidies cover children up to age 13, not just children ages 3 and 4. CCDF received a $2 billion increase from the 2009 American Recovery and Reinvestment Act, but it is as yet unknown how this might have affected enrollment, as it is unclear how the funds were spent and what happened to other sources of child care subsidies, including TANF (Haskins & Barnett, 2010).

With this long history of means-tested public preschool and child care programs, one might expect that the vast majority of children in poverty or near poverty would be in some kind of program. The 2005 NHES still provides the best data (consistent with the 2008 CPS) with which to address that question. As discussed previously, updating the 2005 NHES data does not really change overall enrollment estimates. Table 5.1 presents estimated participation in Head Start and other kinds of center-based preschool programs for children at ages 3 and 4 by family income. The breakout by program type is consistent with data reported by programs if it is recognized that half of the special education and private no-fee programs for age 4 are in state pre-K. The lowest income quintile corresponds closely to children living below the poverty line. Note that these figures are adjusted to represent each age cohort's full participation (i.e., 4-year-olds are those children who will attend kindergarten next year), and the figures are consistent with the estimate that 72% of a cohort would enter kindergarten having attended a preschool program in the prior year based on the CPS. Based on program data and the CPS, I estimate that at age 4, enrollment in state pre-K was 25% and that

CHILDREN FROM MIDDLE-INCOME
FAMILIES NEED AND CAN BENEFIT FROM UNIVERSAL PRE-K

The notion that only disadvantaged children might benefit from public preschool education is not supported by the evidence. Analysis of data from the Early Childhood Longitudinal Study–Kindergarten Cohort indicates that there is no sharp discontinuity in school readiness at the poverty line, nor are there sharp discontinuities in later school success or in social and emotional development (Barnett, 2007). Instead, child development improves steadily and linearly with income. Given the distribution of scores, it is also true that a substantial portion of children in the three middle-income quintiles begin kindergarten with cognitive and social skills below those of the average child in the bottom income quintile. For children in the bottom income quintile, grade retention is 12%, and the dropout rate is 18%; at the median income, these rates are 8% and 12% (Barnett, 2007). Although it might be hypothesized that middle-income children catch up more easily, it turns out that numerically, children in these middle-income families also account for most school failures and high school dropout (U.S. Census Bureau, 2008a). The question then is not whether they need help, but whether they can be helped by public preschool programs.

Universal pre-K in Oklahoma and elsewhere has been found to produce immediate gains for non-disadvantaged children that are at least three quarters the size of effects for the disadvantaged children (Gormley et al., 2005; Sylva et al., 2004). One randomized trial on a small scale has found persistent effects for highly advantaged children from a quality preschool program (Larsen, Hite, & Hart, 1983; Larsen & Robinson, 1989). In Europe, where universal preschool education is more common, programs have been found to improve long-term cognitive and social development for children of all socioeconomic backgrounds (Fuchs & Wossmann, 2006; Osborne & Milbank, 1987; Rindermann & Ceci, 2008; Schutz, Ursprung, & Wossmann, 2008; Waldfogel & Zhai, 2008). Children from middle-income families do not currently obtain the potential benefits from pre-K because they either do not attend a preschool program or the program they attend is not of sufficient quality. Table 5.1 presents the data on participation. In a study of preschool in California, only about one in five preschool classrooms attended by children from higher income families qualified as good based on direct observation, even for families with incomes exceeding five times the federal poverty level (Karoly, Ghosh-Dastidar, Zellman, Perlman, & Fernyhough, 2008).

THE ADDED COST OF UNIVERSAL
PRE-K CAN BE JUSTIFIED BY ITS ADDED BENEFITS

A universal program inevitably has a much higher total cost than a targeted program. Whether the extra cost is worthwhile depends on the benefits. The three ways in which a universal program generates additional benefits that can more than offset the additional costs have been discussed previously. First, a universal program provides more complete coverage of the disadvantaged population. Second, a universal program provides greater benefits to each disadvantaged child served. In addition to the evidence on peer effects, it is difficult to look at results for Head Start and not conclude that programs for poor children often are not very effective programs (Gelbach & Pritchett, 2002; Nelson, 2007; U.S. Department of Health and Human Services, 2010b). Third, children who would not be eligible for a means-tested program also derive benefits from quality preschool education. I estimated the benefits and costs of offering publicly funded pre-K to every 4-year-old using an average cost per child of $6,000, which is more than sufficient to provide a quality program if many children attend for a half day, keeping in mind that preschool special education costs are already paid for separately (Barnett et al., 2009). Similar calculations could be made for 3-year-olds, but it is unlikely the nation will be ready to take such a step for quite some time.

To estimate the added costs and benefits, it is first necessary to estimate changes in enrollment from replacing the current set of means-tested programs (from the 2005 NHES data) with a universal program. I assume that enrollment would increase to near 100% for the two lowest income quintiles but would reach only 90%, 85%, and 80% in the next three quintiles moving up the income ladder as some of these children continue to attend private programs. Overall, this yields a public preschool participation rate of 91%. This level of enrollment is consistent with kindergarten enrollment and slightly higher than what has been achieved in Oklahoma (taking state and Head Start programs together). However, the high enrollment rates for low-income families will only be possible if there is substantial outreach and programs are designed to meet their needs (e.g., at least coordinated with child care and providing transportation if this is an obstacle). Taking into account the extent to which state pre-K already pays for some private enrollment, the cost is roughly $14 billion per year. Topping off state pre-K funding to reach $6,000 per child for the 25% of 4-year-olds currently enrolled would cost slightly more than $1 billion. Head Start is currently funded at a much higher level than $6,000 per child. The rest of the cost is to bring public enrollment up from just below 40% to just over 90% at age 4.

Benefits for disadvantaged children are estimated assuming the 10-to-1 return found for the Chicago Child-Parent Centers for children in lower income families. This equals $60,000 per child in lifetime present value for those not currently enrolled in the bottom income quintile. For children in the middle three income quintiles, this figure is cut in half consistent with the estimates discussed previously; for children in the top quintile, it is reduced by half again. To estimate benefits for children currently served in private programs and Head Start, I cut these figures in half, despite the disappointing results from these programs that suggest larger gains from moving to a high-quality state-funded pre-K. Under these assumptions, a universal program produces benefits of $70 billion. The current means-tested approach may or may not have a higher rate of return per dollar invested given imperfect targeting and the small effects produced by some programs. In any case, it forgoes what is potentially a very large net benefit from a universal program. This is more than four times the estimated additional cost—a substantial margin for error—and it does not take into account any possible cost savings through reductions in other public funding now devoted to 4-year-olds in private preschools, including tax credits and subsidies through CCDF, TANF, and other programs.

CONCLUSION

Four advantages are set out for universal over targeted preschool education. Such an approach requires public funding, but can rely substantially on private provision, as is the case with many state-funded pre-K programs (Barnett et al., 2009). The greatest disadvantage of a universal program is undoubtedly its cost. The advantages are better coverage of the disadvantaged population, larger educational gains for disadvantaged children, education benefits for nondisadvantaged students, and a substantial economic return flowing from those first three advantages. To achieve these advantages, pre-K policy will have to be designed to facilitate high rates of participation by children from low-income families and to maintain reasonable levels of effectiveness. State pre-K programs have shown that this can be done, so this is not setting an unrealistic goal for public programs (Applewhite & Hirsch, 2003; Gormley et al., 2008).

Universal pre-K could be carefully tailored in ways that might improve the returns. Parents could be charged fees on a sliding scale with income to recoup some costs. Children could receive more or less intensive services within the program depending on their needs. It might also be argued that means-tested programs also could be improved—with better targeting and greater effectiveness. This has been tried for over 40 years, and while some improvements are possible, the advantages cited are exclusive to a universal approach. It is time to try something new.

CHAPTER 6

About Everyone's Child
Winning Public Support for Early Learning

David Lawrence, Jr.

Here is a brief but valuable history lesson for advocates trying to establish or expand publicly funded early learning programs. In 1988, in what was then called Dade County—the largest county in Florida with a population greater than that of 16 states—State Attorney Janet Reno (later to become Attorney General of the United States) and other community leaders campaigned for a dedicated source of funding for early intervention and prevention programs. The top leadership of this campaign included some of the most prominent, most caring child advocates and civic leaders in Miami. Their argument was that the voters ought to raise their property taxes to fund early education and health programs to help the most at-risk children and families in the community's most distressed neighborhoods. It made sense. Besides, who doesn't love children? Who wouldn't be willing to do almost everything for them, especially those in the most dire straits who will have a hard time succeeding in life without our special attention? However, the outcome was overwhelming rejection. The votes were 2–1 against the measure.

Fourteen years later, in 2002, it was time to try again. Would it be possible to pass? What will make this time different? Advocates had learned from their stunning defeat and studied up on how public perception is shaped and how to frame issues to elicit favorable responses. In short, they adopted a very different way of looking at things: Their campaign would be about all the community's children—not about *those* children but rather *our* children, about everyone. They realized, of course, that certain children and families needed more help and it should be available to them. But the campaign would not be framed as being "on the side of the angels"—although certainly this is heaven-inspired work—but rather would be a genuine political campaign. Therefore, they needed to raise real money to mount a campaign built on real political strategy. The outcome in 2002 was a 2–1 victory.

To give the cause and the outcome a better chance, a 5-year sunset was put on the ballot. In essence, the voters were told, "Try this for 5 years. You will have a chance to vote again. If you like it, then you can vote for this to be for perpetuity. Don't like it? It's gone." So in August 2008, it was time to vote again. The economy was beginning to tank, and Miami-Dade County had become a national example for excesses in housing prices. Gas cost more, and so did most everything else. The partial collapse of the national economy was felt especially hard in South Florida, so it was an especially difficult time to get people to vote for higher property taxes.

On the positive side, there was not one hint of a scandal with a single dollar of the more than $100 million available each year for the early intervention and prevention initiative which was not coincidentally named the Children's Trust. Indeed, *trust* was the fundamental issue. Could people trust their dollars to be wisely invested in the lives and futures of the children of the community? Would the whole community benefit, including those who did not have children? Would the investment in children pay off in a safer, more successful community for everyone?

Advocates had a great story—indeed, many stories—to tell about where the people's money was being spent: incentives for high-quality, brain-stimulating child care; millions for programs to help children with special needs; the dollars to pay for more than 100 school health teams, including not only a nurse or nurse practitioner but also someone with a master's in social work; and the addition of parent skill-building programs, after-school programs, and much more. A skilled political strategist—Sergio Bendixen, a Miamian with a national reputation—ran the campaign. In addition, enough money was raised—more than $1.5 million—to run a substantive campaign using broadcast and print media as well as grassroots advertising.

As a result, the Children's Trust was reaffirmed in perpetuity by an 85.4% margin. Voters were willing to pay taxes forever to help the children—all the children—succeed in school and in life. The two biggest factors in this success were advocates relentlessly promoting the initiative as being about *everybody's* child and keeping the public's trust.

Whether taxpayer dollars should be spent on services that are universal or be reserved for children who are most at risk is a national question. The choices are either to focus the dollars and the efforts on those children who most need the extra help and attention, or to aim for everyone, knowing that extra funding should and will need to be spent on the children with greatest need. At first glance, the obvious choice is the first choice: put limited resources to work where the need is greatest. However, the second choice is the path with by far the best chance of success.

However, this is not how government sees the situation. Government, both national and state, operates on a level of means testing—for example, 150% of the federal poverty level or some other benchmark. No one I know outside of government thinks that way. Rather, most people think about what all children need regardless of whether they are being raised in impoverished or affluent households, stressed or strong families. For example, all children need to play and experience the great outdoors, so governments have few issues with providing parks and playgrounds. My five children were raised according to what I now understand to be the principles embracing the right blend of health and education and nurturing and love. All children need the same.

It is never a good strategy to attempt to divide Americans. Social Security would never have passed if it had been about some senior citizens and not others. Medicare was for everyone older than 65; it could not have passed any other way. It was the same with prekindergarten (pre-K) for Florida 4-year-olds and funding for early intervention and prevention in Miami-Dade County.

I don't live in an especially enlightened state. Our indicators are plain embarrassing in health and education—toward the top in high school dropout rates, more than 800,000 children without health insurance, mediocre investment in public education at all three levels (elementary, secondary, and higher education). Yet back in 2002, with the full leadership of Miami-Dade Mayor Alex Penelas, 722,000 Floridians signed petitions to put a constitutional amendment on the ballot that called for every 4-year-old to have access to a publicly funded, "high-quality prekindergarten experience delivered according to professionally accepted standards." The voters of Florida passed it, with 59% voting in favor of the amendment. That constitutional amendment and voluntary universal pre-K went into effect in the 2005 school year. Today, the state spends more than $350 million each year on this program, with approximately 161,000 enrolled 4-year-olds.

Is the program good enough? No, it is nowhere near good enough (albeit of enough basic quality for tens of thousands of parents to want to sign up their children). The current version of Florida's pre-K program lacks a data-driven discipline, needs to face up to the matter of fully qualified teachers, needs to require research-based curricula in all settings, and should require pre- and post-assessments for 4-year-olds in the program, which can both inform instruction and be shared with parents who can help if they know where their children have gaps and how they can contribute to their success.

So would I rather take smaller, even baby steps toward the highest quality program, or take the constitutionally mandated approach that creates a large enough program to have room for all children? I choose the latter. Along with other Floridians, I will work hard to get the program up to the quality that all children deserve. What we are trying to build for children is a movement.

But what do I mean by *movement*? When one thinks of the lessons of history, what comes quickly to mind may be the civil rights movement or the feminist movement. Both of these movements initially were marginalized by the majority. They were frequently ridiculed and sometimes cruelly beaten back. Yet eventually, when most people came to understand that these were movements that spoke to every person and an American sense of equality, they came to be recognized as part of the founding principles of this country. Do not think it is coincidental that at least half the seats in most law and medical school classrooms in this country today are occupied by women. This progress is a direct consequence of the struggle for women's rights and the feminist movement. That movement was about standing up for the rights of all Americans—assuring that everyone has equal opportunity and is spared from discrimination. Likewise, the civil rights movement was not only about African Americans but about all Americans and the essence of American egalitarianism.

Kindergarten is an example of a movement. Frequently, I ask audiences to guess when public kindergarten began, and usually I hear back that it was in their lifetimes or that of their parents, which demonstrates most people's perspective on history. In fact, kindergarten was created in 1837 and came to America in the 1850s. Taking more than a century to become genuinely widespread, kindergarten was frequently fought as unnecessary and even antifamily. For decades, kindergarten was seen as mostly for society's worst-off and best-off children. Only when it became a movement on behalf of everyone's children did it become a full reality. Today, a high-quality kindergarten experience delivered in the public schools has become an expectation on the part of almost all parents for their 5-year-olds. Kindergarten is still not mandatory in two thirds of the states, but it would be difficult to find a parent of a 5-year-old today who wants his or her child's first exposure to school to be first grade.

Using that same logic, common sense and the lessons of history tell me that a real movement for school readiness will never be built unless it is for everyone's child—regardless of socioeconomic status. Too often, this is not the way most people do it. Instead, people often focus on one corner of the community or another, as witnessed by the majority of the states that offer public pre-K only to certain children or in certain neighborhoods. Then, the rest of the community may say, "Oh, I understand.

Finn (2009) argued that limited resources should be used to produce high-quality programs for the children who are most in need of services, particularly if the goal of pre-K is to close the achievement gap. Others contend that public funding of all services to 3- and 4-year-old children would displace programs already operating in the private sector (Besharov & Call, 2008). Universalizing pre-K fosters the public assumption of private sector expenditures by subsidizing preschool for upper-middle and upper class families who can well afford to send their children to private programs without government support.

Effectiveness for Low-Income Children   Complementing the cost-effectiveness argument is research suggesting that children from low-income families benefit most from high-quality services. Although studies have found that all children can benefit from preschool, the most significant gains are often demonstrated by those from low-income and minority families (Gormley et al., 2005; Magnuson, Ruhm, & Waldfogel, 2007a). The evidence of greater gains for low-income children fits squarely with policy trends toward eliminating the achievement gap, solidifying a call for targeting services at those who benefit most.

Neutral Issues

Some issues are used by both advocates and opponents of universal pre-K to justify their stances, such as accountability and standardization. Critics fear that trends toward increased accountability in the K–12 system will discourage the child-centeredness that has long marked early education (Fuller, 2007). Accompanying this concern, early educators fear that the curriculum will be "schoolified" and that the pedagogical freedom traditionally accorded to early educators will lose out to more standardized pedagogy and content. In short, there is a fear that universality means uniformity—that universal pre-K will curtail flexibilities that accommodate the diversity of American children's needs (Fuller, 2007).

Others contend that the presence of universal pre-K, especially when housed in public schools, will serve to alert elementary personnel to the unique needs of young children and the importance of the early years. They strongly support a continuum that embraces pre-K through third grade in hopes of fostering continuity and more effective learning environments for all children in their primary years (Takanishi & Kauerz, 2008).

Even this very brief review of the stances for and against universal pre-K suggests that there is no paucity of sentiment. Less clear, however, is the undergirding challenge—one that we suggest is buried in decades of history.

CHANGING THE DEBATE: MOVING FROM DEFICITS TO RIGHTS
The Historic Stance: Deficit

With the exception of elementary and secondary education, American society has traditionally viewed its obligation to young children and their families from a deficit perspective. From 19th century infant schools to Head Start's founding in 1965, public programs for young children have been designed for those deemed to be at risk because of developmental or family circumstances (Beatty, 1995). Unlike other countries with which America routinely competes economically and intellectually, the United States does not entitle its young to environments that optimize their social, emotional, intellectual, and spiritual development. To the contrary, public investments in the young must be justified as meeting a greater social or economic good. Conceptually, the movement toward universality has sought to redress the impact of this deficit orientation by seeking to provide common access. Practically, however, the movement from deficits to rights has focused primarily on one aspect of rights—that of universal access. We propose that a genuine movement to rights must be predicated on the right to quality as well. Moreover, it must be grounded in a robust understanding of rights.

The Universal Plus Stance: Rights

A rights position is predicated on two different meanings of the word *rights* (Kagan, 1993). The first meaning, often rooted in research, is concerned with what is correct in judgment, opinion, or action. Aiming to advance what is good, proper, and correct, it asks what is appropriate for young children and their families in order to ensure optimal development. Taking a different frame, a right can also be an entitlement: one that confers privilege via a legal guarantee, a just claim, or a moral principle. Often rooted in legality or morality, this meaning asks: To what are children rightfully entitled? Universal Plus combines the two, bringing what is right and appropriate for children (the first question) into alignment with their rightful entitlements (the second question).

Operationally, moving from a deficit to a rights framework has two major consequences. First, rather than beginning with piecemeal approaches to policy, which are framed and limited by political and fiscal realities, a rights orientation begins with a vision of what one believes all young children deserve, and then one creates policy options to reflect that vision. The rights orientation acknowledges that policy is incremental and that such entitlements may not come overnight. Yet, it demands situating all policy within the context of both definitions of rights—what is appropriate and what is to be entitled.

Emanating from this first consequence and specifically germane to Universal Plus, the second consequence suggests that universality cannot be equated with quality, nor can quality be presumed or subsumed under universality as it is presently construed. As a result, and stated from a rights perspective, any approach to early childhood expansion must focus equally on entitling all children to both access and quality. Moreover, given the vulnerability of young children and the diversity of familial values, parents of young children have rights as well; they are entitled to choice in whether their children should attend preschool and in their selection of those preschools. In other words, within a rights framework, on the supply side preschools must be universally available and be of high quality; on the demand side, participation must remain voluntary, with options and choice made available for parents.

UNIVERSAL PLUS: THE RIGHT TO QUALITY

Such a rights framework may seem too far a stretch—too idealized, too romanticized, and above all, too remote from reality. Skeptics might ask how both universal access and universal quality can be achieved. Universal Plus suggests that rather than focusing on access to the near exclusion of quality, all initiatives—no matter how large or small—should be infused with a commitment to both. To elaborate how this might unfold, we discuss the infrastructure, or the core, as a prelude to describing the services that should be offered to all children and families.

Universality within a Rights Framework: The Core

Conventionally, universality has been associated primarily with the quantitative aspect of service provision, notably increasing the number of slots rendered available to children. We twist that notion: Universality must also visibly and intentionally embrace the qualitative dimensions of early childhood provision, notably focusing on the proven characteristics of quality services.

Guidelines and Standards   Early learning and development guidelines and program standards are both effective elixirs of quality. Early learning and development guidelines specify what children should know and be able to do and provide the framework for an integrated approach to quality early education. Program standards, for decades, have been linked to quality, with more stringent requirements related to high-quality services.

Coordinated Professional Development   With a work force that is characterized by low levels of education and compensation and high levels of turnover (Kagan, Kauerz, & Tarrant, 2008), a commitment to universality necessitates the improvement of professional development opportunities for all. Coordinated professional development that embraces new approaches to supporting adult learners is essential to providing higher quality programs to young children.

Integrated Governance Body   Given the siloed nature of early childhood services, a formalized mechanism for planning and coordinating resource allocation, service delivery, and program and child monitoring needs to become a standard element of universal service delivery. Such governance entities should transcend individual programs and create the platform of program quality and comparability, with a particular focus on fostering transitions among and between child supporting environments: home, preschool, school, and community, including community health and mental health services.

Durable Funding Stream   Although increases in federal and state funding for early childhood has generally characterized the early 21st century, considerable inconsistency prevails across and within states regarding funding amounts and mechanisms. Moreover, as state budgets have decreased, states are experiencing challenges in sustaining their funding, often with initial investments in universal services being partially sacrificed (Pew Center on the States, 2009). A durable, dedicated funding stream is a necessary element of universality.

Universality within a Rights Framework: The Services

Coexisting with these four core elements of the infrastructure and building on the comprehensive model advanced by Zigler et al. (2006a), we suggest that the following array of services be rooted in the following principle: Beyond the universal provision of quality preschool for 3- and 4-year-old children, all other services described below should be made available first and free to all low-income children, with services offered to other children on a sliding fee basis.

Prenatal to Age 3   Given the importance of early development and the criticality of parents to that development, we recommend that parenting education and family support services be made available. In addition, health passports and the preventive services attendant to them should be created for all children. Nontoxic, safe environments where nutritious food is obtainable and affordable should be an essential component of Universal Plus.

Age 3–5 Years   All the infrastructure and services for children from birth to age 3 apply to this age group as well. As noted, quality preschool education and services should be made available to all on a voluntary basis. In addition, such programs should consider the unique needs of dual-language learners and children with disabilities.

Age 6–8 Years   Incorporating all previous items, the needs of children as they make the transition into kindergarten and the primary school must be addressed by each of the four elements described under the infrastructure. Moreover, specific efforts that foster pedagogical, programmatic, and policy alignment must characterize the experiences of, and learning and living contexts for, this age group.

ACHIEVING UNIVERSAL PLUS

Fully recognizing that American early childhood policy is incremental and that the Universal Plus approach represents a more ambitious than usual stance, we recommend a phased implementation strategy. A suggestion for how such a strategy might unfold is presented in the following sections.

Phase I: Getting Going

Policies aimed both at enhancing the provision of direct services to 3- and 4-year-old children and at enriching the infrastructure elements deserve commensurate attention. At the base, there is a need to better understand precisely who is (and is not) being served by which programs and services. With the goal of discerning a true count, states are creating unique identification numbers for all children that will enable the tracking of both the services received and, in some cases, the progress of children derived as a result of those services. Any effort toward universality must have clear unduplicated counts of children and services at hand. Moreover, this suggests developing the data system's capacity to collect, analyze, and use the data.

Phase II: Moving Forward

Service expansion will occur more rapidly and more efficiently once a viable infrastructure is in place. Although it begins in Phase I, building an infrastructure is the focus of Phase II. Taking the four elements of universality presented previously, we call for the development of aligned early learning guidelines for children from birth to age 8. We also support the development of optional national early learning guidelines that states could adapt to fit their context. Program standards and their enforcement should be universalized, with some exceptions rendered depending on climate, geography, and resource availability. Integrated approaches to professional development, largely in the form of quality rating systems, should be undertaken, as should the supports necessary to render them effective. Taking cues from many states, governance mechanisms need to be developed and legitimated either by the legislative and/or executive branches of government. Such entities should have the authority and the accountability to effect critical fiscal and programmatic changes across the evolving early childhood system. Efforts to convert piecemeal funding streams into a unified funding mechanism, such as using the K–12 funding formula, need to be advanced. Not ancillary to universality, these infrastructure elements are central to its efficient and effective evolution.

Phase III: Getting It Right

This is not a short-term phase; these efforts will take time to evolve. En route, there must be mechanisms to assure that everyone is on the right track to a rights-based approach. To that end, strategies for evaluating the growth and progress of children and programs must be planned and implemented. Teacher quality must be ensured, with coaching, mentoring, and professional development opportunities abundant. Such accomplishment must be rewarded financially while the compensation levels of all early childhood personnel are enhanced. Systems of child, program, and teacher evaluation need to be linked, with a clear goal of enhanced child outcomes across all domains of development as the goal.

CONCLUSION

Universal Plus, as described herein, does not negate the importance of universal pre-K, nor does it espouse our current controversial and variable approach to universality. By changing the debate—and hence the framework for universality—from one that is deficit oriented to one that is rights based, we regard the provision of universal pre-K as one that must focus as much on quality enhancements as it does on slot provision. In the rights paradigm, universality must come to fruition with commensurate attention accorded the direct services and the infrastructure that makes rendering the services worthwhile. As such, Universal Plus actualizes the mantra that whatever is worth doing is worth doing well.

Teacher Credentials versus Competencies and Supports

STUDY QUESTIONS

- What qualifies someone to teach pre-K? Who should make these decisions? Based on what criteria? Use specific evidence from the text to support your argument.

- What areas of focus should be included in teacher preparation courses in terms of content knowledge? How have the expectations of what teachers need to know in terms of child development changed since the 1980s?

- How are teacher quality and teacher effectiveness defined and measured? How does distinguishing between those two terms factor into the teacher qualifications debate?

CHAPTER 8

Minimum Requirements for Preschool Teacher Educational Qualifications

W. Steven Barnett

One of the most vexing questions in early childhood policy is how much education should be required for teachers in publicly funded programs. The issue is vexing for several reasons. First, it significantly affects costs. Second, every program is a jobs program, and the higher the minimum educational qualification for a job, the fewer the people who are eligible for it. Third, research findings regarding the value of teacher educational qualifications are mixed. Policy makers confront contradictory research-based claims about the efficacy of a preschool teacher's education level. This chapter aims to help policy makers sort through the evidence and provide a basis for better decisions about requirements for a teacher's education. First, however, the basic rationale for requiring preschool teachers to have a 4-year degree and the current educational requirements of the various public preschool programs are described.

The argument for requiring a 4-year degree is that teaching young children is a cognitively complex task requiring both general and specialized knowledge and above-average cognitive abilities (Bowman, Donovan, & Burns, 2001; Cunningham, Zibulsky, & Callahan, 2009). Adults cannot readily pass on to children vocabulary, discourse patterns, mathematics and science knowledge and skills, and general knowledge that they do not possess or comfortably use often in ordinary interactions. Identifying the particular needs of each child in order to deliver a highly individualized education one to one, in small groups, and in large groups is a complex and demanding activity. The knowledge and skills required are so extensive that 4 years seems hardly enough. Better educated teachers also are more able to learn from professional development as they move from novice to expert teachers and adapt to advances in knowledge about learning and teaching.

BACKGROUND

There is relatively little variation in minimum requirements for public school teachers of children beginning at age 5 years. Every state requires public school teachers to have at least a 4-year college degree (i.e., bachelor's degree) and some specialized education for the teaching profession. Specialization requirements and how they may be obtained (e.g., alternate routes) vary considerably and are not a primary focus of this chapter. Salaries for public school kindergarten teachers (not including special education) average more than $50,000 for a 10-month school year. Teachers in private schools earn somewhat less and may not be required to have a bachelor's degree, but the vast majority of kindergarten teachers work in public schools. Teachers in Grades 1–6 make slightly more, perhaps an additional $2,000 per year.

Only about half of the states with prekindergarten (pre-K) programs require all public pre-K teachers to have a bachelor's degree (Barnett et al., 2009). Some have lower qualifications for teachers who work outside the public schools and others have lower qualifications for all public pre-K teachers. Many states require that preschool teachers in the public schools be paid public school teacher salaries; a few require this for all teachers if they are state funded. Assistant teachers who are employed in most programs alongside lead teachers are rarely required to have formal education beyond a high school diploma or equivalent. In several states, state-funded pre-K teachers are generally paid at the same level as public school teachers, whether or not they are in public schools, but in most states they are paid at the same rate only if they work in public schools (Barnett et al., 2009).

Public school preschool special education teachers are all required to have at least a bachelor's degree and meet certification requirements. Frequently, although not always, these teachers are paid on the same scale as other public school teachers. This can present issues for inclusion of children with disabilities in general education classrooms in state pre-K where teachers are not similarly qualified and paid. Parents and special education professionals may be reluctant to place children with disabilities in classrooms where they do not consider the teachers to be educational professionals.

Head Start teacher qualifications and pay are low compared to those of public school kindergarten teachers. The 2007 Head Start reauthorization mandated that all teachers have at least an associate's degree by 2011 and at least 50% have a bachelor's degree by 2013 (U.S. Department of Health and Human Services, 2008). In 2008, 41% of teachers held at least a bachelor's degree and 34% had an associate's degree (Center for Law and Social Policy, 2011). However, Head Start teachers with a bachelor's degree were paid only about $29,000, teachers with an associate's degree were paid $24,000, and teachers with less education averaged $22,000 (National Education Association, 2010; U.S. Department of Health and Human Services, 2009a). Head Start salaries are very similar to the salaries of teachers in private child care centers, suggesting that these are not separate markets. However, child care teachers often have larger classes and less support from administrators and other support staff, including instructional leaders.

If public pre-K teachers were required to have a bachelor's degree without adopting public school salary levels, the financial consequences would be minimal. Allowing for fringe benefits, the cost would be $300–$400 per child for a full-day program. However, such a policy would be foolish. There would be a shortage of qualified teachers. New teachers with bachelor's degrees would be much weaker than those in the public schools, and turnover rates would rise. These problems would be most serious for programs in the most disadvantaged and troubled neighborhoods. Higher qualifications only make sense if accompanied by higher pay. Raising pay to the level of the public schools would cost state pre-K programs perhaps $600 per child (although this would vary from state to state), or $300 where teachers have two half-day sessions. For Head Start, the cost would be $1,500–$1,800 per pupil for a full day, or half that for teachers with two half-day sessions.

RESEARCH ON THE EFFECTS OF PRESCHOOL TEACHER QUALIFICATIONS

The substantial body of research on the effects of preschool teacher qualifications on teaching, learning, and child development has yielded mixed results. Some studies find that teachers with more education are better teachers and have stronger effects on learning, while others do not. A 2007 meta-analysis of the literature found a modest positive effect (standard deviation of 0.15) of teachers with a bachelor's degree compared to those with less education (Kelley & Camilli, 2007). Most of the studies looked at effects on teacher beliefs, knowledge, and practices rather than child outcomes. Of course, the only way in which one would expect a teacher's level of education to produce larger gains in children's learning and development would be through changes in thinking that led to changes in practice and, therefore, children's experiences.

Not surprisingly, results from the research on teacher qualifications are mixed. Researchers have addressed different questions with different methods, and different specifications of the model relating learning outcomes to inputs (including teacher education) to the early learning process. In addition, differences in education levels may capture different aspects of teacher quality (e.g., differences in attitudes and abilities, the content and rigor of course work) depending on the geographic and other contexts of studies. Studies of the effects of a bachelor's degree within a particular state may not yield the same results as studies in another state. These same problems afflict the more extensive literature on the estimation of the effects of teacher qualifications, class size, and other dimensions of K–12 education set by policy (Imbens & Angrist, 1994; Todd & Wolpin, 2003, 2007). I discuss these with particular reference to the preschool teacher qualifications literature.

Studies of the effects of preschool teacher education levels have employed techniques ranging from simple correlations to complex statistical analyses that account for many different variables to structural models that model nonrandom assignment of students to teachers and the ways in which teachers may affect classroom experiences. Some even allow for interactions between classroom and home experiences. Unfortunately, there are not any randomized trials, although some randomized trials that examine the effects of preschool programs provide information relevant to the teacher qualifications issue. Studies that employ different research designs and methods do not address the same questions. The simple correlation addresses the question of the effect of teacher qualifications, letting everything else vary. This approach is problematic because other variables associated with teacher degree (e.g., whether the program is in a public school) might be responsible for the association. Other methods that control for extraneous variables can have their own problems. Many studies inadvertently control out the effects of teacher education in the process of using this method. Examples include holding salary constant, controlling for all effects of state policy first (including policies regarding teacher education), and controlling for the child care center's fixed effects by limiting comparisons to teachers within the same center, which is a problem if teachers influence each other or if hiring is based on a target salary and budget constraint regardless of teacher qualifications. Some researchers have even examined the effects of teacher education level while controlling for variations in teacher attitudes, beliefs, or practices but do not explain what other mechanism could possibly transmit the effects of teachers to students.

In deciding what approach to take and how to interpret a study, it is essential to specify the policy question carefully. Is it the effect of raising teacher qualifications, holding all else constant? Is it the effect of raising teacher qualifications and pay, holding other elements of program structure constant? Is it the effect of raising teacher qualifications as part of a broader set of policy changes adopted together and including pay, in-service training, and child–staff ratio? These program features are unlikely to be independent within a budget constraint and may interact even if the budget constraint is relaxed.

A major challenge for any study of the effects of teacher qualifications on learning and development is proper specification of the model. In addition to the issues discussed, few studies have measures of the part of the production process that takes place in the home. Simply including family background measures as proxies is not necessarily good enough to remove bias. Nonrandom classroom assignments based on students' abilities and growth can seriously bias the estimates of value-added models that relate teacher characteristics to child learning over a year (Rothstein, 2008, 2009). Studies also need to take into account the nonindependence of teachers and other characteristics. A teacher's performance may depend on the performance of the other teachers with whom that teacher works and on other supports and working conditions. Studies rarely take into account assistant teacher characteristics and pay, even though these may systematically vary (perhaps inversely) with teacher characteristics and pay. Studies comparing different comprehensive packages of policies might get us further than studies that seek to identify the independent contributions of program features that are not independent.

A few studies deserve specific discussion because they are well known and have obvious strengths. The oldest of these is the Cost, Quality, and Outcomes Study of child care (Cost, Quality and Outcomes Study Team, 1995; Peisner-Feinberg et al., 1999; Phillipsen, Burchinal, Howes, & Cryer, 1997). Higher levels of teacher education and pay were associated with higher quality as measured by structured observations, and children's cognitive test scores were associated with quality. Howes (1997) found that teachers with more education were associated with higher classroom quality scores and higher children's test scores. Reanalyses controlling for location and center find no differences between teachers with bachelor's degrees and those with only an associate's degree or high school diploma (Blau, 2000). However, if location controls for regulatory and budget constraints and programs assign more difficult-to-teach children to more highly qualified teachers, and if teachers help each other, or if programs hire teachers at roughly the same ability level and pay regardless of degree, then such models are inappropriate.

The National Institute of Child Health and Human Development (NICHD) study of early care and education has an advantage over most other studies in that it includes measures of education in the home so that it can more completely model the processes that contribute to a child's learning and development. It also has measures of learning and development over multiple years and not just over a few months. Several NICHD studies have found that teacher education contributes to children's learning and development, including one that explicitly modeled the effects of teacher qualifications on teaching practices as the mediator of effects on children while including effects of parenting (NICHD, 1999, 2002b). Modest positive effects were found, but it should be kept in mind that this is in the context of private child care with its poor pay and working conditions.

A number of studies have reported finding no relationship between teacher qualifications and teaching practices on children's learning. These studies have larger sample sizes than many past studies, which is a distinct improvement. However, they have other serious limitations, including the general problem of specifying the production function correctly. None of the studies model teacher assignment, implicitly assuming that it is random. None of the studies include measures of home learning processes. All employ linear models in which program features contribute additively to output. One of these studies focused on child care centers and had a very limited range of teachers in the sample; only 30 of 964 had annual salaries above $30,000 (Torquati, Raikes, & Huddleston-Cass, 2007). Although the study had 964 teacher interviews, it had only 223 observations of quality, which suggests that only about 7 teachers with salaries over $30,000 contributed to the estimates of the relationship of education to quality. Therefore, I do not discuss it further, as few teachers in the study are likely to be highly qualified. Several other studies looked at state pre-K programs and included measures of children's learning as well as program quality (Early et al., 2006; Howes et al., 2008; Mashburn et al., 2008). The most comprehensive includes an analysis of the data from the state pre-K studies and analyses of data from six other studies (Early et al., 2007). These studies have been widely interpreted as finding that a bachelor's degree has no effects on teaching and learning in preschool programs.

The state pre-K and seven study analyses all employed models that include state- or site-fixed effects. Thus, they control for state and organizational policies regarding teacher qualifications and funding (which implies a budget constraint) and only look at the effects of variations within those. Within these constraints, programs trade off various aspects of teacher quality against each other and against other structural features. For example, they may trade off natural abilities and personality characteristics, general education, and specialized training in early childhood education. Even within general education level, there is the potential to trade off a 2-year degree from a strong institution against a 4-year degree from a weak institution within a given salary constraint. This likely obscures any association between level of education and quality or child development. The studies find a lack of significant relationships with any program features, not just teacher education level. The lack of an education effect is not limited to the bachelor's degree; no level of education beyond a high school diploma has positive effects. More generally, no features of program structure consistently predict learning and development.

My reading of the evidence from the seven study analyses leads to a conclusion that is not as dismal as the authors' interpretations. Their analyses of state pre-K data find children make greater gains in prereading and math if their teachers have at least a bachelor's degree. Although they did not look at social outcomes, another analysis of the same dataset reported larger gains in social competence when teachers had a bachelor's degree. More generally, the seven study analyses estimated 27 relationships with the bachelor's degree, of which 19 were positive and eight were negative. This is unlikely to have occurred by chance, and across all these studies, the hypothesis that the bachelor's degree is not associated with quality or child learning is rejected at the conventional level. (A simple binomial test rejected the null hypothesis that the bachelor's degree is not associated with quality or child learning, with $p = .026$). The estimated effects are not large, but the estimated effect sizes in these studies may not be a good guide given all of the problems (discussed previously) that may have attenuated the estimates. In addition to all of the limitations already noted, the average time between pretest and posttest is far less than a full school year, and measurement error afflicts both dependent and independent variables (e.g., teachers without bachelor's degrees may have substantial credits toward the degree, programs vary in rigor and content).

It is by no means clear how far any of these correlational studies will get in the field. Large scale randomized trials would get us much further but would be an expensive proposition. To truly test the effect of education level, there would have to be a long-term commitment to supporting this policy on a substantial scale.

The closest thing available to a randomized trial is a natural experiment that was created by the New Jersey Supreme Court when it ordered high-quality preschool education to be provided to all children in 31 districts with high percentages of low-income families. Their prescription included a bachelor's degree with early childhood certification and maximum class size of 15. This was implemented in a public system in which most children were served by private child care centers under contracts with school districts. Prior to implementation of the court's order, the overall quality in these private programs was low. The state provided scholarships so that teachers in private programs who lacked the necessary credentials to serve children in the court-ordered program could become degreed or certificated. The reward for this was not just keeping a job but the much higher salaries provided to teachers who met these public school standards even though they remained in private programs. After teachers had time to acquire degrees and certification, observed quality increased so that most programs were good to excellent, and there was no difference in quality between the public schools and private centers (Frede, Jung, Barnett, Lamy, & Figueras, 2007; Frede, Jung, Barnett, & Figueras, 2009). Increased education accompanied by a pay increase was not the only change, as there was also extensive on-the-job professional development, but I know of no instance where professional development alone produced these kinds of permanent improvements on a large scale.

OTHER RELEVANT RESEARCH ON PROGRAM EFFECTIVENESS

Finally, it is possible to approach the question from another perspective. What can be learned about teacher qualifications from preschool programs that have produced substantial gains in learning and development in rigorous studies? A review of the literature finds that virtually all reports of large effects on learning with highly rigorous designs are due to preschool programs in the public schools with licensed teachers who have bachelor's degrees (Barnett, 2008). This includes the randomized trials of the Perry preschool and Institute for Developmental Studies programs, the Chicago Child-Parent Centers study, and the study of universal pre-K in Tulsa (Deutsch, Deutsch, Jordan, & Grallo, 1983; Gormley et al., 2005; Reynolds, 2000; Schweinhart et al., 2005).

The Tulsa study broadens the scope of the evidence (Gormley et al., 2008). In Tulsa, Head Start programs participate in universal pre-K by having public school teachers staff their classrooms. The educational effects of Tulsa Head Start for disadvantaged students are much larger than the average findings for Head Start in the National Impact Study. Tulsa Head Start's effects are identical to the effects of the Tulsa Public School pre-K for mathematics but somewhat smaller for literacy. This suggests that teachers account for part—but not all—of the advantage of Tulsa's universal pre-K program over typical Head Start programs. There may be additional benefits to effectiveness from being part of the public school system (Reynolds & Temple, 2008). The Tulsa study's findings resonate with those for New Jersey's Abbott pre-K program discussed previously, and it is noteworthy that the Abbott program also produces robust benefits for children's learning and school success at the end of preschool and beyond.

To my knowledge, the only study close to a counterexample is of California state pre-K. The study found strong learning gains for children, even though only about half the teachers had 4-year degrees and another 40% had 2-year degrees. However, this study obtained permission to collect data in only half the classrooms selected for study, raising questions about bias, as only the best may have agreed to participate in the study (Barnett et al., 2009).

The national randomized trial of Head Start provides another relevant set of findings. Head Start is well funded relative to state pre-K programs and child care (Puma et al., 2005, 2010). Class sizes are low and staffed by a teacher and an assistant. The program has extensive performance standards, administrative structures, requirements for specialized training in early childhood, and supports for professional development. Supportive services for children and families outside the classroom and for children with special needs within the classroom are notable program features. A substantial number operate within public school systems. The one glaring difference relative to other programs found to produce large educational gains for children is that Head Start teachers have relatively low levels of formal education and pay. Nevertheless, Head Start had small initial effects on children's learning and development, and the study found no gains in language, literacy, or math by the end of kindergarten. As noted previously, Head Start in Tulsa, using licensed teachers with bachelor's degrees who were paid public school salaries, produced much larger gains than Head Start nationally, further implicating teacher education and pay.

CONCLUSION

Education research rarely provides a basis for certainty. Still, one can be quite certain that costs will rise if teachers are required to have bachelor's degrees and pay comparable to that of public school teachers generally. The estimated amount ranges from $300 per child for part-day state pre-K to $1,500 per child or more for Head Start. There is less certainty about the benefits of requiring a bachelor's degree and higher salaries. The evidence is mixed, and much of the research has serious limitations. However, there is less uncertainty about the qualifications of preschool teachers who have consistently produced strong gains for young children in rigorous studies. Almost without exception, these have been teachers with bachelor's degrees who were paid public school salaries. This is relevant because the programs that produced large educational gains for children produced much larger economic benefits than other programs. The difference in benefits is an order of magnitude greater than the difference in costs. If we assign a probability greater than 50% to a bachelor's degree with higher pay producing large gains in learning and development, then the expected value of requiring a bachelor's degree and adequate pay is quite large. This does not mean hiring just anyone with a bachelor's degree and ignoring actual abilities and knowledge or the quality and content of a degree, nor does it mean that other program features including in-service professional development and supervision are unimportant. Policy must focus on real competencies, the teacher preparation curriculum, and the other program features that support effective teaching. In addition, attention must be paid to the conditions under which teacher preparation matters, which involve compensation and working conditions as well as curriculum, support, and supervision. Otherwise, policy makers could end up requiring bachelor's degrees without producing benefits for children.

If policy makers want greater certainty than the existing evidence provides, then different sorts of studies will need to be funded. This will require true experiments to be conducted. One type of experiment would be large-scale randomized trials raising teacher qualifications and pay in some school districts or Head Start programs and not others. Such experiments are very expensive compared to statistical analysis of extant data. However, they are inexpensive compared to the cost of a bachelor's degree requirement for Head Start or state pre-K if the policy is not educationally effective or the cost of failing to implement the policy if it is effective. For example, if Head Start lost benefits equal to even two thirds of the benefits generated by the preschool portion of the Chicago Child-Parent Centers, this costs $50,000 per child (the estimated benefits are about $75,000 per child, so I am assuming Head

Start generates $25,000 per child in benefits; Temple & Reynolds, 2007). Assuming 400,000 children in each age cohort attend Head Start, the total cost of not requiring a bachelor's degree would then be $20 billion annually. Similarly, Florida serves more than 135,000 in its state pre-K program with no requirements for teacher higher education. The estimated annual lost benefits for Florida pre-K could be $6.75 billion per year. These estimates are hypothetical but not implausible. A few large experiments can be afforded. What cannot be afforded is persistent needless expenditure or underperformance by public preschool programs.

CHAPTER 9

Bachelor's Degrees Are Necessary but Not Sufficient

Preparing Teachers to Teach Young Children

Barbara T. Bowman

The number of young children enrolled in early childhood programs has risen dramatically in recent years. More than half of 3- and 4-year-old children attend some form of early education program (U.S. Department of Education, 2007). The enrollment has been stimulated, in part, by research showing that early experiences greatly influence later social-emotional and cognitive processes (Shonkoff & Phillips, 2000) and the precursors of literacy and math acquired during the preschool years play an important role in school achievement (Ramey et al., 2000; Reynolds, Temple, Robertson, & Mann, 2001; Schweinhart et al., 2005). In addition, the public has responded to economists who have shown that the social and academic benefits of preschool attendance yield significant educational and economic returns. Estimates of the cost–benefit ratio in preschool vary, but few researchers question its potential savings (Barnett, 2004; Heckman, 2000a). This means that early education is not only good for individual children but is also good public policy.

As the number of programs and expectations for early education increase, one of the recurring issues is determining the kind of investment that is necessary to realize the projected benefits. The answer is highly correlated with the preparation of teachers because the smaller group size and teacher-to-child ratios in early childhood programs raise personnel costs well above those for older students. Are the benefits of the better educated teacher worth the cost? Which degrees or certificates (if any) best prepare early childhood teachers to teach young children? Much hangs in the balance; yet, differences of opinion are sharp and significant.

Most of the human service professions require a minimum of a bachelor's degree, usually with a mandatory higher degree for professional training (Grossman et al., 2009). In some professions for which certification for practice is given at the bachelor's level (e.g., K–12 teachers), both general education (liberal arts) and professional courses are required. Also, the bachelor's degree with teacher certification usually requires field experience and evidence of practice competency.

At present, early childhood teachers (teachers of children from birth to 5) are not required to have much education or training for several reasons. Many believe that because early childhood teachers do not generally teach academic subjects in a formal way, they need little preparation for teaching. Head Start, the largest program for low-income children, traditionally has had low education requirements for teachers, often giving employment preference to low-income parents. In most states, educational requirements for preschool teachers and child care workers are low, rarely consisting of more than a few college courses. Even so, because of the high adult to child ratio, the cost of early care and education is high, exerting downward pressure on wages and providing little incentive for additional education.

Teaching young children, therefore, is a job open to those without much formal education or skills and has been used by states as employment opportunities for women poorly prepared for the work force.

Many advocates believe it is time to change. There is a huge body of evidence showing that, when teachers have more education and training, they are more likely to do the things that lead to good outcomes for children. For example, teachers with bachelor's degrees have richer language, more sensitive and less punitive teacher–child relationships, and more engaged children than teachers with less education. When teachers have more education and specific training and when they are well compensated, classroom quality is better (Barnett, 2004; Bowman et al., 2001; Whitebook, Gomby, Bellm, Sakai, & Kipnis, 2009).

THE EARLY CHILDHOOD TEACHER CONTENT KNOWLEDGE

The expanded knowledge base is one of the prime reasons why teachers of young children need at least a bachelor's degree. Child development, the traditional content for early childhood teachers (Bredekamp, 1987), has exploded since the 1990s. Development is vastly more complex than was once thought. Instead of unfolding in a predetermined, biologically driven, and orderly fashion, experience interacts with genetics to create endless variation in developmental structure and design. This is quite different from the romantic or naturalistic orientation of the mid-20th century, when children were seen as developing at their own pace and in their own way and teachers had simply to watch them unfold. It also differs from the belief of the late 20th century that children would construct most of their knowledge on their own, given an interestingly equipped classroom and the opportunity to explore. In the 21st century, essential teacher knowledge includes a broad range of fields and content areas: from genetics and neurobiology to nutrition and health, from maternal attachment and stranger anxiety to teacher and peer relationships, from mathematics and science to sociology and economics—just to name a few.

Another component of the early childhood knowledge base is social context and its effects on children's learning. Both macrosituational and microsituational variables shape how children develop and what they learn, with numerous permutations of how to teach. Instead of assuming one developmental model (e.g., middle-class Caucasian) to define what is normal for all children, teachers must know how to assess and respond to a variety of cultures that mediate what and how children learn. Cultural awareness and the ability to tailor teaching to different groups of students are now considered essential knowledge for teachers.

Not only has understanding of child development changed, but expectations for children have changed as well. As the economic and social future of the country increasingly depends on its human capital—that is, the educated citizen—school achievement is increasingly important (Heckman, 2000a). The effectiveness of teacher preparation must be judged against the achievement of expected learning outcomes for children. Early learning standards are seen as a guide for teachers of young children as they are for older students. This contrasts with the traditional perspective in early education in which young children were not thought to be ready for formal curricula. Although some early childhood educators are reluctant to orchestrate learning outcomes for young children, many states are moving in this direction as they recognize the need to align preschool with K–12 standards. Teachers are now expected to know strategies to ensure children master the precursor skills for school achievement.

New expectations have encompassed groups traditionally left behind in educational ventures who are now expected to meet the standards. Because the children most in need of preschool education are those most at risk of school failure, it is assumed that early childhood teachers will be prepared to support school readiness for children already on a downward achievement spiral (Duncan, Ludwig, & Magnuson, 2009). This means that early childhood teachers must expand their knowledge base to meet the challenge of diverse learners. For example, vocabulary disparities, which are already apparent by age 3 (Hart & Risley, 1995), require a high-quality intervention if children from low-income families are to catch up with middle-class children. Similarly, children whose home language is not English are likely to be at risk for poor school achievement unless special efforts are made. Other groups of children at risk include immigrants, children with special needs, children from minority groups, and children whose families are unable to provide a stable environment (e.g., homeless children, foster children)—all of whom have special threats and supports about which teachers must learn.

Today, teachers must understand the complexity of development and the learning expectations for all children. They must also know how to set both individuals and groups of children on the path to school success. The new model of preschool teaching is an intentional teacher who actively interacts with children and uses extensive knowledge of both individual and group developmental patterns and learning capabilities—skills and knowledge unlikely to be acquired outside of a high-quality collegiate-level teacher preparation program. This is the reasoning behind the recommendation of the Committee on Early Childhood Pedagogy of the National Research Council. After their review of the research covering teachers of children between 2 and 5 years of age, they wrote,

> Each group of children in an early childhood education and care program should be assigned a teacher who has a bachelor's degree with specialized education related to early childhood (development psychology, early childhood education, early childhood special education). (Bowman et al., 2001, p. 13)

CONTENT RECOMMENDATIONS OF PROFESSIONAL ORGANIZATIONS

Professional organizations are another source of information about what teachers should know and be able to do. The National Board for Professional Teaching Standards (2001) listed the following as essential knowledge for teachers: understanding young children; promoting child development and learning; and implementing integrated curriculum, assessment, and multiple teaching strategies. The National Association for the Education of Young Children (2001) has a similar set of recommendations, as well as increased emphasis on the following aspects: communities in which children live, the complexity of assessment issues in educational settings, a continuum of teaching strategies and developmentally effective approaches, linguistic and cultural diversity, and inclusion. The Committee on Early Childhood Pedagogy of the National Research Council (Bowman et al., 2001) also recommended that teacher education programs provide students with specific foundational knowledge of development of children's social and affective behavior, thinking, and language; knowledge of teaching and learning and child development; information about how to provide rich conceptual experiences that promote growth in specific content areas; and knowledge of effective teaching strategies, subject-matter content, assessment procedures, and the variability among children. Each organization proposed extensive content knowledge in preparation for teaching young children.

Although the research in favor of more education for early childhood teachers is substantial, the evidence supporting the bachelor's degree is not conclusive. Possible reasons for this include the diversity in what is taught in university courses, the broad expanse of ages covered in these courses (birth to age 8 is common), and the goals and objectives of the programs where teachers work. At the university level, there is little standardization in the content of courses, in their rigor, or the qualifications of faculty who teach. Degrees and certification rarely connote the same education within states, much less between states. The age range of programs for which teachers are being prepared is wide. Depending on the state, teachers may work with any combination of infants, toddlers, preschoolers, kindergartners, and primary-grade children. The goals of early childhood programs are also extremely diverse. Some teachers provide highly structured curricula addressing cognitive skills. Others adhere to a more indirect teaching style that focuses on play and social interaction, whereas other teachers do not plan an educational program but simply care for children safely. The acceptance of early childhood standards, greater emphasis on accountability and specificity by accrediting organizations, and the acceptance of Quality Rating Scales by states should provide more guidance for teacher training institutions.

WHAT ELSE IS NEEDED?

Increasing recognition of the expanded knowledge base, the achievement gap, and the special needs of some children requires the field to look more carefully at what teachers should be expected to know and do. Part of the difficulty is in the unique staffing pattern in early childhood programs. All adults in a classroom are called teachers, and they are often trained together with no differentiation of skills and knowledge. The field needs to look more carefully at roles, responsibilities, and the knowledge necessary for each. One solution is to develop a lead teacher's role in early childhood classrooms—a role that includes planning, supervision, and assessment. This would make the expanded knowledge base of well-educated and trained teachers available to other staff, as well as to children and families.

Like other professionals, early childhood teachers need a strong general education background. Although most adults have an operational knowledge of the early childhood curricula, many do not fully understand the underlying concepts that affect children's learning—concepts drawn from science, math, the social sciences, and the arts, as well as child development. The precursors of math and science in particular require a solid understanding of the essential concepts, yet many early childhood teachers' inadequate basic knowledge prevents them from designing or adapting curricula.

What is the proper balance between general education and pedagogy in teacher preparation? Some critics of the K–12 system contend that public school teachers are not effective because teachers lack content knowledge. According to this perspective, depth of discipline knowledge in math, science, literature, and the social sciences is more important than teaching methods, which can be learned on the job. A number of states now provide alternative certification in which teacher applicants are judged by their general knowledge rather than their participation in a formal teacher education program. According to the Carnegie Foundation for the Advancement of Teaching, the solution is not to abbreviate one or the other but to unite professional competence with the intellectual dimensions of the liberal arts (Sullivan & Rosin, 2008).

Teachers need more than an extensive knowledge component; they also need a time and place to develop practice skills. This part of teacher's education must be done in the field, with opportunities to learn specific management and teaching methods and with time for reflection on practice. Some educators suggest the practice component can be completed on the job, making alternative pathways to teacher status a viable alternative. Others see a license to practice as an essential step in teacher education that needs to be supported by higher education. In any case, it is incumbent on the field to avoid placing poorly trained practitioners in the workplace.

Teachers must constantly make decisions that involve the future of students (Darling-Hammond & Bransford, 2007). The better prepared teachers are to do this, the more likely students will be to succeed in school and in life. Investing in the youngest students makes the best economic and social sense (Heckman, 2000a). Early childhood teachers need bachelor's degrees, teaching certificates, and programs that provide them with the information and skills necessary to start children out right.

CHAPTER 10

College Credentials and Caring
How Teacher Training Could Lift Young Children

Bruce Fuller

Policy makers on Capitol Hill have long worried about how to raise the quality of teachers who serve children in preschool classrooms, ever since questions were raised in the 1970s over the benefits of Head Start. The aim of quality improvement has returned, addressed by President Barack Obama's push to award $10 billion in challenge grants to states and integrate federal and state preschool programs. One potential way to boost the quality of education for young children has surfaced among some early childhood advocates who have pitched it to congressional leaders, governors,

Special thanks are given to Daphna Bassok, Diane Early, and Edward Zigler for helpful comments on earlier drafts of Chapter 10. My research team's work has been generously financed by the MacArthur, McCormick, Packard, and Spencer Foundations; the U.S. Department of Education; and the U.S. Department of Health and Human Services. Any errors or misinterpretations stem from the author's own thinking.

and state legislators. These well-meaning proponents would mandate that every preschool teacher in the country acquire a 4-year college degree, despite the fact that a variety of independent studies revealed no consistent link between children's early learning and whether their preschool teacher has a bachelor's degree.

This chapter explores several questions. First, whose interests are served by pressing the bachelor's degree remedy? That is, why would an empirically futile remedy gain such traction in the halls of government? Policy actors—from U.S. senators to local school boards—influence how early educators and researchers view bachelor's degrees as a remedy to buoying preschool quality. Second, what is known about the education of preschool teachers and subsequent benefits for children? This question leads to a third topic: How can the teaching practices or social mechanisms that lift child development be addressed in 4-year preservice programs? In addition, how do the outer bounds of such improvements compare with the cost-effectiveness of alternative strategies aimed at lifting quality? These questions lead to a collateral issue that prompts reflection on the underlying ideals regarding child development: What defines high-quality teaching practices and caregiving skills, and how do these approaches match the diverse cognitive and social goals held by America's increasingly diverse families? The first section explores how government defines its interests when it comes to preschool quality.

LIFTING TEACHER QUALITY: THE STATES' INTERESTS AND CHILDREN'S GROWTH

In Washington, D.C., bland yet bustling cafeterias serve uninspiring meals to hundreds of staffers, beneath congressional offices that are linked by a labyrinth of corridors. Despite this institutional aesthetic, rich and animated conversations often fill these dreary dispensaries. For example, Roberto Rodriguez explained how Senate leaders hoped to lift the quality of Head Start and allied state programs. "My boss believes that we need a similar system for all young children," Rodriguez said, referring to his senate mentor at the time, Edward Kennedy. When I asked specifically about the wisdom of mandating the bachelor's degree for all teachers, something Kennedy had been pushing legislatively, he said, "I know, the evidence isn't consistent" (Fuller, 2007).

Later that day, I spoke with Grace Reef, Senator Christopher Dodd's longtime aide. "I think the evidence is mixed, [but] my boss believes that people self-select into community colleges versus 4-year colleges," Reef said, explaining how bachelor's degree programs work as a screening device, but not necessarily by awarding teacher candidates a stronger ethic of caring or effective classroom skills (Fuller, 2007). In the 1990s, Congress pushed Head Start teachers to attain a 2-year college degree. Then in 2007, Congress upped the ante, requiring that half of all Head Start teachers attain a 4-year college degree by 2013. Some governors and state legislators are enamored with this remedy as well, as 27 states required in 2008 that preschool teachers obtain a 4-year degree, up slightly from a decade earlier (Barnett, Epstein, et al., 2008).

I will soon turn to the lack of evidence supporting this costly policy drift. But first, I examine one prior fact and a pair of theories that explain why interest groups and the political players they inform have come to interpret the 4-year degree as such a powerful tool in boosting preschool quality. The prior fact is that the quality of preschool—and not increasing access to it—is now seen as the leading policy challenge. As Rodriguez told me that afternoon over forgettable cuisine, "Now that we are up to over 60% of (4-year-olds) enrolled, quality becomes the issue" (Fuller, 2007). Access barriers do remain high for subgroups of children, especially Latino youngsters from poor families. But Rodriguez is right in that census data show that almost 70% of all 4-year-olds currently attend some kind of preschool center (Fuller, 2007). As President Obama's chief education advisor, Rodriguez is one architect of the $10 billion in state grants that are focused on raising quality.

So, given the federal and state governments' interest in elevating preschool quality, the question becomes how to frame the problem and advance policy options that gain political traction. One account from political sociology argues that the government works from a long-term interest in regulating various periods of children's lives (Fuller, 1999; Grindle & Thomas, 1991). This includes consequential efforts to improve women's prenatal practices and reduce risks facing newborns, to creating and regulating public schools. This regulatory mentality, emanating from Washington, D.C., can be seen in education reforms such as the No Child Left Behind Act of 2001 (PL 107-110), which attempts to simplify classroom curricula and even regularize teaching methods. On the political left, advocates of an active, pro-equity government often concur, pushing for a tighter, more efficient system to ensure stiffer accountability and uniform indicators of performance, such as the No Child Left Behind Act's emphasis on standardized testing in math and English.

Working from this logic of government regulation, the Foundation for Child Development now advocates for tighter alignment in learning goals and teaching practices between preschool and elementary schools (Bogard, Traylor, & Takanishi, 2008). Child care centers should now be defined as prekindergarten classrooms. As the system's proponents gain legitimacy, bringing preservice training for preschool teachers into conformity for the training of K–12 teachers makes eminent sense. (I will return to the empirical debate over how best to train new K–12 teachers.) So, if the government now regulates teachers to advance basic literacy and numeracy skills inside elementary classrooms, shouldn't preschool teachers be prepared in the same way to emphasize this tightly aligned agenda? Given that about 40% of preschool teachers nationwide currently hold bachelor's degrees, it is tempting to define this as a problem when compared against K–12 traditions (Hart & Schumacher, 2005; Whitebook, 2002).

The government's drive to regulate in standardized fashion also serves to attract a new mix of interest groups and their lobbyists who share an organizational interest in this novel conception of preschool and how the next generation of early educators should be prepared. Because preschool may now be designed to add two new grade levels inside public schools rather than be operated largely by community-based organizations (CBOs), as is presently the case in the United States, K–12 interest groups are suddenly eager to be at the table. Teacher unions in particular see the potential of tens of thousands of new jobs (and dues-paying members) on the horizon. When universal preschool advocates placed an initiative on the California ballot, labor unions spent millions of dollars to support its passage, to no avail (Fuller, 2007).

This brings us to a second account for the sudden ascendance of the bachelor's degree as a quality fix—what economists and sociologists call *public choice theory*. Proponents of this model argue that the government acts to arbitrate among the policy options that gain the greatest political support. Organizations and associations arise to protect their ideals and economic interests and in turn push politicians to back their framing of the problem and preferred remedies. That is, organizations choose to optimize their utility or well-being, just as individuals behave in markets (at least according to neoclassical thinking).

CBOs have historically dominated the organized field of early care and education, going back to the settlement house movement of the early 20th century. Groups like the National Association for the Education of Young Children grew from this institutional base, a mix of practitioners who worked inside CBOs and, as state preschool programs sprouted in the 1970s, in public schools. The creation of Head Start, which was dedicated in part to community organizing and job creation in poor neighborhoods, further strengthened the legitimacy of CBOs and certain ideals, such as developmentally appropriate practices. These ideals sparked innovations like the Child Development Associate certificate and associated career ladders, which explicitly balanced work-force diversity with the alleged benefits of college credentials. Daphna Bassok's (2009) work showed a significant decline in the count of parents employed as classroom aides in Head Start preschools as escalating credential requirements have taken hold.

These institutional arrangements clearly display weaknesses at times. For example, the political influence of CBO associations has been uneven over the past two generations, certainly not rivaling the clout of teacher unions. The field in general has not policed itself well, guarding against preschools that manifest low quality. Many programs serve poor families, but state governments often show limited will to even regulate quality rigorously. Given these persisting concerns, it is understandable why the most recent generation of preschool advocates—who push free and universal access for all families, regardless of their means—has moved to build coalitions with K–12 interest groups. But once these interests are at the table, lobbying and contributing to the campaigns of congressional leaders and state officials, pressure builds to regulate preschool quality with the same policy tools that hammer on K–12 educators. Public choice theorists warn, however, that the policy options that stick are the ones that gain the greatest political support, whether they are effective or not.

Initiatives from the Obama Administration have aimed to combat public choice pressures. Under the Race to the Top program, the U.S. Department of Education is pushing states to link data on teacher characteristics to student achievement results, providing the opportunity to systematically study whether preservice programs for K–12 teachers contribute to their children's growth curves (U.S. Department of Education, 2010). In addition, rather than linking teacher promotion policies to credential and experience levels, the administration has pushed to understand what teachers need to know and how they deploy these skills in classrooms. In this light, there may be waning congressional interest in seeing credentials as a meaningful proxy for teacher quality.

DOES A BACHELOR'S DEGREE LIFT CHILDREN'S DEVELOPMENT?

Does a bachelor's degree lift children's development? The short answer is no. This does not mean that 4-year programs—ideally focusing on child development—cannot potentially advance the cognitive and social-emotional growth of 3- and 4-year-old children. However, it does mean that given the present quality of college-level programs, public dollars are wasted by requiring this credential. Much is known about the qualities of adults (including parents) who care for young children, as well as how those qualities contribute to child development. These qualities include beliefs and behaviors that can be acquired in schools and colleges, such as the use of rich language, curiosity about children's own talk and feelings, and the capacity to build trusting and affectionate relationships. Exposing young children to adults with low levels of education, say a high school diploma, slows early development (Burchinal, Cryer, Clifford, & Howes, 2002; Loeb et al., 2004).

Beyond a 2-year degree in child development, a number of researchers have failed to find increased value for completing a 4-year degree program. Other policy options, aimed at improving quality and child benefits, do yield significant effects, such as enriching the ratio of adults to children in preschool classrooms and increasing the character of social interactions (Blatchford, Goldstein, Martin, & Brown, 2002; Clarke-Stewart & Allhusen, 2005; Zaslow, 1991). Researchers argued through the 1980s that teacher education at any level was associated with higher child outcomes within preschool centers. However, research designs ignored potential selection biases, such as when higher income parents select preschools that employ highly credentialed teachers. These researchers made the risky inference that higher child outcomes (causally) resulted from being served by teachers with higher credentials. Instead, stronger outcomes could stem indirectly from the home practices of higher income parents.

Stronger research designs emerged in the 1990s that minimized the risk of selection bias, included large samples of young children, and tapped multiple measures of preschool and teacher quality, which were important for isolating discernible effects from teacher education or credential level. Scientists examining longitudinal effects from a variety of child care arrangements in the 1990s, conducted by the National Institute of Child Health and Human Development, found that the education level of caregivers was correlated with developmental outcomes, but the bachelor's degree per se showed no association after taking into account other facets of quality, including staffing ratios. A similar study by Janet Currie, tracking children who attended Head Start preschools, came to the identical conclusion, even when looking at the trajectories of siblings, only one of whom experienced Head Start. This approach minimized selection bias introduced by parents who are more or less likely to enroll their children in preschool (Currie & Neidel, 2007).

Later work suggested that specialized training in child development may energize positive social mechanisms that mediate the skills of preschool teachers and child outcomes. Howes, Phillips, and Whitebook (1992) compared the classroom behaviors of three groups of teachers—two groups with bachelor's degrees (one subgroup with specific child development training and the other subgroup without) and a third group with 2-year degrees in child development. The two groups with specialized training displayed the most sensitive caregiving and relied less on harsh discipline practices, compared with those with a general bachelor's degree with little child development training. Similarly, Henry et al. (2004) found no differences in teachers holding a bachelor's degree versus those with a 2-year degree in child development in a universal preschool program. This null effect was attributed to strong on-the-job teacher mentoring and in-service training.

The most exhaustive investigation to date was conducted by Early et al. (2007), who reanalyzed data from seven independently conducted studies that included near-identical measures of preschool teacher education and credential levels. The statistical modeling strategy was very similar across datasets, and stringent controls were used to take into account the prior attributes of children and teachers. Five of the seven original studies drew on nationally representative data. The team found few associations between teachers' overall school attainment or attainment of a bachelor's degree with the quality of care they provided. Data from two of the seven studies found that holding a 4-year degree was predictive of stronger caregiving or teaching behavior, but analysis of the remaining five datasets found negative or no effects. Most importantly, benefits for children were no more promising. When estimating children's early language or math proficiencies, the majority of the studies found no significant effect from being in a classroom with a teacher who held a bachelor's degree (negative effects were observed in two studies). Other studies confirmed these findings (Burchinal, Howes, et al., 2008; Loeb et al., 2004).

Similar results have emerged from research on teachers in elementary schools. One review concluded that of the variability in student performance observed in K–12 schools overall, about one third of a standard deviation could be explained by teacher characteristics (Nye, Konstantopoulos, & Hedges, 2004). Two thirds of this effect size was linked to observable teaching practices; the remaining one third was attributable to prior background attributes, including the teacher's own school attainment and credential level. Nearly identical results were observed among first-grade students by Palardy and Rumberger (2008), who detailed how teachers significantly advance young children's growth in reading and mathematical understandings, but credential level per se is relatively unimportant. At the same time, specific pedagogical practices are influential, including classroom time in which children are reading, practicing vocabulary and phonemic awareness, and engaging in writing exercises. Such practices can be facilitated by certain qualities of classrooms, including small numbers of students and peer composition (Betts, Zau, & Rice, 2003; Stipek, 2004). The question of where beneficial practices and organizational skills are acquired, if not from 4-year or credential programs, remains an open question.

HOW MIGHT COLLEGE LIFT NEW TEACHERS AND PRESCHOOLERS?

Preservice programs at 2- and 4-year colleges might yield discernible benefits for teachers and children if they advanced the human scale practices that are known to contribute to young children's development. The first way to define how college may raise the likelihood of producing teachers that display these beneficial mechanisms is to see the university institution as providing multiple screens through which teacher candidates move. Students with stronger verbal skills, cognitive agility, and perhaps social proficiencies (e.g., persistence) are differentially screened in or out as they move through community colleges or 4-year degree programs. Downstream economic or status incentives, attached to various teaching jobs, likely influence students' decision making. The institutional problem is that students and parents reason that staying in college longer helps to retain one's place in the labor queue, as everyone else behaves in a similar manner, independent of whether obtaining the credential effectively imparts the caring qualities and pedagogical skills that are wanted from young teachers (Dore, 1976). A more efficient alternative is to recruit and select preschool teachers who display the caring qualities, verbal proficiencies, and engagement with children that are known to advance development. This is already happening in many preschool classrooms where effective teaching practices are used, independent of credential levels.

A second way to think about boosting the benefits of preservice training is to ask how these degree programs can reinforce such effective social mechanisms inside preschool classrooms. Research has shown developmental benefits when teachers structure learning activities, offer steady facilitation and feedback, express care and curiosity about children's utterances and viewpoints, and offer emotional support when youngsters experience stress or conflicts with peers (Mashburn et al., 2008; Pianta & Stuhlman, 2004). My team's work similarly found that children's cognitive growth was stronger between

2 and 4 years of age when exposed to teachers who regularly hunkered down to the child's level to listen carefully, recognize success on a task, and actively reason with the child when social or cognitive problems arose (Loeb et al., 2004).

Related work also revealed how many preschool teachers fail to organize classroom time effectively. Early et al. (2010) detailed how a large share of observation segments involved no structured learning activity. This could be useful where activity centers are used to nurture peer interaction and children's intrinsic motivation. My team's work inside centers and family child care homes also revealed large chunks of time in which children wandered about, not carefully engaging any specific activity (Fuller et al., 2004). Early et al. (2010) found that classroom time was spent in about three equal parts dedicated to teacher-assigned activities, free choice time, and meals and other daily routines. Teachers engaged in didactic interaction with children three times more frequently than scaffolding up from the child's own work. Again, context matters in conditioning how teachers organize classrooms and their own practices. Teachers in classrooms with larger shares of African American or Latino children allocated more time to directed activities, but engaged less often in rich and stimulating tasks, compared with those serving primarily Caucasian children.

ALTERNATIVE DEFINITIONS OF EFFECTIVE TEACHERS

This chapter points to the importance of aligning preservice training with the human scale teaching practices and social mechanisms that are known to elevate children's early development in social and cognitive spheres. The government tacks back and forth depending on the historical era, shifting on the particular child outcomes that fit ideological or economic imperatives. So, how preservice training is meshed with effective classroom practice involves debate over ideals (i.e., ideologies) regarding how young children should be nurtured. It is not simply a technical exercise that delineates the skills required at the elementary level and then determines how preschool teachers can instrumentally advance government-defined human competence.

An analysis by Mashburn et al. (2008) found that none of nine preschool quality indicators used to judge states' progress by the National Institute of Early Education Research (including a bachelor's degree requirement) were empirically correlated with children's expressive language skills. Therefore, a reputable institute backed by national foundations seems to pitch easily regulated indicators of quality that have little to do with children's actual growth inside preschools. In short, these indicators are based on well-meaning yet unsubstantiated ideals.

Mashburn et al. (2008) used the Classroom Assessment Scoring System™ (CLASS™; Pianta, La Paro & Hamre, 2008), an observation measure that focuses on features of teacher–child interactions, including teacher sensitivity and responsiveness to children's cues, scaffolding up from children's own performances, and emotional support. They found significant effects on children's language and social development. Yet the forms of language, kinds of social skills, and character of social interactions valued in elementary school are contested in ideological—not only positivistic—terms. One item on the social-development scale—*participates in class discussions*—sounds desirable, except that under the current governmental press for learning known facts (often through didactic pedagogy), it is not clear that all elementary teachers would weigh this as a desirable classroom behavior.

In addition, teachers under pressure to boost test scores may not necessarily take the time to respond to students' cues or anxieties. I am certainly not endorsing the current articulation of the government's interest, as backed by some influential funders. My point is that how one defines the practices of young preschool teachers—and tries to improve the preservice programs they move through—must include candid ideological debates, not simply the technical exercise of predicting context-free child outcomes from isolated conceptions of "effective" practice.

CONCLUSION

By now it should be clear that the government, as well as some preschool groups that influence policy, express regulatory habits and political interest in selling indicators of preschool quality that simply do not predict more robust growth for children. I am not arguing against mindful regulatory standards—when they are shown to lift children's growth curves—but the bachelor's degree mandate is costly for taxpayers and low-paid caregivers alike. It well serves the ideals of politicians, foundation officials, and K–12 interest groups eager to win a material slice of the early education pie (Fuller, 2007). The mandate may serve to advance the status or salaries of early education professionals, but whether this yields a stronger pool of aspiring teachers over time remains an open empirical question as well. Why not simply raise salaries to ensure a living wage and more competitive recruitment?

Another pressing question is whether high-quality bachelor's programs either screen in stronger teacher candidates or impart richer competencies. This would allow one to estimate the outer bounds of child-level benefits to improving preservice programs. The eventual answer may be that high-quality 2-year programs are more cost effective than 4-year programs. But first the benefits resulting from stronger 4-year credential efforts need to be tested.

The related comparison is whether high-quality in-service training or mentoring efforts yield more distinct gains in teaching practices and for children when compared with costly preservice programs. Some promising models have enjoyed careful study, even involving random assignment of participants to differing in-service strategies (Johnson, Pai, & Bridges, 2004; Koh & Neuman, 2009). Several states are experimenting with incentives for in-service training. Still, little evidence has come to light regarding how these efforts alter teaching practices and caregiving skills at a magnitude that advances child development. Incentives, rather than mandates, do serve to advance the most committed teachers, create mentoring and peer support structures, and supplement income, rather than imposing costs on staff associated with mandates.

As early educators, policy makers, and scholars seek to enrich the quality of preservice and in-service training, one should be sensitive to the colorful variability of children and families who now enter America's preschools. The forms of language, social behavior, and accompanying cognitive demands that are presently invoked by preschool teachers (not to mention by parents) differ greatly across programs and neighborhoods. Developmentalists often hope to identify universal teaching practices or caregiving behaviors that advance children's growth. The government, too, holds this habitual interest in pushing universal remedies. But researchers are just beginning to grasp how children's social-emotional growth and cognitive facilitation are conditioned by parents' differing goals when it comes to raising their children, along with the social collectives to which youngsters are expected to contribute—be it the family, classroom, or ethnic community.

The research community should design more careful studies that isolate on the discrete benefits stemming from alternative forms of preservice training. Similar to teacher research in the public schools, it is difficult to fully partial out other attributes of early educators who obtain a bachelor's degree. At the same time, it is unlikely that teacher candidates can be convinced that wise scholars should randomly assign them to different training conditions. Quasi-experimental designs with population data would move beyond prior work, although not fully eliminate endogeneity issues. Perhaps a more informative line of work would be to identify what caring qualities and pedagogical skills teacher candidates are learning within 2- and 4-year degree programs and see how they predict children's developmental trajectories. Obtaining a credential is a very rough proxy for the competencies and compassion that it is hoped preschool teachers will acquire during their preservice training.

The rising debate over whether to require all preschool teachers to attain a bachelor's degree brings these issues to the fore. The controversy serves to clarify the dominating interests of the government versus the interests of children's own development. It also prompts reflection over whether researchers simply assume that all children should grow and be socialized along a single cultural or "middle-class" pathway. The debate also should remind researchers that their work is usefully shaped by contested ideals and scientific evidence. Ideology is certainly no stranger to the reasoning advanced by policy makers, foundation officials, and scholars themselves. This does not mean that scientific inquiry cannot distinguish sound policy from bad, but it does suggest that mindful practitioners must clarify their ideals and distinguish them from the accumulation of scientific evidence.

CHAPTER 11

A Degree Is Not Enough
*Teachers Need Stronger and
More Individualized Professional
Development Supports to Be Effective in the Classroom*

Robert C. Pianta

The loosely organized system of educational and developmental opportunities to which young children are exposed in child care, state-funded prekindergarten (pre-K) programs, Head Start programs, and a host of other settings increasingly is intended as a point of leverage for addressing low levels of (and gaps in) K–12 achievement. How to ensure the training and expertise necessary to support the value of early education poses a serious challenge for scientists and policy makers. Critically important to realizing the promise of early education is coming to grips with the needs of teachers for support that enhances their effectiveness in the classroom. The debate needs to shift from whether a preschool teacher should have a bachelor's degree; instead, it should focus on building and delivering proven and effective supports for teachers that lead to improved outcomes for children (Pianta et al., 2005; Powell, Diamond, Burchinal, & Koehler, 2010). Arguing about degrees is a distraction from the central issue of designing, testing, and implementing the supports that teachers need to be both knowledgeable and effective, regardless of their level of formal education.

There is little evidence that accumulating course credits, advancing in terms of degree status (e.g., from associate's degree to bachelor's degree), or attending workshops directly contributes to teachers' actual skills in the classroom and to children's achievement. In fact, a comprehensive analysis of seven major studies of child care and preschool showed no evidence whatsoever of a link between a higher level degree, experience, or accumulated course credits and child outcomes (Early et al., 2007). Moreover, observational studies show that even in state-sponsored pre-K programs with credentialed teachers with bachelor's degrees, variation in observed curriculum implementation and quality of teaching is enormous. Observed instruction, interaction, and quality of implementation were essentially unrelated to teachers' experience or education (Pianta et al., 2005). There is simply no evidence, even in correlational studies, that degree status matters for child outcomes if these degrees reflect the present offerings in higher education. Requiring that the non-bachelor's work force enroll in current early childhood education offerings to attain a degree does not seem to be supported by evidence.

Researchers should move on from this sticking point. If degrees are desired because of factors such as work-force professionalization or salary parity, then those reasons should be the basis of the argument, not that degrees produce child outcomes. Of course, to the extent that formal education remains a goal and is incentivized by policy and resources, then using the vehicles of degrees and formal education credits (and associated funds) to incent teachers and reward teachers' participation in effective professional development would be sensible. However, to argue that a bachelor's degree is necessary or sufficient for teachers to be effective and for children to learn is, in my view, a distraction from what should be the focus—to connect teachers to professional development supports (either in teacher preparation or in-service contexts) that work.

In this chapter, I outline perspectives and evidence gleaned in support of this contention from work that draws from direct observations of teachers' practices in classrooms and a range of efforts to leverage from observation to effective professional development.

Contemporary evidence does provide support for certain forms of professional development that produce children's skill gains (see Bierman et al., 2008; Landry, Swank, Smith, Assel, & Gunnewig, 2006; Pianta, Mashburn, Downer, Hamre, & Justice, 2008; Powell et al., 2010; Raver et al., 2008). What these approaches have in common is an alignment of skill targets for children with teacher–student interactions that produce gains in these skills, as well as professional development supports that foster gains in these teacher–child interactions. Work in my laboratory by Susan Landry, Doug Powell, Cybele Raver, Karen Bierman, and others very clearly indicates that effective supports to teachers are very closely tied to practice in their current classroom (Bierman et al., 2008, Landry et al., 2006, Powell et al., 2010). Delivered in small repeated doses over time, they provide opportunity for practice and feedback in contexts that are small and meaningful to the teacher. Whether described as coaching or consultation, these approaches usually combine knowledge about development in a target area (e.g., language, self-control) with explicit exposure to modeling and feedback on teacher behaviors that foster development. These approaches are often very specific (about developmental domains and teacher behaviors) and explicit, and often they are directly tied to a set of measures that allow the teachers to know if they and the children are making progress. These are not the typical vehicles through which teachers accrue degrees or certification, but if such experience and outcomes can be delivered and incentivized through accumulating credits toward a degree, or if direct assessments of teacher competency derived from this work were woven into certification structures, then degrees and certification might matter more.

Much of what I discuss in this chapter is a consequence of my involvement in a program of research involving standardized descriptions and measurements of teachers' practices in early education classrooms and experimental studies of a cluster of interventions designed to improve their practices and interactions with children. This program of work emanates from both a strong conceptual and empirical base in developmental psychology and early education, but also from an interest in engineering a scalable approach to supporting teachers in classrooms. I have relied on observation as the leverage point of this work, largely because I believe that if one could observe (across many classrooms) practices of teachers that could be shown empirically to contribute to children's developmental gains, then those observed behaviors could and should become the target of professional development. The descriptive basis for identifying what teachers do that matters drew from two of the largest studies of the early education system conducted to date: the National Institute of Child Health and Human Development (NICHD) Study of Early Child Care and the National Center for Early Development and Learning Multistate Pre-K study (e.g., Pianta et al., 2005). The development and testing of professional development interventions has taken place in two major professional development studies: the MyTeachingPartner (MTP) study of the NICHD School Readiness Consortium and the National Center for Early Childhood Education professional development study, funded by the Institute of Education Sciences (Pianta et al., 2008). Collectively, this work has involved well over 3,000 early education classrooms and child care settings from all across the United States, varying in economic, geographic, cultural, racial, and language background. In my work, I have regularly attended to whether the results or conclusions were different across groups from these various backgrounds; to date, I have no evidence that this is the case.

Effective teaching in early childhood education, not unlike in the elementary grades, requires skillful combinations of explicit instruction, sensitive and warm interactions, responsive feedback, and verbal engagement and stimulation that is intentionally directed to ensure children's learning, while embedding these interactions in a classroom environment that is not overly structured or regimented. These aspects of instruction and interaction uniquely predict gains in young children's achievement, have been directly tied to closing gaps in performance, and are endorsed by those who advocate tougher standards and more instruction and by those who argue for child-centered approaches. But unlike for older children, effective teachers of young children must intentionally and strategically weave instruction into activities that give children choices to explore and play, engage them through multiple input channels, and are embedded in natural settings that are comfortable and predictable. The best early childhood teachers are opportunists—they know child development and exploit interests and interactions to promote it, some of which may involve structured lessons and much of which may not.

Therefore, it is not surprising that measures of teacher–child interactions account for the value of enrollment in preschool and contribute to closing performance gaps. A cluster of experimental and well-designed natural history studies show a return to achievement from observed teacher–child interactions of between a half and a whole standard deviation on standardized achievement tests, with greater effects accruing to children with higher levels of risk and disadvantage (Pianta et al., 2009). Experimental studies, although few and involving far fewer children, have shown similar effects. In fact, findings are almost uniform in demonstrating significant and meaningful benefits for enrollment in early education settings in which teacher–child interactions are supportive, instructive, and stimulating (e.g., Pianta et al., 2005). Unfortunately, the odds are stacked against children getting the kind of early education experiences that close gaps. Overall, observational studies including several thousand settings (Pianta et al., 2009) indicated that young children are exposed to moderate levels of social and emotional supports in their preschool classrooms and quite low levels of instructional support—levels that are not as high as those gap-closing, effective classrooms. The quality of various aspects of teachers' instructional interactions (Pianta et al., 2005), particularly those that reflect stimulation of language and conceptual thinking/understanding and use feedback to the child as a means of eliciting more advanced knowledge and skill, are particularly low. The average levels hover around 2 on a 7-point scale.

These realities about the level and distribution of high-quality early education classrooms in the United States probably reflect the convergence of at least three factors. First, teaching young children is uniquely challenging and is not easy. Second, many of the publicly funded early education programs that are included in large-scale studies (e.g., Head Start, state pre-K) are composed of a high percentage of children who live below the poverty line. These children may bring with them a collection of features that make teaching even more challenging, especially when concentrated in a classroom. Third, the system of early education operates on a shoestring of support. The degree to which a teacher (or program) can provide gap-closing social and instructional interactions is a product of balancing the teacher's capacity and skills with the needs of children in the classroom. Researchers have observed that even the best teachers' interactions with students are drawn down when faced with a particularly challenging classroom—what the best teachers do over time is "right the ship" and more importantly, weaker teachers in tough classrooms show a decline over the year in the quality of their interactions with children (Pianta et al., 2008). This suggests that the value added by a teacher (or classroom experience) to a young child's development is determined by both the teachers' capacity (e.g., knowledge, skill) and children's needs—an equation that poses serious challenges to policies that target fixed features such as a degree. Therefore, regulation and policy should focus on providing every teacher the support (individual or classroom level) he or she needs to be effective rather than focusing on fixed attributes of the adult in the room.

Professional development should focus on supporting teachers to skillfully use instructional interactions, implement curricula effectively and intentionally through teacher–child interactions, and provide language-stimulation supports in real-time dynamic interactions that operate at the intersection of children's developing skills and the available instructional materials or activities (Pianta et al., 2008). This approach aligns (conceptually and empirically) the requisite knowledge of desired skill targets and developmental skill progressions in a particular skill domain (e.g., language development or early literacy) with extensive opportunities for the following items: 1) observation of high-quality instructional interaction through analysis and viewing of multiple video examples; 2) skills training in identifying appropriate and inappropriate instructional, linguistic, and social responses to children's cues; 3) skills training in how teacher responses can contribute to student literacy and language skill growth; and 4) repeated opportunities for individualized feedback and support for high quality and effectiveness in one's own instruction, implementation, and interactions with children. Conceptually, this is a system of professional development supports in which a direct path can be traced from inputs to teachers, to teacher inputs to children, to children's skill gains. I describe this system briefly in the following paragraphs, starting with skill targets for children's development.

Teacher training that focuses on interactions and quality of implementation of instructional activities in language and literacy must be based on a way of defining and observing interaction and implementation that has shown strong links to growth in child outcomes—in this case, language and literacy development. In the National Center for Research on Early Childhood Education (NCRECE) professional development approaches, teachers learn to observe others' effective and ineffective interactions and their own interactions with children and receive feedback and suggestions related to improving quality and effectiveness of interactions. These supports are anchored in a metric for observing interactions that predicts child outcomes in the desired skill targets—the Classroom Assessment Scoring System (CLASS; Pianta et al., 2008). The CLASS focuses on teachers' instructional, language, and social interactions with children. In large-scale studies of pre-K through Grade 3 classes, higher ratings on CLASS dimensions predicted greater gains on standardized assessments of academic achievement and better social adjustment, even adjusting for teacher, program, and family selection factors (e.g., Pianta et al., 2005). Thus, my professional development models rely on the CLASS as one of the central targets for teachers' knowledge and skill training. In the Landry, Powell, Raver, and Bierman models (Landry et al., 2006, Powell et al., 2010, Raver et al., 2008, Bierman et al., 2008), there are parallels in anchoring professional development supports to a metric for teacher–child interactions, whether in the form of implementation of a curriculum or of a particular aspect of instruction.

The MTP system of professional development supports for teachers is designed to foster skillful use of instructional interactions and effective implementation of curricula by offering extensive opportunities for observation of high-quality instruction through analysis and viewing of multiple video examples; skills training in identifying appropriate and inappropriate responses to children's cues and how these contribute to literacy and language skill growth; and repeated opportunities for individualized feedback and support for high-quality instruction, implementation, and interactions with children. These outcomes are achieved through delivery mechanisms that include didactic and skills-focused coursework, web-based video exemplars of effective practice, and consultation and feedback focused on a teacher's own classroom interactions (Pianta et al., 2008).

The MTP web site exposes teachers to knowledge about and observations/exemplars of others' high-quality interactions. Teachers are provided detailed descriptions of the CLASS dimensions of high-quality teacher–child interactions and a library with numerous annotated video examples of teachers demonstrating each dimension within their classrooms, which helps teachers become critical observers of classroom behavior and more attuned to the effects that teachers' behavior have on children. Importantly, these annotations are very specific and focus on moment-to-moment analysis of child cues and teacher behaviors in that clip that exemplify that CLASS dimension. MTP consultancy provides observationally based, nonevaluative, practice-focused support and feedback for teachers through web-mediated remote consultation, providing individualized support wherever teachers work, without consultants having to visit classrooms (a potential cost savings). Teachers record their classroom interactions during a learning activity and send the recording to a consultant. The consultant edits that tape into smaller segments that focus on indicators of quality teaching identified by the CLASS and posts those segments with written feedback (which is again very specific) to a secure web site where they are viewed and responded to by the teacher, whose comments are automatically sent to the consultant. The teacher and consultant then discuss teaching practices on the telephone or by video chat.

My team then developed a 3-credit course offered in partnership with university or community college programs (Hamre, Pianta, Burchinal, & Downer, 2010). The course is an intensive, skill-focused didactic experience in which students learn how the development of language and literacy skills targets is linked to features of interactions with adults (using CLASS as the focus) in family and early education settings, as well as how high-quality implementation of language and literacy curricula and activities leads to skill growth (again using CLASS as the focus). Teachers learn to identify behavioral indicators of high-quality and effective teaching on CLASS dimensions and to identify such indicators in their own teaching.

Each one of these forms of professional development has been shown to increase levels of teacher–child interaction as measured by the CLASS and the consultation approach produces skill gains in children. (The course has not been evaluated in relation to child skill gains.) Teachers who showed greater exposure to the web site resources (when the web site was the only resource they had available) also interacted more effectively with children as a result. Early career teachers and teachers working in very high poverty classrooms were more effective when they were exposed to the higher intensity supports of the consultation approach, but the web site resources were not associated with gains for those groups of teachers or their students. Finally, evidence indicated that the course produced significant changes in teachers' knowledge of language and literacy skill targets, knowledge of teacher–child interactions linked to gains in these targets, competence in identifying interactive cues and behaviors, and in their provision of instructionally supportive interactions during literacy activities (Hamre et al., 2010). These results are consistent with the work of others regarding the value of ongoing practice-focused coaching and feedback to teachers (Bierman et al., 2008; Landry et al., 2006; Powell et al., 2010).

All these improvements in practice and child outcomes occurred via professional development that was not tied to a degree, to course credit (except for the course), or to a professional career ladder or pay. Clearly, it is not too much of a stretch to envision professional preparation and credentialing models based on aligned professional development that is practice focused, ongoing, and classroom or teacher sensitive. To the extent that these models of support and education for teachers can be demonstrated to produce gains in teacher competencies that, in turn, produce child outcome gains, then it seems critical to build such opportunities for professional preparation back into the preservice sector. More important, for the bachelor's degree debate, consider awarding credit to teachers for their participation in effective professional development and certifying them on the basis of their demonstration of competence. Perhaps teachers' performance in classroom settings, specifically their interactions with children, could be a credentialed dimension of career advancement.

Teachers need more support. Courses, credits, and degrees matter when they provide that support. However, these factors will not provide enough support if such experiences do not meet the following criteria: 1) based on an explicitly aligned model of professional development anchored in a measure of practice that is linked to children's gains in a developmental domain; 2) tied directly to practice in the classroom in which the teacher is working; 3) provided in ongoing, regular, small doses; 4) focused explicitly and specifically on teacher–child interaction; and 5) titrated in intensity relative to the teacher and classroom.

Courses, credits, and degrees can provide the vehicles and incentives for participation in and delivery of such supports. But in the end, teacher competency and effectiveness will be more a matter of the blend of supports and teacher capacity than it will be a fixed attribute of a teacher. Perhaps the most important qualification of lead teachers is their skill in seeing and detecting interactive cues as opportunities to teach and learn, and participating in support that fosters those skills.

CHAPTER 12

B.A. Plus
Reconciling Reality and Reach

Sharon Lynn Kagan and Rebecca E. Gomez

Sound social policy needs to be imbued with a dose of both reality and reach; that is, it must understand the present and envision the future simultaneously. True for policies affecting teacher quality in general, the need for reality and reach is particularly pressing when considering the quality of teachers and teaching required for and by young children. Given the vulnerability and rapid pace of young children's development, this has always been true; arguably, however, given escalating attention to and investment in young children, the press for serious focus on the individuals who care for and educate young children is even more critical now. This chapter is about those individuals and the rankling debates surrounding their education, experiences, and the credentials required for them to teach. It is also about the need to reconcile reality and reach; it aims to do so by delineating each as it addresses three pivotal questions. As we answer the questions, we raise provocative issues and render recommendations regarding specific ways to address them. At the outset, it is important to note that this chapter is about the bachelor of arts (B.A.) degree debate; in addressing it, however, we suggest that although the B.A. may be a fashionable proxy for the reach, achieving it alone, however necessary, is insufficient for the challenging realities at hand.

WHO ARE THE CURRENT
TEACHERS AND WHAT ARE THEIR CAPACITIES?

There exist disparities among the credentials early childhood teachers currently hold and the qualifications they need to be considered "highly qualified." In addition, the definitions of teacher quality in early childhood are changing rapidly.

The Reality

A good deal is known about the early childhood work force, notably its scope and composition, the range of qualifications required, and the compensation and stability of early childhood teachers. In examining these facets, clear patterns emerge (Kagan et al., 2008). Early childhood teachers are predominantly females in their late 30s to early 40s. The majority of teachers do have some formal education—usually an associate's degree. However, there is still great variability in the credentials states require teachers to possess. In general, entry requirements for preschool teachers have been, and continue to be, far lower than those expected even for kindergarten teachers who may be working with children just a year older. Preschool teachers have extremely high rates of turnover, in part due to extremely low levels of compensation. In concert, these realities—high turnover and low compensation—predict and help perpetuate the overall low quality found in early childhood settings and consequential limitations on children's positive achievement (Child Care Services Association, 2008; Kagan et al., 2008; Kreader, Ferguson, & Lawrence, 2006; LeMoine, 2008).

The Reach

Despite increasing public will for high-quality early childhood programs, the nexus of the above realities (poor preschool quality, high turnover, low salaries, limited child achievement) has hindered the field's ability to respond efficiently and effectively (Goffin & Washington, 2007). In noble responses to this knotty situation, many have called for a viable, visible solution by requiring a B.A. for all who work with young children (Bowman et al., 2001). Indeed, for many, the B.A. has become the contemporary reach to help assuage the preschool quality problem. Although we are not negating this stance, we suggest that beyond reaching for ready-made solutions, early childhood educators and advocates need to examine both the assumptions undergirding this stance as well as their applicability to the realities of preschool teaching. There is an assumption, for example, that the B.A. breeds quality at both the preschool and school levels. At the school level, some vigorously doubt that this is the case (Decker, Mayer, & Glazerman, 2004; Goldhaber & Brewer, 2000; Humphrey, Weschler, & Hough, 2008), while at the preschool level, the assumption is complicated by several still-pondered questions. First, who is a preschool teacher? Given that most early childhood classrooms are staffed by a lead teacher and an assistant, it is necessary to discern whether both are teachers with equal roles and responsibilities as was once advocated or whether there are different roles and functions associated with each title—the more accepted contemporary stance. The former stance regarded distinguishing teachers from teachers' assistants as undesirable and inequitable; the two needed to work in complete harmony, with their teaching likened to a well-orchestrated dance. Today, more removed from the civil rights era, discerning differences in roles and expectations for preschool teachers is seen as necessary. Nonetheless, old traditions die hard, and much consideration needs to be given to precisely who will be required to achieve the B.A. and with what consequences to the teaching partnership.

A second assumption is that early childhood educators know what constitutes, and have cogently defined, quality teaching. Although some definitional agreement was reached in the past, the press for accountability has raised new considerations regarding quality teaching, with many assuming that to be of quality, teaching must yield effective outcomes for children. Certainly true for elementary and secondary education, this has led some to distinguish between teacher quality and teacher effectiveness, with teacher quality generally defined as the positive actions and behaviors of teachers and teacher effectiveness regarded as the impact teachers have on the accomplishments of children they teach (Kagan et al., 2008; Weber & Trauten, 2008). Yet, the debate ensues, evoking reconsideration of what it means to be a quality and/or effective early childhood teacher. Lacking a consensus on the definitions, functions, and responsibilities of the quality contemporary early childhood teacher makes it difficult to unequivocally declare that any single strategy is privileged in achieving it.

A third assumption undergirding the debate about teacher quality tilts the focus from the teacher alone to the interaction between the teacher and child. Are the qualifications for quality teachers the same for teachers of infants, toddlers, preschool, and primary school-age children? Can one definition of teacher quality transcend all 8 years of the early childhood spectrum, the stage of life when learning and development are the most rapid? Moreover, are the quality specifications precisely the same for teachers of children with diverse learning and linguistic capabilities? And are they the same for early childhood teachers who work in family child care homes and centers where working conditions are different?

Not intending to stymie the press for the B.A., we call for the field to augment this quest by examining underaddressed assumptions about what the B.A. can render. As a field, early educators must question for whom, when, and under what conditions the B.A. is most appropriate in early education. Upon examination, the metric of the one-size B.A. (or any single quality elixir) might be too generic a reach; to make the concept of the B.A. maximally applicable to the early childhood field, its requirements and entitlements may need to be specified and tailored.

WHAT IS REALLY KNOWN ABOUT WHAT WORKS?

More information is needed about what types of professional development yield the highest quality teaching. To that end, we discuss here four promising practices in early childhood professional development.

The Reality

Data on early childhood teachers and teaching are not moribund. Indeed, a great deal is known about teacher qualifications, certification effects, and—although still somewhat contentious—the B.A. impact. Detailed discussions of these findings are elaborated elsewhere; for the purposes of this chapter, we note that a number of variables are associated with quality and improved child outcomes (Bowman et al., 2001). There is general agreement that some relate to what adults do with young children in that they provide warm, nurturing, and stimulating child–adult interactions (Shonkoff & Phillips, 2000). Others relate to what adults know: they have solid knowledge of child development (Shonkoff & Phillips, 2000) and knowledge of what constitutes developmentally appropriate practice (Bredekamp & Copple, 2008). But beyond this knowledge, others (Kagan et al., 2008; National Child Care Information Center, 2009; Zaslow & Martinez-Beck, 2006) suggest that more information is needed in order to address questions about the right dosage of professional development to cultivate these characteristics. For example, more information on the personal characteristics of the teachers, including their motivation, disposition, and socioeconomic variables would enable the field to better discern the impact of professional preparation on teacher quality.

With regard to professional preparation, the literature indicates that high-quality teaching most frequently occurs when teachers participate in professional development opportunities that are "intensive, continuous or ongoing, individualized—sometimes accomplished by embedding the training in the person's job, inclusive…and focused, covering specific content rather than a range of topics" (Weber & Trauten, 2008, p. 3). Although these descriptors do shed light on the indicators of effective professional development for early childhood teachers, they do not provide a concrete definition for what professional development needs to be, something the field struggles with still (Buysse, Winton, & Rous, 2009; Goffin & Washington, 2007).

Raising the question of what constitutes effective professional preparation, scholars have noted an erosion in work-force quality (Center for Family Policy and Research, 2009; Herzenberg, Price, & Bradley, 2005). Continued low status, low compensation, and inconsistent quality in early education have prompted a strong press for more rigorous credentials, notably the B.A. degree. The rationale for this stance is strong. The B.A. is universally recognized; it is a clear and ubiquitous condition of public school teacher employment. Accompanying this requirement, higher salaries and more comprehensive benefits—sometimes directly and often indirectly linked to degree levels—are normative in public schools when compared with most preschools. Moreover, the B.A. is regarded as a comparatively standardized metric of professionalization and quality; it stands tall as a barometer of a level of formal education deemed essential to effective teaching.

Beyond values, research fortifies these stances. Early research, for example, suggested that a B.A. in early childhood or related field provided teachers with the skills and knowledge to be effective teachers. These early studies (Clifford & Maxwell, 2002; Cost, Quality, and Outcomes Study Team, 1995; Saluja, Early, & Clifford, 2002) suggested that teachers with bachelor's degrees and certification in early childhood had the highest quality classrooms, substantiating the ethos that the bachelor's degree semi-automatically catalyzes quality teaching. Leveraging the data and the emerging ethos, proponents of the B.A. have advocated for its utility, recommending it as the key to quality teaching and increased continuity of care in classrooms (Bogard et al., 2008; Child Care Services Association, 2005). Indeed, the B.A. has become the gold standard for teacher preparation (National Child Care Information Center, 2008), with many policies embracing movement toward its achievement. The 2007 reauthorization of Head Start required 50% of teachers to obtain B.A. degrees by 2013; many states are following suit, with some calling for the B.A. in publicly funded programs.

Not without concerns, this press for the B.A. degree has triggered debate. Opponents argue against its viability on grounds of precedent, variability, and inconclusive data. With regard to precedent, they contend that because much of early education takes place in the private sector, it is inappropriate and perhaps even illegal to mandate B.A. degrees and state certification for this sector in total; they note that no such requirements exist for teachers serving in America's private elementary and secondary schools. The lack of precedent is also argued on the basis of the uneven levels of funding accorded to different early education programs; without resources, how can low-funded programs be expected to hire more expensive B.A. teachers? Opening the issues related to variability, this stance is accompanied by concerns with the high levels of variability that currently characterize state certification requirements. Legion among early childhood programs, great variability exists in states with regard to the certification ranges and the knowledge base associated with them. Conferred by the states, certificates range from those covering kindergarten through Grade 3 or birth through age 8. Such inconsistency in requirements for teaching children birth through age 8 complicates the transportability of the certificate; it also legitimizes differences in the scope of knowledge and skills necessary to be a qualified early childhood teacher throughout the nation.

Beyond precedent and state and programmatic variability, opponents of the universal B.A. suggest that the research is inconclusive regarding B.A. efficacy (Fukkink & Lont, 2007; Maxwell, Field, & Clifford, 2006); some studies suggest that there is little or no correlation between formal education and child achievement (Early et al., 2006; Weber & Trauten, 2008), and little correlation between formal education and teacher quality. Both contradictory findings and a paucity of research have led many to call for more research on the nature and dosage of professional development (Fukkink & Lont, 2007; Weber & Trauten, 2008; Zaslow & Martinez-Beck, 2006) as well as on the potency of the B.A. itself. Gaining currency, the call for the B.A. is reality; its achievement, however, remains a reach.

The Reach

Although a great deal of angst and data propel the press for the B.A., there are a number of efforts to advance professional development currently taking hold. Not able to discuss them all here, we present four efforts that take different approaches to the reach. Some may stand alone or complement the B.A. approach, whereas others might act as an interim strategy until states and programs discern their consensus position on early childhood teacher requirements. The four approaches vary in their degree of implementation and refinement. In presenting them, we suggest that each reach breeds interesting questions about the impact of professional development on teacher quality and offers potential tools for achieving a highly qualified work force.

Relationship-Based Professional Development   Recognizing that formal education is expensive and is not the only way to inculcate capacities and values, the field has turned to onsite, relationship-based professional development (National Child Care Information Center, 2008). In relationship-based professional development, early childhood teachers work with coaches or consultants over time; goals are set and the coach/consultant provides the teacher with field-driven pedagogical guidance (Minnesota Center for Professional Development, 2009). Sometimes called coaching, the approach has also been used successfully with new teachers (when it is typically referred to as mentoring). Whatever the label, these efforts provide ongoing, intensive, and individualized professional development, giving teachers the opportunity to work with more seasoned colleagues (Pennsylvania Cross-Systems Technical Assistance Workgroup, 2007). They also have been effective at staving teacher turnover (Kagan et al., 2008) and breaking the isolation commonly associated with the teaching profession (Buysse & Wesley, 2005). Gaining popularity rapidly, the onsite, relationship-based professional development efforts are often nested within states' professional development systems and are being incorporated into reform efforts, including quality rating and improvement systems.

New Approaches to Formal Teacher Education   Working to enhance the quality and continuity of formal teacher education, numerous efforts are taking hold. To promote continuity of experience and overall affordability, for example, states and their institutions of higher education are promoting continuous career pathways to help prospective teachers navigate the inconsistencies of degree-conferring institutions. Often formalized into articulation agreements, these arrangements permit students to begin their higher education at logistically and financially accessible community colleges and then transfer credits to 4-year institutions without repeating or taking extra coursework. To assist individuals with experience, many states are now providing college credit for field experience, thereby legitimizing the fact that knowledge and skills gained on the job are valid and can be a valuable accompaniment to more conventional knowledge transfer that occurs in college classrooms. A variant of this approach accords independent study opportunities as a means of blending theory and practice.

Differentiated Staffing Model   Another strategy being considered acknowledges the value of the B.A. degree; it suggests that en route to achieving the goal of every lead teacher having a B.A. in a related discipline from an accredited institution of higher education, differentiated staffing patterns could be established in center-based programs that provide access to, and mentoring by, such a credentialed individual. One differentiated staffing approach suggests that two classrooms be paired, with each pair having one teacher with a bachelor's degree who oversees two classrooms, two teachers with an associate's degree in early childhood education, and one teacher with a Child Development Associate (CDA) certification. Given adequate time for planning, this differentiated staffing pattern provides multiple opportunities for team and collaborative teaching, field-based coaching and modeling, and the development of equity-driven collegiality. Moreover, the differentiated staffing model could be operationalized within existing programs as policy makers press for more dramatic advancements in teacher education, certification, and professional development.

New Approaches to Teacher Credentialing   Relying on the B.A. as a quality elixir has been greeted with mixed reactions by some who sense that the B.A. might remain inaccessible and too costly for individuals to pursue, too reliant on conventional institutions and approaches, and too uneven in its requirements and applicability to early childhood education. To combat these concerns, consideration has been given to developing a national early childhood credential that would mirror the strategy used in the nursing profession. Such a credential would be required of all those wishing to take on the lead teacher roles in center-based early childhood programs, irrespective of level of formal degree achieved. The credential would be competency based, much like the CDA credential and the National Board for Professional Teacher Standards credential, but would lie between the two in terms of competence demanded for passage. Through a series of written and performance assessments, it would assess the competence of an individual to work with young children. National in scope, the credential would be highly portable across state lines and would be accompanied by increased compensation and recognition. Explicated elsewhere (Kagan et al., 2008), the early childhood credential represents a reach to be considered.

In short, in summarizing the responses to this question—what is really known about what works—the B.A., although gaining increased currency, should not be considered as the sole elixir of, or proxy for, quality. It will not and cannot stand alone; rather, it must be conceptualized within the context of the emerging approaches to professional development that are being developed.

WHAT SHOULD BE DONE NOW?

The path to achieving teacher quality in early childhood is not straightforward but, rather, multipronged and rife with both complexity and opportunity.

The Reality

As the previous discourse indicated, there is no lack of contention regarding the strategic next steps. Moreover, there is no lack of field-based activity and inventive ideas that could accompany the development of the B.A.. These efforts cannot and should not be curtailed. Rather, they need to be considered as a more comprehensive strategy for teacher quality and teacher effectiveness is mounted. No single strategy will be sufficient. To that end, our reach is for the B.A. Plus.

The Reach

Dodging the tough defining issues will keep the field in a state of perpetual disequilibrium. To that end, the professionals need to develop the mechanisms to define the field and to render far more precision to the professional capacities and competencies necessary to get the job done. Such get-smart/get-together strategies need to recognize the realities of the diverse early childhood field—the needs and diversities of today's young children. In short, to define the scope and nature of professional development, the profession needs to be defined.

Important as they are, ideas alone will not move the agenda. They need to be married with strategically planned research-driven efforts. Such efforts acknowledge that a myriad of strategies, together evoking unplanned natural variation, already exists. As an alternative that builds on the rich history of the field, we recommend that a planned variation strategy be implemented. Such a strategy demands that the nature of professional development and certification efforts being advanced by states are systematically varied and incentivized. Each state's approach would be subject to rigorous evaluation so that the nation could learn which strategies, implemented under which conditions, work best for whom. States who have the resources and inclination to implement the B.A. should do so. In some cases, they might elect to require the B.A. as their primary professional advancement strategy; in other cases, they might enrich the B.A. with mentoring and coaching efforts. States who see the B.A. as a desirable but a presently unattainable goal might adopt other forms of professional development and/or credentialing. Whatever the case, such efforts should be richly and rigorously evaluated to discern their comparative merit. Our guess is that some combination of the B.A. plus other strategies will win the day. In rendering this bet, we note that any plan to achieve teacher quality must be imbued with reality and reach; we think that is good.

CHAPTER 13

Competencies and Credentials for Early Childhood Educators
What Do We Know and What Do We Need to Know?

Margaret Burchinal, Marilou Hyson, and Martha Zaslow

State and federal governments use high-quality preschool experiences as one way to address achievement gaps between children from low- and middle- to high-income families, relying on research that demonstrates that high-quality early childhood education (ECE) improves academic and social skills in children from low-income families. Research evidence also suggested that teachers with baccalaureate degrees tended to provide a high-quality educational experience, so some have urged policy makers to require these degrees. Although no one doubts that the quality of the classroom teacher matters,

Chapter 13 was originally published as Burchinal, M., Hyson, M., & Zaslow, M. (2008, Spring). Competencies and credentials for early childhood educators: What do we know and what do we need to know? *NHSA Dialog Briefs*, 11(1), 1–8; reprinted by permission. A publication of the National Head Start Association.

evidence raises questions about whether standards based primarily on teacher education degrees are producing the desired results. This evidence suggests that a greater focus on the content of pre- and in-service training is needed to create a better-prepared and more effective early childhood work force.

QUALITY IN EARLY CHILDHOOD EDUCATION: EARLIER EVIDENCE

Children who experience high-quality ECE tend to start school with stronger language, academic, and social skills (Vandell, 2004). Experimental studies demonstrated that high-quality ECE experiences produced stronger cognitive and academic skills at entry to school; in turn, these translated into better adolescent and adult outcomes (Campbell et al., 2002; Lazar & Darlington, 1982; Martin, Brooks-Gunn, Klebanov, Buka, & McCormick, 2008; Nores, Belfield, & Barnett, 2005). Descriptive or quasi-experimental studies (i.e., studies that did not involve random assignment to ECE conditions) provided further support with larger, more representative samples (Gormley et al., 2005; Howes et al., 2008; National Institute of Child Health and Human Development Early Child Care Research Network, 2005b; Peisner-Feinberg et al., 2001; Reynolds et al., 2002). Based on this relatively consistent evidence, both state and federal governments have focused on funding high-quality preschool programs for children from low-income families to address the growing achievement gap in this country.

Policy makers have also turned to the research community to determine how they can ensure that their preschool programs are of high quality. Observational research has found an association between higher quality care and both teacher education and training. These associations were observed in both large studies (Burchinal et al., 2002; Clarke-Stewart, Vandell, Burchinal, O'Brien, & McCartney, 2002; Howes, Whitebook, & Phillips, 1992; Kontos & Wilcox-Herzog, 2001; National Institute of Child Health and Human Development Early Child Care Research Network, 2000; 2002a; Phillipsen et al., 1997; Scarr, Eisenberg, & Deater-Deckard, 1994) and small ones (Burchinal et al., 2000; de Kruif, McWilliam, Ridley, & Wakely, 2000; Vandell, 2004). A review of this research literature by Tout, Zaslow, and Berry (2005) concluded that higher levels of teacher education, especially education that focuses on early childhood, are generally related to higher quality but that no evidence existed indicating that a certain education level (e.g., bachelor's degree) will ensure high-quality ECE.

Based on this research evidence and recommendations from early childhood advocates (Barnett, Hustedt, Robin, & Schulman, 2005; National Research Council, 2001; Trust for Early Education, 2004), state and federal policies have focused on requiring that ECE teachers receive training and obtain college degrees. As of 2005, 17 of the 38 states with public prekindergarten (pre-K) programs required that all lead teachers hold a bachelor's degree and another 12 states required a bachelor's degree of some pre-K teachers. Similarly, the Improving Head Start for School Readiness Act of 2007 (PL 110-134) requires that at least 50% of Head Start teachers in center-based programs nationwide have a bachelor's degree.

LIMITS TO THE EVIDENCE BASE

The link between program quality and teacher education is clearly not perfect. There are highly skilled and effective teachers who do not have any college training, and there are teachers with advanced college degrees who are neither responsive to the needs of the children in their care nor very stimulating.

Analyses of data from three large projects—the Cost, Quality, and Outcomes Study; the National Center for Early Development and Learning Multi-State Study of Pre-Kindergarten; and a study of child care programs in Massachusetts, Virginia, and Georgia (Blau, 2000; Early et al., 2006; Phillips, Mekos, Scarr, McCartney, & Abbott-Shim, 2000; Phillipsen et al., 1997)—showed an association between higher quality care as measured by direct observation and higher levels of teacher education. However, once other characteristics of the early care and education setting such as classroom size and child–teacher ratios were taken into account, this association was no longer statistically reliable (Blau, 2000; Early et al., 2006; Phillips, Mekos, Scarr, McCartney, & Abbott-Shim, 2000; Phillipsen et al., 1997).

Such findings raise questions about whether observed associations between teacher education and classroom quality were due to education effects (i.e., college education courses may have taught early childhood educators to be better teachers) or individual effects (i.e., individuals who had obtained college degrees may have had a different set of attitudes and practices even before they attended college, and those attitudes and practices may have then led to higher quality care). However, because different researchers have often used different measures of teacher education (e.g., degree attainment, number of years of education, certification in early childhood), it has been difficult to determine whether differences in research results are attributable to measurement differences, or whether there is a genuine lack of association between teachers' education and program quality when other features of the environment are taken into account.

To address such concerns, data from seven large studies of the early care and education of 4-year-olds (Early et al., 2007) were reanalyzed using the same definitions of teacher education and classroom quality and the same analytic methods across all major large child care study datasets. The datasets included three studies of public pre-K programs, three studies that either exclusively or primarily examined Head Start classes, and one study that primarily focused on community child care. Using the same analyses for all seven datasets, the researchers examined the association between teacher education and classroom quality as measured by either the Early Childhood Environmental Rating Scale–Revised (ECERS-R) or the Observational Record for Childcare Environments (ORCE) and language and academic child outcomes. Various indices of teacher education were examined: highest degree level, whether the teacher had a bachelor's degree, highest educational level among teachers with ECE major, and ECE major among teachers with a bachelor's degree. No consistent pattern of association was found between any index of teacher education and either classroom quality or child outcomes.

Early et al. (2007) offered several possible explanations for this lack of association, including the newness of some early childhood education training programs and the possibility that reverse selection occurred, resulting in degreed teachers who were of lower quality remaining in preschool classrooms while other, higher quality degreed teachers were selected by their school systems to move up into the higher grades. At the same time, it may be that the highest quality teachers without college degrees or teaching certificates are promoted within preschool programs and the lowest quality noncertified teachers may be replaced.

EMERGING PERSPECTIVES

Emerging research adds further complexity to the question of associations between teachers' educational degrees and classroom quality. Although degrees do not guarantee quality, this research suggests that in certain contexts college degrees may make an important contribution.

A study in California found that the importance of having a bachelor's degree to observed quality varied by type of early care and education setting (Vu, Jeon, & Howes, 2008). Having a bachelor's degree predicted quality where there were fewer resources and supports, as in community-based child care, but not in the more resourced and supported settings.

Other researchers have questioned whether it is enough to focus on the education of the lead teacher in isolation from the broader context. Ginsburg et al. (2006) studied professional development for early math instruction; Dickinson and Brady (2005) considered approaches to strengthening the skills of early childhood educators in early language and literacy instruction. Both studies noted the importance of taking a team approach to early childhood professional development. They discussed the value added by providing professional development to all of the early childhood educators in a school or program together and of emphasizing the role of the director or administrator in supporting the implementation of professional development.

The quality of early childhood teacher preparation programs is another important factor that may underlie inconsistencies in the association between professional development and observed quality. The requirement for lead teachers with bachelor's degrees and ECE teaching certificates in pre-K and Head Start programs has created a huge increase in the demand for higher education to prepare these teachers. Many of these teacher preparation programs are small, have limited resources, and may have had a different target audience in the past. They have been expected to make major changes to accommodate public demand for preschool teachers with college degrees.

To examine how the programs have been meeting such demands, Hyson, Tomlinson, and Morris (2008) conducted a national web-based survey of ECE higher education programs. A random sample of approximately half of the directors in all 1,126 higher education programs in ECE yielded a 45% response rate, with about half of the responding baccalaureate programs being accredited by the

National Council for Accreditation of Teacher Education and the National Association for the Education of Young Children.

The survey showed both positive efforts toward quality improvement and areas for concern. Many of these programs reported relying on national and state standards in determining their course and fieldwork. Programs cited a top priority to be helping their teachers learn to implement quality curricula effectively. However, only 37% of baccalaureate programs cited a top priority to be teaching students to engage more frequently in developmentally supportive teacher–child interactions (a key practice in producing quality and positive outcomes). Only 29% listed a program priority to be helping students know about and use research in their practice.

Capacity issues appeared to constrain the quality improvement efforts of many programs. Most programs reported needing more faculty members, having a primarily part-time faculty, needing more professional development for faculty, and having heavy and often overwhelming course loads. These findings suggest that overburdened, underresourced baccalaureate programs may not be able to provide the level of professional development that will translate into high-quality practices once the graduates start teaching in ECE settings. This work emphasized the need to consider not just whether early childhood educators have completed a bachelor's degree but also the quality of the degree-granting program.

Research has also emphasized the potential importance of ongoing training, defined here as professional development focusing on helping early childhood educators implement specific practices in interacting with children. A meta-analysis of published papers from 1980 to 2005 showed that specialized training improved the competency of child care providers and children's outcomes and that in-service training or training workshops were most effective when training was manualized and tailored to the specific audience (Fukkink & Lont, 2007).

Several studies provided further indications that important aspects of effective professional development may occur outside of a bachelor's degree program. Much of this work focuses on the provision of feedback on early childhood educators' interactions with children through technical assistance or coaching. A process that involves reviewing videotapes of the teacher interacting with children while delivering a well-defined curriculum may be especially promising in helping teachers become both more sensitive and effective in providing stimulating instruction (Dickinson & Caswell, 2007; Lonigan & Whitehurst, 1998; Pianta et al., 2008). Programs in which the new teacher receives onsite mentoring also appear to improve and maintain the entry-level teacher's skills when she or he begins to teach in a setting that can have a very different orientation toward teaching than the teacher learned during preservice training. Several intensive curricula combined with coaching are also showing promising results in terms of both improved classroom quality and child outcomes (Clements & Sarama, 2007; Dickinson & Caswell, 2007; Pianta et al., 2008). Many of these findings, drawn from studies of ongoing training and professional development, have potential to improve the quality of preservice higher education programs as well.

CONCLUSION

The quality of early education and care can be improved when teachers receive carefully selected and implemented professional development (either training outside of an institution of higher education or via higher education courses). However, at this point in time, the data suggest that quality is not necessarily higher when teachers have a college degree. It is likely that many higher education programs currently lack the capacity to ensure that their graduates are able to provide high-quality early care and education. In addition, evidence suggests that going beyond preservice education to consider in-service training may be important in assuring that quality is reached and sustained. We may also need to move beyond considering the lead teacher and his or her education as the lone support for quality, focusing instead on providing professional development jointly to all program personnel who interact with children. The impact of the academic degree may vary by context and may especially vary depending on the extent to which the new graduate's work in an early care and education setting continues to be monitored and supported. Finally, early childhood educators may benefit from the background knowledge that formal education provides but may also need direct, ongoing feedback on the nature of their interactions with children in order to ensure high quality.

Overall, before it is reasonable to expect higher education to produce high-quality ECE teachers, more attention should be paid to the content and quality of the degree-granting program, the context the early educator is teaching in, and the supports the educator receives in the teaching setting. These, and not the degree alone, are likely to lead to improved outcomes for children.

CHAPTER 14

The Importance of Early Childhood Teacher Preparation

The Perspectives and Positions of the National Association for the Education of Young Children

Barbara A. Willer, Alison Lutton, and Mark R. Ginsberg

Working to improve the qualifications of early childhood teachers and standards of practice in programs for young children has been the primary focus for the National Association for the Education of Young Children (NAEYC) since it was founded in 1926. In fact, the association's first publication, *Minimum Essentials for Nursery Education* (National Association for Nursery Education, 1929), was written in response to concerns about the lack of standards and risk of unqualified teachers in the burgeoning nursery school movement.

Today, NAEYC's vision centers on four key goals:

1. All children have access to a safe and accessible, high-quality early childhood education that includes a developmentally appropriate curriculum; knowledgeable and well-trained program staff and educators; and comprehensive services that support their health, nutrition, and social well-being, in an environment that respects and supports diversity.

2. All early childhood professionals are supported as professionals with a career ladder, ongoing professional development opportunities, and compensation that attracts and retains high-quality educators.

3. All families have access to early childhood education programs that are affordable and of high quality and actively participate in their children's education as respected reciprocal partners.

4. All communities, states, and the nation work together to ensure accountable systems of high-quality early childhood education for all children.

One of the key strategies NAEYC uses to achieve this vision is to set standards and implement systems for assessing and recognizing programs that meet these standards. NAEYC recognizes early childhood associate's degree programs in institutions of higher education through its Early Childhood Associate Degree Accreditation program and early childhood baccalaureate and advanced degree programs in schools of education accredited by the National Council for Accreditation of Teacher Education (NCATE). Similarly, the NAEYC Academy for Early Childhood Program Accreditation accredits programs serving children birth through kindergarten that meet NAEYC's early childhood program standards. Both sets of standards address the critical role of the early childhood teacher and the importance of specialized qualifications for these individuals for ensuring high-quality experiences for all young children. In addition, they contribute to the association's goal of building an effective professional work force that reflects the diversity of children and families served.

This chapter outlines NAEYC's commitment to ensuring that a diverse work force of early childhood teachers have the knowledge, skills, and experiences needed to provide high-quality early childhood education to all young children and describes the research base for this position. NAEYC standards are designed to be living documents that are periodically revised and updated to reflect new understandings from research and practice. Therefore, this chapter also highlights emerging issues under review as the standards are revised.

IMPROVING TEACHER QUALIFICATIONS THROUGH STANDARDS FOR PROFESSIONAL PREPARATION

NAEYC joined the National Council for Accreditation of Teacher Education in the late 1970s and began the work of developing teacher education guidelines, initially for 4- and 5-year programs and later for advanced degrees as well as for associate's degree programs. Through its membership in NCATE, NAEYC has reviewed and recognized baccalaureate and advanced degree programs in early childhood education for many years. Although guidelines (now standards) for associate's degree programs have been in place since 1985, the formal accreditation process for such programs has only been operational since 2006.

NAEYC's standards for early childhood professional preparation have taken various forms over the years. In a major revision in the late 1990s, NAEYC and other postsecondary accreditation standards moved away from an emphasis on descriptors of structural program components, or inputs, toward student performance standards, or program outcomes. The current standards, adopted by the NAEYC Governing Board in 2009, outline a common framework across all degree levels, identifying six core standards that describe what all early childhood professionals should be prepared to know and do, as described in the following sections.

Standard 1: Promoting Child Development and Learning

Students prepared in early childhood degree programs are grounded in a child development knowledge base. They use their understanding of young children's characteristics and needs and of the multiple interacting influences on children's development and learning to create environments that are healthy, respectful, supportive, and challenging for each child.

Standard 2: Building Family and Community Relationships

Students prepared in early childhood degree programs understand that successful early childhood education depends on partnerships with children's families and communities. They know about, understand, and value the importance and complex characteristics of children's families and communities. They use this understanding to create respectful, reciprocal relationships that support and empower families and to involve all families in their children's development and learning.

Standard 3: Observing, Documenting, and Assessing

Students prepared in early childhood degree programs understand that child observation, documentation, and other forms of assessment are central to the practice of all early childhood professionals. They know about and understand the goals, benefits, and uses of assessment. They know about and use systematic observations, documentation, and other effective assessment strategies in a responsible way, in partnership with families and other professionals, to positively influence the development of every child.

Standard 4: Using Developmentally Effective Approaches to Connect with Children and Families

Students prepared in early childhood degree programs understand that teaching and learning with young children is a complex enterprise, and its details vary depending on children's ages, characteristics, and the settings within which teaching and learning occur. They understand and use positive relationships and supportive interactions as the foundation for their work with young children and families. Students know, understand, and use a wide array of developmentally appropriate approaches, instructional strategies, and tools to connect with children and families and positively influence each child's development and learning.

Standard 5: Using Content Knowledge to Build Meaningful Curriculum

Students prepared in early childhood degree programs use their knowledge of academic disciplines to design, implement, and evaluate experiences that promote positive development and learning for each and every young child. Students understand the importance of developmental domains and academic (or content) disciplines in early childhood curricula. They know the essential concepts, inquiry tools, and structure of content areas, including academic subjects, and can identify resources to deepen their understanding. Students use their own knowledge and other resources to design, implement, and evaluate meaningful, challenging curricula that promote comprehensive developmental and learning outcomes for every young child.

Standard 6: Becoming a Professional

Students prepared in early childhood degree programs identify and conduct themselves as members of the early childhood profession. They know and use ethical guidelines and other professional standards related to early childhood practice. They are continuous, collaborative learners who demonstrate knowledgeable, reflective, and critical perspectives on their work, making informed decisions that integrate knowledge from a variety of sources. They are informed advocates for sound educational practices and policies (NAEYC, 2009b).

Some may question why NAEYC does not advocate a separate standard for inclusion and diversity. NAEYC's standards are deliberately designed so that inclusion and diversity must be addressed in each of these six standards. The phrase *each child* emphasizes that every standard includes children with delays and disabilities; gifts and talents; culturally or linguistically diverse backgrounds; and unique learning styles, strengths, and needs. Similarly, NAEYC is committed to building a diverse early childhood work force that reflects the diversity of children and families served (LeMoine, 2008).

In order to become NAEYC-accredited, early childhood degree programs demonstrate that they offer a curriculum of learning opportunities and assessments aligned with these standards, collect and monitor student performance data from these key assessments, and use that data to develop and improve the program. This could mean analyzing subgroups of students to identify and respond to special strengths, opportunities, and challenges. In addition, it requires particular attention to structural components that support recruitment, retention, and successful degree completion for specific demographic groups such as first-generation college students, students with very limited economic resources, adults who cannot leave jobs and families to attend distant universities, and adult English language learners (NAEYC, 2009b).

Although these things can be perceived purely as barriers to building the work force that is needed, they can also be perceived as opportunities for early childhood degree programs to lead to innovations that could benefit teacher education reform efforts as a whole. For example, baccalaureate degree program completion for adults already working as teachers or aides in child care, Head Start, or primary schools is critical, but these adults face multiple barriers in teacher education degree programs.

IMPROVING TEACHER QUALIFICATIONS THROUGH STANDARDS FOR PROGRAMS FOR YOUNG CHILDREN

NAEYC established its accreditation system for programs for young children in the early 1980s to help families find the best care for their young children and to provide the early childhood education field with a credible means by which to identify and meet standards of excellence. The system underwent a major reinvention process, which was completed in 2006. The reinvented system of NAEYC accreditation is designed to facilitate program improvement, but its primary goal is to reliably and consistently recognize programs that meet its measure of quality—the 10 NAEYC Early Childhood Program Standards—through consistent performance of the accreditation criteria associated with each standard (NAEYC, 2005).

Teacher qualifications have always been addressed through NAEYC accreditation of programs for young children. Prior to the reinvention, the expectation was that teachers have the minimum of a Child Development Associate (CDA) credential or an associate's degree in early childhood education/

child development or the equivalent, with a preference stated for a baccalaureate degree in early childhood education/child development (NAEYC, 1998). Few programs that achieved accreditation met this criterion, but they were able to demonstrate substantial compliance with the criteria overall and thus able to achieve NAEYC accreditation.

Since the reinvented system went into effect in 2006, programs must meet each of the 10 NAEYC Early Childhood Program Standards as demonstrated through their performance of the accreditation criteria associated with each standard. By Standard 6, teachers should address the importance of teacher education and training, as well as the contributions of professional development to high-quality care, effective teaching, and children's development:

> The program employs and supports a teaching staff that has the educational qualifications, knowledge, and professional commitment necessary to promote children's learning and development and to support families' diverse needs and interests. (NAEYC, 2005, p. 52)

This standard is addressed through criteria that are organized in two topic areas—first, preparation, knowledge, and skills of teaching staff; and second, teachers' dispositions and professional commitment (see Ritchie & Willer, 2005, for specific background on this standard).

The criterion specific to teacher qualifications is 6.A.05:

> All teachers have a minimum of an associate's degree or equivalent. At least 75% of teachers have a minimum of a baccalaureate degree or equivalent in early childhood education, child development, elementary education, or early childhood special education, and this training encompasses child development and learning of children birth through kindergarten; family and community relationships; observing, documenting, and assessing young children; teaching and learning; and professional practices and development. (NAEYC, 2005, p. 53)

Because the expectations stated in the criterion were so much higher than under the previous system, a timeline was established to phase in the expectations over time by setting stepped up percentages for the number of teachers with associate's and baccalaureate degrees at 5-year intervals between 2005 and 2020 to meet the criterion, with some leeway by program size. In general, the expectations that went into effect in September 2010 are for all teachers to have an associate's degree, with some proportion having or working on a baccalaureate degree.

As under the previous system, programs can achieve NAEYC accreditation without meeting the specific criterion addressing staff qualifications (and many continue to do so), as long as they demonstrate meeting at least 80% of the criteria on which they are assessed within Standard 6. (Note that the criteria specific to qualifications are always assessed.) The remaining criteria within the standard address whether teachers demonstrate specific knowledge and skills; whether they have received appropriate orientation to the program; and whether they have specialized college course work, professional development training, or both in key areas related to good practice. In essence, this approach has been necessary to acknowledge the current realities that present barriers to achieving the desired educational qualifications for teaching staff.

While acknowledging the realities, with reinvention, new steps were introduced to encourage more staff to pursue degrees through NAEYC accreditation. Because the system still allows programs to not specifically comply with the criterion for teacher qualifications, new candidacy requirements were also established. These require programs that do not meet the qualifications for teaching staff as listed in the criteria to describe in a detailed professional development plan how they are ensuring that early childhood expertise is being provided to guide curriculum and learning. In addition, such programs must also meet specified minimum educational requirements for the teaching staff and program administrator that require that at least 75% of teachers meet one of the following: 1) have a minimum of the CDA credential awarded by the Council for Professional Recognition or equivalent; 2) be working on an associate's or higher degree in early childhood education, child development/ family studies, early childhood special education, or elementary education with a concentration in early childhood education or the equivalent; 3) have a degree (associate's or higher) outside the early childhood field and 3 or more years of work experience in an NAEYC-accredited program; or 4) have a degree (associate's or higher) outside the early childhood field with 3 or more years of work experience in a program not accredited by NAEYC and at least 30 contact hours of relevant training during the past 3 years. Programs that cannot demonstrate that they meet these requirements are denied candidacy, and are therefore not eligible for NAEYC accreditation. Currently about 10% of applicant programs fail candidacy, mostly due to failing to meet staff qualification requirements.

THE RESEARCH BASE BEHIND THE STANDARDS

Both the professional preparation standards and children's programs standards are grounded in research and professional knowledge. Literature reviews are conducted whenever the standards are periodically reviewed and revised. Historically, the reviews have found strong support for higher qualifications for teachers. In 2000, two comprehensive literature reviews were published by the National Academy of Sciences, *Eager to Learn* (Bowman et al., 2001) and *From Neurons to Neighborhoods* (Shonkoff & Phillips, 2000), specifically considering the linkages between qualifications and effective teaching. Both studies, completed under the auspices of the prestigious National Academy of Sciences National Research Council, stressed the importance of baccalaureate degrees with specialized training in child development and early childhood education for preschool children, although *From Neurons to Neighborhoods* added the caveat that "staff–child ratio may be relatively more important for infants and toddlers and that the educational level of the teacher may become more important as children move beyond the infant years into toddlerhood" (Shonkoff & Phillips, 2000, pp. 315–316).

As noted by Whitebook (2003b), additional evidence for the importance of the bachelor's degree was also demonstrated by the fact that teachers in model programs demonstrating long-term benefits for children have all held baccalaureate or higher degrees. This evidence affected the burgeoning state-funded prekindergarten (pre-K) movement in the early 2000s; by 2006, more than half of the states had publicly funded pre-K programs that required lead teachers to have baccalaureate degrees (Barnett, Hustedt, Friedman, Boyd, & Ainsworth, 2007). Similarly, Kelley and Camilli (2007) found more positive outcomes for children when teachers had bachelor's degrees.

NAEYC's review of literature that guided the development of the 2005 criterion for teacher qualifications (Ritchie & Willer, 2005) noted that much of the existing research tended to confound formal education and specialized training. The level of degree attainment does not necessarily indicate the level of specialized early childhood preparation. The six core NAEYC professional preparation standards are used across associate, baccalaureate, and graduate programs. Accreditation guidance materials include examples of the level of early childhood–focused learning opportunities and student assessments that are expected as teacher candidates progress from initial to more advanced levels of preparation. Students may begin initial early childhood teacher preparation in associate, baccalaureate, or graduate programs. Advanced early childhood coursework will always be at the graduate level and builds on prior early childhood knowledge and experience, preparing candidates for roles as master teachers, researchers, administrators, and teacher educators.

As newer research has attempted to disentangle these effects and to utilize more complex analytic tools, it has become increasingly clear that a more nuanced understanding is needed to consider the importance of teacher qualifications. For example, a research review by Tout et al. (2005) found that higher levels of teacher education—and specifically those focused on early childhood development— were associated with higher levels of program quality, but that it was not possible to link specific levels of education, such as a baccalaureate degree, to higher quality. Several studies found relationships between the level of teachers' education and quality that later disappeared when controlling for other variables (Blau, 2000; Early et al., 2006; Phillips et al., 2000; Phillipsen et al., 1997).

To tease apart the relationships between various aspects of teacher qualifications, Early et al. (2007) reanalyzed data from seven large studies of early childhood programs serving 4-year-olds, including three studies of public pre-K programs, three studies focused largely on Head Start programs, and one study focused primarily on community child care programs. The researchers considered the highest degree attained by the teacher, whether the degree was in early childhood development, and how these were related to measures of program quality as well as specific child academic skills. They found largely null or contradictory associations, concluding that "solely increasing teachers' education will not suf-fice for improving quality or maximizing children's academic gains" (2007, p. 558).

Early and colleagues were careful to note that their findings should not be interpreted to mean that teachers' educational levels do not matter but that further research is needed to understand the nature of the relationships. They and others (Burchinal, Hyson, & Zaslow, 2008; Whitebook, Gomby, Bellm, Sakai, & Kipnis, 2009) have suggested potential reasons as to why no relationships may have been found, including the variability in teacher preparation programs both individually and over time, depending on when the teacher was trained; the economic context of early childhood service delivery, in which publicly funded pre-K programs offer higher compensation and benefits than private programs but less compensation and benefits than publicly funded programs serving older children. As a result, it is hypothesized that more skilled teachers without degrees may be sought by the publicly funded pre-K programs while more skilled teachers with degrees leave the pre-K programs for the higher benefits associated with programs serving older children.

IMPLICATIONS OF THE RESEARCH

Taken together, the research findings have important implications for NAEYC's work. To reiterate, NAEYC strives to achieve positive outcomes for children through an effective system of early childhood program delivery that is supported by a strong, competent, and diverse profession. Our goal includes helping the early childhood field achieve the hallmarks of a profession—a dynamic knowledge base, mechanisms to recognizing evidence-based standards of practice, and status that is commensurate with the value of the work, including appropriate compensation.

In no profession is degree completion alone sufficient to ensure high-quality practice. Teacher quality is built, sustained, and increased through career-long professional development with attention to deliberate recruitment of candidates with promise, early experiences that inform and build commitment to the profession, successful degree program completion, and workplace-embedded training, coaching, and peer collaboration.

NAEYC recognizes that there are many challenges ahead, and building a diverse and effective work force will not be easy—but it can be done. NAEYC believes that professional development policies are necessary that recognize both where the field is now and where the profession needs to go. As an example of this type of strategy, NAEYC defined alternative pathways for program administrators to meet accreditation standards not because we see the various pathways as equivalent to an earned degree in a program with a well-designed scope and sequence of study, but because equivalents are sometimes needed to acknowledge people already in the field during a period of change and those whose professional expertise includes degrees out of field.

It is necessary to recognize that both professional degree programs and children's programs are underresourced, working under conditions of high demand with little support to meet those demands. Both need policy supports to meet NAEYC standards. Early childhood policies and systems need better integration across regulatory and funding auspices if degree programs are to be built to prepare teachers for children in child care, Head Start, preschool, pre-K, and early grades.

It is necessary to raise expectations around both qualifications and diversity in the nation's early childhood teachers. Research indicates that the percentage of Caucasian teachers currently working in early learning programs rises as degree requirements and salaries rise, from 63% of child care workers to 78% of preschool teachers and 82% of elementary and secondary teachers. The figures are most striking for Latino teachers. Child care teachers are 16.5% Latino, but just 6% of preschool, elementary, and secondary teachers are Latino (Chang, 2006). Promising strategies are emerging including introductory early childhood coursework in Spanish, early childhood content assignments in adult English language learner classrooms, community-based recruitment of Spanish-speaking students and faculty, and designing programs to produce bilingual early childhood teachers. In some cases, degree programs are simultaneously conducting these experiments while earning NAEYC Early Childhood Associate Degree Accreditation, demonstrating that innovation and accreditation can work hand in hand (Lutton, 2009).

It is necesssary to continue to develop and use program standards, both for professional preparation programs and early learning programs, as more than a checklist—as opportunities for spurring creativity and innovation. Many of the challenges identified in this chapter also make the case for new approaches to early childhood teacher education. Cohort groups, higher education and early learning program partnerships, alignment with national standards across degree levels to promote transfer, baccalaureate degrees offered on local community college campuses, data-driven strategies that respond to the needs of specific demographic groups of college students—all of these are already underway (Coulter & Vandal, 2007; Whitebook et al., 2008).

NAEYC firmly believes in the power of high-quality early childhood education for all children. Teachers hold the key to this power. Early childhood teachers are most effective when they have the specialized education and continuing supports that allow them to meet the diverse needs of all young children and are recognized for the critical contributions they make to the nation's future. Children deserve nothing less.

DEBATE 3
Cognitive/Academic Emphasis versus Whole Child Approach

STUDY QUESTIONS

- What guidance does research provide regarding how much of a program's resources should be devoted to learning and teaching in the classroom versus social and health services for parents and the child?

- What guidance does research provide regarding the appropriate balance between child-initiated activities and direct instruction and the role of intentional teaching during free play?

- What are some limitations to existing measures for assessing the early childhood classroom?

- How can teachers use guided play to instruct children in language, reading, and mathematics?

CHAPTER 15
The Cognitive/Academic Emphasis versus the Whole Child Approach
The 50-Year Debate

Sandra J. Bishop-Josef and Edward Zigler

There is a renewed focus on children's cognitive and academic development, in both K–12 and preschool education. This emphasis has been accompanied by a denigration of play and a lack of attention to other developmental domains, including health and socioemotional development. The policy change resulted partially from findings showing the poor academic performance of many

American children, particularly in comparison to students from other nations (Elkind, 2001). The change also reflects an attempt to eliminate the well-documented achievement gap between children from low socioeconomic backgrounds and minority families and those from higher income, nonminority backgrounds (Raver & Zigler, 2004).

The policies of the George W. Bush administration did much to fuel this emphasis on cognitive development. President Bush spoke often about reforming education (including preschool education) with curricula focused on cognitive development, literacy, and numeracy. The White House Summit on Early Childhood Cognitive Development had a narrow focus on literacy—one cognitive skill out of many related to success in school. The Elementary and Secondary Education Act of 1965 was renamed the No Child Left Behind Act of 2001 when it was reauthorized. The new law added the initiative that all children be able to read by third grade (Bush, 2003). The reading mandate and accompanying testing resulted in further emphasis on literacy training, particularly phonics, in the early elementary grades (Brandon, 2002; Vail, 2003).

The spotlight on cognition also found its way into policies and proposals for preschool, including Head Start. The Bush administration initially wanted to change Head Start from a comprehensive intervention to a literacy program (Raver & Zigler, 2004; Strauss, 2003). This sort of change could be made only by changing the law governing Head Start—a time-consuming process. To move the program in the direction it wanted more quickly, the administration imposed new protocols on how the program should be run (decisions that are within its power). For example, training and technical assistance was diverted from its usual function of helping programs meet quality standards to training teachers in literacy instruction. A new reporting system was instituted that imposed standardized testing of Head Start preschoolers twice a year to assess their cognitive development (language, preliteracy, and premath skills). The results of the testing would be used to determine whether centers were performing adequately. One fear was that funding decisions would be based on children's test scores. Another fear was that Head Start teachers would teach to the test.

In the 2003 attempted reauthorization of Head Start, Congress sought to redesign the program. Among other things, a version of a bill later passed in the House removed language in the law relating to what has always been one focus of Head Start—social and emotional development. Most occurrences of these words were replaced with one word: *literacy*. This version also stopped assessments of children's social and emotional functioning in ongoing national evaluations of Head Start (Schumacher, Greenberg, & Mezey, 2003). Instead, representatives wanted assessments of whether children meet specified goals on preliteracy and premath tests. (These goals prevailed in the bill that eventually passed, although the obliteration of language pertaining to social and emotional competence and evaluations did not.)

Many experts vocally criticized these policy changes, arguing that the overemphasis on cognitive development and standardized testing was inappropriate (Strauss, 2003). Elkind (2001) argued that young children learn best through direct interaction with the environment. Before a certain age, they simply are not capable of the level of reasoning necessary for formal instruction in reading and mathematics. Whitehurst (2001), who was subsequently appointed director of the Institute of Education Sciences at the U.S. Department of Education by President Bush, wrote a counterpoint to Elkind. He claimed that content-centered approaches (i.e., academically oriented) are more likely to facilitate children's literacy learning. Raver and Zigler (2004) disagreed, criticizing the emphasis on cognitive development and standardized testing as being far too narrow and unsupported by scientific evidence on how children learn. They advocated for continued attention to and assessment of children's social and emotional development, viewing this domain as synergistic with intellectual development. Without taking sides on whether emotion or cognition should be primary, more than 300 scholars signed a letter protesting the plan to carry out standardized testing in Head Start, questioning the validity of the proposed assessments (Raver & Zigler, 2004). Related data have shown that many children are failing to meet the inappropriate demands placed on them. For example, the number of children held back in kindergarten in Chicago quadrupled from 1992 to 2001 (Brandon, 2002).

Congress was unable to pass a bill reauthorizing Head Start during the 108th session (2003–2005), so efforts began anew in the 109th Congress. In the 109th Congress, the focus on literacy and numeracy took a backseat to other matters. Despite considerable effort, the 109th Congress also failed to pass a

Head Start reauthorization bill. Finally, in Fall 2007, the 110th Congress passed the Improving Head Start for School Readiness Act (PL 110-134) and President G.W. Bush signed it into law in December 2007. The legislation has several key positive features, including a requirement for a new assessment framework, recommended by the National Academy of Sciences (Snow & Van Hemel, 2008), to replace the national reporting system.

Parents are also increasingly demanding academic preschool content (Bodrova & Leong, 2003; Vail, 2003). One preschool director commented about parents: "All parents want now are worksheets, and they want them in their babies' hands as early as possible" (Bodrova & Leong, 2003, p. 12). As parents are the customers of early childhood programs, programs are likely to eventually succumb to parental pressure and change curricula to reflect parental preferences, even if these are ill advised.

A HISTORICAL PERSPECTIVE

A similar overemphasis on cognitive skills occurred in the late 1950s when American attitudes toward education were seriously affected by the Russians' launching of Sputnik in 1957 (Zigler, 1984). This focus on cognitive skills had nothing to do with new knowledge about child development or education. The Russians beating the United States into space was traumatic for Americans, injuring national pride. The Russians' feat was perceived by many as evidence that the more rigorous Soviet education system was more effective than the American system. A return to the three Rs—reading, writing, and arithmetic—was touted as the way to build American superiority in the global arena.

A prominent spokesperson for this point of view was not an eminent early childhood educator, but an admiral in the U.S. Navy, Hyman G. Rickover. Admiral Rickover made the provocative assertion that young children in Russia were being trained in mathematics while America's young children were busy fingerpainting. The second author of this chapter (Zigler) was trying to forge a middle ground, writing and speaking of the need to nurture all aspects of early development, including the physical, socioemotional, and cognitive systems. Zigler remembers vividly getting a call from Admiral Rickover castigating him for championing a whole child approach instead of encouraging attention to cognition. Thus, the battle line was clearly drawn between academic pursuits and the whole child approach.

By the 1960s, the emphasis on cognition was accompanied by a facile and overstated "environmental mystique" (Zigler, 1970). This view held that minimal environmental interventions during the preschool years could yield dramatic increases in children's cognitive functioning. A book by Joseph McVicker Hunt, *Intelligence and Experience* (1961), was the bible of this point of view and had an immense effect. The environmental theory was glorified through the popular press and bookstores filled with titles such as *How to Give Your Child a Superior Mind* (Engelmann & Engelmann, 1966). Academic prescriptions for infants appeared and were grounded in the argument that, if one started cognitive training early enough, remedial efforts would not be necessary later on. Drill and exposure to educational gadgetry were seen as the activities worthy of children's time and attention.

Another guiding principle of this environmental theory was that intervention programs are most effective if they are administered during a critical period—the earlier the better. This critical period concept was popularized in Benjamin Bloom's (1964) *Stability and Change in Human Characteristics.* Bloom pointed out that IQ scores at age 4 years account for half of the variance in adult IQ scores. Bloom's claim was misinterpreted by the popular media to mean that half of the child's learning is over by age 4. This questionable argument further fueled the infatuation with cognitive development and compelled parents and educators to feverishly teach children as much as possible, as early as possible.

Even Head Start fell victim to the excessive focus on cognitive skills and naïve environmentalism (Zigler, 1970). From its inception in 1965, Head Start has been a comprehensive program, with components to support physical health, nutrition, social and emotional development, education, services for children's families, and community and parental involvement. The founders of Head Start believed that preparing children who live in poverty for school requires meeting all of their needs, not just focusing on their academic skills. However, when researchers began to evaluate early intervention programs, they were drawn to assessments of cognitive functioning, particularly IQ test scores (Zigler & Trickett, 1978). Part of the reason was the zeitgeist of the time (e.g., the work of Hunt [1961] and Bloom [1964]).

Evaluators also became enthralled with the results: Relatively minor interventions—even 6–8 weeks of a preschool program—seemed to produce large increases in children's IQs. These gains were soon found to be caused by improvements in motivation rather than cognitive functioning (Zigler & Butterfield, 1968). Yet findings such as these did not (and still do not) deter the use of IQ as a primary measure of Head Start's effectiveness (Raver & Zigler, 1991; Zigler & Trickett, 1978). This practice is understandable in that measures of IQ were readily available, easy to administer and score, and deemed reliable and valid, whereas measures of socioemotional constructs were less developed. Also, IQ was a construct that policy makers and the public could easily understand, and it was known to be related to many other behaviors, particularly school performance.

Before long, however, researchers lost faith in IQ as a measure of Head Start's success (Raver & Zigler, 1991). In 1969, the Westinghouse Report (Cicirelli, 1969) found that Head Start children failed to sustain their IQ advantage once they moved through elementary school. Investigators began to understand that Head Start children's rapid IQ gains could be explained by motivational factors (e.g., less fear of the test and tester, more self-confidence) rather than by true improvement in cognitive ability (Zigler & Trickett, 1978). Experts also pointed out the numerous difficulties and biases in using IQ to evaluate comprehensive intervention programs (e.g., Zigler & Trickett, 1978).

In the early 1970s, the Office of Child Development (OCD; now the Administration on Children and Families) articulated social competence as the overriding goal of Head Start and encouraged broader evaluations to measure more accurately the program's effectiveness (Raver & Zigler, 1991). However, no accepted definition was available of social competence, much less established measures. Therefore, OCD funded the Measures Project in 1977, a multisite study to develop a battery of measures of the factors making up social competence, including but not limited to appropriate cognitive measures. Zigler and Trickett (1978) also suggested approaches to assessing social competence, arguing that measures of motivational and emotional variables, physical health and well-being, achievement, and formal cognitive ability must all be included.

Thus, by the late 1970s to early 1980s, the naïve cognitive-environmental view had largely been rejected, and a renewed appreciation of the whole child was becoming evident. The second author of this chapter (Zigler) wrote optimistically in 1984, "I am happy to report that the view of the child as only a cognitive system is now defunct" (Zigler, 1984, p. x). Books by David Elkind, *The Hurried Child* (1981) and *Miseducation: Preschoolers at Risk* (1987), argued that children were being pushed too hard and too early, and they were being driven to grow up quickly, especially with respect to intellectual tasks. Elkind saw the consequences of this pressure as severe, ranging from stress to behavior problems and even to suicide. Elkind's books were very popular and were important in moving both professionals and the general public toward a view that social and emotional development is a valuable part of child development and strongly affects intellectual growth.

However, the pendulum had already started to swing back in the opposite direction. In 1982, the Reagan administration cut most of the funding for the Measures Project, supporting only the site that was developing measures of cognitive functioning. In 1991, Raver and Zigler described how, during the Reagan and George H.W. Bush years, the Head Start administration was again focusing almost exclusively on cognitive measures to assess the program's effectiveness. Further, the cognitive measurement system that emanated from the Measures Project (Head Start Measures Battery) was accompanied by a curriculum, which led to concerns about teaching to the test.

The tide began to shift yet again during the next decade (Zigler, 1994). For example, in 1995, the National Educational Goals Panel, a semigovernmental group composed of federal and state policy makers, officially defined school readiness as consisting of five dimensions, including physical well-being and motor development, social and emotional development, approaches to learning, language development, and cognition and knowledge (Bredekamp, 2004; Kagan, Moore, & Bredekamp, 1995). This definition emphasized that these factors are inextricably linked and must be considered in their totality as indicators of school readiness. The 1998 reauthorization of Head Start explicitly stated that the goal of the program is school readiness, similarly defining readiness (Raver & Zigler, 2004). Finally, a sensible middle ground seemed to have been reached, a consensus that learning is fostered by more than cognitive training. However, the tide turned again shortly thereafter, culminating in the prescribed focus on academics described early in this chapter. Once again, the emphasis on cognition was accompanied by a simplistic environmentalism, as when mothers were given Mozart CDs in the hospital with the prescription to play them for their infants to increase their intelligence (Jones & Zigler, 2002).

There have been some signs of hope that the tide is turning and an appreciation for the whole child is being reborn. In response to the overemphasis on cognitive skills, many organizations have advocated for the vital importance of play for children's development. For example, the National Association for the Education of Young Children updated their position statement on developmentally appropriate practice and listed 12 principles of child development and learning that should inform practice, including "Play is an important vehicle for developing self-regulation as well as for promoting language, cognition and social competence" (2009a, p. 14). In addition, several organizations have been founded to advocate for the importance of play, including Alliance for Childhood, American Association for the Child's Right to Play, National Institute for Play, and Play Matters.

There has also been a backlash to the focus on cognitive development in the policy arena. Illinois has passed a law mandating that school curricula include attention to socioemotional learning and a bill focusing on socioemotional learning has been introduced in the U.S. House of Representatives. President Barack Obama, during the 2008 presidential campaign, issued a policy factsheet that explicitly mentioned play. Obama's campaign promises as well as the actions he took since becoming president portend a new drive to advance children's causes, including, it can be hoped, supporting a more balanced view of the child, in both early childhood and elementary education (Obama, 2008).

The foregoing historical narrative demonstrates that the overemphasis on cognitive development is a step backward in our nation's history. It is also a clear illustration of the swinging pendulum that is often evident in American education, where prevailing political winds allow one extreme view to quickly rise to ascendancy, only to be replaced by another view. Clearly, what is needed is a balanced approach that is based on knowledge derived from the best child development research and sound educational practice.

THE WHOLE CHILD APPROACH

Adherents of the whole child approach do not devalue the importance of cognitive skills, including literacy. President George W. Bush's initiative to ensure that every child in America is a proficient reader is laudable. However, reading is only one aspect of cognitive development, and cognitive development is only one aspect of human development. Cognitive skills are very important, but they are so intertwined with the physical, social, and emotional systems that it is myopic, if not futile, to dwell on the intellect and exclude its partners.

Consider what goes into literacy. It involves mastery of the alphabet and other basic word skills. But, a prerequisite to achieving literacy is good physical health. The child who is frequently absent from school because of illness or who has vision or hearing problems will have difficulty learning to read. So will children who suffer emotional problems such as depression or posttraumatic stress disorder. By the same token, a child who begins kindergarten knowing letters and sounds may be cognitively prepared, but if he or she does not understand how to listen, share, take turns, and get along with teachers and classmates, this lack of socialization will hinder further learning. To succeed in reading and at school, a child must receive appropriate education, but he or she must also be physically and mentally healthy, have reasonable social skills, and have curiosity, confidence, and motivation to succeed. This broader view was endorsed in the authoritative book, *From Neurons to Neighborhoods* (Shonkoff & Phillips, 2000), which pointed out the importance of emotional and motivational factors in human development and learning.

The position that social and emotional factors are essential for cognitive development is not new. The founders of Head Start recognized the importance of these factors when they designed the program in 1965. Since that time, a body of research has demonstrated the importance of emotional and social factors for school readiness (Raver, 2002; Shonkoff & Phillips, 2000). For example, emotional self-regulation has been found to be an especially important component of learning (Raver & Zigler, 1991). Children must be able to focus their attention to the task at hand and to control their emotions when in the classroom. They must be able to organize their behavior and listen to the teacher. All of these are noncognitive factors that foster learning. Further, this type of emotional self-regulation can be developed through play when children take turns, regulate one another's behavior, and learn to cooperate (Bredekamp, 2004).

NONCOGNITIVE INFLUENCES ON COGNITIVE DEVELOPMENT: THEORY

The narrow focus on cognitive development contradicts sound developmental theory. The two preeminent theorists of cognitive development of the 20th century, Jean Piaget and Lev Vygotsky, both stressed the essential role of noncognitive factors in cognitive development.

Piaget argued that all knowledge comes from action and that children actively acquire knowledge through interacting with the physical environment. Play, according to Piaget (1932), provides the child with a multitude of opportunities to interact with materials in the environment and construct his or her own knowledge about the world. Vygotsky emphasized sociocultural influences on development, particularly how interactions with people foster cognitive development. Vygotsky (1978) claimed that play serves as the primary context for cognitive development: in play, the child interacts with others (more skilled peers, teachers, parents) and can learn from them.

NONCOGNITIVE INFLUENCES ON COGNITIVE DEVELOPMENT: RESEARCH

Decades of empirical research clearly demonstrate the benefits of play for children's cognitive development; only a very brief summary of major findings is presented here (see Zigler, Singer, & Bishop-Josef, 2004, for more detail). Research has demonstrated the beneficial effects of play on language skills, problem solving, perspective taking, representational skills, memory, and creativity (Davidson, 1998; Newman, 1990; Singer, Singer, Plaskon, & Schweder, 2003). Play has also been found to contribute to early literacy development (Christie, 1998; Owocki, 1999).

NONCOGNITIVE INFLUENCES ON COGNITIVE DEVELOPMENT: PRACTICE

Recognizing the vital importance of noncognitive factors for children's cognitive development, experts have designed curricula using play to enhance cognitive development as well as teach preliteracy and literacy skills (Bodrova & Leong, 2003; Owocki, 1999; Singer et al., 2003). For example, Bodrova and Leong's Tools of the Mind preschool and kindergarten classrooms, based on Vygotsky's theory of cognitive development, use sociodramatic play to foster literacy. These classrooms contain dramatic play areas where children spend a substantial amount of time daily, and dramatic play permeates many classroom activities. Teachers support children's play by helping them create imaginary situations, providing props, and expanding possible play roles. Children, with the teacher's assistance, develop written play plans, including the theme, the roles, and the rules that will govern the play. Studies of the Tools of the Mind curriculum support its effectiveness in promoting literacy and cognitive functioning (Bodrova, Leong, Norford, & Paynter, 2003; Diamond, Barnett, Thomas, & Munro, 2007).

CONCLUSION

The research and practice literature offer unequivocal evidence for a whole child approach in early childhood education. To foster learning, parents, teachers, and policy makers must focus on the whole child. An important point to emphasize is that those who espouse the whole child approach view all systems of development (including cognitive development) as synergistic and, in that regard, as the proper focus of child rearing and education. In contrast, those who believe that the cognitive system merits the most attention are essentially rejecting the needs of the rest of the child. By ignoring the contributions of physical health and the socioemotional system to learning, they promote an educational system designed to fail.

CHAPTER 16

The Importance of Kindergarten-Entry Academic Skills

Greg J. Duncan

I had the pleasure of serving on the National Research Council/Institute on Medicine committee that wrote the comprehensive review *From Neurons to Neighborhoods: The Science of Early Childhood Development* (Shonkoff & Phillips, 2000). One of its most striking conclusions regarding school readiness was that "the elements of early intervention programs that enhance social and emotional development are just as important as the components that enhance linguistic and cognitive competence" (pp. 398–399). Since that time, I have come to doubt the wisdom of this statement, concluding instead that preschool curricula that promote concrete literacy and (especially) numeracy skills are better bets for boosting children's chances of school success than curricula that focus solely on promoting social and emotional development. Effective programs that address persistent antisocial behavior problems during primary school may also enhance children's life chances.

It is important to note that I am not arguing that socioemotional behaviors are inconsequential for a child's healthy development—quite the contrary. Emotional development is wired into the architecture of young children's brains in ways that are highly interactive with circuits associated with judgment and decision—so-called executive functions that underlie problem-solving skills during the preschool years (National Scientific Council on the Developing Child, 2008; Posner & Rothbart, 2000). And we know that the toxic stress of abusive and neglectful interactions with caregivers can impart lifelong impairments to cognitive functioning (Glaser, 2000).

In the spirit of the volume, this chapter addresses a much narrower question: For a preschool choosing between curricula focused on cognitive and academic skills and curricula focused on mental health and emotional development, which is likely to be better able to promote a child's future school success?

Although the socioemotional behaviors children exhibit when they begin school certainly have the potential to influence their future school success, the evidence supporting the National Research Council's conclusion (Shonkoff & Phillips, 2000) is not strong. Consider first the findings of experimental studies. Model programs like Perry preschool and Abecedarian targeted high-risk preschoolers and produced impressive cognitive and academic achievement gains and long-term reductions in referrals for special education services, grade retention, and school dropout, as well as increases in adult educational attainment. (For Perry preschool follow-ups, see Schweinhart, Barnes & Weikart, 1993, and Schweinhart et al., 2005. For Abecedarian impacts, see Campbell et al., 2002. Other examples of model programs include Lazar & Darlington, 1982; Royce, Darlington, & Murray, 1983; Reynolds & Temple, 1998.) But since most of these programs had broad curricula designed to enhance both academic and social skills, it is impossible to determine which of the academic, self-regulation, and behavioral components of the program—taken individually or in combination—were responsible for the long-run school impacts that were observed.

Other experimental intervention programs, however, have targeted individual problem behaviors such as self-regulation or antisocial behavior. The problem is that their evaluations typically assess impacts only on their targeted behavior and fail to relate experimentally induced improvements in behavior to outcomes such as school achievement. One noteworthy exception is the Barnett, Jung, et al. (2008) test of the Tools of the Mind preschool curriculum, which is designed to promote cognitive self-regulation skills through a comprehensive system of activities. The study's control condition was a

Chapter 16 draws extensively from Duncan, G., & Magnuson, K. (2009, November 19–20). *The nature and impact of early skills, attention, and behavior.* Presented at the Russell Sage Foundation Conference on Social Inequality and Educational Outcomes. The research was supported by the National Science Foundation–funded Center for the Analysis of Pathways from Childhood to Adulthood (Grant 0322356) and benefited from comments from Katherine Magnuson.

school district–developed literacy curriculum. As did Diamond et al. (2007), Barnett, Jung, et al. (2008) documented marked improvements in children's cognitive self-regulation and even bigger reductions in behavior problems. However, children using Tools of the Mind scored significantly better than controls on only one of seven tests of achievement and cognitive ability—hardly proving that boosting attention skills is a better strategy for improving school success than more direct instructional approaches in preschool.

Another exception is Dolan et al. (1993), who reported results from a behavioral intervention targeted to both aggressive and shy behaviors among first graders. Their random assignment evaluation showed short-run impacts on both teacher and peer reports of aggressive and shy behavior, but no crossover impacts on reading achievement. A third exception is Tremblay, Pagani-Kurtz, Mâsse, Vitaro, and Pihl (1995), who randomly assigned disruptive kindergarten boys to a 2-year treatment consisting of both school-based social skills training and home-based parent training in effective child rearing. Treatment/control differences in delinquency were evident through age 15, but initially favorable impacts on placement into regular classrooms had disappeared by the end of primary school.

What light can nonexperimental studies shed on links between elements of school readiness and later school success? Many longitudinal studies correlate early socioemotional skills with later achievement, but most of them fail to estimate models that control well for family and child background factors and concurrent achievement (for a review, see Duncan et al., 2007). So, for example, although correlations between school-entry antisocial behavior and later school success are invariably negative, studies rarely ask whether these correlations can be attributed to the fact that children entering school with behavior problems often lack foundational literacy and numeracy skills as well. Perhaps these academic skills, rather than the antisocial behaviors, are the key determinants of future school success.

EARLY SKILLS AND LATER ACHIEVEMENT

The University of Michigan–based Center for the Analysis of Pathways from Childhood to Adulthood provided the infrastructure for a much more comprehensive assessment of the comparative importance of school-entry achievement, attention, and behavior problems for later school achievement. An interdisciplinary team I co-headed with Chantelle Dowsett identified six population-based datasets including measures of reading and math achievement, attention skills, prosocial behavior, and antisocial and internalizing behavior problems taken around the time of school entry, and measures of reading and math achievement taken later in the primary or middle school years. Most of the achievement outcomes came from tests administered between first and eighth grade, although results were similar when we used teacher-reported achievement data. Most of the school-entry reports of socioemotional behaviors were provided by teachers; the rest came from parents. School-entry reading and math skills were measured using tests. One of the datasets provided a computer-based test of attention skills; the rest relied on teacher and parent reports.

Using these data, we regressed the later reading and mathematics achievement measures on kindergarten-entry measures of reading and math achievement, attention, antisocial behavior, and internalizing behavior problems (Duncan et al., 2007). Our most complete models controlled for the child's cognitive skills, behavior, and temperament measured prior to the point of kindergarten entry as well as for family background factors. To establish comparability across studies, all achievement and behavior measures were standardized. All postkindergarten reading and math achievement outcome measures available in the six datasets were treated as dependent variables in separate regressions.

To summarize our results, we conducted a formal meta-analysis of the standardized regression coefficients emerging from the individual study regressions. Average effect sizes from the regressions involving math and reading outcomes are presented in Table 16.1. The effect sizes for reading indicate that—controlling for prior IQ, family background, and concurrent attention skills and behaviors—a 1 standard deviation (*SD*) increase in school-entry reading skills is associated with a .09 *SD* increase in later math achievement and .24 *SD* increase in later reading achievement. Both of these estimates of average effects are statistically significant.

A broader look at the results in Table 16.1 reveals that only three of the six sets of school-entry skill and behavior measures are predictive of subsequent school achievement: reading, math, and attention,

Table 16.1. Effect sizes of school-entry skills and behaviors on later achievement for Grades 1–8; meta-analysis of 236 coefficients

School entry	Math achievement	Reading achievement
Reading	.09*	.24*
Math	.41*	.26*
Attention	.10*	.08*
Externalizing	.01 ns	.01 ns
Internalizing	.01 ns	−.01 ns
Social skills	−.00 ns	−.01 ns

*$p < .05$; ns = not statistically significant (i.e., $p > .05$); number of observations = 236 estimated coefficients.

Source: Duncan et al. (2007).

Note: With the externalizing and internalizing measures scaled so that more positive values indicate more problems, a negative association between each of these measures and achievement is expected. Estimates control for time to test, test/teacher outcome, and study fixed effects; coefficients are weighted by inverse of their variances.

with early math skills being consistently most predictive. Behavior problems and social skills were not associated with later achievement in models in which achievement and child and family characteristics were held constant. Indeed, none had a standardized coefficient that averaged more than .01 in absolute value. These patterns generally held both across studies and within each of the six data sets they examined. (It should be noted that bivariate associations across the studies were as one might expect. Correlations between later achievement and school entry behaviors were: .21 for social skills, −.14 for externalizing behavior problems and −.10 for internalizing behavior problems.)

Not surprisingly, reading skills were stronger predictors of later reading achievement than later math achievement. Less expected was that early math skills (adjusting for prior cognitive skills in five of the six studies) were as predictive of later reading achievement as were early reading skills. Children's attention skills appeared to be equally important (and several dimensions of socioemotional behaviors uniformly unimportant) for reading and math achievement. Further analysis showed that these results were robust to a host of potential problems: adjustments for error in measuring attention and socioemotional skills had little impact on the results; maternal reports of attention and behavior were nearly as predictive as teacher reports of later academic achievement; worries proved unfounded that the models may overcontrol for achievement-related impacts of attention and socioemotional skills; bias from shared-method variance was not a concern because test scores were just as predictive of later teacher-reported and test-based achievement measures; the relative importance of school-entry factors was similar for immediate (e.g., first grade) and later (e.g., fifth grade) measures of achievement; and impacts of behavior problems were no larger for entering students with the most problems.

All in all, the Duncan et al. (2007) analysis provided a clear answer to one question about the relative role of school-entry skills and behavior: For later school achievement, early academic skills appear to be the strongest predictor, even after adjusting for differences due to the fact that early achievers score higher on tests of cognitive ability and come from more advantaged families. Early math skills are more consistently predictive of later achievement than early reading skills. A student's school-entry ability to pay attention and stay on task is modestly predictive of later achievement, while early problem behavior and other dimensions of social skills and mental health problems are not at all predictive. If school readiness is defined as the skills and behaviors that best predict later academic achievement, concrete numeracy and literacy skills are decidedly more important than socioemotional behaviors.

EARLY SKILLS, HIGH SCHOOL COMPLETION, AND COLLEGE ATTENDANCE

It is far from clear whether early academic skills matter as much and early behaviors as little for adolescent and early adult school attainment as they do for middle-childhood reading and math proficiency. Finishing high school likely requires a combination of achievement, engagement, and perseverance.

Table 16.2.   Effect of persistent versus no problems at ages 6, 8, and 10 on the probabilities of high school graduation and college attendance

Problem area	High school completion	College attendance
Reading	−.05	−.06
Math	−.13*	−.29**
Antisocial behavior	−.10***	−.24*
Inattention	.01	−.05
Anxiety	−.03	−.18***

*p < .05, **p < .01, ***p < .10

Source: Magnuson et al. (2009).

Note: Problem area is defined as being in the worst quartile of distribution at a given age. Both regressions include all listed variables, plus child and family controls.

Antisocial behaviors in primary school may lead only to inconsequential trips to the principal's office, while such behaviors in middle or high school may result in suspension, expulsion, or even criminal prosecution.

In a second nonexperimental study, Duncan and Magnuson (2009) used two datasets to study links between both school-entry and persistent academic and behavior problems during primary school and high school completion. The two datasets used in this research were the National Longitudinal Study of Youth–Child Supplement (NLSY; Baker, Keck, Mott & Quilan, 1993) and the Entwisle-Alexander Baltimore Beginning School Study (BSS; Entwisle, Alexander & Olson, 2007). For ease of presentation, we focus on results from the NLSY. Persistent antisocial problems were somewhat less predictive of college attendance in the BSS than in the NLSY.

Prior research has suggested that a student's trajectory of behavior problems may be more important than his or her level of behavior problems at any single age in predicting later educational attainment (Kokko, Tremblay, LaCourse, Nagin, & Vitaro, 2006). This may also be true for achievement trajectories.

Duncan and Magnuson (2009) first related high school completion to the same set of school-entry achievement, attention, and behavior problems measures used in the Duncan et al. (2007) study. Early math and reading skills had small, positive effects that were at best at the margin of statistical significance. Interestingly, school-entry antisocial behavior also had modest but significant (negative) effects. School-entry attention and internalizing behavior problems were not predictive.

More powerful relationships between some of these skills and behaviors and educational attainment emerged during the school years themselves. In their most revealing analysis, Duncan and Magnuson (2009) tested the impacts of persistent academic, attention, and behavior problems on high school completion and college attendance. To do this, they categorized children according to their pattern of scores for reading and math achievement, attention skills, antisocial behavior and anxiety during the early school years (age 6, 8, and 10 years). The 75th percentile was chosen as the threshold for a high level of behavior problems, while the 25th percentile was the upper limit for low achievement.

They then formed three groups—never, intermittent, and persistent—depending on whether the child fell into the worst quarter of a given measure's distribution on zero, one or two, or all three measurement occasions. Table 16.2 shows differences in the probabilities of graduating from high school and attending college for children with persistent as opposed to no problems. As with Table 16.1, the two regressions control for child IQ and family backgrounds as well as concurrent problems in other areas.

Just as in the school achievement analyses, math achievement emerged as the single most powerful predictor of educational attainment. Children persistently scoring in the bottom end of the math distribution were 13 percentage points less likely to graduate from high school and 29 percentage points less likely to attend college. Although school entry reports of antisocial behavior problems were not predictive of later school achievement, Table 16.2 shows that persistent behavior problems were indeed correlated with lower attainment. Surprisingly, persistent early reading problems were not predictive, nor were persistent attention problems. A measure of persistent anxiety problems was marginally predictive of college attendance, but this result did not replicate in analyses of the second dataset used by Duncan and Magnuson (2009). Patterns were broadly similar for different socioeconomic statuses and race groups, although they did differ by gender: Antisocial behavior was more predictive of schooling attainment for boys than for girls.

SUMMARY AND IMPLICATIONS FOR EARLY CHILDHOOD INTERVENTIONS

Nonexperimental analyses of six datasets suggest that future school achievement is much less a function of a child's school-entry social and emotional development than concrete literacy and numeracy skills such as knowing letters, word sounds, numbers, and ordinality. Ability to pay attention and engage in school tasks occupies an intermediate position—consistently predicting future achievement, but not as powerfully as early reading and, especially, math skills.

Expanding the conception of school success to include not only doing well on achievement tests but also completing high school and attending college changes the picture somewhat. School-entry achievement and antisocial behaviors were only very modestly predictive of these outcomes. More consequential was whether persistent learning or behavior problems were evident in primary school. Avoiding persistently low achievement mattered the most for positive school attainment, but children with persistent antisocial behavior problems across middle childhood were also at elevated risk of low attainment. Persistent attention and internalizing behavior problems were not predictive of high school completion once family background and concurrent achievement problems were taken into account.

It is hazardous to draw policy implications from nonexperimental studies. Our estimates of the causal influence of early skills and behaviors may be biased. Even if unbiased, estimates of what is most important may point to skills or behaviors that are impossible or very costly to modify. The appropriate intervention policy test involves costs and benefits rather than correlations.

Fortunately, as explained previously, quite a number of targeted preschool curricula have successfully boosted early math, literacy, attention, and behavior skills. Based on our nonexperimental analyses, the best bets for promoting later school achievement would appear to be proven preschool math and literacy curricula, while longer run educational attainments are most likely to be influenced by curricula or other programs that ensure that children avoid persistent achievement and antisocial behavior problems in primary school.

Policy actions should not be based on best bets, however, but rather on convincing evidence from rigorous evaluations of scalable programs. Here the biggest problem is that evaluations of seemingly successful curriculum intervention programs rarely continue for more than a few months beyond the end of the programs and typically fail to measure outcomes other than those targeted by their intervention. Crossover impacts of such items as improving attention skills on math or reading achievement are rarely estimated, nor are follow-ups long enough to estimate impacts on general education attainment outcomes such as school dropout or college attendance. Sorely needed are longer run follow-ups that measure impacts on a diverse set of skills and behaviors, school attainment, and economically significant school outcomes such as special education placement and grade failure.

One of our noteworthy results is that early math skills are the most powerful predictor of later achievement. It is important to discover why. Math is a combination of both conceptual and procedural competencies such as working memory; however, our data do not allow us to examine these competencies separately. Still, our findings provide compelling evidence that future research should be devoted to a close examination of efforts to improve math skills prior to school entry. Random assignment evaluations of early math programs that focus on the development of particular mathematical skills and track children's reading and math performance throughout the elementary school years could help to identify missing causal links between early skills and later achievement.

CHAPTER 17

Academic Preschool

The French Connection

E.D. Hirsch, Jr.

In this chapter, I defend an academic approach to preschool as distinct from a naturalistic approach. That distinction has sometimes been conceived too simplistically. When I was visiting preschools in France—all of which follow a specified academic curriculum—I was struck by the wide range of teaching methods and atmospheres that prevailed in different *écoles maternelles*, with teachers varying in their teaching styles from martinet disciplinarians to relaxed earth mothers yet all meeting set academic goals.

Debates over pedagogical techniques in preschool, while important, have sometimes distracted from the more significant issue: curriculum. The word *curriculum*, whenever connected with 2- to 4-year-olds, has a repellant ring to it. But if curriculum is defined as a sequence of specified learning goals, including cognitive, emotional, physical, and social goals, what else is or should be the aim of preschool than the imparting of a curriculum? A curriculum so defined will exhibit highly successful outcomes chiefly when the social and cognitive-linguistic goals are made explicit in advance and when equally explicit means are taken to impart these goals and probe continually whether they are being met.

At all grade levels, curriculum has become the most important conceptual problem confronting American education. At issue is not simply a purely scientific question about optimal outcomes. Tinged with emotion, the subject needs also to be placed in a historical context. For the last 75 years, American educational thought has been dominated by what could be called an anticurriculum movement. In 1939, Isaac Kandel summarized the dominant view in a memorable way:

> Rejecting … emphasis on formal subject matter, the progressives began to worship at the altar of the child. Children [they said] should be allowed to grow in accordance with their needs and interests…. Knowledge is valuable only as it is acquired in a real situation; the teacher must be present to provide the proper environment for experiencing but must not intervene except to guide and advise. There must, in fact, be "nothing fixed in advance" and subjects must not be "set-out-to-be-learned."…No reference was ever made to the curriculum or its content…. The full weight of the progressive attack is against subject matter and the planned organization of a curriculum in terms of subjects. (as cited in Ravitch & Null, 2006, pp. 401–411)

Under this reigning American conception, the idea of a set academic curriculum becomes more acceptable only gradually as students mature and approach high school. In thinking about very early childhood education, antipathy to an academic curriculum has been tenaciously sustained.

Let us coldly ask, "Has the repudiation of an academic curriculum actually worked in preschool, or for that matter in the grades that immediately follow?" The short answer is *no*. Quite apart from the evidence of continued low national achievement and wide gaps between demographic groups, there are theoretical considerations that explain why the anticurriculum idea cannot possibly work very well either in preschool or in later grades.

To illustrate this point, consider an example from the area of language development. For simplicity, let us ignore growth in syntax and focus our attention on growth in vocabulary, an area where the dreaded Matthew effect bedevils efforts to achieve higher and more equitable achievement across demographic barriers. The *Matthew effect* alludes to a Bible passage: "For unto every one that hath shall be given, and he shall have abundance: but from him that hath not shall be taken away even that which he hath" (Matthew 25:29, King James Version). That is, if a child knows more words to start with, he or she will be able to understand more utterances and will learn still more words thereby. Children with a small vocabulary will have much slower rates of gain and will fall further and further behind. What sort of curriculum will best promote active and passive vocabulary growth in the early years and not only advance the vocabulary size of advantaged children but also enable disadvantaged students to begin to catch up?

Stanovich (1992) has shown that the vocabulary of written text is much richer than that found in movies, television, or ordinary conversation. Hence the common preschool practice of reading aloud and discussing written text along with illustrations is well justified; it is likely to be more vocabulary enriching per unit of school time than other forms of linguistic engagement.

Once that uncontroversial observation is accepted, however, one may ask on what basis should particular read-alouds be selected as the most productive ones in building up the vocabularies of young children? What principles shall guide teachers in choosing texts and putting them in some definite order? It goes almost without saying that teachers will want to choose narratives that engage the interest and pleasure of all the children in the group. But how shall they choose the content and the sequence of content?

Some years ago on the above-mentioned trip to France, I was asked by Professor Eric Plaisance, the preschool expert of the Sorbonne, whether I would like to attend an orientation meeting with American scholars and policy makers who were inspecting the *écoles maternelles*. At the meeting, some of the French school inspectors were explaining to the Americans the various things inspectors look for when they evaluate a preschool. Their remarks were being translated by a young American living in Paris, and at one point I intervened to suggest to him that he not translate the term *programme scolaire* as activities, but rather as curriculum. This occasioned a lively discussion between the French experts and the incredulous Americans who could scarcely conceive that a preschool would have a curriculum in the ordinary academic sense. Yet, that is indeed the case in France, where goals are set with high specificity in mathematics, language, history, the arts, socialization, and physical development. The French, on their side, were equally puzzled that for the Americans *scolarisation des enfants* could or ought to be anything other than what those words explicitly suggested. That momentary impasse said a lot about the basic assumptions about preschool in the two nations.

Indeed, the French Ministry of Education's web site provides the following explanation to parents as to how vocabulary is developed during the 3 years of the *école maternelles* (parents can enroll children at age 2 if they wish):

Each day, in the different activity domains, and through the stories which the instructor narrates or reads, the children understand new words. But simple exposition does not suffice for them to learn the words. The acquisition of vocabulary requires specific sequences of classification and learning of words and re-utilization of the words learned, and the interpretation of unknown words within their context. In connection with activities and readings the instructor habitually introduces new words each week, growing in number in the course of the year and from year to year.

In short, under a definite curriculum set in advance, vocabulary growth is enhanced by being integrated with the sequence of knowledge domains that are carefully mapped out from week to week in the preschool curriculum: arithmetic, history, the natural world, and the arts, in addition to physical and social development. A similar sequence has been mapped out for an American context (Bevilacqua, 2008; Wiggins, 2009).

This cumulative organization has worked quite well in practice, as I shall show in a moment. Before turning to that data, however, I want to provide theoretical justification for developing language through a coherent and cumulative curriculum, starting in preschool when high productivity in the use of school time will pay the greatest dividends in later achievement and equity. Advocates of preschool hold that early learning is critical in raising student achievement and achieving equity across demographic groups by the high school years. Much hinges on whether real gains are indeed made in preschool, especially in language development, and on whether a curriculum-based development of language such as that used by the French is a near optimal use of preschool time.

In this connection, it will be informative to consider the phenomenon of fadeout—that is, the disappearance in later grades of the early relative gains made by low-income students in preschool. This is a disagreeable subject because it calls in doubt the very premise that preschool advocates subscribe to—namely that a good preschool will have enormous later effects on achievement and equity.

The evidence points to two causes of fadeout. The first (and dominant) cause is a lack of coherent and cumulative continuation of preschool gains in K–2, the grades that follow preschool. But the evidence also points to a more subtle cause, as in the case of Direct Instruction System for Teaching Arithmetic and Reading (DISTAR; SRA/McGraw-Hill), a basic skills preschool program that emphasizes explicit phonics. According to the evaluation study, Project Follow Through (Becker & Gersten, 1982), it caused the greatest gains. But Project Follow Through stopped at third grade. When Becker and Gersten compared cohorts later, in fifth and sixth grade, they found that students from DISTAR continued to perform better only on tests of decoding skill. They did not perform significantly better on comprehension and vocabulary. In other words, DISTAR was successful in developing the mechanics of literacy but not in developing a foundation of knowledge that enhanced later vocabulary and comprehension.

This very same pattern of fadeout, and with similar causes, was observed in the results of reading achievement of 17-year-olds in the National Assessment of Educational Progress (http://nces.ed.gov/nationsreportcard/reading). An uptick in the reading scores of fourth-grade students was not followed 8 years later by a rise in the reading comprehension of these students as 12th graders. On the contrary, later scores slightly declined.

Such dissonant results can be understood by considering the nature of the tests that report them, as Professor Joseph Torgesen and his colleagues at the University of South Florida have explained (Schatschneider et al., 2004). In early grades (as in Project Follow Through), reading tests are predominantly—although not exclusively—tests of the mechanics of literacy. In later grades, they become predominantly tests of comprehension and of the background knowledge that enables comprehension. According to this explanation, the phenomenon of fadeout is real but misleading. Gains in the mechanics of literacy persist; they do not fade out. However, when later verbal tests gradually increase their emphasis on knowledge and comprehension, the test results do fade out. Actually, the enabling knowledge was never there. Fadeout is not, therefore, an actual decline so much as an exposure of something that was not adequately tested before. The phenomenon of preschool fadeout has a double cause: the lack of an effective knowledge buildup in preschool and the lack of effective knowledge buildup in the schooling that follows.

Before turning to empirical evidence, I outline one further theoretical consideration that favors an academic preschool as a means of speeding up language gain in students. In a very favorable learning environment, advantaged students will make good gains, but disadvantaged ones will learn relatively even more—and begin to catch up (Hirsch, 2009). This is because a feature of an academic preschool is the carefully planned coherence of cognitive learnings that are imparted from one day to the next. Children stay on a topic or a narrative for several days. For example, under the topic *Scientific Reasoning and the Physical World* and the subtheme *The Importance of Water*, several days can be spent on exploring the properties of water, its different states, its prevalence, what things can and cannot float, and so on. A story such as *The Snowy Day* by Ezra Jack Keats (1976) can be read aloud, and children can see experiments with ice and steam. And while they are learning about water, they are also learning a whole range of words, such as *snow, ice, steam, seasons, solid, liquid, gas, kettle, float, sink, rain, mist, clouds, fog, evaporate, freeze, thirst, drought,* and *dissolve.* These words and many more will not necessarily be taught explicitly. In many cases, their meanings will quickly be inferred by the children because immersion in the subject (and in water!) over several days has made them familiar with the subject matter, and they will learn the words as a matter of course (Alishahi, Fazly, & Stevenson, 2008). Landauer and Dumais (1997) estimated that word learning occurs four times faster in a familiar context—and that may be an underestimate because implicit word learning in unfamiliar instances may not occur at all.

Large-scale studies in France have established that cumulative gains for all students can be made when an academic preschool with coherent curriculum is followed by an elementary school with a coherent academic curriculum. Preschool is universal in France, and one way French researchers have gauged the effects of preschool is by studying the effects on later achievement when students begin preschool at younger or older ages, then stay in preschool for correspondingly shorter or longer times. Indeed, the French have developed three specific academic curricula for the three potential years of preschool, starting at age 2–4. (See http://about-france.com/primary-secondary-schools.htm for more information.)

Table 17.1. The effect of preschool attendance on grade retention

Years in preschool attendance	Percent of sample that repeated a grade
3 years	10%
2 years	14.5%
1 year	18.3%
0 years	30.5%

Reprinted from Hirsch, E.D., Jr. (n.d.). *Equity effects of very early schooling in France.* Available online at http://www.coreknowledge.org/mimik/mimik_uploads/documents/95/ Equity%20Effects%20of%20Very%20Early%20Schooling%20in%20France.pdf

The French wanted to find out whether starting preschool at age 2 was a worthwhile expenditure. Large-scale research had already established that preschool has positive benefits in preventing retention in grade (Hirsch, n.d.). When researchers followed more than 20,000 preschoolers through all grades of elementary school, they found a high correlation between attendance at preschool and the need to repeat a grade (Duthoit, 1988). (Grade retention occurs at third or fourth grade in France, and social promotion is rare.) The results showed that the longer the child attended preschool, the more dramatic were the later results, as indicated in Table 17.1. Because most children who repeat a grade come from the ranks of the disadvantaged, it will be seen simply from these figures that academic preschooling has broad educational as well as equity benefits in France. No fadeout here!

Did entering preschool at age 2 show sufficient gain over starting at age 3 to justify a general policy of expenditure on very early preschool, as contrasted with, for example, a reduction in class size in later grades? The answer turned out to be an emphatic *yes* to the early start, and the French government now sponsors preschool for all children starting at age 2. In fact, it has three specific curricula for the three grades of preschool: *petite section* (ages 2–4), *moyenne section* (ages 4–5), and *grande section* (ages 5–6).

To reach this result, the researchers took a sample size of 1,900 students and made a detailed analysis of the achievement and equity effects of starting preschool at age 2, as compared with age 3 or age 4 (Jarousse, Mingat, & Richard, 1992; for an English translation, see Hirsch, n.d.). A preschooler who enters at age 2 will gain .29 of a standard deviation in language competence over one who enters at age 5 and .24 of a standard deviation in math—remarkable results, again with no fadeout.

Indeed, a remarkable finding of the study is that the long-term pattern in France is one not just of lasting benefit but of increasing magnitude as children progress through the grades. That is to say, the benefit of an earlier start is more marked in fifth grade than it was in first or second grade. And still more remarkable is the social-equity effect, as shown in Figure 17.1. Note that the achievement level

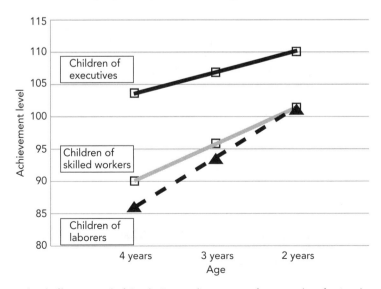

Figure 17.1. Preschool effects at end of Grade 5 according to age of entry and professional category of father.

of disadvantaged (and, in many cases, immigrant) children who entered preschool at age 2 is on a par with highly advantaged children who entered at age 4.

Keeping the American fadeout phenomenon in mind, two notable results of these studies are the following: 1) the relative benefits of an early start in a French preschool increase over time, with the effect being much greater in fifth grade than it was in first grade; and 2) by the end of fifth grade in France, the relative benefit to disadvantaged pupils who start at age 2 rather than age 4 is 7.8 points (over one-half a standard deviation) as compared to a benefit of only 4.6 points for advantaged students. Thus, the long-term gain for disadvantaged students is not only relatively but absolutely greater by a large margin. These significant gains made by disadvantaged children offer further confirmation of Coleman's (1966) finding that disadvantaged children derive relatively greater benefits from effective schooling (and correspondingly greater harm from ineffective schooling). These results from academically oriented preschools confirm the underlying premise (if not the execution) of Head Start programs.

CHAPTER 18

Classroom Practices and Children's Motivation to Learn

Deborah Stipek

Preschool should promote the cognitive skills children need to meet the academic demands of kindergarten. But if teachers undermine children's motivation to learn while they endeavor to increase their academic skills, they may do more harm than good. The debate on appropriate preschool education, therefore, must consider effects on motivation as well as on academic and social skills.

Motivation is important because learning is an active process. To learn, children need to be willing to pay attention, exert effort, persist in the face of difficulty, and deal constructively with the frustration of not understanding or getting something right the first time. They need to want to learn, and they need to have the emotional and psychological tools necessary to engage comfortably and productively in a public learning context.

In this chapter, I review research bearing on the debate about effective preschool education, focusing on motivation as an outcome. I also briefly review what is known about motivating learning environments from research on older children, as the strategies that work for older children most likely work for younger children as well. In the final section, I recommend reframing the debate and discuss the implications of such a reframing for future research.

ASSESSING CLASSROOMS

To assess the effect of different kinds of programs on any child outcome, it is necessary to differentiate programs in some systematic way. Many of the extant studies on the effects of preschool have characterized classrooms in dichotomous terms, such as developmentally appropriate versus developmentally inappropriate, child centered versus teacher directed, academic versus play based, and discovery learning versus direct instruction. Observation measures have been developed to help observers determine which of these categories best describe programs. A typical measure has a series of items describing specific practices; the observer rates the degree to which the practice is seen in the program being observed. Researchers can then examine the effects of different kinds of programs on child outcomes, such as academic skills, social skills, or motivation.

In the past, most preschool observation measures focused more on the social climate of the program than on instruction. Items concerning instruction typically described practices considered to be inappropriate (at least by the person who created the measure), such as whole-class recitation and paper-and-pencil tasks (worksheets) with one correct answer. Very few items have described appropriate instruction. Consequently, on some extant classroom observation measures, as long as worksheets and rote recitations were not seen, a classroom with almost no instruction at all but a positive social climate could receive a respectable score. Studies comparing different kinds of classrooms, therefore, have not yet yielded much information on the effects of the kind of instruction that most early childhood educators currently endorse.

Another challenge to determining the effects of specific practices in preschool on child outcomes is the degree to which different dimensions of programs (e.g., social context, nature of instruction) are associated with each other in the natural world of preschools. In one study of 62 preschool and kindergarten classrooms, my colleagues and I used 47 items to assess 6 dimensions of the classroom environment (Stipek, Daniels, Galluzzo, & Milburn, 1992): 1) the degree to which children were able to choose and initiate activities in a playlike atmosphere, 2) the level of teacher warmth, 3) whether positive behavioral control strategies were used (e.g., clear instructions, absence of threats), 4) the degree to which academic skills were emphasized (with subject matter being clearly differentiated and using commercial materials), 5) pressure on performance (i.e., focus on getting right answers), and 6) prevalence of external evaluation (e.g., grades, stickers). The 47 items assessing these 6 dimensions were highly correlated to each other. Thus, classrooms that provided children with relatively more opportunities to choose and initiate activities had, on average, a more positive social environment and little emphasis on performance or evaluation. Classrooms that implemented more academic instruction and stressed performance and evaluation scored relatively low on child initiation, teacher warmth, and use of positive control. Given this natural coherence of practices, it is impossible to determine which of the six classroom practice dimensions affected child outcomes that were found to vary systematically. The only way to isolate the effects of different dimensions would be to create classroom contexts in which one dimension is systematically varied and others are held constant.

The limitations in the observation measures of classrooms practices used in previous research and the coherences of different dimensions of practice in the real world need to be kept in mind when interpreting the research reviewed next on how different classroom contexts affect motivation.

MOTIVATION

Motivation is seen in students' classroom behavior (e.g., paying attention, getting to work without being reminded, following directions, persisting on tasks until completion) as well as in their emotional expressions (e.g., pride, anxiety, frustration). Researchers have found that beliefs—such as perceptions of competence and expectations for success or about whether the task at hand is enjoyable or worth doing—affect these behaviors and emotions in learning contexts. Thus, for example, children who do not believe they can complete a task may not try at all, or they may give up easily when they encounter difficulty. Children who do not enjoy an activity and see no reason for doing it may pay little attention and work halfheartedly.

Researchers have begun to examine temperament (e.g., impulse control, emotional self-regulation) and underlying cognitive capacities, (e.g., memory, attention) to explain motivation-related behavior, such as following directions and persisting on tasks. Fantuzzo, Perry, and McDermott (2004), for example, found that Head Start children's ability to regulate their emotions (e.g., anger, frustration) predicted their approaches to learning (paying attention, tackling new activities, sticking with activities). Howse, Calkins, Anastopoulos, Keane, and Shelton (2003) similarly found that children's emotional self-regulation in preschool predicted their task-related behavior (e.g., finishing tasks and activities, preferring challenging tasks) in kindergarten. Rimm-Kaufman, Curby, Grimm, Nathanson, and Brock (2009) found strong associations between preschool children's inhibitory control (ability to control impulses and execute appropriate behaviors), which is presumed to reflect memory and attention, and their adaptive behavior (sticking to tasks, working toward goals) in kindergarten. In brief, in addition to beliefs, emotional self-regulation, memory, and attention skills may affect the motivation-related behavior children exhibit in classrooms.

Studies examining classroom contexts have assessed the effects of classroom qualities on both children's behaviors directly, as well as the beliefs and perceptions known to affect behaviors in educational contexts. The effect of classroom contexts on underlying cognitive variables, such as memory and attention, has not, to my knowledge, been studied. I mention them because their associations with motivation-related behavior suggest the value of future research in this area. The review in this next section is limited to studies of preschool and kindergarten.

Effect of Classroom Contexts for Young Children

Rimm-Kaufman et al. (2009) assessed the effect of the quality of the social context, including how classrooms were managed (whether teachers used proactive approaches to discipline, established stable routines, monitored students to keep them involved, and provided hands-on, interesting activities) on kindergarten children's task-related behavior. They found that children in classrooms with relatively high-quality classroom management had more positive work habits (e.g., followed classroom procedures, worked well independently, used time wisely), spent less time off task, and were rated as more engaged in learning than children in classrooms that were relatively less well managed.

The emotional climate has also been linked to children's classroom behavior. McWilliam, Scarborough, and Kim (2003), for example, reported that preschool children in classrooms where teachers were emotionally responsive and relatively less directive or controlling were more highly engaged in their classroom activities.

A few studies suggest negative effects of highly teacher-directed, basic skills-focused instruction on young children's motivation. Burts, Hart, Charlesworth, and Kirk (1990) reported that children in kindergartens implementing developmentally inappropriate practices (e.g., large-group, teacher-directed instruction; use of workbooks, ditto sheets, flashcards, and rote counting) exhibited more stress behaviors, such as fingernail biting, stuttering, and destroying worksheets, than did children in developmentally appropriate classrooms (e.g., high use of games, puzzles, manipulatives, free choice, creative art activities). The stress behaviors were highest when children were in large groups and when they worked on worksheets. A later study revealed higher stress levels among boys but not girls in developmentally inappropriate kindergarten classrooms (Burts et al., 1992).

My former students and I conducted three studies that assessed the effect of different classroom contexts on young children's motivation. The first study (Stipek & Daniels, 1988) was designed to explore a possible explanation for the repeated finding that children begin school with very positive perceptions of their abilities and, on average, progressively develop more negative judgments. Most kindergartners, for example, rate themselves among the smartest in their class. We hypothesized that the decline in later grades could be explained in part by systematic, grade-related differences in the nature of instruction and evaluation. Compared to children in the upper elementary grades, children in kindergarten classrooms generally do not have available to them as much or as salient information about how well they perform relative to classmates. Younger children are less likely to be grouped for ability or to be given grades or scores that facilitate social comparison. Having all students work on the same task in which it is easy to compare performance is also typically less prevalent in kindergarten than in the later grades. (This was true in the late 1980s when this study was conducted. It may be less true of kindergartens presently, given the current pressure to promote academic skills.) We reasoned that young children may be able to maintain positive views of their competencies because they did not have very much information to the contrary. In the later grades, where there is typically ample evidence of how one's own performance compares to peers, it is more difficult for everyone to believe they are the smartest. If our interpretation was correct, then competence ratings would be lower in kindergarten classrooms that looked relatively more like upper elementary classrooms—with frequent, salient, and comparable information on performance.

As we expected, children's perceptions of their competence were significantly lower in classrooms in which evaluation was salient and comparable (e.g., students were grouped for ability and written assignments were graded with checks, stars, and happy faces; letter grades were given on report cards) than in classrooms in which evaluation was not very salient. The study demonstrated therefore that the evaluative context can affect young children's beliefs about their academic competencies, and the age-related decline can be accelerated by making kindergarten more like later grades. (Note that I am not promoting these practices, just pointing out their likely effects.)

In a second study, we compared preschoolers' and kindergartners' motivation on a variety of dimensions in two different kinds of preschool and kindergarten classroom settings (Stipek, Feiler, Daniels, & Milburn, 1995). The study used a modified version of the classroom observation scale described previously, differentiating classrooms in how nurturing and responsive the classroom climate was, as well as the degree to which child-centered instructional approaches (a lot of choice in a playlike atmosphere) were used versus more teacher-directed instruction, with paper-and-pencil activities and stress on performance (getting the right answer).

The findings suggested that the more didactic, performance-oriented approach, combined with the less nurturing social climate, had some negative effects on motivation-related variables. Compared to children in the more child-centered and nurturing classrooms, children in the more didactic classrooms rated their academic competencies lower, selected an easier task when given an option, predicted lower performance on two tasks (a maze and a puzzle), were less likely to smile spontaneously when they completed a task, and were less likely to express pride (e.g., drawing the experimenter's attention to their achievement). They also showed more dependency on the experimenter (requesting permission, opinions, or approval) and claimed to worry more about school.

In a third study of preschool and kindergarten children, we assessed motivation in both an experimental setting, as in the previous study, and in the natural classroom context (Stipek, Feiler, et al., 1998). The results were similar to those of the previous study in that most of the significant differences favored the child-centered instructional approach and social context. The preschool-age children in the more didactic, teacher-directed classrooms also showed more evidence of stress during daily classroom activities than children in the child-centered classrooms. Both preschoolers and kindergartners in the more didactic classrooms were more likely than children in the child-centered classrooms to request the teacher's help or seek approval while they were engaged in activities. They were also less compliant and more likely to be disciplined, and they expressed more negative affect.

It is possible that the more stringent expectations and rules in the basic-skills oriented classrooms gave children more ways to be noncompliant and that the pressure to conform to teacher-determined outcomes and to use teacher-determined strategies made them more dependent on the teacher. If the basic skills-oriented teachers were more strongly committed to getting through their curriculum, they also may have been less tolerant of (and thus more likely to punish) transgressions that interfered with instruction. These side effects of a strong academic focus may be the real cause of any harm done to children's motivation, not the academic challenges themselves.

A few experimental studies conducted by Dweck and her colleagues demonstrated that very nuanced differences in teacher behavior might affect young children's motivation. A study by Kamins and Dweck (1999), for example, found that the way criticism and praise were given to kindergarten children affected their motivation in a role-playing activity. Praise and criticism that focused on the process (e.g., "You must have worked really hard on this"; "The blocks are all crooked and in a big mess; maybe you could think of another way to do it") produced higher ratings of competence, more positive affect, and greater persistence in children's responses to the role-playing situation than praise and criticism that focused on the person (e.g., "You're really good at this"; "I'm very disappointed in you"). In a similar study, Cimpian, Arce, Markman, and Dweck (2007) found that manipulating something as subtle as whether praise was worded generically (e.g., "You are a good drawer") or specifically ("You did a good job drawing") affected preschool-age children's self-evaluations and persistence, with the specific praise having the more positive effects.

In summary, although there is not very much evidence on the effect of different early childhood classroom contexts on young children's motivation, what exists suggests the value of more child-centered instruction and nurturing contexts. It is not known, however, whether a greater focus on basic skills itself undermines motivation or whether the negative effects are due to the performance focus and the less nurturing and supportive social context that typically accompanies a focus on basic skills. The findings are consistent with motivation research involving older children, which I discuss next. The cursory summary of this vast literature in the following section both helps explain findings from early childhood programs and suggests classroom qualities to study in future research on early childhood education.

Motivating Instruction for Older Children

Fortunately, there exists a great deal of research on the kind of instructional environments that promote the cognitions, emotions, and behaviors required for effective learning (see Stipek, 2002, for a review). The qualities of classrooms listed next have been found to promote a variety of positive motivation-related cognitions (e.g., self-confidence, expectations for success), enjoyment, and constructive behaviors (e.g., seeking challenge, persisting in the face of difficulty). Motivating tasks and instruction have the following characteristics:

1. They are optimally challenging—not beyond children's ability to grasp, but requiring some effort. (This necessarily requires some differentiation in instruction, tasks, and expectations because children enter preschool with varying levels of skills.)

2. They are personally meaningful and are related to children's interests and experiences.

3. They provide opportunities for active involvement, including experimentation, analysis, and problem solving. In preschool, this often means manipulating materials; it can also involve asking children open-ended questions and for opinions, predictions, and explanations.

4. They involve choice, as some discretion in choosing or completing tasks gives children a sense of control and an opportunity to be creative and make tasks personally meaningful. Children are likely to select personally enjoyable and also appropriately challenging activities and tasks as long as they are not worried about failure. Instructional goals can be achieved by providing planned options and guiding choices.

Motivating social contexts have the following characteristics:

1. They have a mastery orientation—a focus on learning and understanding rather than getting right answers or performing well relative to peers. Evaluation is specific and is constructive (provides guidance); errors are considered a natural part of learning and information that can be used to guide future efforts; success is attributed to effort and persistence, not ability.

2. They have caring, responsive, respectful adults who build close relationships with children.

3. They have accepting, supportive, and respectful peers.

Note that *fun* or *playful* tasks are not mentioned. If the above qualities of instruction, tasks, and the social context are in place, children will be intrinsically motivated and enjoy preschool. Extra effort to amuse children is not usually required.

Fortunately most of the principles mentioned above have been shown to predict learning as well as motivation (see Stipek, Salmon, et al., 1998). Consequently, the same practices are recommended whether learning or motivation is the explicit goal.

RECONCEPTUALIZING THE DEBATE

As Hyson (2003a) and others have pointed out, the dichotomies often used to characterize classrooms are unnecessary. What is needed is a more nuanced and integrative approach to characterizing and studying preschool classrooms. Consider the play-based versus academic comparison. Play—in the sense of giving children some choice and activities that are meaningful and enjoyable—does not preclude planned and purposeful instruction. Science concepts and vocabulary, for example, can be taught in the context of a nature walk, drawing flowers, or taking care of a garden. Measurement can be taught while baking muffins or comparing the relative length of classmates' arms, legs, and feet. There are many ways in which even free play can be harnessed to achieve basic literacy and math learning goals and in which planned—even teacher-directed—instruction can be playful. For example, teachers can structure play opportunities, including pretend play (e.g., store, post office), to promote literacy and math skills. In such playlike contexts, teachers are deeply involved in "instruction" in the sense that they have very specific learning goals, plan activities and tasks that promote those goals, and assess whether students have achieved them (see Stipek, 2006, for other examples).

The distinction between direct instruction and discovery learning is also a false dichotomy; almost all instruction has components of both. The issue is not whether teachers should give direct instruction—clearly there are situations in which it is the most efficient and effective strategy—or whether children should be allowed to grapple with new concepts. The real question is how and when both strategies are implemented, when opportunities for child experimentation and exploration can be used to enhance learning, and when it is more effective to provide direct teaching of concepts and opportunities to practice newly developing skills. Researchers and expert educators may disagree on the exact mix, but I suspect that no proponents of one strategy would deny the value of the other.

A focus on academic skills also does not preclude attention to other dimensions of children's development. Nonacademic needs of the whole child—such as social skills, emotional competence, and moral development—can be met, even in the context of academic instruction. For example, basic skills instruction can involve cooperative learning opportunities, which is an ideal context for helping children develop such social skills as listening, taking turns, and negotiation. In addition, emotional competence and moral lessons can be embedded in activities designed to develop language and literacy skills.

In brief, the debate should be reframed to examine the appropriate mix of different kinds of instructional strategies. Given the many different skill levels, language and cultural backgrounds, and learning orientations of preschool-age children, it cannot be expected to find one best approach for all children. Rather, one should endeavor to identify general principles that can guide teachers' decisions in their local contexts and train teachers well to apply those principles in ways that are appropriate for their students.

FUTURE RESEARCH

Returning to the issue of motivation outcomes, I propose that future research should seek to identify the kinds of preschool contexts and instruction that support social and emotional development and promote basic academic skills without undermining children's self-confidence and love of learning. It is an ambitious goal, but a more productive one than trying to decide which of important developmental dimensions is most worthy of attention.

To do this, researchers will need better tools for assessing classroom contexts. Some progress has been made in developing observation measures that include information on both the social climate and instruction and that capture the qualities of instruction on which there is broad (although in no way complete) agreement regarding their effects on learning (National Academies, 2008). But there is still much work to be done. Math instruction and learning opportunities are not well represented in extant observation measures and science is almost nowhere to be seen. Moreover, those measures that provide the best information on instruction do not assess (or only weakly assess) the social context, or vice versa. No observation measure, to my knowledge, assesses practices explicitly associated with the motivation principles listed above. To measure the effects of different kinds of instruction on academic skills and other important child outcomes, researchers will need to develop valid measures that assess practices known or hypothesized to foster all of the outcomes they hope to affect.

PRACTICAL IMPLICATIONS

Whatever future studies find, they are almost sure to point to a need for better training for early childhood educators. Direct teaching with a script has been proposed to help teachers promote basic academic skills, in part because scripts provide poorly trained teachers with a tool that they can adhere to regardless of their understanding of the principles of teaching and learning. But teacher-directed, scripted teaching violates most of the basic principles of motivating instruction. A script precludes providing choice, personally meaningful, and appropriate levels of challenge to children with varying interests and skill levels. The kind of teaching that motivation (and learning) research suggests is most effective requires skills in individual student assessment, differentiated instruction based on those assessments, and the ability to make academic instruction meaningful to young children. This kind of teaching requires a great deal of training, which is currently not the norm. If it is to be the norm, much more will need to be invested in the preparation and ongoing support of early childhood educators.

CHAPTER 19

Classroom-Based Intervention as a Way to Support Low-Income Preschoolers' Emotional and Behavioral Development
Pressing Challenges and Potential Opportunities

C. Cybele Raver and Genevieve Okada

In an era of rising poverty and income inequality, policy professionals and educators are increasingly committed to "closing the achievement gap" between children from low-income families and their more affluent peers as early as preschool (Karoly, Zellman, & Li, 2009). Yet practitioners and researchers who have spent their careers working with young children have underscored that preschoolers must accomplish several self-regulatory and social skills in order to take full advantage of the opportunities for learning afforded by preschool classrooms. Put simply, preschoolers' ability to learn and remember preliteracy content or early math concepts during circle time and small-group instruction may depend on the ways that they are able to modulate their own emotions, behavior, and social relationships with others. This central claim—that children's noncognitive skills matter for their progress in educational settings—stands as a driving question motivating our completion of a large, multicomponent classroom-based intervention called the Chicago School Readiness Project (CSRP; Raver, 2003; Raver & Zigler, 2004).

This claim rests on intellectual bedrock on which Zigler and his colleagues founded Head Start over 40 years ago, asserting that educators must focus on emotional and behavioral components of classroom instruction that support the whole child in order to maximize children's chances of school success (Zigler & Trickett, 1978). But critics might raise several challenges to that assertion. First, improving the emotional and behavioral elements of classroom quality may be tougher than researchers might hope: Teachers may not easily be able to establish new patterns of classroom management, and they may have a difficult time building more positive relationships with their students. In short, using the gold standard of cluster-randomized design, the CSRP needed to establish whether it was feasible to make significant improvements in the ways that teachers managed the challenging behaviors of children in their classes. Second, skeptics might argue that children's emotional and behavioral difficulties are likely to be linked to a wide array of poverty-related stressors in children's homes and neighborhoods and that changes in classroom quality may have little, if any, impact on children's emotional and behavioral adjustment. Thus, we also needed to establish whether a classroom-based intervention organized around teachers' support of children's emotional and behavioral self-regulation was ultimately successful in yielding measurable and meaningful improvements in young children's behavioral profiles.

Guided by these questions, the CSRP was launched in 2004–2005. Our aim was to learn whether multiple components of classroom-based intervention significantly improved classroom quality in Head Start centers serving low-income, ethnic minority children in neighborhoods of concentrated disadvantage. Most centrally, we then asked whether our intervention led to lower rates of behavioral difficulty and significantly higher levels of school readiness among young children who faced a serious set of economic and neighborhood risks.

This collaboration offered us a remarkable opportunity to test theoretically driven scientific questions about the ways that classroom-based intervention could support low-income children's self-regulation and school readiness. By targeting teachers' ability to support children's self-regulation, we also learned a great deal about the ways in which classrooms can be understood as behavioral systems. Specifically, we learned that it was important to attend to teachers' needs and stressors in order for our collaboration to successfully improve classroom quality. In this chapter, we first briefly discuss the rationale driving our research questions, as well as the steps we took along the way to implement a fair test of our research questions. We then consider implications of our findings for new models of classroom quality improvement. Finally, we highlight two new pressing challenges that models of classroom-based intervention are likely to face against rapidly transforming demographic, economic, and policy contexts.

THEORETICAL RATIONALE: WHAT WERE OUR RESEARCH QUESTIONS?

Prior correlational research in early childhood has provided clear, consistent support for the value of focusing on the whole child, with children's behavioral, emotional, and social competence identified as key components of school readiness (see Blair, 2002; Hyson, 2003b; Raver, 2003; Zaslow et al., 2003). Preschoolers' behavioral and emotional self-regulation have been highlighted as centrally important as they navigate new contexts of school (Conduct Problems Prevention Research Group, 2002; Dodge, Pettit, & Bates, 1994; Raver, 2002). Emerging findings at the frontiers of developmental neuroscience have highlighted the ways that children's affect, attention, and executive functioning (involving memory, organization, and planning) are bidirectionally and inextricably linked (Lewis & Todd, 2007). These new findings in neuroscience have been paralleled by increased attention to noncognitive factors in early educational contexts. For example, children's regulation of positive affect, attention, and behavior has been viewed through a molar behavioral lens that focuses on their approaches to learning. Children who use more engaged and well-regulated approaches to learning have been found to be rated as more academically skilled than their less well-regulated peers (Fantuzzo et al., 2007; McDermott, Leigh & Perry, 2002; Rimm-Kaufman, Fan, Chiu, & You, 2007).

   The need to focus on children's emotional and behavioral difficulty may be all the more pressing in preschool settings where young children and their caregivers face a daunting set of poverty-related stressors. In the city of Chicago, for example, Head Start programs serve more than 16,000 children, most of whose families have incomes at or below the federal poverty line (i.e., just below $20,000 per year for a family of four, at the time of our study). Most parents with children enrolled in Head Start programs in Chicago are working and have general equivalency or high school diplomas, but a substantial proportion of enrolled families also struggle to make ends meet and to keep their children safe. For example, a large, representative survey of Chicago's preschool programs found that more than 60% of children enrolled in full-day Head Start-funded programs faced three or more poverty-related risks (Ross, Emily, Meagher, & Carlson, 2008). In our interviews with administrators and teachers prior to the implementation of CSRP, early childhood educators repeatedly shared their view that children's behavioral difficulty was part and parcel of their exposure to a wide array of stressors, including high levels of parental stress, household instability, recent eviction, and recent exposure to community violence (for similar findings, see Gorman-Smith et al., 2002; Gross et al., 2003). Exposed to a wide range of psychosocial stressors, children in poor neighborhoods are at greater risk for developing emotional and behavioral difficulties and have minimal access to mental health services (Fantuzzo et al., 1999). In an effort to address this pressing concern, we undertook the CSRP during a developmental period in which young children's behavior problems could be reliably identified and successfully targeted (Carter, Briggs-Gowan, Jones, & Little, 2003; Shaw, Dishion, Supplee, Gardner, & Arnds, 2006)

   In designing the CSRP, we drew on innovative new findings in prevention science and school-based intervention. Specifically, research suggests that targeting classroom processes can be an effective way to reduce children's behavioral problems (e.g., August, Realmuto, Hektner, & Bloomquist, 2001; Conduct Problems Prevention Research Group, 1999; Ialongo et al., 1999; Lochman & Wells, 2003; Webster-Stratton, Reid, & Hammond, 2004). In those studies, elementary school teachers' provision of effective regulatory support to children through emotionally positive, firm, and consistent approaches to classroom management were associated with students' improvements in both cognitive and behavioral domains (for reviews, see Berryhill & Prinz, 2003; Jones, Brown, & Aber, 2008). In short, we sought to support Head Start teachers in improving the ways that they managed children's negative behaviors; we targeted the classroom emotional climate as a key mechanism through which we might best be able to support children's behavioral self-regulation.

THE CHICAGO SCHOOL READINESS PROJECT

To reiterate, the principal aim of the CSRP intervention was to marshal several primary programmatic components to improve low-income preschool-age children's school readiness by lowering their risk of behavioral problems and increasing their emotional and behavioral self-regulation. Our model placed a high premium on work-force development, where CSRP provided teachers with 30 hours of training in strategies (e.g., rewarding positive behavior, redirecting negative behavior) that they could employ to provide their classrooms with more effective regulatory support and better management (Raver et al., 2008; Webster-Stratton, Reid, & Hammond, 2001; Webster-Stratton, Reid, & Stoolmiller, 2008).

Based on prior research that suggested that the benefits may be limited when teachers are offered training alone, CSRP also provided weekly coaching through classroom-based consultation. Coaching and consultation were provided by a mental health consultant (MHC) with a master's degree in social work; the MHC supported teachers while they tried new techniques learned in the teacher training (Donahue, Falk, & Provet, 2000; Gorman-Smith, Beidel, Brown, Lochman, & Haaga, 2003). In addition, we drew from prior research suggesting that preschool teachers face a wide array of competing demands and little control over their work environments. We were worried that teachers in our intervention might have a difficult time in implementing new classroom management strategies if they felt emotionally unsupported and psychologically stressed. Thus, as an additional component, MHCs spent a significant portion of the school year conducting stress reduction workshops to help teachers to limit burnout. Finally, MHCs provided direct child-focused consultation, working directly with three to five children who exhibited the most challenging behavioral problems, with the view that these children might benefit from access to clinical psychological services that could be delivered through the Head Start setting (Perry, Dunne, McFadden, & Campbell, 2008; Yoshikawa & Knitzer, 1997).

Mindful of the role of race, ethnicity, and culture in children's socialization of self-regulation and the importance of model equivalence in developmental and prevention science, careful attention was paid to the design of CSRP as culturally sensitive. In addition, planned piloting steps were followed to assure that the multicomponent intervention met standards of acceptability among Latino and African American teachers and administrators in local community-based agencies.

Through extensive collaboration with community-based Head Start programs in seven of Chicago's most economically disadvantaged neighborhoods, we randomly assigned nine Head Start programs to receive a high-intensity package of intervention services (designated as the treatment group) and assigned another nine programs to receive a lower intensity package of services (designated as the control group). It is important to highlight that randomization at the site level made practical sense to the administrators who were willing to sign their programs on to the CSRP. Random assignment at the site level offered a fair means of allocating costly services such as training and mental health consultation in a policy context where it was not clear whether those additional services were preferable or beneficial to programs. For example, control group programs received the support of a lower cost teacher's aide in the classroom 1 day a week in lieu of the MHC visits and teacher training. For some teachers and administrators, the simpler and easier-to-implement change in teacher-to-student ratio (via inclusion of a lower cost teacher's aide) might be preferable to the higher demands that training and mental health consultation were likely to place on programs. Random assignment to the two different packages of services offered an equitable solution to the problem of who gets what while also eliminating the possibility that CSRP outcomes were driven by potential differences in different administrators' and teachers' preferences.

Although programs were randomly assigned, teachers' preferences still made a difference in other ways. For example, not all teachers who were in the intervention group attended all training sessions. Despite a wide range of efforts to support teachers' participation (including payment of a stipend, the offer of child care, and multiple follow-ups by a talented and engaging program coordinator), teachers assigned to the intervention group attended three of the five trainings on average. Similarly, even though classroom visits were a main ingredient of the intervention package, some classrooms received as few as 21 visits while other classrooms received as many as 40 visits, with an average of 29 visits (or 128 hours of consultation) during the academic year. It is important to highlight that treatment impacts of the CSRP intervention that are reported here are estimated across all teachers and classrooms in the intervention group, whether teachers participated at a high or low level. This is referred to as the intent-to-treat estimate and represents a conservative estimate of CSRP's benefit to the classrooms and children who were enrolled.

PROMISING PRELIMINARY EVIDENCE OF THE BENEFITS OF CLASSROOM-BASED INTERVENTION

The research team relied on independent observers' ratings of classroom quality using a standardized measure called the Classroom Assessment Scoring System (CLASS; La Paro, Pianta, & Stuhlman, 2004). This measure of classroom quality provided an observational snapshot of four aspects of classroom process, including the classroom's positive climate, its negative climate, teachers' level of sensitivity, and teachers' skill in behavior management. Our coding team assessed these dimensions of classroom quality at two points in time, for both treatment and control group classrooms, in September and March of the Head Start school year.

Our first set of analyses suggested that teachers in treatment-assigned Head Start sites showed considerable improvement in the ways that they supported children's emotional and behavioral development, as compared with teachers in the control group. Teachers in the treatment group scored significantly higher on the CLASS dimensions of positive climate and teacher sensitivity than did control group classrooms (Raver et al., 2008). Improvements in those subcategories of the CLASS suggest that teachers in the treatment group were observed to show considerably greater enjoyment of their time with children, greater enthusiasm for teaching, and a more emotionally secure base for children than were teachers in the control group. Similarly, classrooms in the treatment group were observed to have significantly lower ratings of negative climate than were control group classrooms, where observers rated treatment group teachers as less angry, sarcastic, and harsh than control group teachers, on average. Finally, teachers in the treatment group were observed by independent raters to show marginally higher levels of effective behavior management than did control group teachers, where teachers were rated on the ways that they structured the classroom and activities so that the children knew what was expected of them.

With clear evidence that CSRP led to improvements in classroom quality, our next question was whether CSRP led to corresponding improvements in children's behavioral regulation and to lower rates of behavioral difficulty. Our findings were greatly encouraging. Random assignment to participation in the CSRP treatment group translated to clear reductions in children's emotional and behavioral difficulty along several important dimensions, relative to those children in the control group (Raver et al., 2009). Data were drawn from standardized teacher-reported surveys (Achenbach & Rescorla, 2001; Fantuzzo, et al., 1995; Milfort & Greenfield, 2002; Zill, 1990), where we asked teachers to rate children's behavior problems in both fall and spring of the Head Start year.

With these measures, our analyses provide clear evidence that CSRP benefited children in the treatment group as compared to children in the control group. For example, children in the treatment group were reported by their teachers as having significantly fewer internalizing (or sad and withdrawn) behavior problems than did their control group counterparts by spring of the Head Start year. Children in the treatment group were also reported by their teachers to show significantly fewer externalizing (or aggressive, disruptive, and acting out) behaviors than were children in the control group in the spring of the Head Start year. We also found marginally significant differences between treatment and control groups (in the expected direction) on children's observed aggressive/disruptive behavior (Raver et al., 2009).

IMPLICATIONS FOR MODELS OF CLASSROOM-BASED INTERVENTION WITH YOUNG CHILDREN

In designing, implementing, and measuring the impact of the CSRP, we learned about ways to support learning opportunities for low-income children in Head Start settings. Of primary importance was that the CSRP underscored the value of targeting emotional and behavioral processes in the classroom as a complement to innovative new interventions targeting young children's language, preliteracy, and early math skills (Bierman et al., 2008; Diamond et al., 2007; Justice, Cottone, Mashburn, & Rimm-Kaufman, 2008; Pianta et al., 2005). Teachers had a strong interest in learning concrete, easily implementable tools with which to more effectively manage young children's behavioral difficulty. In addition, teachers were able to take advantage of the training that was offered by meeting and practicing those new behavioral skills with their MHC, whom they recognized as a trusted professional from outside the organization. We also learned that the shift from familiar habits and less effective classroom practices to new approaches to classroom management represented a significant risk for many teachers. In short, improvement in the emotional and behavioral support that teachers provide to students is achievable through intervention, but there are likely to be no shortcuts. We are skeptical that the same results would have been obtained had we dropped the coaching component of the intervention, for example.

A second lesson from our experience running CSRP is that, although intervention that targets children's emotional and behavioral development is an important complement to an emphasis on academic achievement, we certainly do not see it as a substitute for efforts to improve young children's language, early literacy, and math skills. Programs enrolled in CSRP were similar to programs in a large, representative 2007 survey of Chicago's preschool programs in that the range of instructional quality across sites was very wide. In that study (Ross, Emily, Meagher, & Carlson, 2008), 4-year-olds in Chicago's preschool settings were found, on average, to score a full standard deviation below national norms on a standardized vocabulary measure (Peabody Picture Vocabulary Test–Third Edition, PPVT-III; Dunn & Dunn, 1997; Zill, 2003) in the fall of the school year. Moreover, children were enrolled in preschool classrooms where the instructional quality (in areas such as teachers' modeling of complex language and support of children's conceptual development) was independently rated as falling in the low to middle range, on average. Our classrooms were similar, showing wide variability in their scores on the standardized CLASS measure of instructional quality at baseline (Raver et al., 2009).

In short, our experiences in CSRP-enrolled classrooms supported the view that children's behavioral difficulty may interfere with their own and their peers' opportunities to learn by limiting teachers' ability to provide cognitively stimulating, well-scaffolded instruction. But after spending a great deal of time in classrooms, we suspect that the reverse is also true: That is, some teachers are not using class time in ways that are cognitively engaging, well paced, and pitched at the level that scaffolds and stretches preschoolers' cognitive skills. In some classrooms, children may be acting out and becoming increasingly disruptive as a consequence of lower quality instruction, rather than the other way around (Arnold et al., 2006). In those classrooms, teachers and students would likely benefit from intervention targeting both instructional support as well as emotional support, as has been demonstrated by other preschool intervention efforts (Bierman et al., 2008; Pianta et al., 2005).

This project also underscored the ways that an emphasis on the whole child may need to be matched with an emphasis on the whole teacher when implementing a comprehensive classroom-based intervention. When we entered classrooms on a typical weekday, we found teachers who were clearly facing a very large number of demands. On a typical school day, we witnessed teachers trying to cover a wide range of bureaucratic details such as attendance, the number of meals served, and whether health practices were maintained. Teachers also juggled the interpersonal details of communicating with parents, co-workers, administrators, and (not least) with a large number of small children. In the midst of these competing demands, teachers were expected to cover the instructional details of having a clear and implementable lesson plan, materials ready for the day's whole-group and small-group activities, and assessments of children's skills completed. Despite these multiple demands, teachers in our study were generally upbeat and positive about their roles in their classrooms and deeply dedicated to their students' well-being (Li-Grining et al., 2010). That said, a substantial number of teachers also reported high numbers of work-related stressors; it was clear that for an emotionally and behaviorally focused intervention to stick, teachers' capacity to regulate their own feelings of frustration, burnout, and fatigue needed to be addressed (Li-Grining et al., 2010). Earning incomes of approximately $30,000 on average in full-day Head Start programs, Chicago's early educators try to meet the emotional and cognitive needs of their students while many of those teachers are themselves facing significant economic challenges (Raver, 2004; Ross, Emily, Meagher, & Carlson, 2008). In light of those economic challenges, it was important for teachers to be offered stress-reduction strategies along with more concrete strategies in managing children's more challenging behaviors. Researchers continue to learn more about the key role of teachers' stressors in predicting whether interventions are successfully taken up or disregarded by teachers (Pianta et al., 2008; Zhai et al., in preparation).

NEW CHALLENGES IN THE FACE OF
RAPID DEMOGRAPHIC AND ECONOMIC TRANSFORMATIONS

Educators and researchers alike have highlighted dramatic shifts in the demographic characteristics of young children in the United States. Latinos now make up the largest ethnic group in the United States, representing 15% of the population, as compared to African Americans, who make up 12% of the population (U.S. Census Bureau, 2006). Issues surrounding immigration and acculturation have clear implications for early childhood programs such as Head Start. In 2006, Latinos made up 34% of the Head Start population, the largest single ethnic minority group in the program and only slightly less than the number of Caucasians in Head Start, who represent 39% of children (Administration for Children and Families, 2007; Magnuson & Waldfogel, 2005).

The increasing diversity of children's immigration, cultural, and linguistic experiences has real implications for interventions implemented in preschool programs in large urban centers such as Chicago. As teachers reach out to recently immigrated families within their classrooms, not only must teachers be sensitive to linguistic differences, but they must be aware of and sensitive to cultural differences (Calfee, 1997; Gonzales, Knight, Birman, & Sirolli, 2003; Schmitz & Velez, 2003; Wehlage, Smith, & Lipman, 1992). As a first step in meeting these needs, many researchers have recommended specific guidelines for how programs can be more culturally sensitive to ethnic minority children and families (Acevedo-Polakovich et al., 2007; Andres-Hyman, Ortiz, Anez, Paris, & Davidson, 2006; Boyce & Fuligni, 2007; Fisher et al., 2002).

In addition, the changing demographic profile of Head Start families may have significant implications for models such as CSRP that include mental health consultation as a key component of service provision. Some research has shown that Latinos, in general, are less likely to use mental health services and that Head Start may be an effective means of providing those services (Hough et al., 1987; Vega, Kolody, Aguilar-Gaxiola, & Catalano, 1999). Moreover, it will be important to examine within-group differences among Latino children to detect whether benefits of intervention are associated with families' recency of immigration and/or patterns of acculturation (Keels & Raver, 2009). In short, interventions targeting both social, emotional, and behavioral components of children's school readiness must increasingly determine "for whom the intervention works best" in addition to testing whether the intervention demonstrates efficacy overall (Raver et al., 2009). Such questions must be expanded to include children's ethnic category membership and their status as the children of immigrant parents. Although they may share the same ethnic category membership, Latino and immigrant children may reside in substantially different sociocultural contexts and may have differing language, economic, and cultural backgrounds and strengths (e.g., Kellam & Van Horn, 1997; Knight & Hill, 1998; Raver, Gershoff, & Aber, 2007). The need to understand why and how Latino children differ from not only African American children but from others within their ethnic group is underscored given the demographic trends within urban centers such as Chicago and throughout the United States.

SERVING CHILDREN IN A TIME OF RISING ECONOMIC HARDSHIP

Economic data indicate that the number of children younger than the age of 6 from poor families is rising, with increases in the use of services such as food stamps skyrocketing in some parts of our nation (Isaacs, 2009). This has grave implications for communities serving large numbers of poor residents, with the likelihood that programs will be expected to serve more children while also facing significantly large cutbacks in their own budgets (Johnson, Oliff, & Williams, 2009). Job growth in the next few years is likely to be slow and families may be less well-off, financially and psychologically, as parents struggle to cope with layoffs, foreclosures, and tightening credit. In past recessions, these economic strains within households have translated to greater difficulties experienced by children in out-of-home settings such as school (for a review, see Stevens & Schaller, 2009). In short, Head Start teachers and administrators may find that, on average, entering cohorts of preschoolers in their programs are manifesting higher levels of sadness, withdrawal, and acting-out behaviors than did previous cohorts as low-income families navigate these troubled economic times.

In the face of these bleak economic prospects, what will need to be known in the fields of child development, public policy, and early intervention? First, it is necessary to have a clear understanding of both baseline and rising prevalence of behavioral difficulties among children in different classroom settings, across city and county delegate agencies, so that classrooms that are hardest hit by economic downturn can be most effectively targeted with staffing and training support. Our findings suggest that children's behavioral difficulty has implications not only for their own learning but for others' learning as well, and that investment in teacher training and mental health consultation may forestall some of those negative sequelae for individual children and classrooms as a whole.

In addition, models of intervention such as CSRP are likely to need to be adapted to meet these new economic and policy constraints. Just as it may not be possible to generalize from a given program model to multiple sociocultural contexts, so too may there be limited generalizability of the efficacy of a given intervention model across economic conditions that shift dramatically. For example, the CSRP model offers a promising means of working to support children in emotionally positive classroom settings as supportive and safe social contexts in the face of ongoing household and neighborhood stressors. That said, our model may need to be adapted to help teachers to help children to cope with worries and concerns specific to increased parental psychological strain, heightened financial worry, parents' sudden loss of jobs or homes, and concomitant housing instability. It will also be increasingly important to find innovative ways to strategically do more with less, as agencies face significant cutbacks in the money they can spend on teacher training, coaching, and consultation. The use of online consultation by sensitive and supportive coaches in the MyTeachingPartner intervention (Pianta et al., 2008) offers just one example of innovative solutions to the challenges that Head Start programs are likely to face as federal, state, and local budgets are tightened.

CONCLUSION

In the face of these challenges, there is a remarkable set of new opportunities in the fields of child development, public policy, and early intervention. For example, the U.S. Departments of Education and Health and Human Services have made several major investments in rigorous randomized controlled trials on increasing school readiness among young children (Interagency Consortium on School Readiness, 2003; Preschool Curriculum Evaluation Research Consortium, 2008). The fields of early childhood education, prevention science, and policy analysis continue to yield a range of new intervention and analytic tools that help teachers to take clear steps to support young children across socioemotional, behavioral, and cognitively oriented domains of development. Intervention models such as the CSRP help identify concrete steps that teachers, administrators, and policy makers can take to improve children's chances of school success. Rising economic hardship across urban, rural, and suburban communities in the United States heightens the need for swift action to put science to work by supporting young children's school readiness.

CHAPTER 20

The Great Balancing Act

Optimizing Core Curricula Through Playful Pedagogy

Kathy Hirsh-Pasek and Roberta Michnick Golinkoff

The Capulets and Montagues of early childhood have long battled over their vision for a perfect preschool education. Should young children be immersed in a core curriculum replete with numbers and letters or in a playful context that stimulates creative discovery? Cast as a feud, many have come to believe that the two approaches are incompatible. It is, however, time for allegiances to give way to empirical findings. Playful learning offers one way to reframe the debate by nesting a rich core curriculum within a playful pedagogy. The data are clear: Young children thrive in settings with a strong curricular base that expose them to foundational skills that will be learned in school. Research also suggests that they learn best through the kinds of meaningful engagement and exploration found in play. Curricular goals need not constrain pedagogical practices; children can learn and learn well in playful classrooms.

THE CASE FOR A CORE CURRICULUM

There is no question that academic advancement is cumulative. The roots of children's competencies begin in infancy and early childhood. By way of example, toddlers' oral language skills not only predict how well they will communicate in school, but also how well they will learn the alphabet and understand written texts (Dickinson & Freiberg, in press; National Early Literacy Panel, 2009; National Institute of Child Health and Human Development, 2005c; Scarborough, 2001; Storch & Whitehurst, 2001). Learning to count and to master concepts related to numbers (big and small) are also critical to later mathematical understanding and to flexible problem solving (Baroody & Dowker, 2003). Finally, a bounty of research findings now link early social competencies to later academic achievement (Raver, 2002). Training in emotional regulation that helps children control their behavior and plan effectively is related to both academic outcomes and social gains (Diamond et al., 2007). These facts alone compel us to design curricula for preschoolers that expose children to language, literacy, and early number and social skills.

A wealth of empirical data tell the same story. Importantly, many of these studies have evaluated the short- and long-term effects of preschool on disadvantaged children (Campbell, Pungello, Miller-Johnson, Burchinal, & Ramey, 2001; Campbell & Ramey, 1995; Campbell et al., 2002; Reynolds, Ou, & Topitzes, 2004; Schweinhart, 2004; Weikart, 1998; Zigler & Bishop-Josef, 2006). A large survey of six longitudinal data sets from Britain and the United States examined precursors for school readiness (Duncan et al., 2007). Using meta-analyses across thousands of children, researchers concluded that mathematics, emergent literacy scores, and attentional skills were the best predictors of later academic success. These results held for children from low and high socioeconomic niches and equally for boys and girls. Thus, researchers are zeroing in on exactly the kinds of curricular goals that will align preschool education with later primary school subjects.

Although there has been enormous progress in understanding precursors to several academic outcomes in school (reading and math), warring factions still dominate the question of how to teach these and other competencies to America's youngest citizens. Worried about the discontinuity between preschool and elementary school pedagogy, many early education curricula are taught using what Bowman (1999) referred to as "traditional practices, which emphasize basic skills and whole-class, direct-instruction, even in preschool." An Alliance for Childhood Report (Miller & Almon, 2009) found that as these direct-instruction methods gain traction, playtime is being all but eliminated. Observing 200 kindergarten classrooms in New York and Los Angeles, they found that 25% of the teachers in Los Angeles reported having no time for play in their classrooms. What was replacing this activity? Test preparation! In New York and Los Angeles, a whopping 80% of the teachers spend time each day in test preparation. These findings are consistent with Elkind's (2008) claim that children have lost up to 8 hours a day of free playtime since the 1990s and that 30,000 schools in the United States have given up recess time to ensure that children have more time for academic study. This reduction in playtime is a barometer for a much deeper debate in our society about the value of play in children's lives.

In this chapter, we argue that the optimal preschool environment contains rich content delivered in a playful, whole-child approach to learning. Using the best available data as our foundation, we introduce the idea of guided play and suggest that young children learn language, reading, and mathematics

The research in Chapter 20 was supported by Temple University's Center for Re-Imagining Children's Learning and Education that the authors co-direct, by Eunice Kennedy Shriver National Institute of Child Health and Human Development Grant 5R01HD050199; National Science Foundation Grant BCS-0642529; Spatial Intelligence Learning Center Grant SBE-0541957; and National Institutes of Health Grant 1RC1HD0634970-01. Thanks to Kelly Fisher for reading earlier drafts of this chapter and for suggesting ways to make the piece stronger and Aimee Stahl for help with the references.

as well or better when they have a combination of free and purposeful play than when they are trained with methods of direct instruction. Our argument is based on a set of well-established learning principles (Hirsh-Pasek, Golinkoff, Berk, & Singer, 2009) that illustrate how children master academic and social competencies through play. Finally, we use these principles to describe how looking at learning through play offers us a broader perspective on the skill sets that young children must develop to be successful in school and in the global world beyond the school walls. In short, the debate must no longer be about learning *versus* play. Rather, curricula should stress learning *via* play. A whole-child perspective enhances children's social, academic, and creative development; allows for accountability; and can easily align with early childhood education (Bogard & Takanishi, 2005).

EMPTY VESSELS OR CHILD EXPLORERS AND DISCOVERERS?

The direct-instruction approach to preschool curricula builds on a well-worn metaphor of child development viewing children as empty pails to be filled with information. Teachers become environmental agents, charged with pouring in facts as children passively absorb information. In this view, children learn best via explicit pedagogy. The notion of school readiness is often limited to cognitive learning (Stecher, 2002) and developmental dimensions like physical and motor growth, social skills, or the range of skills and habits that enable children to learn in the classroom (e.g., the ability to sustain attention) are often not addressed (Kagan & Lowenstein, 2004; Kagan et al., 1995). Derived from a more behaviorist approach to learning, the empty vessel metaphor often uses worksheets and memorization of facts and drill. Increasingly, this kind of approach is being adopted to teach children emergent literacy skills such as letter-sound correspondence and vocabulary acquisition, along with mathematical competencies in counting (Miller & Almon, 2009). Undoubtedly, children can and do learn in multiple ways, from both direct instruction and playful, guided learning (Datta, McHalle, & Mitchell, 1976). However, research suggests that direct instruction often leaves children feeling stressed and not liking school (Stipek, Feiler, et al., 1998).

The whole-child perspective is exemplified by a philosophical approach assuming that the child brings much to the learning environment. Teachers are guides; learning is not compartmentalized into separate domains because all learning is inextricably intertwined (Froebel, 1897; Piaget, 1970). As Zigler wrote, "The brain is an integrated instrument. To most people the brain means intelligence. But the brain mediates emotional and social development. Emotions and cognition are constantly interwoven in the lives of children" (2007, p. 10).

This view suggests that the whole child integrates cognitive and emotional information in meaningful ways with the help of a rich environment and supportive adults (Vygotsky, 1934/1986). This view presupposes that children seek meaning in all they do and that through play they not only practice and hone their social skills but engage in cognitive acts that expand their repertoires (Piaget, 1970). Play is a prominent and integrative experience for young children in which they use both social and academic skills. Thus, scientists such as Roskos and Christie (2002, 2004), Zigler et al. (2004), and Singer, Golinkoff, and Hirsh-Pasek (2006) make compelling arguments for the central role of play as a medium for promoting school readiness in a whole, active child. In her review of the Abecedarian program (e.g., Campbell et al., 2001), the HighScope Perry preschool project (Schweinhart, 2004; Weikart, 1998) and the Chicago Child-Parent Center Project (Reynolds et al., 2004), Galinsky (2006) noted that each of these successful programs viewed children as active experiential learners using a pedagogical approach that was aligned with playful learning.

WHAT IS PLAYFUL LEARNING?

Playful learning is a whole-child approach to education that includes both free play and guided play, each of which is related to growth in academic and social outcomes. Researchers generally agree that free play—with objects, fantasy play, make-believe, or physical—is pleasurable and enjoyable, has no extrinsic goals, is spontaneous, involves active engagement, is generally all-engrossing, often has a private reality, is not literal, and can contain a certain element of make-believe (Christie & Johnsen, 1983; Garvey, 1977; Hirsh-Pasek et al., 2009; Hirsh-Pasek & Golinkoff, 2003). The merits of free play in early education have been well documented (e.g., Singer et al., 2006).

Guided play is distinct from free play. Here educators structure an environment around a general curricular goal that is designed to stimulate children's natural curiosity, exploration, and play with learning-oriented objects/materials (Fein & Rivkin, 1986; Hirsh-Pasek et al., 2009; Marcon, 2002; Resnick, 1999; Schweinhart, 2004). Guided play offers educational scaffolding in which adults enrich the environment in two ways. First, they populate the child's world with objects and toys that promote a variety of developmentally appropriate learning experiences (Berger, 2008). A room filled with books encourages children to explore print and a room with balance beams encourages children to experiment (Siegler, 1996). Second, in guided play, teachers may enhance children's self-discovery by commenting or asking open-ended questions about what children are finding, thereby encouraging children to think beyond their own self-initiated exploration. Although guided play may appear to defy the play criterion of no external goal, children continue to be the active drivers of learning. Learning is child directed and not adult controlled. Guided play is not direct instruction dressed in playful clothes.

Fisher (2009) identified two orthogonal continua that define guided play. The first varies according to who initiates the learning: either the teacher or the child. In free play, for example, the child determines what to explore. In direct instruction, the teacher controls the agenda. The second dimension is loosely defined through the structure of the learning experience. Free play is unstructured while direct instruction is a structured learning experience. Under guided play, a teacher can have well-formed curricular goals but present them in ways that stimulate children's discovery and engagement. This mixture of goal-oriented experiences with whole-child learning offers a new alternative—guided play—that meshes core curricula and playful pedagogy.

Having described the model previously, it is worth seeing how it might be adopted in practice. A teacher may embed a variety of shapes in the free-play area to promote the exploration and learning of shapes in preschool. After initial free-play activities, the teacher asks children to play explorer and find shapes. The teacher may enrich conceptual understanding by asking children to compare their shapes in a show-and-tell activity.

To date, a number of studies have examined playful learning. The studies have been observational and correlational and have included strict random assignment experimental settings. Furthermore, the research spans areas as diverse as cognitive and academic learning and social development. The results are uniformly positive: Children's learning through free play and guided play is as good as, if not better, than their learning under direct instructional methods. A review of the literature makes this point (Hirsh-Pasek et al., 2009).

FREE PLAY AND ACADEMIC OUTCOMES

Through playful investigations, children develop rudimentary mathematic and science concepts (Sarama & Clements, 2009a, 2009b; Tamis-LeMonda, Uzgiris, & Bornstein, 2002). In one observational study, Ginsburg, Pappas, and Seo (2001) found preschool children spend over half of their playtime in some form of mathematic or science-related activity: 25% was spent examining pattern and shape, 13% on magnitude comparisons, 12% focused on enumeration, 6% explored dynamic change, 5% compared spatial relations (e.g., height, width, location), and 2% of the time was spent classifying objects. Similar findings were evident in Siegler's (1996) observation that those children who played with a balance beam became experimenters who discovered the rules of weight and balance.

Free play activities thus provide opportunities to explore, practice, and refine early math and science skills. Children who engage in these activities with high frequencies also show stronger academic gains (e.g., Ginsburg, Lee, & Boyd, 2008; Wolfgang, Stannard, & Jones, 2003). Those participating in manipulative activities (e.g., block play, model building, carpentry) or playing with art materials do better in spatial visualization, visual-motor coordination, and creative use of visual materials (e.g., Caldera, McDonald Culp, Truglio, Alvarez, & Huston, 1999; Hirsch, 1996; Wolfgang et al., 2003).

A growing body of evidence suggests that free play also relates to the development of language and literacy. Symbolic play, in particular, consists mostly of enacted narratives that share vital aspects that underlie literacy, such as the identification of characters, creation of a coherent storyline, and the use of props and contextual descriptions to foster a story-related reality (Dickinson, Cote, & Smith, 1993; Nicolopoulou, McDowell, & Brockmeyer, 2006; Pellegrini & Galda, 1990). This kind of play predicts language and reading readiness in kindergarten (Bergen & Mauer, 2000; Dickinson & Moreton, 1991; Dickinson & Tabors, 2001; Pellegrini & Galda, 1990). Additional experimental research is necessary to isolate the specific elements of symbolic play that promote different aspects of literacy development.

GUIDED PLAY AND ACADEMIC OUTCOMES

A wealth of empirical data also shows that teachers can enrich learning through children's play by adding math- and literacy-related materials into school environments (e.g., Arnold, Fisher, Doctoroff, & Dobbs, 2002; Christie & Enz, 1992; Christie & Roskos, 2006; Einarsdottir, 2005; Griffin & Case, 1996; Griffin, Case, & Siegler, 1994; Kavanaugh & Engel, 1998; Roskos & Christie, 2004; Saracho & Spodek, 2006; Stone & Christie, 1996; Whyte & Bull, 2008). For example, Cook (2000) found preschool children engaged in more talk and activities relating to mathematical concepts when number symbols were embedded within play settings. Neuman and Roskos (1992) also noted that the incorporation of literacy props in preschoolers' free play environments increased literacy-related activities compared to a control group. Taken together, these findings demonstrate how simple interventions that augment the academic content in free play environments stimulate academic outcomes.

In the examples above, guided play takes the form of *supplementing* environments that encourage children's discovery. Teachers can also subtly structure play activities (Singer, 2002) as they co-play with children, guiding them toward imaginary activities and games that match with curricular goals (e.g., going on shopping trips, doing math). Parent–teacher training programs designed to enhance learning-oriented co-play, for example, enhance children's imaginative play, prosocial skills, task persistence, positive emotions, and academic skills (Singer et al., 2003). Thus, guided play sparks enriched, meaningful learning experiences while still maintaining children's sense of curiosity, autonomy, choice, and challenge. Taken together, the literature suggests that playful learning, in the form of both free play and guided play, leads to strong academic and social outcomes for children.

LONG-TERM EFFECTS OF PLAYFUL PEDAGOGIES

The real measure of learning comes not only from immediate mastery of information but also from long-term retention and transfer. Here, too, the evidence suggests that playful learning is an important pedagogical tool. Marcon (1993, 1999, 2002), for example, compared three preschool models on a variety of academic, behavioral, and social measures. Children in the child-initiated learning environments showed superior social behaviors, fewer conduct disorders, enhanced academic performance, and retention beyond children who experienced didactic, direct instruction or mixed methods in sixth grade (didactic instruction and play learning). Other researchers have documented similar gains in social and academic development of child-initiated learners over didactic learners (Burts, Hart, Charlesworth, & DeWolf, 1993; Lillard & Else-Quest, 2006).

Research on social outcomes of playful learning comes from the now classic HighScope project (Schweinhart & Weikart, 1997; Schweinhart, Weikart, & Larner, 1986). By age 23, individuals who had attended play-based preschools were eight times less likely to need treatment for emotional disturbances and three times less likely to be arrested for committing a felony than those who went to preschools where direct instruction prevailed. To paraphrase Schweinhart, HighScope's director, direct instruction does not cause these problems (Brown, 2009). Rather, not giving children the opportunity to develop socially is the unintended side effect. In other words, social problems arise when early education does not focus on the whole child.

WHY DOES PLAYFUL LEARNING WORK?
SEVEN DEVELOPMENTAL PRINCIPLES

In 2009, Hirsh-Pasek et al. articulated seven developmental principles that summarize accumulated knowledge about how young children best learn. These same principles appear in a series of now classic books (Berk, 2001; Bowman et al., 2001; Bransford, Brown, & Cocking, 2000; Hirsh-Pasek &

Golinkoff, 2003; Hirsh-Pasek et al., 2009; Shonkoff & Phillips, 2000; Zigler et al., 2004), among others, and largely reflect the developmentally appropriate practices espoused by the National Association for the Education of Young Children (Copple & Bredekamp, 2009). Perhaps it is not surprising that pedagogies consistent with these principles endorse a whole-child approach and embrace playful learning rather than direct instruction:

1. All policies, programs, and products directed toward young children should be sensitive to children's developmental age and ability as defined through research-based developmental trajectories. Developmental trajectories and milestones are better construed through ranges and patterns of growth rather than absolute ages.

2. Children are active, not passive, learners who acquire knowledge by examining and exploring their environment.

3. Children, as all humans, are fundamentally social beings who learn most effectively in socially sensitive and responsive environments via their interactions with caring adults and other children.

4. Children learn best when their social and emotional needs are met and when they learn life skills necessary for success. Self-regulation, flexibility and compromise, and the ability to take the perspective of the other are skills to be nurtured.

5. Young children learn most effectively when information is embedded in meaningful contexts that relate to their everyday lives rather than in artificial contexts that foster rote learning.

6. The process of learning is as important as the outcome. Facilitating children's language, attentional skills, problem solving, flexible thinking, and self-regulation is crucial to children's academic success and to accountability. Settings that promote these skills prepare confident, eager, engaged, and lifelong learners.

7. Recognizing that children have diverse skills and needs as well as different cultural and socioeconomic backgrounds encourages respect for individual differences and allows children to optimize their learning.

There is virtual consensus surrounding these principles of learning for children in prekindergarten to third grade (Bogard & Takanishi, 2005). Playful learning is one of the strong characteristics of both the successful Tools of the Mind curriculum (Diamond et al., 2007) and of Montessori programs (Lillard & Else-Quest, 2006). Playful learning also encourages sensitivity and responsiveness in teachers—characteristics that are hallmarks of high-quality programs (e.g., Galinsky, 2006). These seven principles, based in developmental and learning science, suggest that playful learning—not direct instruction—will maximize children's ability to learn and to transfer what they have learned.

REAPING THE BENEFITS OF PLAYFUL LEARNING

We have suggested that prekindergarten to third grade education would be best served by a peace treaty between the educational Montagues and Capulets. Broad curricular goals can be achieved using playful pedagogy, and the scientific evidence is consistent with this recommendation. Indeed, Copple and Bredekamp gave guidance on how we might achieve this end:

> Education quality and outcomes would improve substantially if elementary teachers incorporated the best of preschool's emphases and practices (e.g., attention to the whole child; integrated, meaningful learning; parent engagement) and if preschool teachers made more use of those elementary-grade practices that are valuable for younger children, as well (e.g., robust content, attention to learning progressions in curriculum and teaching). (2009, p. 2)

Herein lies a partial recipe for achieving the great balancing act. Playful pedagogy offers a model for how students can be better prepared to be lifelong learners who will enter a world that is increasingly relying on global, socially sensitive, and creative thinkers. Research linking play with creative and flexible responses has been available for decades (Pellegrini, 2009).

CONCLUSION

Children in preschool today will be the future work force. To best support them, we must return play to childhood and ensure that as more content is added into preschool curricula, we use a playful learning pedagogy. Just when children need to discover the pleasure of learning and the importance of taking the perspective of the other, just when children should be maximizing their problem-solving and creative abilities, research suggests that direct instruction reduces children's ability to adapt in school, acquire crucial social and emotional skills, and respond to school's demands (Hirsh-Pasek et al., 2009). In contrast, when children have the opportunity to participate in free play, to be treated as whole children with brains and hearts, and to experience learning in a playful and engaging way, they learn and they thrive. Learning and play are not incompatible. For young children, learning is best achieved *via* play.

DEBATE 4
Public Schools Only versus Other Sites

STUDY QUESTIONS

- How do public school systems support an affordable, accessible, and quality system of preschool education nationwide?

- In what areas is the public school system lacking in its ability to provide high-quality preschool programs?

- How might existing programs in private settings be blended with the public school system?

- What is a mixed delivery model, and what are its advantages and disadvantages?

CHAPTER 21
The Case for Public Preschool

Kathleen McCartney, Margaret Burchinal, and Todd Grindal

In contrast to most Western industrialized countries, the United States has built a fragmented, mixed-delivery preschool system rather than a system in partnership with the public schools. Rose (2007) has described it as a patchwork quilt consisting primarily of community and for-profit child care centers, Head Start, and public preschools. Preschool in the United States has evolved as a family matter, a largely private system with an unstable financial structure that threatens the work force as well as the early care and education of young children. Some early childhood advocates continue to promote the value of a mixed-delivery system despite the serious limitations in availability, affordability, and quality. We believe these problems can only be addressed by rebuilding preschool in partnership with the public schools.

The current preschool policy is rooted in the history of Head Start. When Head Start came of age in the 1960s and 1970s, preschool was an uncommon experience for most American children. Although some children from economically advantaged families attended part-time nursery school programs, most children did not begin formal schooling until kindergarten. Head Start was created as part of President Lyndon Johnson's antipoverty agenda. The architects of Head Start believed in the power of community organizing to eradicate poverty. Schools at the time were racially segregated, and many constituents were skeptical about the ability and willingness of public schools to meet the needs of the poor (Rose, 2007). This is a key point. The Johnson administration's decision to provide preschool services through community-based agencies essentially reflected a lack of trust in the public schools.

President Richard Nixon's 1971 veto of the Child Care and Development Act cemented the disconnect between preschool and public school. The purpose of this bill was to build a legislative framework for universally available child development services, including child care. Although Nixon was initially favorably inclined toward the bill, he decided to veto it to garner support from the right wing of the Republican Party. The veto ensured a private, open market for early care and education with a minimal role for the federal government. Furthermore, it prevented the United States from building an iterative policy agenda to meet the needs of employed families, in stark contrast to continental European and Nordic countries, which provide significantly greater supports not only for early education but also for parental leave and other child benefits (Waldfogel, 2006).

WHY PRESCHOOL BELONGS IN PUBLIC SCHOOL

Despite their history, the public schools have demonstrated the capacity to serve young children. When large numbers of women began working outside of the home during the Second World War, federal funds provided care for many of their children through the local public schools (Youcha, 1995). Demonstration projects in the 1960s and 1970s showed that public schools can meet the complex needs of preschool children and their parents (Caldwell, 1986). Today, public schools serve preschool children enrolled in Head Start and state prekindergarten (pre-K) programs across the country. In fact, some estimates suggest that nearly 1 out of every 4 U.S. child care programs is operated by the public schools (Neugebauer, 2003). There is a growing recognition among educators and policy makers that public schools, both charter and traditional, can and should provide high-quality preschool. Expanding the role of the public schools will offer the best opportunity to ensure that quality preschool is available to every child.

Perhaps the best argument for placing preschool in public schools is that it would guarantee an alignment of curriculum and standards and thereby ensure a more seamless transition to kindergarten (Bogard & Takanishi, 2005; Kauerz, 2006; Vecchiotti, 2003). When preschool is offered in the public schools, it is typically referred to as pre-K. There is some evidence that communication between community-based preschool teachers and public school teachers is logistically difficult (Horan, 2009). When preschool teachers work in elementary schools, they have regular opportunities for formal and informal collaboration with their colleagues who teach older children. Aligning curricula, sharing assessments, and coordinating practices and professional development are just simpler when people work under the same roof.

An equally important reason for public schools to offer pre-K is universal access. From 2001 to 2008, annual funding for state preschool programs more than doubled to over $5 billion, with state programs in 38 states serving more than 1.2 million 3- and 4-year-old children (Barnett, Epstein, et al., 2009). Nevertheless, universal access to affordable quality preschool remains a serious limitation across the country (Brauner, Gordic, & Zigler, 2004). Worst of all, the patchwork system leaves children from poor families—those most at risk for school failure—more likely than other children to be enrolled in low-quality preschool programs (Fuller et al., 2004). Public schools are universally accessible and therefore represent a logical source for pre-K delivery. Although quality and funding levels may vary by school districts, access to school does not.

The third reason is cost. Preschool was once a luxury, but today it is a public good for children and for parents (Gormley, 2005). Yet, the cost of private preschool is a financial challenge for poor and middle-class families alike. Since the Nixon veto, finding affordable child care has remained a challenge for most American families. Increasingly, both parents in two-parent families as well as single parents are employed for financial reasons, to comply with public policy employment provisions, or for personal reasons, especially gender equity (Abramovitz, 2000; Haskins, 2006). Between 1970 and 2007, the percentage of mothers with children younger than 6 years who worked outside of the home rose from 30% to 62% (Annie E. Casey Foundation, 2008; Sandberg & Hofferth, 2001). As a result, more than 11 million U.S. children under the age of 5 years are in some form of nonparental child care every week (National Association of Child Care Resource and Referral Agencies, 2008). Costs to parents vary widely by setting, region of the country, and age of the child. In 2008, the average annual fees for a 4-year-old to attend center-based pre-K ranged from $4,560 in West Virginia to $11,678 in Massachusetts. Clearly, public pre-K that is free of cost to parents would eradicate the affordability issue with a guaranteed steady source of funding from states and the federal government. In contrast, current public early education programs have been "notoriously susceptible to funding cutbacks" (Lubeck, 1989, p. 8).

High costs for parents do not translate into high wages for preschool teachers. The U.S. Bureau of Labor Statistics (2010) estimated that preschool teachers earn on average $22,120 per year (excluding special education teachers). Salary and benefits vary across the country and by program type. Individuals who provide educational services do earn more than those who provide custodial care. Nevertheless, there can be little argument that levels of compensation for all types of early care and education providers are embarrassingly low. It is therefore not surprising that attracting and retaining a quality early childhood teacher work force is a challenge (Barnett, 2004; Whitebook, 2003a). Perhaps as a consequence, the quality of U.S. early care and education programs is unacceptably poor (Early et al., 2007; Fuller et al., 2004; Pianta et al., 2005). Public schools offer an opportunity to address many of these structural challenges. They provide teachers with a living wage and benefits. In fact, preschool teachers who work in public schools earn up to 50% more than their colleagues working in independent and community-based preschools, with the mean annual wage for preschool teachers in public elementary schools being $37,800 (U.S. Bureau of Labor Statistics, 2009). Public schools are regularly monitored and accountable for the quality of their classrooms. They ensure that teachers have training before working with students and provide regular opportunities for experienced teachers to improve their practice. Thus, public pre-K eliminates the unfair preschool subsidy provided by teachers to parents by virtue of low wages and lack of benefits.

POTENTIAL CONCERNS ABOUT PUBLIC PRE-K

Continued lack of confidence in the public schools regarding the politics of race remains a serious concern. In the 1980s, the National Black Child Development Institute (NBCDI) warned that public school sponsorship of pre-K programs posed potentially calamitous consequences for African American children. Noting the historically high rates of suspension, retention, special education designation, and underachievement among African American children in public schools, NBCDI scholars worried that public pre-K would reflect white cultural biases and expand the system of separate and unequal education (Moore & Phillips, 1989; NBCDI, 1985). Concerns about racism in the public schools across all grades remain; however, we argue that the current mixed-model child care system has not lived up to its promise to meet the needs of preschool children of color.

A second, long-held concern is that public schools cannot provide developmentally appropriate practice (Elkind, 1988; Goldstein, 1997). Because private preschool was originally designed as a "middle-class" experience, Lubeck (1989) argued that it has been influenced by class-based values, beliefs, and practices, such as active exploration and discovery. In contrast, preschool interventions for poor children have focused on academics—the purview of public schools—to promote achievement to set the stage for school success. Today, there is near consensus that public schools can provide developmentally appropriate early childhood education when they hire teachers with appropriate training (Frede & Barnett, 1992). Thankfully, the National Association for the Education of Young Children has embraced not only a child-centered curriculum, but also direct instruction (Copple & Bredekamp, 2009). The standards movement, however, may reignite this debate (Meisels, 2007).

A third concern is purely logistical. With their limited hours of operation, public schools are largely unable to meet the needs of working parents (Neugebauer, 2003). Of course, this concern applies to the elementary school years as well, which is why many public and independent schools offer after-school care. Although public schools could extend their hours, many cash-strapped districts would likely balk at any unfunded public policy mandates, and as such it will be critical to identify new revenue sources for public preschool (Andrews & Slate, 2001), such as fee-based extended learning programs (Gabrieli & Goldstein, 2008).

THE EVIDENCE ON PRE-K

Evaluations of pre-K programs suggest that they are successful in improving children's academic skills. The most rigorous assessment of their effectiveness is a multisite evaluation by a research team from the National Institute for Early Education Research (Wong et al., 2008). The research team conducted regression discontinuities studies in five states with mature pre-K programs by comparing children entering pre-K programs with children entering kindergarten from the same school districts. Results indicated significant differences between children with and without the pre-K experiences on language skills, math skills, and print awareness.

In a second important study (Mashburn et al., 2008), the National Center for Early Development and Learning (NCEDL) examined pre-K programs in 11 states with large mature programs. They randomly sampled 50–100 programs per state, one classroom per program, and four children per classroom. Gains during the pre-K year were computed on measures of skills in language, reading, math, and social skills, adjusting for nesting of children in classrooms, amount of gains expected due to age, and family characteristics. Results indicated that there were significant effects in language, reading, math, and social skills. Effects were larger for children whose mothers had less education, especially larger gains in receptive language and larger declines in problem behavior.

Unfortunately, these studies do not speak to the effectiveness of public pre-K per se because most states allow or mandate a combination of settings for their pre-K programs. For example, the majority of states include community child care programs as sites for public pre-K. In our opinion, the main reason for this is that it represents a political compromise for pre-K advocates, who represent the nonprofit and for-profit child care industry. Two other reasons are worthy of note: specifically, a conservative agenda to limit government programs generally, as well as space constraints in some overcrowded schools.

Howes et al. (2008) tested whether children benefited more when pre-K programs were located in public schools using data from the NCEDL study. About 60% of the sampled programs across 11 states were located in public schools, and about 40% were not. The programs in public schools were more likely to have a teacher with a bachelor's degree as the lead teacher (84% when programs were in public schools and 48% when they were not) and were likely to provide half-day rather than full-day programs (35% of programs in public schools were full day, whereas 65% of other programs were full day). Whether the program was located in a public school was not strongly correlated with measures of global classroom quality or the proportion of time spent in instruction. Observations of public school teachers yielded mixed results. Compared with other teachers, public school teachers provided more sensitive teacher–child interactions and they spent more time in reading and math activities; however, they were also rated as providing lower quality instruction. Regardless, children's academic and social skills were not statistically related to whether or not the pre-K program was located in a public school.

The NCEDL team believed their findings reflected the current early education context. Many school districts in their study had completely separate standards and programs for their early childhood classrooms and for their K–12 classrooms. The early childhood programs have different criteria for hiring, different standards for teaching and for promotions, and different supervision. The state early childhood specialists interviewed believe that the early childhood programs tend to be regarded as less important programs within many schools (M. Burchinal, personal communication, December 11, 2009). Why would districts want to build two separate education programs? The answer is principals, who are not typically trained in early childhood education and may not believe that pre-K belongs in public schools. Moreover, standards-based reform has ushered in a greater focus on testing. Early education is viewed by some principals as a diversion—or worse. In some schools, the principal was not aware that there was an early childhood program in the school, which was apparent when the NCEDL team contacted him or her to discuss the school's pre-K program.

The Tulsa pre-K study provides compelling evidence that public pre-K can be effective when the context is right. In 1998, Oklahoma established voluntary universal pre-K by offering incentives for every 4-year-old who enrolled. By 2002, 91% of school districts were offering either half-day or full-day pre-K programs to families. Teachers were required to have a bachelor's degree and an early childhood certificate, and the ratio of students to teachers was 10:1. Regression discontinuity design controlled for potential selection bias in the studies to evaluate the effectiveness of the Tulsa pre-K program (Gormley et al., 2005; Gormley & Phillips, 2009). Specifically, they compared kindergartners with pre-K experience with children currently in pre-K of a comparable age by restricting the sample to children who fell near the cutoff date for pre-K eligibility. The effects for pre-K were significant and dramatic. Children with pre-K experience scored higher on the Woodcock-Johnson Tests of Achievement III (Woodcock, McGrew, & Mather, 2001) for letter–word identification, spelling, and applied problems, with effects ranging from a 5- to a 9-month advantage. Effects were larger for children who were eligible for free lunch, which suggests that pre-K can level the playing field for poor children. To understand the size of the pre-K effects, it was compared with the effects for race, free lunch status, mother's education, and presence of the biological father in the home. The effect of pre-K was larger than any of these family background variables. The Tulsa study offers powerful evidence of the promise of public pre-K for two reasons: Oklahoma implemented pre-K universally, and the researchers evaluated this intervention using strong causal methods.

BUILDING POLITICAL WILL

In this chapter, we argue that current conceptions of public preschool are linked with a history that has resulted in the largely dysfunctional mixed-delivery model that exists today. This model does not meet the needs of parents, teachers, or children. We agree with Bogard and Takanishi (2005) that for early childhood education to be effective it must be connected to a broader system, like public education. We do not doubt that many private and community-based preschool programs are staffed by effective and dedicated teachers. We simply believe that the public schools are in the best position to provide the logistical, monetary, and pedagogical supports necessary to create an affordable, accessible, and quality system of preschool education nationwide.

Lingering questions about whether preschool generally is a public or private responsibility must be laid to rest as Americans build political will for a 21st-century early education system. There is emerging consensus on critical components—educated teachers with training in early childhood education, continuity and alignment of curriculum standards, and incentives for parent involvement. Going forward, a deepening commitment on the part of public schools to young children must be a critical component of serious school reform efforts.

CHAPTER 22

Preschool Programs Should Be Coordinated in the Public Schools with Supports from Head Start and Child Care

Walter S. Gilliam

School readiness is the primary goal of preschool education. Although preschool programs may also play an important role in providing safe and reliable child care for working families, the primary purpose is to help young children develop the social, emotional, and cognitive-linguistic skills they will need to be successful in elementary school, to smooth the transition from the home to school environments, and to provide parents an opportunity to develop important working relationships with the type of professionals who will be educating and caring for their children throughout the rest of their formative years.

This is no small task. To accomplish this important work, preschool environments need to be warm, friendly, inviting places staffed by caring professionals who are able to smooth the transition from the home to school environment. In other words, effective preschools need to have all of the supports and resources available to a high-quality elementary school packaged within an environment and relationships that resemble the comfort and familiarity of home, fostering relationships between the parents and teachers that are both professional and personal, and setting the stage for continued family–school collaboration and educational success. It is for this reason that effective preschools are very special places—they are neither home nor school, but in many ways both at the same time.

In addition to facilitating the transition from the home to preschool environment, effective preschools work to smooth the transition from the preschool environment to the typically more highly structured elementary school environment. This transition from preschool to kindergarten represents a challenge for most children:

> As children enter elementary school after preschool, they and their families experience a substantial shift in culture and expectations, including more formal academic standards, a more complex social environment, less family support and connection, and less time with teachers due to larger class size and more transitions during the day. (Pianta & Kraft-Sayre, 2003, p. 2)

Providing services to assist children and families in bridging the transition from preschool to kindergarten is essential to preventing loss of effects achieved during preschool (Pianta & Cox, 1999; Ramey & Ramey, 1998b; Ramey, Ramey, et al., 2000; Reynolds, 2003; Shore, 1998). In a review of four extended early childhood interventions, programs that provided transition and follow-up services from preschool into kindergarten and the early grades were found to "promote more successful transitions to school than preschool interventions alone" (Reynolds, 2003, p. 188). Transition services can take many forms and must be tailored to the needs of a particular population and their community. However, those that conform to a developmental-contextual model by continuing to provide connections between children's home and school environments, as well as curricular and pedagogical continuity between programs, are likely to be the most effective (Hodgkinson, 2003; Kagan & Neuman, 1998; Reynolds, 2003).

It would be fortuitous, indeed, if one particular type of preschool setting were able to guarantee the perfectly balanced mix described above. Unfortunately, with the well-documented degree of variability in quality across and within different early education and child care settings, such guarantees seem unlikely. Rather, the more reasonable course may be to identify the types of settings most likely to provide the greater amount of the essential ingredients of an effective preschool program and supplement those settings with the additional supports needed to provide a high-quality early education experience.

SMOOTHING TRANSITIONS THROUGH A PREK-3 FRAMEWORK

The importance of the transitional role of effective preschool services for 3- and 4-year olds cannot be overstated. This transitional role requires a thoughtful alignment of purpose, quality, work force, and technology between preschool and elementary school, as well as the centrality of families and effective home–school collaboration for continued school success. This is best accomplished through an integrated preschool through early elementary grades (PreK-3) framework.

Takanishi (2010) offered five priorities for developing a viable and effective system of PreK-3 education. First, primary education must consist of high-quality preschool education for 3- and 4-year-olds, equally high-quality full-day kindergarten, and excellent educational experiences in Grades 1–3. Second, accountability systems must embrace the importance of prekindergarten (pre-K)/early learning programs, K–3 educational settings, and families as equally important to student outcomes by Grade 3. Third, there must be alignment between the standards, curricula, and assessment from PreK-3. Fourth, all early education teachers should possess a PreK-3 teaching credential, helping to align teacher training throughout the PreK-3 range, and assistant teachers should have at least an associate's degree and be working toward teacher certification. Fifth, families need to be viewed as an important component by promoting parent literacy and parent involvement throughout the PreK-3 range. Clearly, within this

PreK-3 framework, effective preschool programs are seen as being fully aligned with both the expectations of elementary school and the needs and goals of the family, representing a transitional period in and of itself between the home and school.

WHY SCHOOLS ARE AN EXCELLENT SETTING FOR PRESCHOOL SERVICES

There are many reasons why locating preschool in the public school system makes practical and political sense. Arguably, the most important domestic policy issue today is education reform. It is widely accepted that the public schools must do a better job by children and families in the United States today. No Child Left Behind Act of 2001 (PL 107-110) was a small, if flawed, step in that direction. Real and lasting educational reform must begin with preschool. Publicly funded preschool located in the public school system should serve as the foundation for broader school reform and should be the basis on which all subsequent layers of school reform efforts are built. Also, public schools are already staffed by teachers with bachelor's degrees and teaching certificates, school psychologists, social workers, and other support personnel who are paid a wage commensurate with their training, and the public schools have developed links to services necessary for children and families with disabilities and/or chronic health problems. As part of a comprehensive array of services infused in public schools through the highly successful School of the 21st Century model, preschools provide both a solid educational foundation for early learning and needed child care for working families (Finn-Stevenson & Zigler, 1999). These reasons are further discussed in the following sections.

Public Schools Are Already a Major Venue for Preschool

Public schools have been used extensively by many state-funded pre-K systems, and the value and feasibility of schools as preschool settings are supported by research. For examples, Oklahoma's state-funded pre-K program and the Chicago Child-Parent Centers—both well-regarded and highly successful preschool models—are administered by the public school system. In a study of the effectiveness of Oklahoma's pre-K system, Gormley and Phillips demonstrated that the public schools are a "viable and effective vehicle for delivering educational services to young children" (2005, p. 77). Similarly, the well-regarded and highly successful Chicago Child-Parent Centers (Reynolds, 2003; Reynolds & Temple, 1998; Reynolds et al., 2001) are located in and administered by the Chicago public school system, providing an organizational structure that "strengthens continuity of service delivery in several ways, including providing centralized oversight by the school principal and having geographic proximity between preschool/kindergarten and school-age components" (Reynolds, 2003, p. 176).

Similar to the Oklahoma model, many other state-funded pre-K systems are administered by the public schools and locate many or all of their classrooms in school settings. Sometimes location in the public schools is mandated. For example, in its landmark 1998 decision, the New Jersey Supreme Court mandated that children in the 30 highest poverty districts in the state, known as the Abbott districts, receive a high-quality preschool education beginning at age 3 and that school districts would primarily be responsible for the provision of this service (Frede et al., 2009).

A nationally representative study of 3,898 teachers in state-funded pre-K classes randomly selected across all 40 states that funded pre-K in 2003–2004 highlighted the extent of public school involvement in pre-K (Gilliam, 2008). Weighted frequencies across these 40 states indicated that 68% of all state-funded pre-K classes are located in a public school, of which 9% were in a public school setting that was also a Head Start grantee. The rest of the pre-K classes were located across a wide array of other settings, such as Head Start centers that were not in the public schools (9%), for-profit child care centers (7%), nonprofit service agencies (7%), private or nonpublic secular schools (7%), and various faith-affiliated settings (2%). The sizable overlap within state pre-K systems between the public schools and Head Start is expected, given that 17% of all Head Start grantees are public school systems (Administration for Children and Families, 2005). Moreover, all but 3 of the nation's 51 state-funded pre-K systems (some states have more than one system) are administered through or in coordination with a state department of education, and in at least 65% of all state systems the public school is the most common pre-K setting (Barnett, Epstein, et al., 2009).

Public Schools Have the Capacity to Build an Educated Preschool Teacher Work Force

Preschoolers learn best in classes taught by well-trained teachers (Bowman et al., 2001). Classrooms led by more highly educated teachers with specialized training in early childhood education provide a more developmentally appropriate, stimulating, and supportive environment (Burchinal, Howes, & Kontos, 2002; Clarke-Stewart et al., 2002; Early & Winton, 2001; Whitebook, 2003b). Many researchers in the early care and education field agree that a teacher with a bachelor's degree in early childhood education is the best standard (Maxwell & Clifford, 2006; Whitebook, 2003a), although recent research in pre-K classes suggests that the relationship between teacher educational level and child outcomes has been overestimated (Early et al., 2007). Although assistant teachers are an important part of the teaching staff, very little is known about them except that most hold no more than a high school diploma; in addition, they tend to assume greater teaching responsibilities when their educational level is closer to that of the lead teacher and there is adequate scheduled planning time available for the lead and assistant teachers to coordinate their roles (Sosinsky & Gilliam, in press). Teacher compensation also matters, with better compensated teachers being associated with better child outcomes (Bowman et al., 2001; Howes, Phillips, et al., 1992; National Institute of Child Health and Human Development [NICHD], 1999; Peisner-Feinberg et al., 1999). Unfortunately, the median annual salary of a preschool teacher in 2009 was $24,540, only slightly better than child care providers ($19,240) and far less than kindergarten teachers ($47,830; U.S. Bureau of Labor Statistics, 2009).

Preschool teachers in public schools have more years of college education and more years of education specifically in early education relative to state-funded pre-K teachers in any other setting (Gilliam, 2008). About 90% of state-funded pre-K teachers in public school settings hold a bachelor's or master's degree, whereas these degrees were far less likely in similar teachers located in Head Start (37%) and other (57%) settings. Although the proportions are lower, the overall pattern is the same for degrees and training specifically in early childhood education: 40% of public school pre-K teachers reported holding a bachelor's degree or higher in early childhood education, as opposed to 13% in Head Start and 17% in other settings. Also, relative to their peers in other settings, preschool teachers in public schools tend to earn far higher salaries and achieve a level of compensation far more similar to kindergarten teachers. Additional analyses of the data presented by Gilliam (2008) indicated that state-funded pre-K teachers in public schools earned an average yearly salary of $35,193, which is significantly higher than state-funded pre-K teachers in Head Start centers ($28,499; $d = 0.49$) and for-profit child care centers ($25,250; $d = 0.73$). Although lead preschool teachers in the public schools held a higher degree than lead teachers in other settings, this is not true for assistant teachers. Assistant teachers in public school-based preschool programs tend to be more likely to hold no more than a high school diploma, and they spend fewer scheduled hours planning with the lead teacher (Sosinsky & Gilliam, in press).

Although states are making strides in requiring teachers to have higher educational credentials, pre-K teachers still fall far behind kindergarten teachers in this respect. The majority of state-funded pre-K classrooms meet the standard that requires a lead teacher to hold a bachelor's degree (Barnett, Epstein, et al., 2009). Yet, although all 50 states require kindergarten teachers to have at least a bachelor's degree, only 20 states and the District of Columbia require similar credentials for teachers in state-funded pre-K programs (Doherty, 2002). A greater proportion of public schools providing pre-K services may lead to a greater proportion of preschool teachers with bachelor's and master's degrees, helping to bridge the training and compensation gap between the preschool and kindergarten and elementary school work forces.

Public Schools Provide Greater Access to Special Education Supports

Greater access to special education supports infused into preschool settings benefits young children with special needs by facilitating early identification, allowing for greater access to needed support services and supporting greater integration of young students of varying learning needs. Nationally, 10.5% of preschoolers in state-funded pre-K systems are identified as qualifying for special educational services, and 61% of all classrooms have at least one identified child (Gilliam & Stahl, 2008). Data from the National Prekindergarten Study (Gilliam, 2008) indicate that state-funded pre-K teachers in public school settings and Head Start, relative to teachers in for-profit child care centers, report greater access to special education teachers (90% and 93% versus 67%), physical and occupational therapists (83% and 83% versus 55%), and speech/language therapists (95% and 95% versus 88%). Although the rate of access to these special education supports is similar for pre-K teachers in public school and Head Start centers, public schools are more likely to have these services on site, whereas Head Start centers are more likely to have these services provided by off-site providers who are accessed on an as-needed basis. This greater access to special education teachers and therapists in school-based pre-K classes is likely due to these services already being present and mandated in the school for the elementary school students. Locating preschool programs in the public schools takes advantage of the extant special educational support staff already available in this setting.

Public Schools Reduce Access Barriers

For a preschool program to meet the needs of all families, barriers to attendance such as transportation must be addressed. Just as transportation is provided for children attending public elementary schools, adequate transportation should be provided for children attending preschool. In addition, arranging transportation to schools for parents who are volunteering, observing, or meeting with staff facilitates parent and family involvement by making it easier for parents to take advantage of the broader array of services provided. Another obvious potential barrier for participation is parent fees or tuition.

In the National Prekindergarten Study (Gilliam, 2008), teachers in state-funded pre-K programs were asked whether any child in the past 12 months had to leave the program because of poor transportation or difficulties paying fees or tuition. Although the classrooms were in a variety of settings, all of the programs were state-funded pre-K centers. Nationally, teachers in public schools (21%) and for-profit child care centers (20%) reported at least one child dropping out because of transportation problems compared to Head Start (26%). Also, fewer teachers in both public schools (8%) and Head Start (6%) reported far fewer instances of at least one child dropping out because of a family's inability to pay the fees compared to for-profit child care centers (29%). Overall, children in public schools were less likely to experience one or the other of these two barriers to participation.

AREAS WHERE PUBLIC SCHOOLS NEED SUPPORT

There are caveats, of course, to recommending that all public-funded preschool programs be located in the schools. First, no single setting holds a monopoly on quality. In a study of state-funded pre-K programs in Connecticut (Gilliam, 2000), pre-K programs located in the public schools evidenced higher levels of average quality on the Early Childhood Environment Rating Scale–Revised (Harms, Clifford, & Cryer, 1998) relative to state-funded pre-K programs in child care centers. However, the most striking finding was that all setting types had their fair share of programs that scored extremely high and extremely low on this measure of overall quality. Although faith-affiliated and for-profit child care centers scored the lowest on average, there were several instances of high-quality programs in each of these setting types. It would not be wise to exclude these high-quality classrooms and centers from participating in a public-funded pre-K system just because they are not located in a public school.

Second, although pre-K classes in the public schools tend to have teachers with higher credentials and compensation, Head Start classes tend to outperform public school classes on providing various comprehensive services for children and families and on observing recommended group sizes and child–teacher ratios (Gilliam, 2008). Although child health, family well-being, and parent involvement are widely believed to be important facets of early childhood education and development, as well as integral components with regard to children being ready for school, the role of schools in providing comprehensive services is debated. Teachers in Head Start classes reported a greater mean number of comprehensive services in the areas of developmental screening, social services, health screenings, and meals relative to pre-K teachers in public schools (Gilliam, 2008). Teachers in the Head Start classes also reported greater provision of comprehensive services, relative to teachers in the public schools, across all 13 comprehensive services measured.

A considerable amount of research suggests that group size and student–teacher ratios are important markers of quality in early childhood education programs. Lower student–teacher ratios are associated with better classroom quality across all age ranges of young children—infants, toddlers, and preschoolers (Phillips et al., 2000; Phillipsen et al., 1997). In addition, lower student–teacher ratios are associated with increased responsiveness by teachers, leading to a host of positive outcomes for young children, such as improved language skills, social-emotional functioning, behavior, and play skills (Howes, Phillips, et al., 1992; NICHD, 1996, 2000; Phillips et al., 2000). For classrooms serving mostly 4-year-olds, both the National Association for the Education of Young Children (1998) and the Head Start Bureau (Administration for Children and Families, 2010) have recommended group sizes no greater than 20 and ratios no greater than 10 students per teacher or assistant teacher. Teachers in public schools reported larger class sizes than teachers in Head Start classes (based on October 1 enrollment), typical daily attendance, and maximum past year enrollment. Specifically, public school teachers were significantly more likely to report an October 1 enrollment greater than 20 (21.7%) relative to Head Start (6.7%). Similar to the class size variables, teachers in public schools reported significantly higher typical student–teacher ratios and higher highest daily ratios, relative to Head Start. The proportion of public school teachers reporting a typical student–teacher ratio greater than 10 (27.6%) was more than twice that of Head Start (13.2%).

Third, preschool programs can and should play an important role in the provision of safe and affordable child care for working families. Not all forms of child care can be considered educational, but combining both early education and child care into a single setting can be a highly effective use of public dollars (Brauner et al., 2004). In order to do this, preschool programs must provide care for a sufficient number of hours per day and weeks per year that can be individualized to the varying child care needs of diverse working families. Nonexperimental research with Head Start and kindergarten children has shown that children who participate in full-day classes show greater benefits in early academic skills than children who participate for only part of the day (Administration for Children and Families, 2003; Gullo, 2000). The evaluation of Oklahoma's pre-K program revealed that for certain subgroups of children—particularly ethnic minority children and children with low socioeconomic statuses—participation in full-day preschool was more effective at raising children's language and cognitive test scores than part-day only (Gormley & Gayer, 2005; Gormley & Phillips, 2005). A flexible system such as this is necessary to promote the school readiness of all children. For children who are not in child care, such a system would provide a developmentally appropriate early school and socialization experience that would facilitate the transition between home activities and kindergarten. For children and families who need child care, such a system can provide a solution to the tremendous heterogeneity of quality in child care that currently exists within the United States by offering educationally meaningful, school-based care (Brauner et al., 2004; NICHD, 1996, 2000; Young, Marsland, & Zigler, 1997). However, for such a program to be a truly viable option for working parents, a model is needed that meets their needs: programs must offer full-day and summer care that match the standard working day of the majority of parents. Unfortunately, analysis of data from the National Prekindergarten Study (Gilliam, 2006) shows that 35% of pre-K classes in the schools provide only half of a school day's worth of care and only 22% are open for extended hours. Likewise, only 16% are open for 11 or more months, as compared to 35% of Head Start classes and 71% of for-profit centers participating in state-funded pre-K systems.

CONCLUSION

Linking preschool to local schools achieves several important objectives: It makes school-based child care more physically accessible for families; it familiarizes children with the school environment at an early age and thus diminishes apprehension about entering school later on; and it allows the school facilities to be used more efficiently, thus making schools a more cost-effective community investment (Zigler & Jones, 2002). In many geographical areas, public schools have already reached maximum student capacity for their existing physical space, particularly in more urban and disadvantaged communities. Also, many excellent preschool programs exist in settings that are not in the public schools, and young students should certainly continue to have access to these services. Therefore, it is likely not feasible or advisable that all preschool programs be located in public school settings. Rather, preschool will likely need to continue to be provided through a variety of community institutions. However, all should have established links to the elementary public schools to create a seamless transition into kindergarten and to the K–12 educational system, and all must meet standards of quality (Zigler et al., 2006a).

One solution worth serious consideration is blending the educational work force and access to special educational and support staff of the schools with the comprehensive services of Head Start and the hours of care provided by most child care centers. Combining funding streams currently available through state-funded pre-K systems, Head Start and child care subsidies would lead to a better array of options for parents (Brauner et al., 2004; Gilliam, 2008) and would eliminate the current need for families to choose between the educational benefits often found in the schools, the comprehensive services and parent involvement that are the core of the Head Start experience, and the workable child care arrangements provided by most child care centers. This blending of early education, comprehensive health and family services, and affordable child care within the public schools has been successfully implemented across more than 1,300 schools as part of the highly successful School of the 21st Century model (Zigler & Finn-Stevenson, 2007). A mixed-delivery system that keeps the public schools as a stabilizing centerpiece, makes best use of public funds across early education and child care funding streams, and is coordinated through the local public school system is the best option for providing the full array of services our children and families need.

CHAPTER 23

Public Schools as the Hub of a Mixed-Delivery System of Early Care and Education

W. Steven Barnett and Debra J. Ackerman

Preschool education in the United States is provided by a mix of public and private providers dependent on public and private funds. The different funding streams and regulatory structures have resulted in what appear to be largely separate silos—public schools, Head Start, and private preschools and child care delivering services in parallel. Although the field is roughly divided in this way, there is a substantial overlap that has been increased as state prekindergarten (pre-K) programs have grown. A substantial portion of Head Start services have been delivered by public schools for many years, but as state pre-K programs have grown to become the largest sector for 4-year-olds, they have relied on Head Start and private child care programs to deliver services (Barnett, Epstein, et al., 2008). Increasingly, the silos are separate as funding streams and regulatory agencies, but the distinctions have become blurred in programs delivering services. As public policy makers look for ways to coordinate across programs, we suggest that they make the public schools the hub of a system that integrates these programs into a high-quality system of preschool education.

Most of these programs emphasize improving children's kindergarten readiness, even those with a primary emphasis on meeting parents' needs for child care (Zigler et al., 2006a). To reach the first goal, programs must be educationally effective (Ackerman & Barnett, 2006). In designing policies to coordinate and support preschool programs, a good place to begin is by asking what programs need in order to be educationally effective. We then consider the capacity of each program or silo setting to offer effective preschool education and what must be done to ensure that capacity is adequate.

CHARACTERISTICS OF EDUCATIONALLY EFFECTIVE PRESCHOOL PROGRAMS

We begin with the assumption that a primary goal of every preschool program should be to contribute to children's learning and development. This is particularly important for the many children who would otherwise start school poorly prepared to succeed. The field does not have a precise input formula for ensuring a preschool program will be educationally effective for specific groups of children. However, programs have demonstrated substantial gains in learning and development in rigorous studies. These programs share at least four key features (Frede, 1998):

1. They employ well-educated teachers (typically with at least a bachelor's degree) who are adequately paid (typically at public school levels). If they do not already have specialized training in the education of children, they receive ongoing, intensive training and support for this development (a point to which we return).

2. Class sizes and the presence of multiple adults in the classroom permit teachers to work with children in small groups and individually.

3. There is a focus on intentional teaching or instruction, as well as a curriculum that prepares children for success in school. This includes discourse patterns and daily activities that give children scripts to help them understand school and how they should behave to succeed there. The curriculum emphasizes rich language development but does not neglect other domains of learning and development.

4. Teachers receive strong supervision and mentoring to assist them in reflective teaching and teacher–child interactions.

This is part of a systematic approach to continuous improvement in the classroom that includes systematic, rigorous assessment of teaching practices and children's learning (Ackerman & Barnett, 2006; Frede et al., 2007).

THE CAPACITY OF EACH AUSPICE TO OFFER PRESCHOOL

Program capacity includes all of the human and physical resources that contribute to providing an educationally effective preschool program, including professional capacity. Professional capacity refers to the knowledge and skills possessed by individuals and their organizations (Johnson & Thomas, 2004). Child care, Head Start, and public schools can contribute valuable capacity to the provision of effective preschool education. However, public schools possess unique capacities and have other strengths that suggest the system of preschool education should be built around a public school hub.

Private programs serve more children younger than 5 years than public programs, although their share of the market is much lower for 4-year-olds, who are the primary focus of state pre-K. The most obvious capacity they bring is physical space. In addition to being conveniently located for parents, many also offer convenient schedules for parents who need full-day, year-round child care. They also have many directors, teachers, and assistants who are committed to serving young children, and more of their teaching staff shares the language and cultural backgrounds of the children served than in public programs. Unfortunately, federal and state policies emphasize safe custodial care at low cost, and state standards for teacher qualifications, class size, and ratio are minimal (Zigler, Marsland, & Lord, 2009). Many staff have little formal education and training, and they are poorly paid (Ackerman, 2006). Directors often lack any background in education and support for reflective practice is extremely limited. Class size is completely unregulated in 17 states (Barnett, Epstein, et al., 2008). Often there is little real attention to education, as opposed to custodial care, and there is no formalized curriculum (Ackerman & Sansanelli, 2008; National Association of Child Care Resource and Referral Agencies, 2009). Organizational support for children with special needs or behavior problems is lacking. Even children from higher income families attend private programs that provide little support of learning and development, and positive effects on learning are very small, at best (Karoly et al., 2008; National Institute of Child Health and Human Development, 2002b).

Head Start is much better funded than child care, especially given its much shorter operating hours in a year; it also has more human and organizational capacity than private child care. In 2008, 41% of lead teachers held a bachelor's or graduate degree and 34% had an associate's degree (U.S. Department of Health and Human Services, 2009a). The 2007 Head Start reauthorization mandated that all teachers have at least an associate's degree by 2011 and at least 50% have a bachelor's degree by 2013 (U.S. Department of Health and Human Services, 2008). However, Head Start teachers with a bachelor's degree are paid only 53% of the average public school teacher's salary, severely limiting the ability to recruit and retain well-educated teachers (U.S. Department of Health and Human Services, 2009a; National Education Association, 2010). Program standards limit class size to 20 for 4-year-olds and 17 for 3-year-olds, with at least two staff members per classroom. Head Start has a child outcomes framework, a technical assistant system, and teachers must use a curriculum and are supervised by an education coordinator (U.S. Department of Health and Human Services, 2000). Head Start also serves children with disabilities (about 10% of enrollment), attends to the health and social services needs of children and families, and emphasizes parent involvement.

Despite its relative strengths, Head Start produces very small improvements in children's learning and development (U.S. Department of Health and Human Services, 2010b). The inadequate qualifications and compensation of Head Start's educational staff are strongly implicated. In addition, Head Start's emphasis on comprehensive services may distract the program from a focus on education. Isolation of many programs from public education may also play a role.

Public school's strengths begin with teachers required to have a minimum of a bachelor's degree—and in many states, specialized certification—and much higher salaries and benefits than the rest of the field. Public school teachers are accustomed to using a district's or state's curriculum and aligning their instruction with state learning standards and in focusing on instruction (Council of Chief State School Officers, 2010). Public schools are organized to provide substantial supervision, support, and professional development, and significant resources are available to assist with children who have educational difficulties or special needs. Public schools serve more than 400,000 preschoolers with disabilities, and integration of them into regular education is much easier when schools serve both populations (Barnett, Epstein, et al., 2008). Public schools can facilitate a preschool to Grade 3 approach (Foundation for Child Development, 2008), providing more schoollike experiences and increasing continuity for children and parents (Reynolds, 2000). Public schools also provide for democratic governance and accountability for results.

Of course, public schools also have drawbacks. Developing new facilities is time consuming and expensive compared to doing this in the private sector (Sussman & Gillman, 2007). Teachers are less likely to be from the same cultural and linguistic background as the children. Optimal decisions for preschool can be sacrificed in the interests of the larger system, such as placing teachers without any early childhood expertise in preschool classrooms. Class sizes and ratios often are less favorable than in Head Start, and a few states place no limits on them (Barnett, Epstein, et al., 2008). The larger scale of the public schools can limit choice and competition, at least for parents with the resources to select from among private providers.

In rigorous studies, public school preschool programs have produced substantially larger effects than Head Start and child care (Barnett, 2008). They include well-known programs like the Perry preschool program and Chicago Child-Parent Centers. The Perry preschool program was so small, intensive, and costly that it is far from typical, but the Chicago programs were similar in cost and design to better programs today. Some of today's statewide programs have been found to produce strong results (Gormley et al., 2008; Wong et al., 2008). These highly effective programs had the features of effective programs we enumerated earlier. However, by no means do all state pre-K programs—or even all of those operated in the public schools—have these features, and many of them are likely to be less effective as a result (Barnett, Epstein, et al., 2008).

CAPITALIZING ON CAPACITY IN ALL AUSPICES

One response to the circumstances we have depicted would be to provide all publicly funded preschool education through the public schools. We doubt that this would be politically possible in many states, and we do not believe it would be good policy either (Ackerman et al., 2009). Each sector has important capacity to offer, and the early childhood sector does not suffer from overabundant resources. Instead, we propose that public schools become the hub of a system that links and supports programs from all auspices to serve young children and families. At the local level, this approach has been pursued by the Schools of the 21st Century model (Finn-Stevenson & Zigler, 1999). A similar statewide model is New Jersey's Abbott program, in which districts contract with private and Head Start programs to deliver services at the same standards as the public schools, employing certificated teachers paid at public school scale (Frede et al., 2007). State and local boards of education provide governance.

New Jersey's Abbott Preschool Program is offered to 3- and 4-year-olds living in 31 of the state's poorest school districts. About two thirds of children are served in private child care centers and Head Start. The education program is funded entirely by the state at about $11,000 per child (the state tops up funding for Head Start–eligible children enrolled in Head Start). There is considerable variation across districts in the extent of contracting. In large districts making extensive use of this approach, parents can have substantial choice among private providers. All participating providers are held to the same program standards and expectations for what children should learn after enrollment. Teachers also receive the same professional development and technical assistance (Barnett, Epstein, et al., 2008).

The Abbott program operates 5 days per week, 6 hours per day during the academic year. However, providers can receive additional funds from the state's Department of Human Services to offer extended-day and extended-year services. Children also receive breakfast, lunch, and a snack, as well as access to health services and vision, hearing, health, and developmental screenings. Although many private programs were of poor quality prior to participation, after several years private provider quality equaled that in public schools (despite increased quality there as well), and the quality of both sectors was high and producing substantial educational gains (Frede et al., 2007, 2009).

An obvious advantage of this mixed-delivery model is the opportunity to provide for much more choice (and competition) than is typical of the public schools. In preschool, this includes more convenient locations and teachers with greater knowledge of the child's home language and culture (Howes, James, & Ritchie, 2003). The need for more linguistic and cultural capacity is substantial and growing (Garcia, Arias, Harris Murri, & Serna, 2010). In New Jersey Abbott context, diversity was preserved by providing scholarships and guidance so that those already teaching in child care could acquire the degrees and early childhood certification required by public education and by providing higher pay and benefits once they completed these requirements (Ryan & Ackerman, 2005). Master teachers employed by the districts provided substantial in-service training to all teachers, facilitated by the use of a single curriculum in each district.

CONCLUSION

The complex nonsystem of federal, state, and local government programs that support public and private providers of early care and education services is far from optimal. Replacing all of the existing programs with a single approach is highly unlikely (Kingdon, 1995). When examined through a capacity lens, using all three auspices to provide preschool education would appear to increase the chances of realizing high rates of enrollment, meeting children's and parents' needs, and raising the quality of all three auspices. Yet, this can only happen if they are somehow brought together under a single governance system. We propose to use the existing public schools for this purpose. An alternative approach would be to form interagency councils and give them the task of coordination. We would not expect this approach to work, as fully independent agencies compete for control and resources.

The approach we suggest will not be easily implemented. Private providers and Head Start centers are accustomed to a much greater degree of financial, programmatic, and administrative autonomy. Public schools are used to more direct command and control. They will have to learn to be supportive partners, albeit partners with the authority to dismiss programs that fail to perform adequately over several years. We believe that negotiated contracts between them are likely to lead to favorable, if initially uncomfortable, circumstances all around. Policy makers will have to resist the temptation to permanently exempt private providers from higher standards that apply to the public schools and will have to pay for everyone to attain those standards. The higher cost is the major stumbling block. In return, taxpayers will get better results for children.

CHAPTER 24

Applying Choice-Based Multivenue Education Concepts to Preschool Education

Daniel E. Witte

Advocates of choice-based multivenue precollege education face a constant challenge. A system of that kind has not been available to the general public in the United States on a widespread basis since about the mid-19th century. Modern Americans struggle to contemplate a lifestyle that has generally faded from the contemporary collective memory.

The available body of data and recent historical experience in education seem much better suited to demonstrate what approach does *not* work—a compulsory government monopoly in education—than to prove what precise approach actually does work as a refined proactive systemic solution. Yet for the United States to reverse disturbing educational trends and avoid national diminution on the world stage, it must somehow effect bold change in a policy arena where the political dynamic favors inertia and persistent gradual decline.

In this chapter, after a broad-brush depiction of a conceptual Jeffersonian system of choice-based multivenue precollege education, I discuss specific application of the general concept to the early education and Head Start context. I then identify three fault lines between proponents and opponents of choice-based multivenue approaches, as such pertain to any discussion about the advantages and disadvantages of choice-based multivenue early childhood education.

A CONCEPTUAL JEFFERSONIAN SYSTEM OF CHOICE-BASED MULTIVENUE PRECOLLEGE EDUCATION

In a very general sense, many advocates of educational choice simply believe that American precollege education (early childhood education, elementary education, and high school education) ought to be handled like modern American higher education (colleges, universities, trade schools, community colleges). In other words, at every stage of development, families and students of all demographic backgrounds should have reasonable access to government schools, private schools, religious schools, and home education or self-education (including apprenticeships). Parents should enjoy the freedom to select the best option(s) for their own children from a complete menu of alternatives.

Currently, educational choice is reliably available only to the rich elite—including many government officials who support compulsory attendance at government institutions for every child except their own. But with surprisingly simple changes to existing government schemes, meaningful educational choice could be extended throughout society, including demographic minorities and the economically disadvantaged.

Most policy makers are at least vaguely familiar with the operational schemes of private schools, religious schools, and home schools. But few policy makers—or even academics—have considered how government public schools could operate in the Jeffersonian tradition alongside the private educational options.

Thomas Jefferson advocated a system of tax-subsidized government public schools to provide a ladder of opportunity for people of all economic classes (Witte, 2010a). However, Jefferson's support was sustained only if such schools actually operated in a manner somewhat akin to the modern public library or modern voluntary community education program—as a community resource available for purely voluntary use. Jefferson also believed that tax-subsidized schools should be collectively controlled by the local parents of the children attending each particular school—imagine parents as

The author acknowledges research assistance and feedback from Donald E. Witte, M.S.W. The author also acknowledges valuable feedback and research leads from the following reviewers: Bryce Christensen, Ph.D., Professor of English, Southern Utah University; Allison Cowgill, Head Reference Librarian, Fresno State University; William C. Duncan, Esq., Director, Marriage Law Foundation; Paul Mero, President, Sutherland Institute; Derek Monson, Manager of Policy, Sutherland Institute; and Stan Rasmussen, Director of Public Affairs, Sutherland Institute. A presentation of material in Chapter 24 with extended detail and endnotes is available; see Witte (2010a).

shareholders of a public corporation, directly electing all of the corporate directors each year—and not by federal, state, municipal, or special governmental authorities. Schools were to be a resource made available on a wholly voluntary basis. Compulsory education, compulsory attendance, legal coercion, and abrogation of parental custody or control of a child were utterly unacceptable to Jefferson. Any attempt to standardize education or obtain a uniformity of worldview in the population was also viewed to be inappropriate. Finally, Jefferson believed that education and law should operate through families and parent–child relationships, and not in subversion of them.

Modern Jeffersonian government schools, borrowing some inspiration from Benjamin Franklin's mostly enlightened attitude toward the education of minorities (Ryan & Cooper, 1998; Witte, 2003, 2009, 2010a), would be subject to strict antidiscrimination laws. Disclosure laws, fiduciary laws, safety laws, dress codes, and discipline standards would apply. Admission guidelines would be designed to provide a safety net and open-door option somewhere in the government system for all noncriminal, nondangerous children.

Ideally, it would be possible for students to attend any government school at any geographic location in the same state, provided that open slots remained after all children in the local geographic area had been afforded a preferential opportunity to apply. Government schools and private schools would negotiate voluntary transfer-of-credit agreements for academic work. Cooperation with regard to extracurricular competitions would often occur. Government schools would ideally also be required to admit otherwise-qualified local athletes into cost-intensive sports, music, and extracurricular programs, unless the government school could prove that a separate program of equivalent quality (using standards similar to those for Title IX) had already been adequately tax funded for the exclusive use of private, religious, and home education students. Government schools would ideally permit part-time or mixed enrollment.

State governments would determine how much of a (per-pupil) state government subsidy to provide to each student for schooling, much like the current system. States might opt to fund schools uniformly through the state budget, use a system of local property taxes or other revenues, or use a combination of funding sources. If the federal government provided any funds at all for precollege education—and many advocates of choice oppose any form of federal involvement in education—the federal government could provide such supplementary funds in a formulaic multivenue manner analogous to the college Pell Grant program.

Any per-pupil expenditure from the state and federal governments would be equal in amount for all similarly situated students, regardless of whether they attended a government, private, religious, or home school. In order to optimize privacy, orderly administration, and educational flexibility, parents in most states would use their state and federal tax returns to claim the children's educational subsidies in the form of a refundable tax credit (analogous to the earned income credit). Refundable tax credits would be preferable to less desirable but still plausible and beneficial choice approaches that merely involve vouchers, grants, scholarships, or tax deductions. These alternative funding approaches tend to dilute the equal benefit effect, implicate more difficult legal issues, and facilitate government–school harassment of competitors.

Taxpayers would be required to submit a form or affidavit to claim the refundable tax credit, analogous to the system already in place for claiming college tuition expenses on federal income tax forms. Submission of false documentation would expose a taxpayer to prosecution for tax fraud and any other additional penalties prescribed by law.

By law, any nongovernmental educational program could entirely opt out of any participation in a government-sponsored tax credit choice program. A nongovernmental program would also have the option of requiring additional tuition for enrollment.

THE CONCEPTUAL IDEAL SYSTEM OF CHOICE-BASED MULTIVENUE PRECOLLEGE EDUCATION AS SPECIFICALLY APPLIED TO EARLY CHILDHOOD EDUCATION

In its current form, Head Start and most state-funded prekindergarten (pre-K) systems (referred to in this chapter as early childhood education) are multivenue programs, because they are hosted by local public, private nonprofit, or private for-profit agencies and created with a wide variety of membership delineations, including a wide variety of geographic locations and boundaries. In many respects, some early childhood education programs such as Head Start afford transparency. Early childhood education is not currently imposed on families by compulsory attendance laws. However, the Platonic design (Witte, 2003, 2009, 2010a) of Head Start and some state-funded pre-K systems do not afford choice because parents of participants are not the ultimate arbiters of critical program characteristics, including political philosophy, funding allocation, pedagogy, personnel selections, institutional evaluation criteria, participant performance criteria, curriculum, institutional termination, and so on (Head Start Statute, 2009). Instead, all of these aspects are ultimately dictated by federal and state statutes, regulations, and administrations. Head Start and some state-funded pre-K systems have some organizational features designed to facilitate input from parents, community leaders, state governors, and tribal leaders, but nothing approaching Jeffersonian direct control or subsidized opt-out substitute choices for parents.

Conceptually speaking, many advocates of choice-based multivenue precollege education would say that early childhood education should be managed consistent with the general Jeffersonian principles outlined above. If there was to be any government-subsidized early education at all—and many choice advocates would strenuously insist that no such programs should exist at either the local or (especially) federal level—parents would be able to choose from a wide variety of approaches and programs. Parents who wished to stay home with their own child for home education during the early childhood phase would not suffer government-sponsored discrimination (Dutcher, 2007; Gardenhire, 2007; Witte, 2010a; Witte & Mero, 2008). Such parents would instead be entitled to the same amount of funds as those parents who chose to outsource child raising to government, private, or religious institutions (Oklahoma Senate Bill 861, Sec. 8, 2007; Oklahoma Tax Commission Chapter 50, 2009).

Educational innovation is best accomplished through the FARM approach—Flexibility through reduced regulation, Accountability through absolute collective parental ability to hire and fire school principals, Representation through direct and total parental control over selection of all organizational trustees, and Modularity allowing students to transfer between programs or institutions (Witte, 2010b).

ADVANTAGES AND DISADVANTAGES OF CHOICE-BASED MULTIVENUE EARLY CHILDHOOD EDUCATION

The advantages and disadvantages of choice-based multivenue education are numerous and fiercely disputed. Rather than attempting an exhaustive list or discussion of all advantages and disadvantages, this chapter concludes with a brief examination of the three most important fault lines between those in the universal compulsory government institution camp (universalists) and those in the multivenue choice camp (choicers).

Choice Promotes Ordered Liberty and Constitutional Compliance

Universalists often prefer to imply—unsuccessfully to this point—a right to education into the federal constitution or federal law (*San Antonio Independent School District v. Rodriguez,* 1973). They believe federal involvement is necessary to ensure universal protection of this right and to facilitate universal access to educational benefits (Ripple, Gilliam, Chanana, & Zigler, 1999).

Many critics of universalists believe that federalized education is unconstitutional because—in contrast to, for example, the U.S. Postal Service, the U.S. Navy, or the U.S. Patent and Trademark Office as mentioned in Article I, Section 8—the Tenth Amendment reserves power over education to the states or (in certain respects) only to the people. From a structural standpoint, these critics believe that the federal government lacks legitimate authority to engage in revenue sharing between states or regulate education.

Moreover, many critics of universalists also raise concerns invoking constitutional provisions designed to limit the government's ability to infringe on individual liberties. These critics believe that the captive audience paradigm is inherently unconstitutional because students are coerced without parental consent into conditions of physical confinement and informational servitude. The captive audience concept violates, among other things, various provisions in the federal constitution, including the First, Third, Fourth, Fifth, Ninth, Tenth, Thirteenth, and Fourteenth Amendments, as well as Article I, Section 9 and Article IV, Section 2, Clause 1 (Witte & Mero, 2008).

Ultimately, this first fault line concerns differing perspectives about the proper role of government, the proper definition of liberty, and the proper application of the rule of law. It is a matter of legal and political philosophy.

Choice Accommodates and Facilitates Desirable Diversity in Demographic Background, Pedagogy, Economic Behavior, and Biological Behavior

The second fault line consists of issues related to healthy civic community: the proper definition of community, the relative importance of pluralism, the need for diversity, the competing interests of various individual and institutional interests, and the proper balance between national, community, and individual interests.

Advocates of compulsory government education tend to favor a worldview that stresses collectivism, central government planning, common identity, paternalistic oversight, uniformity, social engineering, regimentation, de facto economic monopoly, and imposed assimilation. In various other writings, the author has documented through historical review that such an approach is ultimately inimical to individual well-being, incompatible with personal liberty, economically inefficient, socially divisive and destructive, oppressive to demographic minorities, inclined toward corruption and exploitation, and susceptible to widespread human rights abuses needed to maintain social control. These abuses have on various historical occasions included mass confinement, forced relocation, ethnic cleansing, sexual and physical abuse, informational servitude, property seizures, child abduction, and homicide (Mero & Sutherland Institute, 2007; Witte, 1996, 2009, 2010a; Witte & Mero, 2008).

To the extent that a national government education system produces temporarily tolerable results in any locality, satisfaction tends to be manifest in compact jurisdictions that are overwhelmingly demographically homogenous. Japan, Korea, Singapore, Taiwan, Hong Kong, and Nordic nations of Europe are examples of places where traditionally regimented government education has produced high student achievement with relatively harmonious homogenous populations—although many of these countries are gradually adopting multivenue approaches (Delaney & Smith, 2000; Witte, 2010a). Indeed, the United States once had a homogenous educational environment dominated by Caucasian Protestants, which was artificially maintained by excluding or suppressing various demographic minorities. The current U.S. government school system was built on the conversion-by-the-sword pedagogical foundation created by General Richard Henry Pratt and his contemporaries in the latter half of the 19th century (Witte, 1996, 2009, 2010a; Witte & Mero, 2008). Pratt's penological paradigm—a coerced, captive audience of reticent school children and parents—has continued to derogate America's core constitutional values without interruption, although the imposed worldview of government education is now secular rather than sectarian.

Choice-based education is the only viable long-term strategy for a contemporary American society with breathtaking demographic diversity. Attempts to coerce uniformity in child raising and education in a diverse society produce bitter, immobilizing political discord, not generalized academic success. Choice fosters a vibrant, diversified portfolio of child-raising practices, which encourages innovation and hedges American society against pandemic (and often iatrogenic) dysfunctions.

Practitioners of early childhood education and Head Start should carefully study the cautionary tale of General Richard Henry Pratt (Witte, 2010a; Witte & Mero, 2008). They should be disquieted by data suggesting to some researchers that African American and Latino children do not benefit from Head Start as much as children of Caucasian descent (Fryer & Levitt, 2004; Isaacs & Roessel, 2008; Stewart, 2009; Witte, 2010a). This is especially true given Head Start's special emphasis on low-income and minority populations.

Families from all backgrounds—including families from demographic minorities—should enjoy self-determination. They should be able to choose early childhood education approaches that are compatible with their own unique needs and with their own racial, religious, cultural, ethnic, philosophical, pedagogical, geographic, and vocational traditions. A true, equal, and respectful choice-based multivenue approach would provide what demographic minorities desire—without pitting minority parents squarely against majority parents—and thereby enhance the satisfaction and student achievement for all demographic sectors at all levels of child development.

Choice Optimizes the Potential of Early Childhood Education to Enhance the Academic and Emotional Well-Being of Each Individual Child

The third fault line arises because of pragmatic questions about pedagogy, student achievement, and economic efficiency. Here the issues are technical rather than abstract: What means tend to best achieve desirable empirical results for the well-being of children and society? Researchers fiercely dispute the answer to this question, including the criteria to be used and the proper interpretation of accumulated data.

The most common empirical criticisms of the federal, centralized, universalist approach to Head Start hold that the program yields only mixed, small, illusory, or very short-term positive effects; any positive effects are mostly nonacademic in nature; and any positive results are only achieved with excessive opportunity cost. Supporters of Head Start tend to dispute these assertions, often emphasizing perceived incremental academic gains or nonacademic benefits.

Head Start and many state-funded pre-K systems have been around for decades and have relatively uniform, federal and state-inspired, government-monitored designs. In contrast, existing multivenue choice programs are typically diverse in design, localized in their implementation, and longitudinally immature. (An important exception is the United States' well-regarded, well-proven, nationwide, choice-based system for higher education.) These features arguably make it more difficult to extrapolate general empirical conclusions about multivenue education for younger children. Critics of choicers assert that existing multivenue empirical data do not demonstrate clear positive results for student achievement (e.g., Lubienski & Weitzel, 2008). However, taken as a collective whole, various studies of various choice programs do seem to suggest positive results for academic achievement and civic education (Campbell, 2008; U.S. Department of Education, 2009a; Walberg, 2007; Warren, 2002; Witte, 2010a; Wolf, 2008, 2009). At a minimum, choice does not appear to inflict significant harm.

The existing early childhood education system and the various current multivenue programs share a common retrograde feature: no allowance for a bona fide independent home education option, which in turns means de facto discrimination against home educators (Witte, 2010a). This is unfortunate because academic achievement and social wellness in home education is exceptionally high, outperforming both government and private schooling in many respects (Basham, Merrifield, & Hepburn, 2007; Ray, 2009; Rudner, 1999; Witte, 2010a). Research also indicates that preschoolers raised by a stay-at-home parent usually are better off in various ways than those in child care (Bell et al., 1989; Holmes, Morrow, & Pickering, 1996; National Institute of Child Health and Human Development, 2003; Witte, 2010a). It also appears that home education works for families of modest backgrounds and helps such families overcome the potentially negative effects of certain socioeconomic factors (Basham et al., 2007). Home education produces these results with a median annual per-pupil expenditure of about $400–$599, in contrast to about $9,644 per child in government schools and about $3,500 per child in government Head Start (Basham et al., 2007; Currie & Duncan, 2009; Ray, 2009). These findings should raise questions about what could happen if home educators were afforded access to an equal share of the tax revenues allocated for education at all age group levels.

Some advocates of Head Start and pre-K believe that differences in school quality between Caucasians and minorities help to explain racial test score gaps in general knowledge and the fading benefit pattern often attributed to Head Start (Fryer & Levitt, 2004; Witte, 2010a). If this is true, a choice-based approach to early childhood education, elementary education, and high school education may provide a strategy for generating child achievement and well-being during the early education stage and then preserving a pattern of gains until high school graduation.

CONCLUSION

Because of international competition, demand for educational innovation, and new electronic distance-learning technologies, choice-based multivenue approaches will probably become increasingly important in the United States. At minimum, the choice-based trend will have to be taken into account by advocates of Head Start and other forms of government-sponsored early education. But choice-based multivenue innovation should be seen as more than a mere feature of the educational landscape. Choice-based strategies provide a potential avenue for enhancing the quality of early childhood education actually received by America's children.

PART II

The Issues

ISSUE 1

How Can Quality and Accountability in Preschool Programs Be Ensured?

STUDY QUESTIONS

- What are the key characteristics of highly effective early child care programs?

- What types of resources for parent involvement are integral to a program's success?

- Explain the primary approaches to evaluating early education systems.

CHAPTER 25

A Model Preschool Program

Edward Zigler

Bronfenbrenner's (1979) widely accepted bioecological model of human development centers on the contributions of environmental factors to directing the child's life course. These factors extend from proximal factors, such as the home and neighborhood, to more distal factors, such as national policies and world events. For practical application, the model can be distilled into four key, synergistic systems that weigh the most on a child's developmental progress and can realistically be addressed by circumscribed programs. By far the most influential system is the child's family. The other systems are health, education, and child care, where many children spend a significant amount of time before and after they reach school age. An effective preschool program should be designed to have an impact on all four of these systems to ultimately benefit the child.

The preschool model presented in this chapter is a modified version of the program recommended by Zigler, Gilliam, and Jones (2006a). To reassure myself that our model was backed by solid research and sound theory, I assessed it against three admirably comprehensive reviews of those preschool components that are clearly instrumental in enhancing child outcomes (Barnett, Friedman, Hustedt, & Stevenson-Boyd, 2009; Karoly, Kilburn, & Cannon, 2005; Nelson, Westhues, & MacLeod, 2003). I also wanted to be sure that the model was a realistic one that could be scaled up nationally and could be delivered at a cost that is not prohibitively expensive. Evidence that our program is not just wishful thinking is contained in the fact that a similar model is already in place in 1,300 Schools of the 21st Century (called Family Resource Centers in Connecticut and Kentucky, and hereafter referred to as 21C schools) operating in 20 states (Zigler, Gilliam, & Jones, 2006b).

The goal of preschool education is greater school readiness. The logical extension of this goal is better educational outcomes, which should eventually influence life success. (Of course, these results depend on factors way beyond preschool such as the quality of K–12 education and the family's support of learning.) There is wide consensus that to launch this series of achievements, the preschool program absolutely must be of high quality. Quality, however, may not be enough if children only experience the program for a short time. Although repeatedly warned, decision makers appear to remain enamored with the inoculation model in which preschool education is viewed as a magic potion. They expect a

136

small dose to produce huge benefits. This view was carried to its extreme at the birth of Head Start, which began as a 6- or 8-week summer program. This brief interlude in the life of a child was fully expected to have a dramatic impact on later life performance.

In the optimistic 1960s, the inoculation view received some scholarly legitimacy in a widely read book by Joe Hunt (1961), *Intelligence and Experience*. Hunt's position was that even minimal environmental enrichment experiences could enhance children's cognitive development. In support of his hypothesis, Hunt conducted some studies that reported large gains in developmental quotient (an intelligence measure formerly used for infants) following relatively effortless interventions. Behavioral scientists now know that cognitive development is not nearly as pliable as Hunt espoused. Poverty in particular has devastating effects on children's cognitive growth that cannot be erased by quick intervention or a short stint in preschool.

Despite the evidence (and indeed, common sense) to the contrary, the lure of the inoculation model has proven hard to overcome. Perhaps because kindergarten is one academic year long, many decision makers and education administrators have concluded that preschool should also be a 1-year program. Yet, most preschool educators have always viewed the preschool period as encompassing ages 3 and 4 years. Nonetheless, the national Head Start program and most state prekindergarten (pre-K) programs are generally offered for a half-day for 8 or 9 months. (Some Head Start children receive 2-year and/or full-day programs, as do some children in the states of Illinois and Connecticut, where public preschools enroll both 3- and 4-year-olds.) Whereas policy makers may be wedded to the shorter versions of preschool because they are less costly, these nonscientists fail to appreciate the difficulty of changing an at-risk child's developmental trajectory. This is especially true for children living in poverty, who are the focus of all of public preschools, with the exception of a handful of states that have mounted universal programs.

To effectively influence the developmental course of children in poverty, services must be intense and last long enough to make a difference. Years ago, I presented a national plan for extended childhood intervention that contains three dovetailed programs (Zigler & Styfco, 1993). The first extends from conception to a child's third birthday, followed by a 2-year high-quality preschool, succeeded by a program that carries the developmental attainments from preschool through the first three grades of elementary school. The additive effect of these segments has some scientific backing. For example, poor children who were in a home-visiting program from conception to 3 years of age and then had 2 years of preschool education demonstrated the same level of school readiness as more affluent children (Zigler, Pfannenstiel, & Seitz, 2008). This study also showed the value of the elementary school piece from kindergarten through Grade 3. Although the poor and middle-class children were equivalent at school entry, by the end of third grade the poor children had fallen behind (the classic fade-out phenomenon). In the Head Start Transition to School demonstration project, extending services from preschool to third grade resulted in quite positive findings for children living in poverty, without evidence of fadeout (Ramey, Ramey, & Lanzi, 2004). This project and the 1,300 or so 21C schools offer proof that ordinary American schools can run successful programs spanning the entire time between conception and third grade, or about 8 years of age.

Of course, poor children can be expected to profit more from extended intervention than middle-class children, whose development is not at risk and who therefore may not need the additional services. Preschool, however, is the middle piece of the intervention package and the one that middle-class parents have long deemed necessary for their children. The elements of my model preschool program are universal, designed to help children of all socioeconomic levels prepare for kindergarten and beyond. A consensus exists that all of America's students should have better academic performance. Barnett, Brown, et al. (2004) have pointed out that the achievement gap between middle-class and poor children is approximately the same magnitude as between upper-class and middle-class children. Although preschool may have greater benefits for poor children than for those who are more affluent, there are many more nonpoor than poor children in America. Thus the total benefits of a universal high-quality preschool program may well be greater for the middle-class children as a group than for poor children as a group. Indeed, research on the Oklahoma universal program has shown that middle-class children also profit from preschool intervention.

Even though I was concentrating on poor children alone, I unsuccessfully attempted to integrate Head Start across socioeconomic statuses in the early 1970s. My primary reason for this was the publication of the Coleman (1966) report, which showed that the educational performance of poor children is better when they are in integrated classrooms with more affluent children. Forty years later, a consistent body of evidence supports this conclusion (Bazelon, 2008; Dotterer et al., 2009; Henry & Rickman, 2007; Jung, Howes, & Pianta, 2009; Kirp, 2007; Mashburn et al., 2009; Rusk, 2006; Schechter & Bye, 2007). Oklahoma Head Start centers are not limited to enrolling children below the poverty level, which may be part of the reason why poor children in these centers have superior outcomes compared to those found for the national Head Start program. Thus the targeted approach to preschool access ignores a known determinant in improving the educational performance of children living in poverty—socioeconomically mixed classrooms.

Other arguments for the universal approach are that to maintain political support for a program, it is necessary to have a broad constituency whose voices carry weight with decision makers. Some taxpayers view programs for the poor as charity to a group they consider undeserving or beyond help. Compare that opinion with the broad support for the universal K–12 education system, which is considered essential to the future success of students and society.

I also believe that universal preschool will result in higher quality programming than will targeted preschools. Limited access is exactly the course the nation has pursued with Head Start. The result is hardly reassuring. Since Head Start began in the 1960s, only about half of eligible children have been served. Enrollment rates are even worse for Early Head Start, where only approximately 3% of eligible children and families are served. Quality improvement has taken place throughout the life of Head Start, but the program is still far from having consistently high quality across service components and across the nation. As the Oklahoma study showed, the outcomes for attendance in Head Start embedded into a universal program are more impressive than those found for Head Start in general. Better quality is surely largely responsible for this difference.

As for the content of preschool programming, I have always maintained that services must address the developmental needs of the whole child. I believe it is counterproductive to concentrate on academic performance alone, as in the George W. Bush administration's attempts to remake Head Start into a literacy program. Instead, programs must target the child's physical health and social and emotional systems in addition to cognition. These systems are synergistic, with development in each influencing development in the others. For example, a study by economists showing the close relationship between health and academic performance for African American children was showcased by the *Wall Street Journal's* economics editor (Wessel, 2009).

States seem to have resolved the 50-year-long debate between the cognitive emphasis and the whole-child approach (Zigler & Bishop-Josef, 2004) by moving their pre-K programs toward the broader orientation: "Since 2003, the vast majority of states have adopted new early learning standards or revised existing standards to make them more comprehensive" (Barnett, Friedman, et al., 2009, p. 15). In constructing their standards, the states are following the guidance of the school readiness or Goal 1 panel of the Education 2000 legislation, which originated as a joint effort by the 50 state governors and the first President George Bush. The five broad content areas recommended by the panel to affect school readiness were physical well-being and motor development, social-emotional development, approaches toward learning, language development, and cognition and general knowledge (Kagan et al., 1995). Head Start targets all these areas, and the Head Start Transition Project demonstrated that elementary schools can include these services as part of a programmatic design. Likewise, 21C schools either provide health and social services at the school site or employ a resource and referral unit to assist parents in obtaining access. Where possible, neither Head Start nor the 21C school is a direct provider of all the services a child and family may need. Instead, needs assessments are performed and participants are linked to community providers.

The social-emotional or mental health component in the whole-child approach deserves special mention. The high prevalence of mental health and serious behavioral problems in both poor and more affluent young children is well documented (Luthar & Latendresse, 2005). The problem is witnessed by the surprisingly high expulsion rate of children from preschool programs (Gilliam, 2005). This evidence indicates the need for mental health services and behavioral treatments that can help children function better in the classroom and improve pedagogical outcomes. A model preschool would have mental health consultants available to assist teachers in helping children with emotional and/or behavioral problems.

My model preschool program also includes an explicit parent involvement component. Thanks in part to Bronfenbrenner's input, Head Start's Planning Committee committed the program to working with parents and inviting their participation in the preschool education of their children. This decision was unconventional at the time but proved to be prescient. Decades of research has now indicated that the more involved parents are in their children's schooling, the better the children's educational performance (for a discussion of parent involvement at the preschool level, see Henrich & Blackman-Jones, 2006). The education establishment has generally been slow to incorporate this evidence. Preschool is the ideal place to begin because parents of such young children are likely to welcome opportunities to participate.

A continuing debate (discussed as Debate 4 in this book) is the optimal site for preschool. The previous discussion in this chapter suggests that, ideally, the preschool program should be located in the neighborhood school building. Parent involvement at the tender ages of 3 and 4 can more easily transfer to the later grades if both levels of school are in the same place. An added benefit is that placement in the school building will help preschool to be viewed as an integral part of schooling just as kindergarten is now instead of as a lesser form of education.

My model preschool program differs from more typical recommendations in one important way. In addition to providing a good quality preschool education, my ideal program also provides good quality child care. In the majority of American families today, both parents work outside of the home or there is a single parent who is the sole provider. Preschool sessions are typically only a half day, and even those that are "full day" typically end about the same time as elementary school in mid-afternoon. Furthermore, preschools commonly follow the school calendar and are closed for frequent holiday breaks and for the entire summer. This time frame simply does not match the needs of working parents. As a result, many parents place their children in child care centers or family day care homes or utilize kith and kin care rather than enroll them in high-quality preschool programs. There is much evidence that the average quality of care received in child care settings is fair to moderate; some care is so low in quality that it compromises the child's school readiness (Zigler et al., 2009). School readiness is a major predictor of the child's third-grade performance, which in turn predicts performance through the end of elementary schooling (Zigler et al., 2008). Child care, therefore, must not be overlooked as a contributor to children's educational outcomes.

To a young child, there is no difference between high-quality preschool and high-quality child care except for the length of day and year. In both settings, children learn and practice important tasks such as cognitive and motor skills, socialization, and self-control. The network of 21C schools is proof that schools can provide successful full-day, full-year programs that meet the developmental needs of children and the child care needs of working parents. In 21C schools, parents pay a fee calibrated to their income for extended-day child care services. After the preschool stage, these schools provide early morning, after-school, and vacation care for older children. With this relatively simple realignment, schools can provide all of the child care that parents need from preschool through middle school. This is not a new idea but was advanced by education leader Albert Shanker (1987) as long ago as 1970.

The highest priority item in a model preschool program is well-trained and appropriately paid teachers. A cliché in the field of developmental psychology is that human development is the story of human relationships. A child's relationships first with parents and then with teachers are strong determinants of the course of development. There is a great difference in educational outcomes when a child experiences good as opposed to inadequate teachers (Takanishi, 2009). It is therefore imperative that early childhood educators have appropriate training.

Although there is conflicting evidence about the need for lead teachers to hold bachelor of arts (B.A.) degrees, I agree with the views of Maxwell and Clifford (2006), who argued that recommending the B.A. is essentially the conservative approach. Although I have read the contrary evidence on the B.A. issue by respected scholars, I have been swayed by the pro-B.A. arguments advanced by Steve Barnett (presented in this book). I therefore recommend that the lead teacher in a preschool classroom possess a B.A. in early childhood education and the assistant teacher have at least an associate's degree or Child Development Associate certification. Ideally, both will have continuing in-service training to hone their skills and keep current with new developments in the field. Class sizes should be no more than 20 preschoolers. The National Association for the Education of Young Children (1998) has recommended staff ratios of 1:10. At the inception of Head Start, preschool classes were at a 1:5 ratio, which is better, particularly for high-risk children. Since the staff-to-child ratio weighs so heavily on the cost of the program, pragmatics lead me to concede to the 1:10 ratio.

Decision makers have not waited for the B.A. controversy to be resolved. In the 2007 reauthorization of Head Start, Congress legislated that by 2013 at least half of the lead teachers must have a B.A. degree in early childhood education or its equivalent. (This legislative demand has been made before but has been largely unfunded.) Many state pre-K programs, particularly those run by public schools, only hire teachers with B.A. degrees and certification in early childhood education. Evidence indicates they are on the right track. The Head Start program in Oklahoma serves children under the general umbrella of the state's universal preschool program. Like the rest of the public school system, lead teachers in Head Start must have a B.A. and as a result are paid more than their counterparts in more typical Head Start centers. The cognitive improvements among students in the Oklahoma Head Start programs are markedly higher than those reported in the National Impact Study for Head Start as a whole. It is reasonable to interpret these superior outcomes as due in some significant part to the better trained and better paid preschool teachers in Oklahoma (Gormley et al., 2008).

Finally, my model preschool program must include a solid accountability system based on scientifically demonstrated, reliable, and valid assessments. Although I have many reservations about the No Child Left Behind Act of 2001 (PL 107-110), I do concur with its philosophy that educators should have high standards for all the children they teach and that all programs including preschool should be held accountable for meeting their goals. Assessments must also have a feedback loop that helps administrators tweak services to correct any weaknesses the evaluations uncover and helps teachers adjust their practices to meet the needs of individual students (see Chapter 28). Evidence showing the efficacy of public preschool programs can reassure policy makers and taxpayers that their support yields value in terms of improving children's educational performance. For example, one study compared the preschool performance of children in a large number of 21C schools in Arkansas with the performance of preschoolers in high-quality non-21C schools. Children in 21C schools nonetheless achieved higher scores across a broad range of academic measures (Ginicola, Finn-Stevenson, & Zigler, 2008). In 21C schools in Missouri, parents demonstrated lower levels of stress (McCabe, 1995), which is a known contributor to child abuse and neglect. Forthcoming evidence collected by scholars at Washington University in St. Louis indeed shows that families in the 21C schools in Missouri have a marked reduction in the incidence of child abuse and neglect.

Future research may offer cause for me to alter the structure of the model preschool program presented in this chapter. At this place in time, I feel comfortable recommending a model that offers high-quality comprehensive services, invites parent participation, is universally accessible, is responsive to the child care needs of children and their families, and is accountable in terms of child outcomes. Not all the expert contributors to this book agree with me on all these counts. They may ultimately be proven right. I remain an empiricist: Just as research findings to date contributed to the formation of my model, future research may reveal that certain components should be added, subtracted, or modified. Until that research is in, the model presented here will offer children a sound preschool experience that should result in better school readiness than more traditional pre-K programming. Better school readiness is the promise of preschool and our responsibility to children and taxpayers.

CHAPTER 26

How to Make Early
Childhood Programs Highly Effective

Lawrence J. Schweinhart

Many early childhood programs have been found to effectively contribute to children's development of readiness for school (Barnett, 2008). A few studies have gone a major step further to identify early childhood programs that not only effectively contribute to children's development but do so with an intensity that leads to lifetime effects and resultant economic return on investment. They include studies of the HighScope Perry preschool program (Schweinhart et al., 2005), the Abecedarian enhanced child care program (Campbell et al., 2002), and the Chicago Child-Parent Centers program (Reynolds et al., 2001).

Regrettably, several major studies of the effects of early childhood programs have found only modest short-term effects. The Head Start Family and Child Experiences Survey (FACES) study (Zill et al., 2003), the Head Start Impact study (U.S. Department of Health and Human Services, 2005), and a five-state preschool study (Barnett, Lamy, et al., 2005) found only modest short-term effects on children's literacy and social skills and parents' behavior, casting doubt on whether these programs will have worthwhile long-term effects or return on investment. For example, in the Head Start FACES study (Zill et al., 2003) and the five-state preschool study (Barnett, Lamy, et al., 2005), children were found to have gained 4 points at age 4 years on the third edition of the Peabody Picture Vocabulary Test (Dunn & Dunn, 1997), a small effect of about a quarter of a standard deviation, whereas the children in the HighScope Perry preschool program gained 8 points on the original version of this test in their first year, a medium-sized effect of about half a standard deviation (double that of 1 year of Head Start or state preschool programs) and 15 points in 2 years, a large effect of one standard deviation (Schweinhart et al., 2005). In the Head Start Impact Study (U.S. Department of Health and Human Services, 2005), the group difference was trivial, less than 2 points for 3-year-olds and even less for 4-year-olds. On the other hand, the Tulsa study of Oklahoma's universal prekindergarten program holds out promise of long-term effects and return on investment on a program serving all children regardless of income, with large effects of .99 of a standard deviation on letter and word identification and .74 of a standard deviation on spelling, as well as a medium-sized effect of .36 of a standard deviation on applied mathematics problems (Gormley, Phillips, & Gayer, 2008). The combined effect of this magnitude on literacy and mathematics skills could be sufficient to lead to long-term effects and return on investment. Unfortunately, the regression discontinuity design that identified these findings does not permit longitudinal follow-up.

For now, scrutiny of the characteristics of these highly effective programs that have identified long-term effects and return on investment offers guidance on how early childhood programs should be structured and what processes they should follow to achieve this higher standard of lifetime effects and return on investment.

All three studies found economic returns that were much greater than the initial program investment, making them a great investment for the public. Leading economists have viewed this evidence as stronger than the evidence for most public investments (Heckman, 2006; Rolnick & Grunewald, 2003). In addition, Heckman, Moon, Pinto, Savelyev, and Yavitz (2010a) confirmed the long-term effects of the HighScope Perry preschool program using rigorous statistical methods to counter methodological criticisms of the study, such as its small sample size, departures from random assignment, and testing of multiple hypotheses with the same data. Although the long-term effects in the three longitudinal studies varied, at least two of them found improvements in participants' childhood intellectual performance, adolescent school achievement, and high school graduation rates and reductions in their placements in special education, retentions in grade, teen pregnancy, and arrest rates.

These studies differed in time, place, design, and program. They began in different decades—Perry in the 1960s, Abecedarian in the 1970s, and Child-Parent Centers in the 1980s. Perry and

Abecedarian were in college towns, whereas the Child-Parent Centers were throughout Chicago. The Perry and Abecedarian studies were true experiments with random assignment of children to the program or no program and sample sizes of a little more than 100, whereas the Child-Parent Centers study looked at existing classes of some 1,500 children. The Perry and Child-Parent Centers control groups had no preschool program, whereas the Abecedarian control group had typical child care experiences. Perry preschool and Child-Parent Centers served children at 3 and 4 years of age with a part-day, school-year program and strong parent outreach, whereas Abecedarian served children from birth to 5 years with a full-day, full-year program without additional parent outreach. Abecedarian and Child-Parent Centers followed up the preschool portion of the program with school-age services, whereas Perry did not. All this variability indicates the robustness of the general claim that high-quality early childhood programs have long-term effects and returns on investment.

KEY CHARACTERISTICS

All three of these programs and studies focused on improving the development of young children living in poverty. At least two of these programs had qualified teachers, validated a curriculum, engaged in outreach to parents, and engaged in regular assessment of program implementation and children's development. Specific information below comes from the Promising Practices Network web site (2009).

Perry preschool and Child-Parent Centers used state-certified teachers, whereas Abecedarian teaching staff had a range of educational backgrounds. Perry preschool teachers were state certified in elementary and special education. Four such teachers served a class of 20 to 25 children age 3 and 4 years, with the number of children depending on the school year. The Child-Parent Centers were staffed by early childhood–certified teachers and aides, with 8 children per teacher. Each school had three full-time administrative teachers and a lead teacher. The Abecedarian project teaching staff had professional backgrounds ranging from paraprofessional to graduate degrees in early childhood education, all with extensive experience working with young children. Twelve teachers and aides each worked with 3–6 children in the nursery, depending on children's ages. The Perry and Abecedarian projects testify to the value of having teachers with bachelor's degrees in early childhood education, whereas the success of the Abecedarian project shows that close supervision can enable teachers without bachelor's degrees to provide a highly effective program.

Each of the three programs used a systematic curriculum that was validated by the evidence found in the studies themselves. The Perry preschool program used the HighScope curriculum, in which children are recognized and treated as active learners who learn best from activities that they plan, carry out, and reflect on. The Abecedarian program presented the LearningGames child development activities (Sparling & Lewis, 1981) for children up to age 3 and used several standard preschool curricula focusing on communication skills after age 3. The Child-Parent Centers prescribed a literacy curriculum and a specific learning style in other subject areas. The Child-Parent Centers focused on a variety of activities, including individualized and interactive learning, small-group activities, and frequent teacher feedback. Perry preschool and Chicago Child-Parent Centers engaged in extensive outreach to parents, and Abecedarian engaged parents in child care. The Perry program involved parents as partners with teachers through weekly home visits to discuss their children's developmental progress and occasional group activities. The Chicago Child-Parent Centers required parent participation involving volunteering in the program a half-day each week. The Abecedarian project required the style of parent involvement that is essential to providing quality full-day, full-year child care throughout early childhood.

By virtue of the longitudinal studies in which they were embedded, all three programs included extensive assessment of children's development. Although they did not engage in systematic data collection on program implementation, the fact that they were model programs virtually guaranteed that their program implementation was subjected to close scrutiny. All three of the studies collected extensive data on children's intellectual development during their early childhood years. In the Perry and Abecedarian projects, the program leader was also the research leader, thereby providing the program teaching staff with considerable focus and feedback regarding the success of their teaching efforts in improving children's intellectual and social performance.

APPLICATIONS

What would it take for all early childhood programs to become highly effective—that is, to have long-term effects and returns on investment? The evidence presented in this chapter suggests that they would all need qualified and/or well-supervised teachers, a validated curriculum, outreach to parents, and regular assessment of program implementation and children's development. What stands in the way of achieving these characteristics in Head Start programs, school prekindergarten programs, and child care programs?

The central issue is the lack of teacher qualifications. It has been estimated that only 33% of center teachers and 17% of family child care providers have a bachelor's degree or higher (Burton et al., 2002). Lack of credentials follows from low pay: The average hourly wage for U.S. preschool teachers (excluding special education) in 2008 was only $11.48 (U.S. Bureau of Labor Statistics, 2009). The gap between professional recommendations and government regulations regarding child care in the United States is wide. The National Association of Child Care Resource and Referral Agencies (NACCRRA, 2009) recommended that child care center directors have at least a bachelor's degree and that child care center teachers have at least a Child Development Associate credential or associate's degree in early childhood education, but only two and five states have this requirement, respectively, whereas 20 states have no educational requirement and 22 require only a high school diploma or the equivalent. NACCRRA also recommended that states require teachers to get at least 24 hours of in-service training a year, which 5 states do, but 14 states require no more than 10 hours of training a year. As long as the government expects so little of child care teachers, it is difficult for child care directors to insist that more training and professional development are necessary.

The other key characteristics of highly effective programs are also unevenly applied in U.S. early childhood programs. Few of them now use validated educational models that have evidence of their effectiveness, partly because so few early childhood educational models have been subjected to the empirical study that would provide evidence of their effectiveness. A national survey of 400 early childhood educators conducted by Quality Education Data (2005) found that 10% of them used the validated HighScope curriculum as their primary curriculum—the same percentage found a decade earlier by Epstein, Schweinhart, and McAdoo (1996). Few early childhood programs fully engage parents as genuine partners in their children's education through frequent home visits and other meetings, as Perry and Chicago projects did. Head Start requires only two home visits a year.

Publicly funded preschool programs do have a perennial concern for regular assessment of program implementation and children's development. Head Start maintains a schedule of program visits every 3 years by an evaluation team, using a program review instrument that is comprehensive of all aspects of program operation. Assessment of children's development is required for teacher use, but Head Start's effort to collect child outcomes data nationally—dubbed the National Reporting System—was hastily conceived and terminated by Congress pending further study. Standards for children's learning are widespread in state preschool programs, and assessment of these standards is often required.

Publicly funded preschool programs such as Head Start and state preschool programs should upgrade their performance, particularly on the four characteristics of qualified teachers: validated curriculum, outreach to parents, and regular assessment of both program implementation and children's development. These improvements are within their reach. What is required is the political leadership to see them through.

Child care programs are in a more challenging situation because their resources are generally insufficient to achieve the broad standards outlined here. Clearly, no child care should harm children; ideally, child care objectives overlap and coincide with early childhood education objectives. But without a massive shift in social priorities, immediate child care objectives must be more modest: less-than-ideal caregiver qualifications, curriculum articulation, partnerships with parents, and program quality rating without child development assessment. Levels should be set at somewhat arbitrary balancing points between the tolerable and the desirable. Even as the National Institute for Early Education Research early education standards review has had some influence, the NACCRRA child care standards review appears to have gotten little traction. That is partly because state Departments of Education recognize to some extent that preschool programs must aspire to quality to contribute to children's development, whereas state Social Services Departments, by their legislative mandates, may not be able to act on their recognition that child care programs must have a certain level of quality in order to contribute to children's development. Perhaps the lessons of highly effective programs now can only apply to these programs in broader form: that everyone who takes care of young children can and should somehow make use of the scientifically established lessons of early childhood education. Child care teachers need to be qualified, but directors must do the best they can in a market that does not pay for certified teachers. It is a challenge for providers in child care centers and homes to secure the in-service training and program implementation assessment they need to use validated curriculum models as they should be used. National commissions worry that publicly funded preschool programs do not give adequate attention to teacher training in literacy or mathematics (e.g., National Research Council, 2009), while the discussion in state child care agencies is whether the meager number of hours of in-service training permits attention to anything other than children's health and safety. It is difficult to build outreach to parents into programs that serve children whose parents' lives are filled with their employment demands. And how do you assess program implementation and children's development in programs run by providers with little preparation? A massive shift in public priorities is critical to the future of child care in the United States, but until then, early childhood professionals have to do the best they can.

There is a large lesson here about the role of science in politics. Program developers have developed model programs that have been validated by scientific research. In addition to the three mentioned here, David Olds has developed nurse home visit programs that have been found to have similar long-term effects and return on investment (Olds et al., 2004). But as these programs scale up to widespread use, they enter into the political arena, in which many parties have an interest, so that maintaining the vision of any single party—even one with evidence of long-term effects and return on investment—becomes a problem. This principle applies at various levels. For example, some see the purpose of Head Start as contributing to children's development of school readiness, whereas others see it as a means for families to become empowered. Some want children to develop reading skills, whereas others want them to develop in broad cognitive, social, and physical domains. Some teachers see themselves as professionals, whereas others do not. Any single vision of what an early childhood program must accomplish must contend with all these conflicting interests. Even with the strongest scientific evidence, a particular vision of what ought to be done requires powerful, steadfast political support to go very far. Then there is the challenge of validating the vision not only in its original form, but also in the forms that result from its interaction within the political arena. Otherwise, all that remains is the false promise of early childhood programs that do not achieve their potential and the sad knowledge of what might have been. Early childhood professionals need to secure the potential of model early childhood education for all the children who need and deserve to realize its potential and their own.

CHAPTER 27

Why the Child-Parent Center Education Program Promotes Life-Course Development

Arthur J. Reynolds and Cathy Momoko Hayakawa

The positive effects of high-quality preschool programs are well established. Whereas the evidence began to be documented in the 1960s, the amount, quality, and breadth of knowledge have culminated in a high level of confidence that program participation enhances children's cognitive, social, educational, and behavioral outcomes. Although recent research syntheses attest to the volume of evidence for a variety of programs (Burger, 2010; Camilli et al., 2010; Manning, Homel, & Smith, 2010; Reynolds & Temple, 2008), research has increasingly revealed that large-scale programs implemented within public service systems can yield beneficial effects. State-funded preschool programs and other large-scale public programs have been shown to promote school readiness and achievement

(Gilliam & Zigler, 2001; Karoly et al., 2005; Reynolds & Temple, 2008). Other studies also found that not just children at risk benefit from preschool but also children from middle-class families and those at lower risk of school difficulties (Gormley et al., 2005; Zigler et al., 2006a).

Two other dimensions of evidence on the positive impacts of preschool are the breadth of identified effects, which span cognitive, educational, and social and emotional learning, and the length of program impact, which extends well beyond early childhood and into adulthood. Preschool participation has been found to reduce the need for remedial education, reduce delinquency and crime, and promote school completion and economic self-sufficiency (Campbell et al., 2002; Reynolds et al., 2007). Finally—and most consequential for public policy—preschool participation can lead to high rates of economic returns. For every $1 invested in high-quality programs, $3–$17 are returned in social benefits ranging from reduced treatment expenditures and increased economic well-being and health behavior (Reynolds & Temple, 2008; Reynolds, Temple, White, Ou, & Robertson, 2011). These returns substantially exceed most other social programs.

PRINCIPLES OF EFFECTIVENESS

Given the strength of evidence on the positive effects of preschool programs and high economic returns, how and why early education programs can substantially improve life-course outcomes are critically important for research and public policy. In many respects, the goal is to identify key principles of effectiveness, which if followed consistently strengthen the effects of programs and make it more likely that demonstrated impacts from evidence-based programs can be used to generalize to larger populations of participants. They also provide guidelines for funding and increasing program quality.

In the rest of this chapter, we discuss the key principles and elements of effectiveness of the well-known Child-Parent Center (CPC) Education Program. This large-scale evidence-based program has been implemented since the late 1960s in the Chicago Public Schools. Although the principles are likely to generalize to other programs and intervention approaches, there are many reasons for the focus on the CPC program. First, the program has a long record of successful implementation. As the second oldest federally funded preschool program (after Head Start), the CPC program was established in Chicago schools in 1967 and has served well over 100,000 children from low-income families. Second, CPC is a sustained public school program. Key elements of effectiveness are more likely to generalize to state-financed and other large-scale programs that serve millions of children nationwide. Third, the CPC program offers a unique blend of child education and family support services. From the beginning, there has been a consistent focus on school readiness and performance in language arts and math as well as intensive parent involvement in children's education. Fourth, and most important, the CPC program has been extensively researched and has demonstrated enduring effects on life-course development in multiple domains of functioning from improved school readiness and performance to higher educational attainment and economic well-being as well as lower levels of child maltreatment, delinquency, and crime. These impacts also translate into high economic benefits—a return of $11 for every dollar invested (Reynolds et al., 2011).

HISTORY OF THE CHILD-PARENT CENTER PROGRAM

The 1960s was a time of great social change. This was especially evident in central cities as social unrest due to poverty and unequal access to social and educational services spurred a community action movement that created new systems of funding. The Chicago Fact Book Consortium (1995) described the changing and debilitating social conditions of a typical CPC neighborhood:

> Between 1970 and 1980, the population decreased significantly by 30%.... This change was accompanied by a drop in housing units of 28%.... Unemployment rose from 8 percent to nearly 21 percent. At the same time, the number of families living below the poverty line increased from 24 percent to 36 percent and female-headed households doubled to 58 percent.

The CPC program was established in 1967 through funding from Title I of the Elementary and Secondary Education Act of 1965 (PL 89-10) to counteract through educational enrichment the negative effects of poverty and promote academic success. Throughout its history, the 25 CPCs were located in the 20 poorest city neighborhoods. Five of these six neighborhoods have at least one

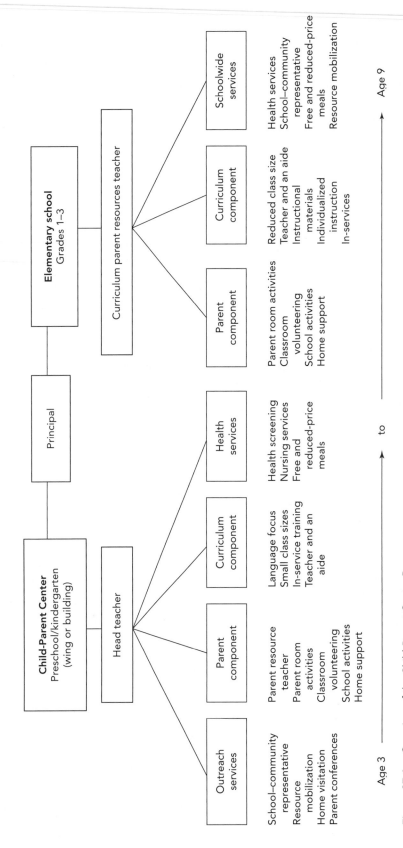

Figure 27.1. Overview of the Child-Parent Center Program.

CPC. Program children were significantly more economically disadvantaged than children in the rest of Chicago. CPC children attended schools, for example, in which 67% of children resided in low-income families compared with 42% for all children (Reynolds, 2000).

PROGRAM DESCRIPTION AND IMPACTS

The CPC program provides comprehensive educational and family support to economically disadvantaged families. The core principles are its school-based structure, emphasis on literacy, and strengthening the family–school relationship. The program has a strong literacy curriculum, in conjunction with approaches to develop other social and emotional development. Similar to grade school, the CPC program focuses on an array of activities, including individualized learning, small-group activities, and frequent teacher feedback. To maximize individual learning opportunities, preschool class sizes are small, and each classroom has a teacher's aide in addition to a regular classroom teacher. The average teacher-to-child ratio is 1:8. This small class size enables an individualized approach to cognitive and social development. The combined literacy and child-focused program within a developmentally appropriate ecological framework is central for promoting child well-being. The program is also unique in that preschool through third-grade services are run by a single school site under the direction of the Head Teacher (see Reynolds, 2000; Reynolds & Temple, 2008). Figure 27.1 shows the program components of the CPC program over ages 3–9 years.

Research on the effectiveness of the CPC program is based on many cohorts of graduates and a diverse set of studies (Reynolds, 2000). The primary one is the Chicago Longitudinal Study (2005), an ongoing prospective study of a complete cohort of 989 children born in 1979–1980 who graduated from kindergarten in 1986 in 20 CPCs, as well as a matched comparison group of 550 children of the same age who attended publicly funded full-day kindergarten in five randomly selected schools and in schools serving the CPC program. The comparison group enrolled in the typical early childhood programs available for low-income children, including Head Start.

Table 27.1 shows that the performance of CPC preschool participants consistently exceeded that of the comparison group at the beginning of kindergarten and into adulthood for a wide variety of indicators of well-being, including cognitive skills at school entry, school achievement, need for remedial

Table 27.1. Effects of preschool participation in the Child-Parent Centers

Domain and measure	Preschool group (n = 950)	Comparison group (n = 523)	Difference	Effect size
School achievement/performance (%)				
Met national norm on cognitive composite at age 5	46.7	25.1	21.6*	0.59
Met national norm on reading achievement at age 14	35.0	22.0	13.0*	0.38
Grade retention by age 15	23.0	38.4	−15.4*	−0.37
Special education by age 18	14.4	24.6	−10.2*	−0.45
Child maltreatment (%)				
Any indicated abuse or neglect from ages 4 to 17	9.9	17.4	−7.5*	−0.35
Any out of home placement	5.2	8.5	−3.3*	−0.25
Juvenile arrest by age 18				
Petition to juvenile court (%)	16.9	25.1	−8.2†	−0.29
Number of petitions to juvenile court	0.45	0.78	−0.33*	−0.30
Educational attainment by age 25				
High school completion (%)	79.7	72.9	6.8*	0.23
Highest grade completed	12.08	11.80	0.28*	0.22
Completed .5 credits at a 4-year college (%)	10.9	7.1	3.8*	0.25

(continued)

Table 27.1. *(Continued)*

Adult crime by age 26				
Any felony arrest (%)	13.3	17.8	−4.5*	−0.19
Number of felony arrests	0.32	0.44	−0.12*	−0.21
Health and mental health (%)				
Reported any depression symptom	12.8	17.4	−4.6†	−0.20
Substance misuse	14.3	18.8	−4.5*	−0.19
Daily tobacco use	17.9	22.1	−4.2	−0.15
Health insurance by age 26	76.7	66.6	10.1*	0.30
Economic status		−		
Number of months of food stamps, ages 18–24	17.50	18.78	−1.28*	−0.21
Occupational prestige by age 24	2.79	2.55	0.24*	0.22

*$p \le .05$. †$p \le .10$.

Note: Effect sizes are in standard deviations. Dichotomous outcomes were converted using the probit transformation. The sample size for the preschool intervention measures ranges from 1,281 for school remedial services to 1,539 for the cognitive composite. National norm is for the Iowa Tests of Basic Skills (http://www.education.uiowa.edu/itp/itbs/). The sample sizes for adult crime by age 26 are provided. Coefficients are from linear, probit, or negative binomial regression analysis. Coefficients are adjusted for the eight indicators of preprogram risk status, gender, race/ethnicity, child welfare history, and a dummy-coded variable for missing data on risk status. Sample comparisons are based on published studies whenever possible. Occupational prestige ranges from 1 to 8, with 4 indicating moderate prestige. The measure of occupational prestige is based on ratings from Davis et al. (1991) and a scale developed by Barratt (2005).

education, high school completion, delinquency and crime, substance misuse, and adult economic well-being (see Reynolds, Rolnick, Englund, & Temple, 2010; Reynolds et al., 2007). Although effect sizes varied by outcome, most were above 0.20 standard deviations, which translate to substantial social benefits (Reynolds et al., 2011).

NINE PRINCIPLES OF EFFECTIVENESS FOR LIFE-COURSE BENEFITS

The demonstrated effects of program participation are primarily due to nine program elements and principles. A summary is provided in Table 27.2. These principles derive from the CPC program theory and the accumulated evidence of impacts across a wide range of analyses. The principles also are generally supported by research on other preschool programs (Campbell et al., 2002;

Table 27.2. Key principles of effective preschool programs from Child-Parent Centers and other programs

Principle	Indicator	Child outcomes impacted
Focus on children at risk	Reside in low-income school areas, high family risk	School achievement, high school completion
Early timing of participation (age of entry)	Entry at age 3 or no later than age 4	School readiness and achievement, maltreatment
Sufficient duration of participation	2 or more years	School readiness and achievement, remedial education
Comprehensive services	Parent involvement, health and social services	School achievement, maltreatment, high school completion
Well-trained and well-compensated teachers	Bachelor's degree (B.A.) or certified teachers	Delinquency and crime, high school completion
Diverse and language-focused instruction	Developmental, activity-based curriculum	High school completion, delinquency, crime
High intensity	Daily contact of 2.5 hours or more, active learning	School achievement, delinquency, crime
Small classes	Seventeen children with a teacher and an aide	School achievement
Transition services (continuity)	Co-located kindergarten, school-age services	School achievement, remedial education, maltreatment

Note: Outcomes are representative and not an exhaustive list. Principles are corroborated by other studies of long-term effects and research syntheses, especially when variability in Child-Parent Center services is low or absent such as for small class size, well-trained and compensated staff, and high intensity.

Reynolds & Temple, 2008) and are consistent with principles articulated in the early childhood field (Ramey & Ramey, 1998a; Reynolds, 2003; Zigler & Styfco, 1993) and in the broader prevention science field (Nation et al., 2003). Because this focus is alterable, factors of program implementation and accountability, including evaluation research, are not included as key principles. See Reynolds and Temple (1998) and Nation et al. (2003) for discussion of the importance of accountability in program impact.

Focus on Children at Risk

This principle indicates that children at higher levels of risk deserve priority in preschool enrollment. Such an emphasis should not discourage universal access, especially in light of evidence that not only economically disadvantaged or otherwise at-risk children benefit from early education (Gormley et al., 2005; Zigler et al., 2006a). It has long been found that children at highest risk of school failure, usually because of poverty and related factors, experience larger effects of preschool than children at lower levels of risk. This is particularly the case for long-term effects (Ramey & Ramey, 1998a; Reynolds & Temple, 2008). The compensatory focus of many programs is partly responsible for this observed pattern. In the Chicago Longitudinal Study of the CPC program, children at higher levels of risk have been consistently found to derive the largest and most enduring effects of preschool. For example, Reynolds et al. (2011) found that the economic returns of CPC preschool were highest for the most socioeconomically disadvantaged children. Although less disadvantaged children benefited as well, for every dollar invested, African American males had estimated benefits of $17.88 versus $2.67 for females, children whose mothers did not complete high school had benefits of $15.38 versus $5.83 for those of high school graduates, and children experiencing four or more early childhood family risk factors had benefits of $12.81 versus $7.21 for those with fewer risk factors.

Early Timing of Participation (Age of Entry)

Across a wide range of social programs for children and youth, the earlier that participation begins (holding other attributes constant), the more likely beneficial effects will be detected. Larger returns on investment also have been found at earlier ages of participation (Reynolds et al., 2011; Reynolds & Temple, 2008). Within the preschool years of 0–5, participation by age 4 and preferably by age 3 has shown to provide the most consistent pattern of effects. Rather than a linear effect of timing such that effects of participation increase proportionally the earlier in life intervention begins, a threshold effect (participation no later than age 4) is most supported by the evidence. In the CPC program, participation can begin at age 3. Other cost-effective programs including the Perry preschool and Abecedarian projects also provide services no later than age 3. (For evidence on the impact of programs prior to age 3, see Olds, Sadler, & Kitzman, 2007; Reynolds, Mathieson, & Topitzes, 2009; Sweet & Applebaum, 2004)

Sufficient Duration of Participation

The third principle of effectiveness is program length (duration): As the number of months and years of program participation increases, so does the magnitude of effects. Most programs showing consistent and enduring effects on child outcomes are at least 9–12 months in length. The CPC program was offered beginning at age 3 so that children could participate for 2 years prior to kindergarten. Preschool length was positively associated with school readiness skills, lower rates of remedial education in the early grades, and lower rates of later child maltreatment (Reynolds et al., 2001). Moreover, the total number of years of participation of CPC preschool and school-age intervention linked to higher school achievement and well-being into adulthood (Reynolds et al., 2007). The three early education programs showing the strongest long-term effects and cost-effectiveness provided at least 2 years of service. This also was consistent for prevention programs for older children (Nation et al., 2003).

Comprehensive Services

A fourth principle of CPC effectiveness is that comprehensive family services are provided to meet the different needs of children. As child development programs, preschools must be tailored to family circumstances and thus provide opportunities for positive learning experiences in school and at home. Consistent with the ecological model (Bronfenbrenner & Morris, 1998), children with special needs or who are most at risk benefit from intensive and comprehensive services. In the CPC program, parent involvement is intensive, as each center has a parent resource room run by a certified teacher and provides school-community outreach. Parents' educational and personal development is an important program goal. Other effective programs, such as the Perry preschool and Abecedarian projects, also provided family services. The Perry preschool had weekly home visits by teachers, and the Abecedarian project provided medical and nutritional services.

Findings in the CPC program have consistently shown that the program increases parent involvement, and this involvement has been linked to long-term effects (Reynolds, 2000). These findings dovetail with the larger literature that parents' involvement in their children's schooling is an important influence on academic success. Parents may become involved in their children's schooling by providing enriched learning opportunities at home or volunteering in their child's classroom. Such involvement strengthens attitudes and values about educational success and prosocial behavior. Two indicators of involvement have been found to be particularly important for school success: parents' high expectations and participation in school (Fan & Chen, 2001; Shumow & Miller, 2001). These are a major focus of CPC and other high-quality preschool programs.

Well-Trained and Well-Compensated Teachers

A fifth principle of CPC effectiveness is that teaching staff should be trained and compensated well (preferably with earned bachelor's degrees and certification in early childhood). These characteristics are much more likely under a public school model of universal access, notwithstanding the need for established partnerships with community child care agencies. It is no coincidence that programs showing the highest economic returns—the CPC and Perry preschools—were implemented in public schools by teachers with at least bachelor's degrees and appropriate certification in early childhood. Due in part to greater training and compensation, staff turnover in school-based programs is also much lower than in other early education settings. Well-trained and well-compensated staff are also key elements of effective home visitation programs.

Evidence from the early elementary grades also suggests that higher levels of preparation, training, and experience in teaching lead to higher-quality instruction and academic performance (Greenwald, Hedges, & Laine, 1996). Support for professional development in reading instruction also has demonstrated beneficial effects (Connor, Morrison, Fishman, Schatschneider, & Underwood, 2007).

Diverse and Language-Focused Instruction

The curriculum—organization and language focus of the learning experiences—is the sixth major principle of effectiveness. The CPC program includes a combination of teacher-directed and child-initiated curricula for the purpose of promoting language and literacy skills necessary for academic success. The teacher-directed curricula approach focuses on teaching basic academic skills that lay the foundation for development in other domains. Another approach, child-initiated curricula, involves the child working independently or in small groups and selecting learning activities. Consistent exposure to the child-initiated curriculum has been associated with substantial positive long-term benefits. Both CPC children in relatively high teacher-directed and relatively high child-initiated curricula (HT/HC) and children in relatively low teacher-directed and high child-initiated curricula (LT/HC) showed significantly higher rates of school achievement, educational attainment (i.e., high school completion and 4-year college attendance), and significantly lower rates of felony arrests compared to programs without a clear indication of curriculum style (Graue, Clements, Reynolds, & Niles, 2004). Moreover, of all curricula, children in the HT/HC curriculum classrooms had the highest rates of high school completion as well as the lowest crime rates by age 24. These findings indicate that one of the strengths of the CPC program that contributes to its long-term effects is the diverse, literacy-rich, developmental instructional approach. This is consistent with findings of other programs (Schweinhart et al., 1986; Stipek, 2004).

High Intensity

Intensity refers to the frequency of classes per week and the number of contact hours per program session. The accumulated literature finds little evidence that programs meeting fewer than 4 days per week or 2.5 hours per session demonstrate consistent short-term and intermediate effects on school achievement and child well-being more generally. Long-term effects and high economic benefits have been found only for programs meeting nearly every day of the week for at least 2.5 hours (minimum of 12 contact hours). The CPC program, Perry preschool, and Abecedarian projects support this key principle. The quality of children's learning experiences including the extent of active and engaged participation also denote high intensity and the CPC program has been found to also satisfy this dimension. Of course, high intensity of instruction is more likely in small classes and in lower ratios of children to adults.

Small Classes

Preschool classes of less than 18 children or with child-to-staff ratios less than 9:1 have been found to be most associated with long-term effects and high economic returns. The CPC program has consistently maintained a maximum ratio of 17 children and 2 staff (teacher and aide). Model programs demonstrating long-term effects into adulthood such as the Perry preschool (24:4) and Abecedarian projects (12:2) had even lower ratios of children to staff. Many state-funded prekindergarten programs have class sizes set at minimum state standards of 20 children with 2 staff (teacher and aide). Although these programs have been found to demonstrate meaningful effects on school readiness and early school achievement, long-term effects and cost-effectiveness have not been found for classes of this size. Small class sizes in kindergarten and the early school-age years also have been found to promote school performance and achievement (Ehrenberg, Brewer, Gamoran, & Willms, 2001; Finn & Achilles, 1999; Krueger, 2003), although, as with preschool length, enrollment for 2 or more years has yielded the most consistent findings.

Transition Services (Continuity)

Often overlooked in the early education field, this ninth principle indicates that the provision of transition services from preschool to kindergarten and during the early school-age years can reinforce preschool learning gains and promote later school performance and achievement. Opportunities for continuous services in the first decade of life provide the optimal level of support for children's learning and development and do not presume that intervention at any stage of development (infancy, preschool, school-age) alone can prevent children from future underachievement.

The core attributes of early childhood programs as an intervention strategy have become increasingly evident as empirical knowledge is established (Foundation for Child Development, 2005; Reynolds, 2003; Reynolds et al., 2011; Takanishi & Kauerz, 2008). Early childhood programs strengthen continuity, organization, instruction, and family support services. A main focus is to enhance the capacity for the organization of services, such as integration of program components within a single site, instructional coordination, curriculum alignment, full-day kindergarten, reduced class sizes, and collaboration among staff and parents.

In the CPC program, children participating in the preschool plus school-age services were found to have higher academic achievement when compared with children receiving only the preschool or follow-on programs (Reynolds, 2000). Extended program participation (4 or more years of services) was associated with lower rates of school remedial services and delinquency infractions (Reynolds et al., 2001). At the age 24 follow-up, extended program participation was associated with higher rates of high school completion and full-time employment, and lower rates of 1 or more years of Medicaid and arrests for a violent crime (Reynolds et al., 2007). Other early childhood interventions also showed positive benefits (Reynolds & Temple, 2008; Zigler & Styfco, 1993).

Given the detrimental effects of school mobility (Mehana & Reynolds, 2004; Temple & Reynolds, 1999), transition services within an early childhood structure can provide school stability and greater consistency in learning that leads to better school achievement (see Figure 27.1). The establishment of a coordinated system beginning at age 3 and continuing through the early school grades within a single administrative system can be an effective approach for promoting continuity and consistency in children's learning. Most preschool programs are not integrated within public schools, and children usually change schools more than once by the early grades. The widely implemented school reform model, Schools of the 21st Century (Finn-Stevenson & Zigler, 1999), extends the system even further by providing prenatal to age 3 home visitation services in public schools.

CONCLUSION

Although evidence of the positive effects of early childhood programs has been widely published, key principles that underlie effective services that lead to life-course and economic benefits have received less attention. The nine principles of effectiveness from the CPC program and related early education programs provide guidelines for continued investments in preschool programs and a framework for helping to ensure that investments can provide substantial benefits many years after the preschool experience.

Our analysis indicates that greater investments are needed in high-quality programs that provide child education and intensive resources for parent involvement. Because the accessibility of high-quality preschool services is not ubiquitous, programs with demonstrative effectiveness warrant emulation. Research on the CPC program and other models suggest the key elements that provide the foundation for long-term effects and cost-effectiveness.

CHAPTER 28

Assessing Accountability and Ensuring Continuous Program Improvement
Why, How, and Who

Ellen C. Frede, Walter S. Gilliam, and Lawrence J. Schweinhart

In this age of escalating accountability and increased public investment in preschool and other early education programs, there is a clear need to design and implement accountability systems that ensure that investments in young children are well spent. Broad interest in the overlapping issues of child and classroom assessment, accountability, and program evaluation is evident in recent publications, such as the combined position statement of national early childhood organizations (National Association for the Education of Young Children [NAEYC], 2003) and the report of the National Task Force on Early Childhood Accountability (Schultz & Kagan, 2007). In addition, the convergence of interest in programs for young children and the large accountability movement are apparent in other initiatives, such as the now-abandoned Head Start National Reporting System (Tarullo et al., 2008), which required that every Head Start child be assessed at the beginning and end of the program year, and efforts by organizations such as the Data Quality Campaign to ensure that early childhood data are included in statewide child level data bases (Laird, 2009).

Policy makers, the early childhood profession, and other stakeholders in young children's lives share the responsibility to regularly engage in program evaluation (NAEYC, 2003). Prior to charting a course for program evaluation as part of an accountability system, state officials and other decision makers must consider the purposes of the evaluations and the audiences to which they are addressed (Patton, 2008). Purposes for program evaluation may vary from obtaining data to inform high stakes decisions, such as determining program funding or child placement, to measuring program quality and/or children's progress for program improvement purposes. Audiences may include policy makers, educators, researchers, and the public in general. Whatever the case, well-conceived program evaluation is a valuable source of information with which to inform decision making in what Campbell (1991) referred to as an experimenting society that strives to rigorously implement and test new initiatives.

No evaluation design is perfect; each has its own set of strengths and challenges (Riley-Ayers, Frede, Barnett, &Brenneman, 2011). Large-scale early education systems have often relied on one of five major design approaches: 1) using extant data, 2) posttest-only designs, 3) pretest–posttest designs, 4) regression discontinuity designs, or 5) randomized controlled trials (RCTs). Although using existing data is obviously fast and inexpensive, major limitations include the strong potential for selection bias; attrition in the data due to the effects of variables that preschool itself may be impacting, such as grade retention, language barriers, special education placement, and absenteeism (Barnett, 1993); and family mobility that may render the data uninterruptable (Barnett, 2006; Olsen & Snell, 2006). For example, state child assessment systems are often used for accountability, but great caution should be taken in forming conclusions about program effects using such data because of these aforementioned limitations (Nichols & Berliner, 2007).

Both posttest-only and pretest–posttest designs may somewhat reduce attrition and mobility problems, but self-selection biases remain and delayed entry to kindergarten may still impact attrition. The addition of a matched comparison group from the community and multiple measures of family background and child characteristics improves the pretest–posttest design, but this still does not fully control for selection bias.

One of the most important issues in evaluation is deciding to whom the participants will be compared in order to determine the effectiveness of the program. Comparison to matched children who are similar to attendees on key variables is far better than using unmatched comparisons or no comparison group at all, but this strategy still falls short of comparison strategies that address selection bias.

The lesser used regression discontinuity design reduces selection bias, but this method requires a large and stable sample, child assessments administered very close to the beginning of the school year, and highly specialized methodological and statistical expertise. This design depends on the ability to identify a variable that predicts group membership but is not associated with other characteristics of the children and families, such as a strict age cutoff for attendance (Barnett, Frede, Mobasher, & Mohr, 1988; Cook, 2008; Gormley et al., 2005).

RCTs directly compare children who attended the program to others who were randomly selected to not attend the program. RCTs afford a high level of internal validity, but this often comes at the expense of external validity. The internal validity of an evaluation refers to the degree of certainty one can have that positive outcomes were actually caused by the intervention itself. Unfortunately, locating programs that are able and willing to participate in a strictly implemented RCT often limits the ability to know that the findings will generalize (external validity) to other programs that were not in the evaluation. This design is very rarely used to evaluate the effectiveness of early education programs, although it offers the strongest protection against selection bias, is easier to interpret, and requires smaller sample sizes (Campbell & Boruch, 1975). Two circumstances that work well for randomization are when there are more children to serve than slots available or during a planned expansion. Of course, RCTs still can fall victim to attrition, and children assigned to the treatment group may fail to participate and those assigned to the control group may access the service or something comparable on their own. Nonetheless, without a well-implemented RCT, baseline differences between children make it difficult to know for certain how effective the program was.

DEVELOPING AN EFFECTIVE ACCOUNTABILITY AND ASSESSMENT SYSTEM

The major issues in accountability and assessment can be broadly distilled to 1) designing the accountability system to be valid and useful for multiple purposes and 2) ensuring that the assessment instruments are valid, administered reliably, and measure useful and appropriate accomplishments.

Designing for Multiple Purposes

Both the purpose of program evaluation and the intended audience(s) affect what should be measured, how it should be measured, and how the findings are presented. For example, if the legislature wants to know whether money was spent as intended, then accountability may include expenditure analyses as well as child outcome studies. For that to happen, however, it is critical that the program standards and outcomes desired already be established (Patton, 2008). If, on the other hand, the accountability question is whether the program is producing adequate child progress, then child learning standards need be agreed upon (Darling-Hammond, 2010), and the relationship between classroom implementation and child progress should be established. As discussed in Chapter 38, it is now true that effect sizes are the coin of the realm. As the collective knowledge base regarding early education has grown, the effectiveness questions have become more nuanced—from "Does it work?" to "Does it work as well as we hoped?" to "Does it work well enough to warrant the cost?"

The challenge is to develop a comprehensive system that provides information for instructional decision making and broad-scale program evaluation that is more efficient and less burdensome than separate systems for each purpose. It is easy to think of improving practice, providing accountability, and conducting program evaluations as if they were completely separate objectives. Perhaps this is because researchers tend to associate each with separate audiences (e.g., providers versus policy makers) and different levels and processes of decision making (classroom versus funding/administrative levels). Rather than thinking about these as separate objectives, it may be possible to think of them as components of one well-integrated system.

Keeping the Main Purpose in Mind The main purpose of all child assessments should be to further educational goals by informing efforts to improve the effectiveness of the services provided to children and families. Assessments may be used by teachers to make classroom- and child-specific decisions regarding educational strategies. Also, assessments may be used by administrators and other decision makers to judge the overall impact of the early education system (or parts of it) and where changes could be made to improve effectiveness. Either way, the goal is to use data to inform decisions about how to improve the educational services provided. Therefore, any early childhood assessment system—whether its focus is at the child, classroom, or larger systemic levels—should have a clearly delineated path running from the data to mechanisms for generating recommendations for clear and observable changes in educational service provision. This continuous improvement system is illustrated in Figure 28.1.

A comprehensive statewide assessment system used for multiple purposes should be multileveled and include more than child assessment data. Information needs to be gathered to inform practice at the individual child, classroom (children and teachers), program (administrator qualifications and practices, as well as other kinds of program support including coaches and parent involvement) and state level if it is to be useful for the purposes of instructional assessment, accountability, and program

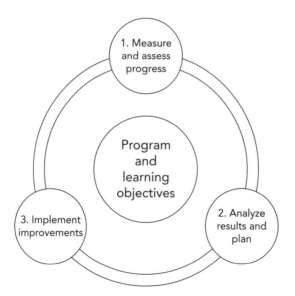

Figure 28.1. The continuous improvement cycle.

evaluation. Also, the timing of the examination of key research questions is essential. Often administrators and policy makers are anxious to determine whether an initiative is having the desired effect, but programs need time to mature before service delivery stabilizes and positive outcomes can be expected (Campbell, 1987a; McCall, 2009). Finally, appropriate evaluation often begins by developing an understanding of the landscape of early education services in a state—what programs are available, who has access, and who is attending. This should include information on who accesses programs and who leaves programs, as well as when and why.

Linking Inputs to Outcomes   In addition to establishing that the services are being used by the intended participants, treatment fidelity should be established to ensure that the program is being implemented as intended. Too often in program evaluations, treatments are labeled without any verification, what Patton refers to as "the problem of labeling the black box" (Patton, 2008, p. 142). For example, a program may report using a particular curriculum or that they are basing teaching practices on the state standards; without verification, the labels become reified. In an evaluation of a state preschool program, Frede and Barnett (1992) found that the program had beneficial effects on children's learning only after controlling for fidelity of implementation of the curriculum. In a national evaluation of implementation and effects of the Comprehensive Child Development Program, Gilliam and colleagues found marked variation in implementation across sites (Gilliam, Ripple, Zigler, & Leiter, 2000).

Implementing a process evaluation will not only ameliorate the problem pointed out by Patton but can also provide insight into the programmatic needs and the cost associated with planning technical assistance if necessary. Campbell (1987b) argued that no program should ever be evaluated until that program is proud. Once proud, a program is best measured through a process evaluation of the degree to which the program is being implemented according to its plan, with adequate levels of both quality of services and degree of participation. An important first step in such an evaluation is the explication of the program's theory of change tied to a detailed logic model that details exactly how the program is intended to impact participants in ways that lead to the desired outcomes (Unrau, 2001). In the case of early education programs, the theory of change and logic model address the questions of how the program developers believe children best learn, how the program is supposed to impact that learning, which key variables are changed along the path toward improved learning, and which variables might impact the ability of the program to achieve these outcomes (e.g., parent participation, teacher skills). As such, the logic model provides a detailed map of all of the variables worth measuring in a comprehensive program evaluation (Gilliam & Leiter, 2003).

With the rise in state-funded prekindergarten programs (Barnett, Epstein, Friedman, Sansanelli, & Hustedt, 2009) and quality rating improvement systems (National Child Care Information Center, 2007), statewide multileveled data collection efforts have become more common. Rigorously designed effectiveness studies that include information on program quality should be one aspect of a comprehensive program evaluation system once the program has reached a reasonable level of treatment fidelity. To date, the majority of state evaluations of preschool programs have been less than rigorous in terms of scientific standards, with many having such flaws that there are severe limitations in interpreting their results (Gilliam & Zigler, 2001, 2004). Table 28.1 presents elements of a comprehensive evaluation system by level, purpose, and data source and gives examples from two state systems.

Ensuring Valid and Useful Assessments

All high-stakes testing is controversial because it represents a snapshot of ability. High-stakes testing of young children is even more controversial, leading several national organizations to criticize universal standardized testing of children under third grade (NAEYC, 2003; National Association of Early Childhood Specialists in State Departments of Education, 2000; for a list of organizations, see National Center for Fair and Open Testing, 2007). Valid assessments of young children are complicated because young children are not always compliant test subjects; their skills are rapidly and unevenly developing and highly impacted by their current context and feelings. For these reasons, results may often be less

Table 28.1.   Elements and examples of multileveled prekindergarten evaluations

Level	Purpose(s)	Data source(s)	Critical elements	State examples New Jersey (NJ)	New Mexico (NM)
Child	Inform teaching for the individual child and across children Evaluate teaching effectiveness	Ongoing, curriculum-embedded individual child assessment that can be aggregated for classroom-level analysis if teachers are trained to reliability on the measure	Ongoing curriculum-embedded performance-based assessments Teachers trained to reliability	Teachers use system based on NJ learning outcomes or a curriculum-specific ongoing assessment system (e.g., Child Observation Record[a])	Teachers use systematic ongoing assessment based on the NM Early Learning Guidelines[b] to observe, assess, document, and plan
Classroom	Inform teaching Evaluate program implementation	Unstructured and structured classroom observations Field notes of coaches	Self-assessment by teaching staff within reflective coaching cycle	One coach for each 15 classrooms uses structured and unstructured observations	Mentor teachers and coaches with focus on child assessment and teaching
Program	Inform planning for technical assistance and professional development Evaluate effectiveness and efficiency	Aggregated data from child and classroom level, if the assessments are conducted reliably Fiscal and program audits	Assessors trained to reliability Element of self-assessment critical to improvement (not a "gotcha" approach)	Programs and state use the Self-Assessment Validation System Higher education consortium assesses sample of classrooms statewide Limited audits of fiscal operations	State personnel monitor programs' contract compliance and adherence with NM Pre-K Program Standards[c]
State	Inform planning for technical assistance and professional development Evaluate effectiveness and efficiency	Aggregated data from child, classroom, and program level, if the assessments are conducted reliably Research with a rigorous design that controls for selection bias and includes classroom and child assessment data Cost and benefit–cost analyses	Rigorous design over multiple years and cohorts Utilization-focused evaluation approach	External evaluation for policy and continuous improvement purpose	External evaluation for policy and continuous improvement purpose

[a] http://www.highscope.org/Content.asp?ContentId=113

[b] http://cdd.unm.edu/Ec/resources/pdfs/ECN/nm_early_learning.pdf

[c] http://www.ped.state.nm.us/earlyChildhood/d108/preK/NMPreKProgramStandards.pdf

than useful for parents and teachers, and the predictive ability of these tests may not be as high as many might expect. A lack of clarity regarding what skills are necessary for school readiness (Meisels, 1999) and the potential to misuse results to deny access to children or punish and reward programs further complicates measurement selection concerns.

In a recent policy report, Darling-Hammond (2010, p. 1) recommended that all student assessment systems should 1) address the depth and breadth of standards as well as all areas of the curriculum, not just those that are easy to measure; 2) consider and include all students as an integral part of the design process, anticipating their particular needs and encouraging all students to demonstrate what they know and can do; 3) honor the research indicating that students learn best when given challenging content and provided with assistance, guidance, and feedback on a regular basis; 4) employ a variety of appropriate measures, instruments, and processes at the classroom, school, and district levels, as well as the state level; and 5) engage teachers in scoring student work based on shared targets.

Which Measures Should Be Used?

Rather than measuring what we value, it may be accurate to say that we all too often value what we measure. Whatever is measured tends to become a focus of concern for preschool providers, policy makers, and the public. Therefore, assessment systems have the potential for driving much of what goes on in early education classes, simply by increasing the saliency of the measured areas of the curriculum relative to the unmeasured (or less well measured) areas. Also, in the absence of a clear mechanism for utilizing assessment data to create meaningfully beneficial changes in educational services at the classroom level (where they are experienced by children), it is hard to imagine any assessment system as being effective.

The effectiveness of any data collection system depends as much on how the data are used as it does on how they were collected. As with program evaluation design, the intended purpose of the assessment should determine the type of assessment being administered (Meisels, 2007). For assessment systems used by teachers for classroom learning purposes, the true test of effectiveness is whether the assessment results actually lead to changes in teaching behaviors that improve children's learning. Likewise, for assessment systems used by administrators and decision makers, the test of their effectiveness should also be whether they yield data that are used to create meaningful improvements in the educational system.

How Many Children Should Be Assessed?

Must all children be assessed, or can only a sample of children be assessed? Data collection on a representative sample of children has the merit of being quicker to obtain, less expensive, and less burdensome to collect, allowing resources to go toward more in-depth assessment, external assessors, and beefed up reliability training to improve the veracity of the data. The limitation is that data may not be useful for instructional planning and accountability at local levels because the sample sizes likely would be too small in each location. Data collection across all children has the merit of being readily applicable for local-level instructional planning (assuming appropriate measures were used by well-trained staff), but the limitation is that this is incredibly expensive in monetary cost, time, and child/staff burden. Attempts to offset the cost and time often come at the expense of the veracity of the data itself (by limiting the resources spent on external assessors, reliability training, and adequate data coding and management systems) and by reducing the amount of time spent in assessment by using tests that are too cursory to provide detailed, useful information on learning and development.

For statewide or large-scale assessment, we recommend matrix sampling, in which children are selected randomly and specific assessment domains are chosen randomly for each child. This design allows one to select the sample size necessary for valid results, while dividing between selected children the full burden of the comprehensive assessment, thus minimizing the overall child assessment burden, as well as the burden for any one specific child. To make sure that enough sample is available to form valid conclusions about children and subgroups, stratification and perhaps oversampling techniques can be used.

Who Should Conduct Assessments?

External assessors administering direct/standardized child assessment tools can generate data to improve instruction, as well as provide for accountability and program evaluation. However, that data should only inform professional development and program improvement efforts at a state or large program level. Typically, results should not be used to make inferences about the effectiveness of teachers, curricula, or other elements of instruction at the individual child or classroom level. It may provide an acceptable basis for inferences about effectiveness at the classroom level if it is part of a very rigorous design that includes random assignment of children to classrooms. At the child level, many safeguards need to be in place, and only a few specific assessment tools are comprehensive and likely to measure state standards.

Typically, it is best not to use teachers to administer on-demand tests for children. Doing so can pervert teaching and lead to incorrect conclusions—especially if teachers believe that their jobs, salaries, or programs are in jeopardy. Teacher-generated observational assessments of children's progress that are used to improve instruction can be used for accountability or program evaluation purposes only when the system implemented has proven validity that meets the same standards as those expected for standardized direct assessments of children, also known as on-demand assessments. Knowledgeable and well-prepared teachers are the best source of information about children's development, but report cards and other checklists that do not have rigorous requirements for data-based conclusions based on systematic observation and documentation over time are regularly found to be inaccurate. The primary purpose of performance-based assessment using teacher ratings is to inform teaching; these should only be used for program evaluation and other purposes when there is sufficient psychometric information to ensure that both the instrument and the administration are valid and reliable (Riley-Ayers & Frede, 2009).

The aggregated results of performance-based assessment should be used for program improvement and overall program evaluation, not for high-stakes decisions regarding teachers or programs or as the sole source of information for placement of children (e.g., referral to special education). Every teacher using the measure must be trained to an acceptable level of reliability, and methods must be in place to ensure that assessor drift does not occur in scoring over time. Finally, teachers should be provided explicit support for using the data to inform instruction.

How Should English Language Learners Be Assessed?   When constructing assessment systems, the special case of English language learners must be considered. Choice of instruments depends to a large extent on the language of instruction and the purpose of the assessment. If the teachers only speak English, then the utility for instruction of knowing more about the child's ability in the home language is limited. Assessment should be conducted in the language of instruction; thus, if the child is in a bilingual setting, bilingual assessments should be administered. If the language of instruction is English, then for program evaluation purposes, it may be appropriate to only use English assessments. In program evaluations, testing in both languages whenever feasible is recommended, although most assessments only exist in English and sometimes Spanish. Some new assessments (Ginsburg, 2008; Greenfield, Dominguez, Fuccillo, Maier, & Greenberg, 2009) can be administered bilingually— that is, the trained bilingual assessor uses the appropriate language throughout the test, responding to the child. Unfortunately, direct translations of English assessments are typically not a psychometrically sound practice (Espinosa, 2010).

CONCLUSION

Programs should perform evaluations both intensively and extensively. For intensive evaluation, the program should conduct (or contract for) a well-designed scientific study collecting data from a sample of program sites. For extensive evaluation, all program sites should collect data on program implementation and children's development. The intensive evaluation should be designed to provide valid estimates of the effectiveness of the program with sufficient precision to guide decisions about the program and should be adequately funded and last long enough for this purpose. The programwide data collection should provide data for teachers and program managers to use to improve teaching and learning. Both types of information can be used together to hold local agencies and providers accountable for performance.

Ideally, local accountability suggests that local agencies and providers contract with outside assessors or the state supplies them. Practically, local accountability is likely to be based on self-monitoring, with teachers collecting program implementation and child progress data that monitors the achievement of benchmarks with the understanding that child assessment data may only weakly support inferences about program effectiveness. If a program is effective statewide and classroom quality in a particular location is comparable to state averages, then the local program may be judged effective locally. It is an obligation to children, parents, taxpayers, and other stakeholders to ensure that programs live up to their promise and use data-based decision making to continuously improve their effectiveness. As the benchmarks set for improvement are reached, it is also imperative that standards are revised so that quality is constantly raised and programs and services for young children are constantly improved.

ISSUE 2
What Should Come Before and After Preschool?

STUDY QUESTIONS

- How can quality of relationships in the early childhood environment be ensured? What types of regulations and supports are needed?

- What are the advantages of building early intervention systems on a foundation of high-quality home-based interventions?

- Does home visitation affect future use of Medicaid and other entitlement programs?

CHAPTER 29
The Link Between Consistent Caring Interactions with Babies, Early Brain Development, and School Readiness

J. Ronald Lally

As Irving Harris, the financial and philosophical catalyst for many of America's infancy initiatives stated:

> The first days of life, first weeks, and first months are absolutely critical to optimal brain development. That is when the brain pathways that eventually lead to curiosity and empathy and trust begin to develop. That is when, in loving interaction with nurturing caregivers, babies learn that they can trust and feel loved and respected…. We must remember. The first few years of life are not a rehearsal. This is the real show. Children do not really have an opportunity to try to get it right later. (1994, p. 6)

Harris understood what the research discussed in this chapter has confirmed—the importance of early relationships. Early relationships are so crucial to the healthy development of the brain that they are—after a caregiver's meeting of basic needs for physical nurturance, health, and safety—the primary environmental ingredient for healthy brain development (Meaney, 2001).

THE RESEARCH

One of the most important discoveries of the early 21st century related to the development of the brain is the finding that the baby's social environment—particularly created together by the mother and the baby, as well as other principal caregivers and the baby—directly affect gene-environment interactions and have long-enduring effects on future development (Schore, 2005; Suomi, 2004). Of particular interest to neuroscience is the influence on development of the early maturing right brain. Beginning in the last trimester of pregnancy and continuing to about 24 months of age when the brain takes on an adultlike appearance, the right hemisphere (dominant in the experience of the emotional and corporeal self) undergoes a growth spurt before the more verbal left hemisphere (Schore, 2001, 2003, 2005; Spence, Shapiro, & Zaidel, 1996).

What the baby experiences during this period of intense right brain activity is brain growth substantially influenced by social experiences, with emotional communications between a caregiver and child indelibly shaping the brain. Specifically, the quality of the care babies' receive from their primary caregivers influences the babies' ability to successfully or unsuccessfully attach to other human beings (Sroufe, 1996), regulate their impulses, learn how to communicate with others, and search for an intellectual understanding of the world into which they are born. Research suggests that the attainment of an attachment bond, competence in emotional communication, and maturation in self-regulation abilities represent the key masteries of early infancy more so than does the development of complex cognitions (Schore, 2005). Only recently has it been learned that the early developing structures of the brain are emotional, and it is upon these emotional foundations that intellectual and language structures grow. For example, communication and language use get stimulated by the emotional need to build, sustain, and use relationships, and intellectual skills get developed to both prolong and efficiently use attachment relationships (Schore, 2001).

The process of building the brain originates in the early social exchanges between caregivers and babies. It has been established that the maturation of the neural mechanisms involved in self-regulation, which are crucial to school success, happens through the experience of critical emotion-based experiences embedded in the attachment relationship (Spence, Shapiro, & Zaidel, 1996). Early brain structures are first shaped, either positively or negatively, by the tenor of a baby's day-to-day interactions with those who are the principal providers of their care. Intellectual and language development are then stimulated by and encapsulated in early emotional development and are influenced by the first interactions babies have with their primary caregivers. Greenspan concluded that early emotional competence establishes the foundation for success in all other developmental domains and that emotional motive drives skill development in other developmental domains: "It is the pleasure and delight that babies get from interaction with people that drive them to relate to people more frequently and more skillfully" (1990, p. 17).

What policy makers and educators must understand is that learning begins in relationships, is informed by relationships, and is stimulated by relationships (Belsky & Cassidy, 1994; Belsky, Spritz, & Crnic, 1994; Honig, 1998, 2002; Shonkoff & Phillips, 2000; Sroufe, 1996). Without careful attention to the quality of the emotional and social exchanges a child experiences during the first 2 years of life, any school readiness or achievement gap intervention will be starting in the wrong place. Rather than being seen as a softer and less significant influence on school success than, for example, the early attainment of numeracy and literacy skills, the emotional foundations of development laid down during the first 2 years of life are now seen by neuroscientists as the first building blocks for learning. Emotional interactions with a familiar, predictable primary caregiver create a sense of security from which learning can take place (Dalli, 1999). A tuned-in caregiver can do amazing things: Through comforting interactions, the caregiver can minimize an infant's negative states; through interactive play, the caregiver can stimulate both positive affective states and an intellectual curiosity that fuels the child's exploration of novel environments (Edwards & Raikes, 2002; Raikes, 1993, 1996; Raikes & Pope Edwards, 2009). Skills that are crucial to success in school, including the ability to inhibit one's urges (inhibition), the ability to hold some information in mind while attending to something else (working memory), and the ability to switch attention or mental focus (cognitive flexibility), are being developed and shaped through the give and take of relationships the baby is

Table 29.1. The role of genes and experience in learning and development

Genes and their early expression play a critical factor in the development of a child's learning capacity, yet genes alone do not dictate that capacity.

Gene release is shaped by experience.

The cellular architecture of the cerebral cortex is sculpted by input from the social environment.

Early experiences with the social environment are critical to the maturation of brain tissue.

The role the adult plays in developing learning capacity is powerful.

The social environment—particularly the one created together by a primary caregiver and an infant—directly affects gene-environment interactions and generates long-enduring effects on child functioning.

Note: Information in this table is compiled from the references cited in the chapter.

engaging in during the first 2 years of life (Thompson, 2009). By age 2 years, structures in the brain have already been created, which influence how children will approach learning. Critical features such as a child's use of relationships in learning, the confidence of a child to engage in the challenge of learning, the ability of a child to persist while learning, and the alacrity to use adult models for learning have already started to take shape (Shonkoff & Phillips, 2000). That is why any serious educational policy initiative that hopes to positively influence what is now being called the achievement gap (for specially defined populations) or school readiness initiatives (for all populations) must begin with an early emotional and relational focus. Any intervention that starts later than infancy and does not pay serious attention to early emotional development will be bad policy—misdirected in thrust and compensatory in nature.

AN OPPORTUNITY

Parents, child care providers, educators, and policy makers can look to basic research for clear direction on best ways to facilitate the growth and development of young children. Research on the early development of the brain seems quite clear (see Tables 29.1 and 29.2). Efforts taken to improve the learning capacities of children should start early and start with attention to the emotional components of a child's first relationships and build from there. Regardless of whether children are cared for at home or cared for outside the home, the type of care they receive should be based on what is known about the early growth of the brain and how the foundations of learning are constructed.

THE ARGUMENT

This chapter does not propose that the infant period is the most important period of life, or that by attending appropriately to the period that some type of an inoculation will take place that makes the child invulnerable to adverse experiences later in life. What happens during the developmental periods of preschool, middle childhood, and adolescence is also very important to developmental outcomes. However, given what is known about the influence of early gene-experience interaction on the development of the brain, school readiness initiatives must change in two ways. First, these initiatives must

Table 29.2. The role of early social interaction in the growth of brain structure

Early brain growth is dependent on social-emotional experience and is influenced by social interaction.

Input from social interactions, which is embedded in early attachment relationships, sculpt the cellular architecture of the cerebral cortex.

The self-organization of the developing brain occurs in the context of a relationship with another self, another brain.

The construction of a child's first sense of self occurs through perceptions gained from caregiver–child interaction.

The early building of crucial structures and pathways of emotional functioning serve as the fundament for future emotional and social functioning and as the bedrock for language and intellectual development that follows.

Early brain growth is fueled by emotional communication and motivated by pursuit of an attachment bond.

The maturation of the neural mechanisms involved in self-regulation is experience dependent and is embedded in the attachment relationship.

Note: Information in this table is compiled from the references cited in the chapter.

start earlier than they currently do, with much more attention given to experiences that happen to children before their second birthday, in the womb, at home and in child care. Second, initiatives that do start early need to be geared to the ways babies learn and not downward extensions of successful practices with older children.

Neuroscience and developmental psychology research about early development and learning reinforces this second point. Alison Gopnik (2009), a leading researcher on infant cognition, discussed this downward extension danger while describing important differences between how babies learn in comparison to older children. According to Gopnik, adults mistakenly believe that infants learn the same way school age children do. In school, adults set objectives and goals for children and try to get the children to focus on the skills and content they should master. However, her research shows that baby learning is different: "Babies aren't trying to learn one particular skill or set of facts; instead, they are drawn to anything new, unexpected or informative" (Gopnik, 2009, p. WK10). Gopnik, Meltzoff, and Kuhl (1999) showed that infants are not very good at planned focus but are very good at the exploration of the real world objects they are interested in and interaction with the people around them. Gopnik concluded:

> Babies are designed to explore and they should be encouraged to do so. Parents and other caregivers teach young children by paying attention and interacting with them naturally and, most of all, by just allowing them to play. (2009, p. WK10)

School readiness initiative for infants should therefore reflect the babies' unique learning style and their need for relationship-based experiences.

THE RECOMMENDATIONS

The following recommended services are supported by neuroscience research to positively influence school readiness.

During Pregnancy

- *Health insurance coverage:* Because critical components of brain development are happening during this period that will greatly influence all future functioning, the healthy development of the child while in the womb needs to be supported.
- *Prenatal care and support:* The negative impact of toxins, stress, mental health problems, and the need for parents to be prepared for both delivery and parenting should be buffered by universally accessible professional and paraprofessional support during pregnancy.

After Pregnancy

- *Extended time period at home with new baby:* Because of the need for the development of attachment relationships for the early development of the brain, it is recommended that paid parental leave be available to all families with a newborn for at least the first 6 months of the child's life.
- *Primary and preventive care:* Because of the fragility of the new relationships being established between babies and primary caregivers and the possibilities for the development of early problems, the following services need to be in place: well-baby home visits, guidance for parents to support children's healthy development, developmental screenings to identify physical and behavioral needs, and special services for families in crisis.

During Child Care

Because many children will be establishing significant relationships during the first 2 years of life with caregivers outside their home who are not members of their family, child care regulations need to be put in place to ensure that care is provided in safe, interesting, and intimate settings where children have the time and opportunity to establish and sustain secure and trusting relationships with other children and with knowledgeable caregivers who are responsive to their needs and interests.

CHAPTER 30

What Should Come Before Preschool
Lessons from Early Head Start

Helen Raikes, Rachel Chazan-Cohen, and John M. Love

Although programs for 3- to 5-year-olds in the United States serve increasing numbers of children, the salience of programs designed to support the development of infants and toddlers living in poverty has waxed and waned over the years, but remains at a very low level. In the mid-1960s, and to some extent subsequently, many of the experiments to determine the potential of early intervention served infants; later, a few specialized public programs (e.g., early programs for individuals with disabilities) were instituted. However, it was not until 1994 that the Early Head Start (EHS) program was authorized, putting into place for the first time a national Head Start program for at-risk infants and toddlers and their families. Approximately 480,000 infants in low-income families receive child care subsidies from the Child Care and Development Block Grant (Matthews & Lim, 2009), although there is limited research on the effects of this subsidized care on the development of low-income infants and toddlers.

After increasing funding levels to 10% of the Head Start budget in 2001, which translated into EHS services for less than 3% of the eligible families nationwide (Center for Law and Social Policy, 2006), the program did not expand until the investment of funds through the American Recovery and Reinvestment Act of 2009 (PL 111-5). In 2010, the number of children served by this prenatal to age 3 program was expected to grow from 65,000 to nearly 110,000. In addition to growth in EHS, many states have invested or will invest in home visiting services under various auspices, including maternal and child health services. The research base has grown both in regards to understanding infant and toddler development and how programs serving children from birth to 3 can contribute in positive ways to early development.

In this chapter, we briefly review the history of infant and toddler programs, take stock of what we know now from research about birth to 3 programs and what that research suggests possibly should happen programmatically before preschool, and identify issues that help frame the discussion about these programs. We emphasize lessons learned from EHS, as well as demonstrate that important lessons about how programs can be designed during this period have emerged from other research as well.

WHAT ARE THE LESSONS FROM RESEARCH ON BIRTH-TO-3 PROGRAMS?

Birth-to-3 programs have been part of early education from the beginning of modern intervention programs. In the early 20th century, experimenters at the University of Iowa demonstrated dramatic IQ gains and different lifetime trajectories among infants who received individualized attention compared with a control group (Skodak & Skeels, 1945). Since the 1960s, a number of programs have demonstrated positive effects for intervention services for children from birth (or prior to birth) to age 3. The programs frequently offered services to both children and parents through centers, home visits, or a combination of these services, such as in the following programs: Ira Gordon's parent education program (Jester & Guinagh, 1983), the Infant Health and Development Program (Brooks-Gunn, Klebanov, Liaw, & Spiker, 1993), the Parent-Child Development Centers (Johnson & Blumenthal, 1985), the Parent-Child Centers (Lazar, 1970), the Yale Child Welfare program (Seitz, Rosenbaum, & Apfel, 1985), Healthy Families America (Daro & Harding, 1999), Nurse Family Partnership (Olds, Henderson, Kitzman, & Cole, 1995), Parent (Mother) Child Home (Levenstein, O'Hara, & Madden, 1983), and Parents as Teachers (Wagner & Clayton, 1999).

The content of Chapter 30 does not necessarily reflect the views or policies of the U.S. Department of Health and Human Services.

Taken together, the programs have demonstrated that birth-to-3 (or sometimes, age 2) programs can have positive impacts on children's cognitive development (Brooks-Gunn et al., 1993; Johnson & Blumenthal, 1985); language development (Brooks-Gunn et al., 1993; Seitz, 1990; Seitz, Rosenbaum, & Apfel, 1985), social-emotional development (Brooks-Gunn et al., 1993), and more frequently on parenting, including improved maternal mental health and reduced subsequent pregnancies (Kitzman et al., 1997), increased parental reading to children (Johnson, Howell, & Molloy, 1993), greater reliance on nonviolent discipline (Heinicke et al., 2001), increased sensitivity in interactions (Olds et al., 2002), and less child maltreatment (Daro & Harding, 1999; Olds et al., 1995, 1997; Wagner & Clayton, 1999). The preponderance of impacts on parents is not surprising given the parenting (rather than child outcomes) focus of many of these early programs. Despite a number of studies of impacts of specific intervention programs, the literature does not clearly answer the question, "What should come before preschool?" Clearly, programs serving children between birth and age 5 can be successful, but what does the literature point to for design of these programs?

LESSONS ABOUT BIRTH-TO-3 PROGRAMS FROM THE EARLY HEAD START RESEARCH AND EVALUATION PROJECT

In 1995, Head Start and other agencies clamored for the new EHS funding. Over 500 agencies applied for the first funding; only 68 could be funded in that first wave, so it was apparent the demand in communities was great. Limited resources also made it apparent that research could contribute by helping the program best focus on what the birth-to-3 contribution should be. Thus, EHS research from the beginning focused on what worked for whom and therefore may be able to shed some light on the question of what the potential of programs for children before ages 3 or 4 is. We have been working on that research project since the mid-1990s, so now we turn the focus for this chapter to what we have learned through the EHS research that may inform program design focused on the period before children enter preschool.

The EHS Research and Evaluation Project began in 1995. In 1995 and 1996, the Administration on Children, Youth and Families (ACYF) selected 17 programs that reflected the characteristics of all 143 EHS programs that had been funded in the program's first 2 years. ACYF selected a purposive sample so that a number of important subgroups could be studied. Sites were relatively balanced in terms of race/ethnicity of families (Caucasian, African American, Hispanic), regions of the country (a balance of rural and urban areas in all regions of the country), and type of EHS prespecified program approaches (whether center based, home based, or those that provided both of these approaches). Center-based programs typically featured full-day, high-quality center-based services; home-based programs conducted weekly home visits and regular group gatherings referred to as socializations. All programs, irrespective of program model, were required to follow the Head Start Program Performance Standards and all provided a variation of a two-generation program, offering parent support as well as direct child services. Each program partnered with a nearby university, which conducted site-specific research as well as participated in the cross-site evaluation. ACYF contracted with Mathematica Policy Research and the National Center on Children and Families at Columbia University to conduct the study.

Across the 17 sites, when families applied to their local EHS program, Mathematica randomly assigned 3,001 families into program and control groups. The evaluation team conducted child assessments, observed parent-child interactions, and interviewed parents when children were 2, 3, and 5 years old and again when they were in the fifth grade. A number of technical reports and publications describe impacts of the program at these times (Love et al., 2005; U.S. Department of Health and Human Services, 2001, 2002, 2006). In addition, many articles from the study published in the peer-reviewed literature provide lessons about the development of low-income children in the context of this program. In the following paragraphs, we present the major lessons from this study. Each paragraph concludes with our assessment of the implications of the finding for what should come before preschool and includes our view of implications from EHS research for optimizing development across the early childhood years for children living in poverty.

When children were 2 and 3 years old, EHS, across all program models, showed impacts on all areas of development and on parenting and parental self-sufficiency and demonstrated that birth-to-3 programs can make a significant contribution to early development. EHS had modest impacts when aggregated across all subgroups, but impacts were notable in that they included all the domains that the program targeted. The findings are consistent with those of earlier studies showing that development and parenting can be affected early in the lives of at-risk children. While impacts were smaller than those from demonstration projects such as Abecedarian (Ramey & Campbell, 1984) and the Infant Health and Development Program (Brooks-Gunn et al., 1993), they are notable in that EHS was implementing a new program in diverse communities with a heterogeneous population on a national scale. In contrast, for example, the Abecedarian program was implemented in a single site where most of the participants were African American. The age 3 impacts for EHS were stronger for those families who entered in pregnancy and in those sites that implemented the comprehensive Head Start Program Performance Standards fully and early. Many early intervention programs do not adequately measure implementation, yet it is vital to determine whether the community-level program is being carried out as designed. The results from EHS suggest birth-to-3 programs are important but that effects will be diluted if the program is not able to achieve full implementation and is not focused on both child and family outcomes.

EHS impacts were sustained through age 5 in the areas of child social-emotional functioning and approaches to learning and for parenting practices. In addition, children who had enrolled in both EHS and formal care and education programs after EHS were faring best at age 5. At age 5, EHS had significant impacts in the areas of social-emotional functioning, approaches to learning, parenting practices, and some risky behaviors of families (e.g., whether children lived with someone who had a drug or alcohol problem). EHS age 3 social-emotional and cognitive impacts mediated children's developmental outcomes at age 5. Specifically, program impacts on the Bayley Mental Development Index (Bayley, 1993) and child engagement in play mediated age 5 impacts on child approaches to learning and observed attention. Growth curve analyses showed that reductions in aggressive behavior problems and gains in cognitive development were maintained and that neither increased after the end of EHS. Finally, those children who had experienced both birth-to-3 EHS and formal care and education (center-based child care, state prekindergarten [pre-K], or Head Start) when they were 3–5 years old were faring best in all areas of development compared to those who had EHS only, formal care and education only, or neither. These findings largely confirm the recommendations of the advisory committee (U.S. Department of Health and Human Services, 1994) that designed EHS, which recognized that early gains would only be consolidated and grow if EHS was followed by other educational experiences; thus the committee charged EHS programs with assisting families with transitions to quality preschool programs. The follow-up study examined where the children (both program and control) went for pre-K and found that EHS had a significant effect on the probability of children entering formal care and education experiences following EHS, although the percentage of program participation between ages 3 and 4 was not as high as expected (49% versus 44% for the control group). However, 82% of both groups enrolled in formal programs between ages 4 and 5, and almost 90% of children in both groups were enrolled in formal preschool programs at some point between ages 3 and 5.

Second, although an optimally rigorous design would have been to randomly assign children to program and control groups during the post-EHS years, it was not possible. Thus, we examined how children and families were faring at age 5 from both an experimental perspective (EHS versus control) and nonexperimental perspective (EHS and formal care and education, EHS but no formal care and education, formal care and education but no EHS, no EHS or formal care and education). Taken together, these analyses showed that EHS contributed to children's social-emotional development, approaches to learning, parenting, and protection of families in regards to risky behaviors (e.g., living with someone who had a drug or alcohol problem). Formal care and education between ages 3 and 5 appeared to contribute to children's achievement-related outcomes such as prereading skills and also to whether children were receiving services if they had a disability. Formal care and education was also associated with an increase in parent reports of aggressive behaviors—a finding reported in other studies as well (National Institute of Child Health and Human Development, 2005a).

When services spanning the birth to 5 age range were looked at together, those children and families who experienced EHS followed by formal care and education fared the best overall, with benefits for most outcomes in the child social-emotional, parenting and home environment, and family well-being domains coming primarily from EHS, and the benefits in achievement-oriented outcomes coming from the preschool programs. Notably, EHS appeared to buffer the unfavorable effects of formal programs on behavior problems.

The results from the follow-up study lead us to two strong conclusions:

1. EHS contributes especially to children's social-emotional development, to parenting practices, and to outcomes that relate to some family support needs. Each of these areas may help children and families to be able to take full advantage of the opportunities for more focused preacademic learning that preschool may offer.

2. Birth-to-3 programs need to be followed by pre-K experiences for children. Although birth-to-3 programs such as EHS have sustaining impacts, they are not inoculations and the range of results is best enhanced and maintained in the context of continuity of early education.

Impacts at age 3 suggested that programs providing both home visits and center-based services had the largest and greatest number of impacts, but impacts at age 5 were stronger for children and families who had attended formal preschool programs following their EHS home visiting. EHS programs select one of several prescribed program models after they complete an assessment of their community needs. These programs may be center based, home based, home visits, or some combination of these approaches (which was referred to in the research as a mixed approach). Because programs select their models, it is not possible to randomly assign families to program approach. Thus, the question that can be answered is whether each program approach is better for the families served in that way than is true for families in the same communities who did not receive services. We also conducted analyses of differences in patterns of impacts between approaches, which showed that the mixed-approach programs had the strongest and broadest pattern of impacts across child, parenting, and self-sufficiency outcomes when the program ended.

The follow-up study showed a different pattern, however. At age 5, it was the home-based programs that showed the strongest pattern of impacts, including child social-emotional outcomes, parenting, and parent self-sufficiency (income). These findings lead us to conclude that the supports for parenting that occur in home-based programs may be contributing to the sustained and enhanced parenting and to the sustained impacts in children's social-emotional functioning that were seen. It is likely that whatever comes before age 3 in the early childhood spectrum of services needs to include a focus on parents during this formative parenting time that is so closely linked to children's development, especially given known linkages between the parent–child relationship and children's social-emotional development (Shonkoff & Phillips, 2000).

EHS had stronger and more lasting impacts on African American children and parents than on other racial/ethnic groups. EHS impacts for African American children and families were broad and substantial when children were age 3, with many outcomes for both children and parents showing effect sizes in the .3–.5 range. A number of impacts were sustained for this group to age 5, including reduced behavior problems, more positive approaches to learning, better observed emotion regulation and attention, and better receptive vocabulary. In addition, the former EHS parents had more books for their children, were observed to be more supportive during play, spanked less, and had fewer depression symptoms than control group parents. That EHS had sustaining impacts on African American children and families is consistent with earlier studies of demonstration programs that included African Americans (e.g., Ramey & Campbell, 1984). The effectiveness of EHS for this group may be due to several factors. First, the African American control group scored lower than other groups so there was more room for the program to have an impact. Next, results may have been sustained because African Americans were significantly more likely to be in formal care and education in the preschool years than other groups, so the early gains were supported by continued services.

The impacts for Hispanic children were fewer at age 3 but some were seen at age 5, including child positive approaches to learning, Spanish vocabulary, and engagement during play (a trend). In addition, the Hispanic former EHS parents more often attended meetings and open houses at the child's school, and there were trends for these parents to read more often to their children and to be employed. One implication for what comes before preschool is that programs seem to know better how to serve African American children and their families than other groups, particularly Hispanics. Thus, programs need to develop more effective approaches for serving the growing number of Hispanic children and families, particularly those who do not speak English.

EHS had stronger impacts at age 3 for children in families with a moderate level of risk, but at age 5 some impacts emerged for children in highest risk families. The EHS Study created a risk index, summing across five demographic risk factors—whether parent was a teen parent at the time of the child's birth, unmarried, not a graduate of high school, neither working nor in school, and receiving cash assistance. The impacts at age 3 for children in the moderate-risk group (three risks) suggest that this was the group EHS was best able to serve. At age 3, lack of impacts for higher risk (four or five risk factors) families may have been related to their being less likely to be enrolled in fully implemented programs and having erratic engagement and attendance patterns. However, a nonexperimental analysis showed that when highest risk families did attend and engage in EHS, some positive outcomes at age 3 were seen (Kisker, Raikes, Chazan-Cohen, Carta, & Puma, 2009).

Two years after the end of the program, positive impacts on parenting emerged for the highest risk group, demonstrating that positive change was likely in motion but took until age 5 to manifest itself. For the highest risk group, the program had a negative impact (trend) on Peabody Picture Vocabulary Test–III (Dunn & Dunn, 1997) scores at age 3; by age 5, there was a negative impact on Woodcock-Johnson letter word identification (WJ-LW). However, for this group, Head Start attendance was associated with positive growth in WJ-LW scores at age 5, controlling for involvement in EHS. For children in highest risk families, having intensive service such as EHS seems to improve outcomes but not immediately, whereas the follow-up years of pre-K services (e.g., Head Start) may allow the effects to be consolidated.

Our studies lead to a number of hypotheses in regard to birth-to-3 programs and demographic risks, as follows:

1. Comprehensive programs for infants and toddlers who are all from low-income families should prioritize children in families that have a high and moderate number of risk factors.

2. Among the highest risk families, programs need to be very careful not to introduce more pressures on these most fragile of families to avoid possible negative program effects.

3. Although it is often hard to maintain a focus on child development in the face of continued family crises, programs must maintain this dual focus in order to obtain positive outcomes for children.

4. Programs need to ensure family engagement among all families, but especially highest risk families whose engagement/attendance is often erratic.

5. Program services for highest risk families likely require intensive and sometimes expensive supplemental family support, including, potentially, mental health, substance abuse, and domestic violence prevention services.

6. Among families in the high and moderate risk groups, birth-to-3 services need to be followed by high-quality care and education during the years 3–5, although the types of services may be different at different ages. For the highest risk families, there may remain a need for intensive and comprehensive family services, which are possible through a comprehensive preschool program like Head Start.

Descriptive results from the Educare evaluation (Yazejian & Bryant, 2010) show that children who have highest quality, intensive center-based services beginning in infancy enter school near national averages in language and cognitive development, while those who begin at ages 3 or 4 make progress but are further from national averages. Educare programs are EHS and Head Start full-day, full-year center-based programs. These programs, now in some dozen cities across the United States, have built on the Head Start model but add features such as bachelor-level teachers in every classroom, master teachers who provide coaching and support to classroom teachers, continuous improvement evaluation, and other core features. An evaluation coordinated by researchers at the FPG Institute at the University of North Carolina, in connection with local researchers at each site, collects pre–post data each school year, as well as standardized assessments of infants and toddlers at ages 2 and 3. Educare children who begin services before age 2 show PPVT-IV scores averaging 95.8 at age 3 and 96.2 by spring before kindergarten entry (Yazejian & Bryant, 2010).The Educare descriptive findings, soon to be more rigorously tested in a clinical trial, show advantages in early cognitive and language development when birth-to-3 services are followed up with 3-to-5 services, and that cognitive and language effects for children who receive the birth-to-3 services exceed those who have only 3-to-5 services. The Educare findings should be watched carefully as more rigorous evaluation design is employed for this program.

SUMMARY AND IMPLICATIONS FOR SERVICES BIRTH TO AGE 5

In summary, the EHS Research (supplemented by Educare descriptive findings) suggest that birth-to-3 programs can make significant and lasting contributions to children's early development. These programs particularly seem to contribute to lasting social-emotional development and parenting practices, but nonexperimental analyses suggest that cognitive and language gains from birth-to-3 programs are enhanced relative to children who receive only 3-to-5 services.

The EHS studies raise a number of questions about the role that birth-to-3 services can play in a birth-to-5 context. A program model that addresses family development, parent self-sufficiency, and parenting practices is an important component of the birth-to-3 service mix, offering critical support to parents as their parenting styles are forming and setting a tone for the ongoing relationship with their child. The EHS Research and Evaluation Project does not clearly point to a specific program model as preferable for this period, although family needs for employment and other services may best be met through center-based child care. The age-5 findings for the home-based approaches, however, suggest the importance of incorporating a parenting component while maintaining a strong focus on both parent and child.

A second issue is whether birth-to-3 programs are equally effective for all racial/ethnic groups. The EHS study indicates they may not be at present but that there is potential for this equity. The EHS studies show that the mix of birth-to-3 service that EHS affords for African American children and families seem to be on the right track today. There may be multiple reasons for this, perhaps primarily that there is a longer history in implementing birth-to-3 programs for these families than for some other racial/ethnic groups, that African American children are more likely to receive 3-to-5 follow-up services than other groups, and that without a program like EHS, African American children perform at lower levels than Caucasian children (as seen in EHS control group data). In addition, there is much to learn about delivering early services to Hispanic children, particularly given Hispanic families' preferences for using informal care while their children are very young (Capizzano, Adams, & Ost, 2007), and a more limited history of birth-to-3 programs in serving this group. The descriptive Educare evaluation, showing strong language and readiness outcomes for Spanish speaking children by age 5, suggests possibilities for non–English-speaking children during very early interventions, and the EHS age-5 findings for Hispanics suggest the birth-to-3 component can make a contribution to children's early language learning.

A third issue, in a resource-limited world, is when to begin services and who should receive continuous birth-to-5 services versus 3-to-5 services only. EHS studies showed that children who began EHS prenatally had stronger impacts than those who began later; the Educare study showed strongest results for children who began before age 2. Irrespective of when they began, the EHS study showed that children who received the combination of EHS and formal care and education between 3 and 5 fared best; the Educare evaluation showed continued advantage and test scores near national norms for children who stayed in Educare to age 5. Finally, EHS studies that examined impacts by level of family demographic risk suggest that comprehensive EHS services might be most effective when offered to families with moderate and higher levels of risk, as is the program mandate, and that the highest risk children may be the best candidates for continued comprehensive Head Start services after leaving EHS. Further research is necessary on how to deliver the needed services to families at these highest levels of risk, but services likely need to include mental health and substance abuse prevention in addition to addressing the demographic risk factors included in the EHS risk index. Meanwhile, children in other risk groups would likely benefit from continued services through part- and/or full-day pre-K programs that do not provide comprehensive services.

Clearly, differentiation of services according to family and other characteristics is a more nuanced way of thinking about birth-to-3 services in a birth-to-5 context than the field has embraced thus far. The implications our studies suggest are, at best, hypotheses for the future. We are hopeful they may be tested systematically over the next decade. Particularly urgent is the need to test models within the context of comprehensive services (e.g., EHS plus Head Start) for effective treatment of parents at highest levels of risk who are encountering mental health, substance abuse, and other conditions that critically affect early development and to find ways to provide safety nets for children in these toxic situations as parents receive needed services. Additional innovation is also needed to better serve English language learners. Certainly, research about early neurological, emotional, language, and cognitive development has taught us about the critical importance of the years birth (and before) to age 3.

CHAPTER 31

Home Visitation

Deborah Daro

A common vehicle for reaching children as early as possible—before preschool or other formal early education efforts become available—is offering pregnant women or new parents home visitation services. Although other methods for reaching new parents exist, no other service model has garnered comparable levels of political support or generated more controversy (Haskins, Paxson, & Brooks-Gunn, 2009). Today, home visitation is viewed by some as a critical lynchpin for a much-needed coordinated early intervention system and by others as yet another example of a prevention strategy promising way more than it can deliver (Chaffin, 2004; Daro, 2009).

To be certain, the seminal work of David Olds and his colleagues showing initial and long-term benefits from regular nurse visitation initiated during pregnancy and continued through a child's first 2 years of life has provided the strategy's most robust empirical support (Olds et al., 2007). Although impressive, it is unlikely these findings would have sparked broad interest in the topic had the political and practice climates not been primed to receive the empirical good news. Hawaii's success in establishing the first statewide home visitation system in the 1980s and the long-standing efforts of national models such as Parents as Teachers (Winter & Rouse, 1991), the Parent-Child Home Program (Levenstein, Kochman, & Roth, 1973) and Home Instruction for Parents of Preschool Youngsters (HIPPY; Westheimer, 2003) shaped the policy landscape by demonstrating that home visitation programs could be established in diverse contexts and embedded within existing educational systems. These efforts also demonstrated that many new parents, regardless of socioeconomic circumstances, were receptive to offers of voluntary support.

On the political front, the U.S. Advisory Board on Child Abuse and Neglect, through a series of reports in 1990 and 1991, called for a universal system of home visitation for newborns and their parents: "Complex problems do not have simple solutions.... While not a panacea, the Board believes that no other single intervention has the promise that home visitation has" (1991, p. 145). In response to this report, the National Committee to Prevent Child Abuse developed Healthy Families America (Daro, 2000) in the early 1990s and aggressively promoted the strategy through its chapter network and state Children's Trust and Prevention Funds. As Healthy Families America and other models expanded, the notion of a home visitation field took shape, in part because of the evidence but also in part because states were now looking for ways to build the type of early intervention systems the Advisory Board had promoted.

This chapter outlines the unique advantages of building early intervention systems on a foundation of high-quality home-based interventions. Although I present an excellent approach for improving child outcomes, how to develop and sustain a comprehensive network of targeted or universal home-based interventions is far from self-evident. The chapter concludes by addressing the contextual and environmental challenges inherent in attempts to broaden the availability of early home-based interventions and to effectively link this system to high-quality early education programs.

THE HOME VISITATION FRAMEWORK

Many home visitation models reflect the belief that one can reduce negative outcomes for children by strengthening early parent–child relationships and linking new parents with needed health care and social services (Daro, 2009). Within this paradigm, early home visitation is an intervention with its own mission and service portfolio as well as a gatekeeper to other community resources. These other resources include not only the immediate health services for infants and mothers common in public health nurse visiting programs but also the therapeutic and concrete services necessary to insure a mother's continued ability to provide a safe and nurturing environment for her developing child. Some of the models extend their outreach to all new parents or pregnant women; some target populations presenting specific risk characteristics such as young maternal age, single parent status, or low income; and others embed more intensive, targeted services for those parents facing specific challenges within a universal system of initial assessment and referral (Daro, 2006).

In addition to a number of national models (e.g., Parents as Teachers, Healthy Families America, Early Head Start [EHS], Parent-Child Home Program, SafeCare, HIPPY, and the Nurse Family Partnership), more than 40 states have invested in home visitation and the infrastructure necessary to insure that home visitation services are of high quality and are integrated into the broader system of early intervention and support (Johnson, 2009).

Home visitation programs primarily involve the delivery of services in a participant's home, although a proportion of these visits may occur in other settings such as parks, recreation centers, restaurants, and other public venues. Services are one-to-one and are provided by staff with professional training (nursing, social work, child development, family support) or by paraprofessionals who receive training in a given model's approach and curricula. The primary issues addressed during visits include the mother's personal health and life choices; child health and development; environmental concerns such as income, housing, and community violence; family functioning, including adult and child relationships; and access to services. Specific activities include modeling parent–child interactions and child management strategies, providing observation and feedback, offering general parenting and child development information, conducting formal assessments and screenings, and providing structured counseling.

Of the myriad ways to reach out to newborns and their parents, home visitation has surfaced as a uniquely promising approach, offering a number of advantages for promoting the early intervention mission not found in alternative strategies such as center-based child care or group-based parenting education offerings. These features include the following.

Reaching all new parents in a nonstigmatizing manner: Outside of public education, prenatal and obstetric care are among the most broadly accessed services in the United States. Offering home visitation within a health care framework has the unique advantage of reaching newborns without requiring individuals to be singled out as facing unique difficulties. Such generalized offers of assistance provide a unique opportunity to raise awareness about the importance of early child growth and development and introduce parents to topics and resources they may be unfamiliar with or unclear as to how to access.

Minimizing barriers to service access: Finding and sustaining participation in any intervention can be daunting particularly if a parent has limited experience and skills in navigating complex service delivery systems. The delivery of services in one's home reduces the need for families to locate the appropriate service provider, transport themselves and their children to a centralized location, and adjust their personal schedules to accommodate service availability. Although retention issues in long-term home visitation programs remain a problem across all models, home-based intervention does afford participants a degree of flexibility and ease of access that is difficult to replicate in center-based efforts.

Individualizing the message: Home-based interventions provide the opportunity for providers to tailor core messages in a manner most compatible with an individual's specific knowledge and skills, cultural beliefs, and learning style. Although the most robust home visitation models follow a speci-fied curriculum and establish common learning objectives and skills for all participants, home visitors deliver this material in diverse ways, adapting presentation content and flow to each parent's presenting problems and immediate challenges. This type of tailored assistance is particularly important given the racial, ethnic, and socioeconomic diversity within the new parent population.

Opportunities to evaluate the home environment and engage other caregivers: Although the content and perhaps the relationships and modeling occurring within home-based services can be replicated in center-based environments, delivering services within a participant's home offers a unique oppor-tunity to assess safety and parental needs. In addition to determining the physical safety of a child's most proximate environment, home-based service delivery affords the home visitor an opportunity to discern both spoken and unspoken needs. Repeated visits to a family's home allows for a more nuanced assessment of the home's general stability, the relationships among family members, and the availability of various informal and formal supports. These insights can be particularly important in determining issues of child safety and identifying the need for additional services.

EVIDENCE OF EFFECTIVENESS

Numerous efforts to summarize the broad and ever-expanding research on home visitation efforts have reached different conclusions. Some authors concluded that when home visitation is well imple-mented, it produces significant and meaningful reductions in child maltreatment risk and improves child and family functioning (American Academy of Pediatrics, 1998; Coalition for Evidence-Based Policy, 2009; Geeraert, Van den Noorgate, Grietens, & Onghena, 2004; Guterman, 2001; Hahn et al., 2003). Other authors reached more sobering conclusions (Chaffin, 2004; Gomby, 2005; Howard & Brooks-Gunn, 2009). To some degree, these disparate conclusions reflect different expectations regard-ing what constitutes meaningful change or appropriate methodological rigor.

Although positive outcomes continue to be far from universal, families enrolled in well-planned and carefully implemented home visitation programs, as compared to participants in a formal control group or relevant comparison population, reported fewer acts of abuse or neglect toward their children over time (DuMont et al., 2008; Fergusson, Grant, Horwood, & Ridder, 2005; Healthy Families Arizona, 2005; Healthy Families Florida, 2005; Olds et al., 1995; Sweet & Appelbaum, 2004), engage in parenting practices that support a child's positive development (Healthy Families America, 2005; Love, 2009; Zigler et al., 2008), and make immediate and future life choices that create more stable and nurturing environments for their children (Anisfeld, Sandy, & Guterman, 2004; Healthy Families Arizona, 2005; Olds et al., 1997; Sweet & Appelbaum, 2004; Wagner & Spiker, 2001).

Findings from the 4-year follow-up of the EHS National Demonstration Project lend support to the unique benefits of home-based interventions with new parents. At age 4, mothers with children enrolled in home-based EHS were more supportive, more sensitive, less detached, and more likely to extend play to stimulate cognitive development, language, and literacy than were mothers assigned to the control group or who were enrolled in center-based programs or programs which combined home-based and center-based delivery (Love, 2009).

In general, the outcomes of home visitation programs can be strengthened when the model provides entry to other services or specialized support (Ammerman et al., 2009; Anisfeld, et al., 2004; Daro & McCurdy, 2006; Healthy Families America, 2005). Home visitation programs also may enhance a child's school readiness and academic performance by promoting specific parental behaviors designed to improve cognitive development, as well as increase the probability children will be enrolled in high-quality preschool. Although such outcomes have not been consistently tracked among participants in early home visitation, at least one longitudinal study has suggested that such outcomes do occur. Examining administrative data on 5,721 children enrolled in Missouri public schools, Zigler et al. (2008) observed that early enrollment in Parents as Teachers had both direct and indirect effects on a child's initial school readiness and subsequent academic performance. Strongest outcomes were observed among children with the most extensive enrollment in Parents as Teachers, more frequent early literacy experiences in the home, and enrollment in preschool.

A prime consideration for the unique emphasis on home visitation within the current federal policy debate is the long-term cost savings found in Nurse-Family Partnership's (Aos, Lieb, Mayfield, Miller, & Pennucci, 2004) initial trials. These savings were primarily realized through a reduction in the subsequent use of Medicaid and other entitlement programs as a result of women receiving the intervention entering and remaining in the work force. Although comparable data have not been collected on the other home visitation models, the range of outcomes achieved by many of them suggests similar savings could accrue from them as well. Additional areas for potential savings include stronger birth outcomes among families enrolled prenatally in a sample of Healthy Families New York programs (DuMont et al., 2008), higher monthly household earnings among those who access Early Head Start services (Love, 2009), and better school readiness and a reduced need for special education classes among children enrolled in Parents as Teachers or the Parent-Child Home Program (Levenstein, Levenstein, & Oliver, 2002; Zigler et al., 2008).

CORE CHALLENGES IN MAXIMIZING OPPORTUNITY

For home visitation efforts to merit serious consideration as an appropriate precursor to preschool education, the strategy needs to demonstrate an ability to extend the promise of equal opportunity and access embedded in public education to children in the earliest years of life. In addition, the effort has to reflect the types of social investments valued by the general public and interested policy makers. Such characteristics are particularly important if one assumes that offers to promote early learning will be universal, voluntary, and scaled based on each family's level of need. Although the provision of more intensive and costly home visitation services should be limited to those families facing the greatest risks, all new parents—regardless of economic circumstances and personal resources—should be encouraged to seek out opportunities to address early parenting challenges.

To effectively engage the general population and maximize the opportunity home visitation offers as the entry point for strengthening a child's early learning opportunities, greater focus is needed in addressing the following concerns.

Reaching the highest risk populations: Home visitation programs that have targeted pregnant women or those giving birth successfully serve a troubled and challenged population but often fail to enroll and retain families at highest risk. Pregnant women unwilling or unable to access prenatal care, parents suffering from serious mental illness or substance abuse problems, and families living in the most violent and distressed communities are among those that are more resistant to offers of voluntary services and are often unable to consistently embrace the skills and resources these models promote. It remains unclear if the majority of such parents can ever be fully engaged in voluntary services offered only within the health care framework. Reaching the most distressed populations may well require stronger linkages to child welfare systems and therapeutic resources within a community. Two home visitation models that have fostered these types of relationships and enroll new parents who have a history of child welfare involvement with their older children—Project SafeCare and Family Connections—have demonstrated improvements in targeted parental behaviors and reduced likelihood of future referral to child welfare (DePanfilis & Dubowitz, 2005; Gershater-Molko, Lutzker, & Wesch, 2003). In building comprehensive early intervention systems, it will be important for home visitation programs to utilize these and other diverse methods for identifying and engaging new parents.

Broadening the message to reflect differential concerns: Every newborn presents parents with unique challenges and concerns. First-time mothers often have a range of questions about monitoring their baby's health and meeting basic caregiving responsibilities. In contrast, mothers birthing a second or third child may have primary concerns around differentiating the developmental needs and temperaments of their children or managing sibling rivalry. College-educated mothers and those with higher incomes may be seeking different types and levels of information than teenage parents or those with unstable income sources. Some new parents may be able to easily assimilate suggested behaviors into their routines, whereas other parents will require extended modeling and repetition in order to grasp new concepts. Again, making offers of home visitation attractive and meaningful to the maximum number of potential participants will require more nuanced and segmented messages regarding its value and core content.

Teaching new parents effective consumer skills: The structures of social, health, and educational systems often require that families struggle with a complex set of tasks, each of which requires them to access, process, and ascribe value to what can be conflicting information. Consumers are often required to sort through multiple venues to identify a set of possible service options, to then discern the relative merits of these choices, and finally to use this information to select an optimal course of action. Although many in the population are competent in making such decisions, not all new parents have the experience or capacity to successfully manage complex service delivery systems or determine how and when to access support for themselves and their children. Such skills are particularly important over time as parents need to select appropriate child care, early education programs, and primary school options. Home visitation programs need to explicitly address this need by educating participants on the importance of these skills and providing opportunities to practice informed decision making in securing resources external to the home visit.

BEYOND SERVICE MODELS: BUILDING EFFECTIVE SYSTEMS

Unlike efforts to reform a single institution or expand capacity by building on an existing service delivery system or set of institutional alignments, constructing early intervention systems is more akin to new construction. Proponents are crafting not only the basic service components and interventions new parents will be offered but also building the infrastructure that will support and link these components into a coordinated system of care that can provide adequate coverage and outreach to a broadly targeted population at a level reflective of their needs. Among the strategies that might be used to strengthen the linkages and connections across all elements of a coordinated early intervention system are common work force development opportunities (e.g., initial and ongoing training for direct service providers and their supervisors), administrative data collection and management (e.g., documenting the results of universal assessments, participant characteristics, engagement rates, and service outcomes), and multisectorial partnerships that engage a broad spectrum of agency managers in collective planning and problem solving. In the absence of such explicit linkages, home visitation, as a distinct service model, will be limited in its ability to enhance a child's early development and provide a strong foundation for future academic success.

CHAPTER 32

Economic Benefits of Intervention Programs Implemented in the First Decade of Life

Arthur J. Reynolds, Judy A. Temple, and Barry A.B. White

The positive effects of early childhood development (ECD) programs on well-being have been documented in hundreds of studies (Karoly et al., 2005; Reynolds & Temple, 2008; Reynolds, Wang, & Walberg, 2003; Zigler, Gilliam, & Jones, 2006a). Advances in scientific knowledge have contributed not only to the establishment of early childhood programs but have helped spur recent expansion of programs in states and localities (Barnett et al., 2007; Reynolds & Temple, 2008). Increased attention to the early years of life also has sparked greater interest in the transition to school and experiences in the early grades that can reinforce learning gains and strengthen achievement (Bogard & Takanishi, 2005; Reynolds et al., 2003). The creation of early childhood systems and practices that enhance the continuity of development over the first decade of life is viewed as fundamental to child well-being.

In this chapter, we present evidence on the impact and cost-effectiveness of ECD programs for school readiness, school achievement and performance, and long-term life-course development. The primary focus is birth to age 3, preschool for 3- and 4-year-olds, and early school-age programs.

Two major questions are addressed: 1) What are the effects and economic benefits of ECD programs implemented in the first decade of children's life? and 2) Is there consistent evidence of comparatively greater economic benefits by age or intervention approach?

We define ECD broadly to include the first decade of life, including prenatal and infancy, preschool, kindergarten, and early school-age programs. We emphasize the results of cost–benefit analysis (CBA). There are three reasons for this focus. First, economic benefits relative to costs are the most relevant indicator for policy development. The value of public investments can be judged, at least in part, on efficiency (Heckman, 2000b). This is especially true in a time of scarce resources. Second, in the economic approach, program effects on multiple outcomes can be converted to dollars and cents (Levin & McEwan, 2001). Finally, CBAs emphasize longer-term effects of programs and practices. A focus on immediate and shorter-term effects, although an important first step, is not the ultimate program goal. A major question for social policy is whether short-term effects translate into long-term effects of adaptive life skills and behavior.

HOW EARLY CHILDHOOD DEVELOPMENT PROGRAMS INFLUENCE OUTCOMES

Considerable research has documented that ECD programs impact later well-being through at least one of five pathways (Reynolds, 2000). These can be viewed as the "active" ingredients of behavior change. They have been conceptualized from the beginning of research on early learning programs as primary mechanisms (Bronfenbrenner, 1975; Zigler & Berman, 1983). As shown by the five-hypothesis model in Figure 32.1, the cognitive advantage pathway indicates that the longer-term effects of ECD programs are due primarily to the enhancement of cognitive skills, including literacy, language, and numeracy.

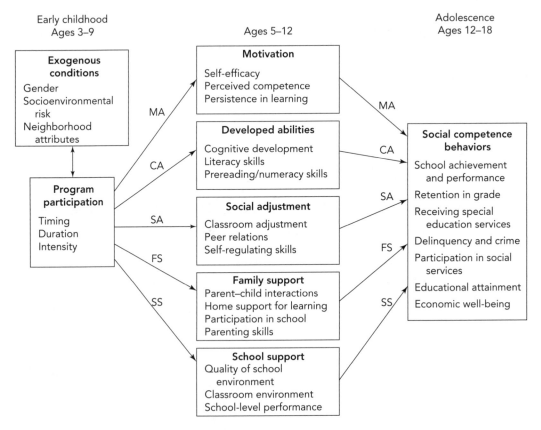

Figure 32.1. Pathways from early childhood programs to long-term outcomes. (*Key:* CA, cognitive advantage; FS, family support; MA, motivational advantage; SA, social adjustment; SS, school support.)

The family support pathway indicates that impacts derive from greater parental investments in children's development, such as greater parent involvement in education, increased parenting skills, and greater supports for parents.

The school support pathway suggests that longer-term effects would occur to the degree that postprogram school experiences reinforce learning gains. Enrollment in higher quality schools and schools with positive learning environments would strengthen or maintain learning gains while enrollment in schools lower in quality would neutralize earlier learning gains.

The social adjustment and motivational advantage hypotheses indicate that noncognitive skills can be the mechanism of effects of ECD programs, such as increased classroom and peer social skills, positive teacher-child relationships, achievement motivation, and school commitment. The greater the magnitude of effect of program experiences on a particular pathway or multiple pathways, the more likely that enduring effects would occur.

Notably, programs that provide comprehensive services would be expected to impact several of the pathways simultaneously. This is one explanation for why comprehensive programs have been found to be more likely to have longer term effects. This principle as well as intensity and dosage are consistent with ecological (Bronfenbrenner, 1989; Bronfenbrenner & Morris, 1998) and human capital (Becker, 1964; Heckman, 2003) theories.

COST–BENEFIT ANALYSIS IN EARLY CHILDHOOD DEVELOPMENT PROGRAMS

CBA is an economic approach for estimating the value of alternative programs and policies relative to costs. Program and intervention investments can be ranked according to their effectiveness per dollar of expenditure. CBA is a major departure from traditional measures of effect size, which take into account only program effects.

The major advantage of CBA is that benefits for multiple outcomes can be summarized in dollar terms, either the net return (benefits minus costs) or return per dollar invested (benefits divided by costs). However, the ability to conduct a CBA depends on whether it is possible to reflect benefits in dollars. Researchers have a long tradition of estimating the benefits of increased graduation rates and reductions in crime. Program budgets often are used to estimate benefits of reductions in special education or child welfare costs. It is more difficult to monetize the benefits of higher test scores or problem behaviors because relatively few studies link test scores or behavior to higher future incomes or fewer crimes (Levin & McEwan, 2001).

EVIDENCE ON ECONOMIC BENEFITS FOR PROGRAMS IN CHILDREN'S FIRST DECADE

At a minimum, the economic return should equal the amount invested in the program—a return of at least $1 per dollar invested. Although not all impacts can be translated into economic benefits and many criteria of a program's worth should be considered, CBA findings are an important metric of efficiency. CBA illustrates the distribution of benefits for different segments of society. Benefits to society at large include the sum of benefits to program participants and the general public. Although societal benefits frequently are emphasized, benefits to the general public (not including the program participants) often are used to justify government investment.

In this chapter, we summarize the societal benefits of programs that have conducted economic analyses by age of program entry. Based on reviews of the extant literature (e.g., Karoly et al., 2005; Reynolds & Temple, 2008), 17 estimates from 16 programs are included. For programs in which there are multiple studies, the most representative and comprehensive estimates from a single study are reported. Typically, these are from the research team of the program study. Table 32.1 provides a summary of the major findings.

PRENATAL AND INFANT PROGRAMS

Home visitation, health, and child care programs in the earliest years of life are associated with positive child development and parenting behaviors, but few long-term behavioral effects have been demonstrated (Reynolds, Mathieson, & Topitzes, 2009; Sweet & Applebaum, 2004). CBA estimates are

Table 32.1. Cost-effectiveness estimates for early childhood programs, birth to third grade

Development stage	Source	Focus	Location	2007 dollars			
				Benefits	Costs	B–C	B/C
Birth to age 3							
WIC	Avruch & Cackley (1995)	Targeted	National	1,206	393	813	3.07
NFP, Low income	Glazner, Bondy, Luckey, & Olds (2004)	Targeted	Elmira, NY	83,850	16,727	67,123	5.01
NFP, Higher income	Glazner et al. (2004)	Targeted	Elmira, NY	25,317	16,727	8,590	1.51
Preschool							
Child-Parent Centers	Reynolds et al. (2002)	Targeted	20 Chicago sites	86,401	8,512	77,889	10.15
Perry preschool	Schweinhart et al. (2005)	Targeted	1 Ypsilanti, MI, site	294,716	18,260	276,456	16.14
Abecedarian	Barnett & Masse (2007)	Targeted	1 site in NC	182,422	73,159	109,263	2.49
RAND study of preschool in California	Karoly et al. (2005)	Universal	State of CA	12,818	4,889	7,929	2.62
National pre-K synthesis for 2050	Lynch (2007)	Targeted	National	20,603	6,479	14,124	3.18
	Lynch (2007)	Universal	National	12,958	6,479	6,479	2.00
Synthesis study	Aos et al. (2004)	Targeted	58 programs	19,826	8,415	11,411	2.36
Kindergarten							
Full-day synthesis	Aos, Miller, & Mayfield (2007)	Universal	23 programs	0	2,685	–2,685	0
School-age							
Tennessee STAR (class size reduction, K–3)	Krueger (2003)	Universal	79 schools	27,561	9,744	17,817	2.83
Synthesis of reduced class sizes, K–2	Aos et al. (2007)	Universal	38 studies	6,847	2,454	4,393	2.79
Synthesis of reduced class sizes, Grade 3–6	Aos et al. (2007)	Universal	38 studies	3,387	2,454	933	1.38
Child-Parent Centers School-Age Program	Reynolds et al. (2002)	Targeted	20 Chicago sites	8,089	3,792	4,297	2.13
Reading Recovery	Shanahan & Barr (1995)	Targeted	General	1,679	5,596	–3,151	0.30
Skills, Opportunities and Recognition	Aos et al. (2004)	Universal	Seattle schools	16,256	5,172	11,084	3.14
PreK-3 Intervention							
Child-Parent Centers Extended Program	Reynolds et al. (2002)	Targeted	20 Chicago sites	47,161	5,175	41,986	9.11

Key: B–C, benefits minus costs; B/C, benefit–cost ratio; NFP, Nurse-Family Partnership; WIC, Women, Infants, and Children.

Note: Findings from the Perry Preschool are at age 40. At age 27, benefit–cost was $141,350 and benefit–cost ratio was $8.74 (Barnett, 1996).

available for two prenatal and home visitation programs in the first 3 years. The Special Supplemental Nutrition Program for Women, Infants, and Children (WIC) provides nutrition education, referrals to social services, and a variety of food supplements to low-income families. A meta-analysis of 15 studies in different states by Avruch and Cackley (1995) found that WIC participation was associated with a 25% reduction in the rate of low-weight births, which significantly reduced hospital costs paid by insurers in the first year of life. The economic return was $3.07 per dollar invested. Devaney (in press) provides a broader review of evidence on WIC and suggests this return may be an upper bound.

The Nurse-Family Partnership (Olds, Henderson, Phelps, Kitzman, & Hanks, 1993) is an intensive nurse home visitation program for young mothers having their first child. For the high-risk sample (unmarried and low-income mothers having their first child), Glazner et al. (2004) found that participation from prenatal development to age 2 was associated with lower rates of criminal behavior for both mothers and target children, lower rates of substantiated child maltreatment, higher earnings capacity for the mothers, and increased projected tax revenues. The estimated economic return was $5.01 for every dollar invested. For the lower risk sample, the economic return was $1.51 per dollar invested. (See Karoly et al., 2005, for additional analyses yielding similar returns of $5.01 and $1.10, respectively.)

Although no CBAs have been conducted for other programs with extensive longitudinal data, including Syracuse Family Development Research Program, Houston Parent-Child Development Center, and Infant Health and Development Program, the pattern of findings are suggestive of lower economic returns than the Nurse-Family Partnership (see Aos et al., 2004; Karoly et al., 2005).

CENTER-BASED PRESCHOOL PROGRAMS

Although short- and longer term effects have been documented for a large number of programs for 3- and 4-year-olds (Gormley, 2007; Karoly et al., 2005), three studies have investigated comprehensively life course impacts and economic returns with strong research designs and low attrition. The Child-Parent Centers (CPC), Carolina Abecedarian Project (ABC), and the HighScope Perry preschool program (PPP) all provided high-quality educational enrichment to children at risk in group settings characterized by small class sizes, a focus on language and cognitive skills, and well-qualified and compensated teachers. ABC was the most intensive and lengthy, providing full-day, year-round care for 5 years (Campbell & Ramey, 1995; Campbell et al., 2002). PPP provided the most established and organized curriculum, which followed the Piagetian principle of child-initiated learning (Schweinhart et al., 1993). CPC provided the most comprehensive services by implementing an intensive parent involvement component, outreach services, and attention to health and nutrition (Reynolds, 2000; Reynolds et al., 2002). It also was the only program to be established in public schools.

The programs showed substantial economic returns into adulthood. Although the costs are significantly different from each other, the returns of each program far exceeded the initial investment. At the age 21 follow-up, the CPC program showed a benefit–cost ratio of $10.15, in part reflecting its relatively lower costs (Reynolds et al., 2002). This is primarily due to higher child-to-staff ratios (8.5:1 versus less than 6:1 for PPP and ABC). Recent analyses of the CPC program, incorporating data on later adult outcomes, suggest earlier projections are robust (Reynolds et al., 2011; White, Temple, & Reynolds, 2010). That a routinely implemented school-based program demonstrates positive returns indicates that wide-scale programs can be cost-effective. PPP showed the highest net present value per child (benefits minus costs) of $276,456 and a return of $16.14 per dollar invested at the age 40 follow-up (Belfield, Nores, Barnett, & Schweinhart, 2006; Schweinhart et al., 2005). Although Table 32.1 reports the recent study of Perry preschool, the age 27 findings were a benefit–cost ratio of $8.74 and a net present-value of $141,350. This earlier age of assessment more closely matches the CPC and ABC studies. Heckman et al. (2010b) also reported findings within this range and conducted an extensive sensitivity analysis.

The consistent findings of these economic analyses, despite differences in approaches, are encouraging for the generalization of preschool effects. Nevertheless, program participants were almost exclusively low-income, African American children. Although there is no comparable evidence from studies of middle-income families or from more diverse samples, research on the short-term effects of seven

state-funded preschool programs shows positive and meaningful impacts that are suggestive of enduring effects (Gormley, 2007; Reynolds & Temple, 2008).

Benefits from Policy Simulations

To estimate the economic benefits of high-quality but routinely implemented preschool programs,
several researchers have conducted cost–benefit simulations that modify assumptions of existing CBAs
from longitudinal analyses of programs such as CPC or PPP or make projections of benefits from
predicted changes in educational attainment, income, or crime using information from other studies
showing correlations between adult outcomes and short-term outcomes such as achievement.

Synthesizing short- and long-term data from 58 evaluation studies published from 1967 to 2003,
Aos et al. (2004) estimated an economic return of $2.36 return per dollar invested for preschool pro-
grams for low-income 3- and 4-year-olds. Karoly and Bigelow (2005) estimated economic benefits of
$2.62 per dollar invested (range of $2–$4) for universal access to 1 year of preschool education at age
4 in California.

A broader national analysis by Lynch (2007) used modified estimates from the CBA of the CPC
program to generalize across states and in the country at large. A high-quality targeted preschool program costing $6,479 (2007 dollars) per child would provide a return per tax dollar invested of $3.18
in government budget savings. For a universal access program, the return per tax dollar invested was
$2.00 for government budget savings. Considering all societal benefits, the long-range annual benefit
per tax dollar was $12.10 for a targeted program and $8.20 for a universal access program.

FULL-DAY KINDERGARTEN

The effects of full-day versus part-day kindergarten are well documented. Many studies have examined
achievement gains at the end of kindergarten and in the early school grades. Aos et al. (2007) synthe-
sized the results of 23 studies of full-day kindergarten for academic achievement. The average effect size
of full-day kindergarten at the end of kindergarten was .18 standard deviation for all children and .17
standard deviation for economically disadvantaged children. This small advantage largely disappeared
by first grade and did not reemerge. Other studies support this pattern (see Reynolds & Temple, 2008).
Although no CBAs are available, the lack of long-term gains would be expected to yield a benefit–cost
ratio close to zero.

CLASS SIZE REDUCTIONS

In the most extensive study of class size reduction, Project STAR in Tennessee experimentally investigated the impact of statewide enrollment in class sizes limited to 13–17 students from kindergarten to
third grade. Although 1 or more years in small classes was associated with higher achievement in the
short-term, longer term effects by eighth grade were found only for students with 3 or 4 years in small
classes. The 3-year group had median effect sizes of .17 standard deviations in Grades 4–8. The 4-year
group had median effect sizes of .25. Only low-income students with 3 or 4 years had higher rates of
high school graduation (Finn, Gerber, & Boyd-Zaharias, 2005). Based on Krueger (2003), Project
STAR was found to have an economic return of $2.83 per dollar invested.

As shown in Table 32.1, these findings are consistent with a synthesis of 38 studies of small classes
(Aos et al., 2007). The economic return of small classes in kindergarten through second grade was $2.79
per dollar invested and $1.38 in third through sixth grades. Similarly, the school-age component of CPC,
which primarily reduced class sizes, had a return of $2.13 per dollar invested (Reynolds et al., 2002).

OTHER SCHOOL-AGE PROGRAMS AND PRACTICES

The Skills, Opportunities, and Recognition program (Hawkins, Catalano, Kosterman, Abbott, & Hill,
1999), formerly the Seattle Social Development Project, is designed to promote social and emotional
skills. Starting in Grade 1 and continuing to Grade 6, the supplemental classroom-based program
includes cooperative, developmentally appropriate teaching practices and optional parent education
classes. Participation was associated with higher achievement, lower rates of delinquency, and lower
rates of alcohol misuse. The economic return was $3.14 per dollar invested.

Reading Recovery, an instructional tutoring program for first-grade students, provides 30 minutes of one-to-one daily instruction with a teacher outside of the regular school class. Findings from more than 30 studies are generally consistent in that significant short-term gains are substantially reduced by fourth grade (D'Agostino & Murphy, 2004). Shanahan and Barr (1995) estimated that the program would be expected to return $0.30 per dollar invested through reductions in special education.

PRESCHOOL-TO-THIRD GRADE PROGRAMS

A key rationale for transition programs and practices in the early school-age years is that elementary schools play an important role in sustaining the benefits of early childhood programs, and follow-on services into the primary grades will promote successful transitions. Preschool-to-third grade (PreK-3) programs are one of the most comprehensive approaches for promoting ECD and learning. Programs and services implemented during the entire first decade of life also are recommended (Reynolds et al., 2010; Zigler & Styfco, 1993) with Schools of the 21st Century being a widely used model (Finn-Stevenson & Zigler, 1999).

Although several PreK-3 programs have shown evidence of positive effects on achievement-related behavior (Reynolds & Temple, 2008), only the CPC extended intervention has had CBA. Compared to participation in less extensive services (0–3 years of intervention), the CPC program returned $9.11 per dollar invested through reduced remedial education and child maltreatment, lower juvenile arrest for violence, and higher levels of educational attainment.

SUMMARY OF BENEFITS AND COSTS

Findings show that most of the ECD investments are associated with positive economic returns. This is illustrated in Figure 32.2 as the economic return per dollar invested for the reviewed programs as a function of the age of entry into intervention. Age 0 corresponds with prenatal development (WIC and the Nurse-Family Partnership). Preschool programs for 3- and 4-year-olds have had the most research and generally show the highest returns from both cohort studies and economic simulations. The variability of contexts, service systems, and curriculum philosophy strengthens this evidence. Ratios ranged from $2 dollars per dollar invested to more than $16 dollars per dollar invested. The average return was $6 per dollar invested. Programs beginning prenatally or in early infancy ranged from $1 to $5 returned per dollar invested and an average of $3 per dollar invested. Early school-age programs varied substantially, with small classes and social skills training showing the highest returns at $2 to $3 per dollar invested. The returns of small classes were highest for low-income children enrolling for 3 or 4 years (Finn et al., 2005). Although not shown, the pattern of findings based on net program benefits (benefits minus costs) is similar: Preschool programs for 3- and 4-year-olds show the largest benefits.

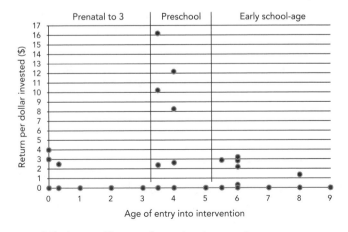

Figure 32.2. Return per dollar invested by age of entry into intervention.

LIMITATIONS OF EVIDENCE BASE

A number of qualifications to these findings are notable. Relatively few studies of economic benefits have been conducted, especially using program cohort studies. Overall, only 16 studies were identified. Consequently, reported returns do not necessarily define the benefits of particular intervention types (e.g., home visitation, prenatal nutrition). Returns would be expected to vary by the quality of program implementation and intensity of services as well as population characteristics.

Second, the assumptions and approaches to economic analyses varied considerably across studies. This was especially true for length of assessments, scope of measured outcomes, and the balance of projected versus actual benefits. Findings from WIC, for example, were based only on medical savings in the first year of life linked to lower rates of low-weight births. Benefit estimates for class size reductions, social skills training, and preschool policy simulations relied almost exclusively on projections from shorter term outcomes.

A third qualification is that the possible benefits of combining programs such as PreK-3, prenatal to preschool, and preschool and small classes in the early grades have not been fully investigated. These and other synergies warrant further effectiveness and cost-effectiveness studies. Interventions across ages should be viewed as complementary.

Finally, cost-effectiveness or CBA is one of many criteria for prioritizing programs for public investment. Social importance, program cost, feasibility, and capacity for sustainability also are important to consider in policy making.

KEY PRINCIPLES OF EFFECTIVENESS OF EARLY CHILDHOOD DEVELOPMENT PROGRAMS

Our synthesis indicates that greater investments in high-quality ECD programs can lead to positive long-term effects and economic returns. The cross-age programs we assessed provide effective models for strengthening quality and continuity of learning. As shown in Figure 32.1, attention to the causal mechanisms of change also can strengthen programs. The accumulated research suggests four major principles of effectiveness:

1. Coordinated systems of early childhood should be in place no later than preschool and address school transitions.

2. Teaching staff should be trained and compensated well, preferably with bachelor's degrees and competitive salaries. Most programs with high returns followed this principle.

3. Educational content should be responsive to children's learning needs, but special emphasis should be given to children's learning in multiple domains and in small groups.

4. Comprehensive family services should be tailored to meet the different needs of children.

Each of the cost-effective programs are ecological and provide service breadth. These principles are consistent with others in ECD (Ramey & Ramey, 1998a) and prevention (Nation et al., 2003).

FUTURE DIRECTIONS

As much as knowledge has advanced, greater commitment to cost-effectiveness is needed. Because CBA is rarely conducted, full consideration of the effects of alternative programs is difficult to achieve. Paramount in conducting CBA is the availability of longitudinal cohort studies that prospectively assess a wide variety of benefits using multiple sources of data. Only four of the studies we reviewed had these attributes; they are most likely to accurately assess societal benefits. In addition, studies are needed that address differential effects across a range of child, family, and program attributes. This will require larger sample sizes than those of most previous studies. Although less comprehensive than cohort studies, research syntheses and economic simulations provide complementary evidence that can strengthen generalizability. The dissemination of cost-effective interventions also will advance as registries of effective programs include economic analyses as inclusion criteria. Most registries treat such evidence as supplemental to basic design and effectiveness data (Kellam & Langevin, 2003). Financial efficiency is a major goal to which all programs should subscribe.

CHAPTER 33

Transforming America's Primary Education System for the 21st Century
Integrating K–12 Education with Prekindergarten

Ruby Takanishi

On November 18, 2009, Arne Duncan, the first U.S. Secretary of Education to address the the National Association for the Education of Young Children, made a historic speech that may change the ways in which educators think about the current primary education system (kindergarten to Grade 4) in the United States. Rather than perpetuating the two separate silos of early learning (i.e., prekindergarten [pre-K]) programs and K–12 education, Duncan (2009) argued that both must be linked to create a birth through postsecondary learning continuum (P–16/20) to prepare all children for the demands of the 21st century: "Now if we are to prevent the achievement gap and develop a cradle-to-career educational pipeline, early learning programs are going to have to be better integrated with the K–12 system."

In his keynote address, Secretary Duncan (2009) concluded with two clear messages. First, early learning programs must be better connected with K–12 education reform, especially through the third grade, than now is the case. Second, policy makers and professionals must move from focusing on program inputs to child outcomes, the first benchmark beginning at the end of third grade. For historical and policy reasons, as well as interprofessional rivalries, both of these goals will be difficult to achieve. However, if America's goal is to raise the achievement level of all children and to narrow the troubling achievement gap between groups of children, the essential connections between early learning and K–12 education will be necessary.

President Barack Obama also argued for the transformation of the American education system to meet the needs of the 21st century. Learning, he affirmed, begins at birth and continues throughout a person's lifetime. His ideas initially did not reflect the needed connections between pre-K and K–12 education reform. Within his first year in office, however, the position of his administration shifted to a more integrated, multiyear strategy (Duncan, 2009). Like everything, the devil—implementation—remains in the details.

PRE-K INTEGRATION IS NOT NEW

Starting in 1965 when Head Start was first launched, efforts to connect pre-K programs and to build on their impact began with the short-lived Follow Through programs. Project Developmental Continuity, initiated in the late 1960s and early 1970s, was another effort to sustain the gains of effective early learning programs. Both were ended because of lack of funding and implementation woes (Zigler & Styfco, 2004).

After these attempts, the early learning universe continued to evolve through expansions of Head Start, state pre-K programs, and the growth of private preschools. Early learning programs became predicated on a birth-to-5 framework, accepting the fact that most children attended formal schools starting with kindergarten and ending with high school or postsecondary education. Early learning programs did not see themselves as—nor did they necessarily desire to be—part of the public universal education system.

Since the 1960s, advocates, researchers, and policy makers have carved up the experience of children into two largely separate camps: what comes before kindergarten (birth to 5) and what comes after it (kindergarten to postsecondary education). People create social institutions such as educational systems and programs. There is no essential logic to the current situation, nor is it based on increased scientific knowledge about how children develop and learn—which, if used, could change how children are now educated (Shonkoff & Phillips, 2000). Research, education, and advocacy organizations—all part of the American democratic system—proliferated along the lines of the two camps. All have accepted the silos of early learning and K–12 education. This situation is only beginning to change, and the outcomes are not yet clear.

Key states with pre-K programs such as Florida, Georgia, New Jersey, and Oklahoma are prime places for connecting better their pre-K programs with their K–12 education system. All of these states have high rates of participation in their pre-K programs; New Jersey and Oklahoma have high standards for program quality, including teacher qualifications. Washington State, which does not have a state pre-K program, has made important progress due to philanthropic investments by The New School Foundation and The Bill and Melinda Gates Foundation. These investments are supported by strong nonprofit leadership.

REIMAGINING AMERICAN EDUCATION

To understand a PreK-3rd approach, we can visualize an educational pipeline that begins with pre-K programs for 3-year-olds and extends at least until postsecondary education. Right now, this pipeline is sprouting leaks early on from pre-K into the end of Grade 3. Just about 30% of all American children are reading at grade level at the beginning of Grade 4, when they are first tested by the National Assessment of Education Progress (NAEP). The leaks continue into the Grade 8 assessment, and by the end of Grade 12, almost half of students, especially those from low-income backgrounds, have left the education system. The overall performance of students at the two NAEP assessments at Grades 8 and 12 does not change significantly from the first one at the beginning of Grade 4 (Foundation for Child Development, 2008). By the end of college or postsecondary education, the flow of students through this education pipeline is a small trickle. African American, Hispanic/Latino, and American Indian children are not proportionately represented among the college-educated population.

No corporation with its eyes on the bottom line would tolerate these poor outcomes. No country with our aspirations for equity should tolerate the leakage of human potential that has been occurring for decades. This country faces a civil and human rights scandal of major significance.

This visualization of American education as a pipeline means that educators should aim for a steady and successful flow of students with few, if any leaks, from pre-K into postsecondary education. In this picture, PreK-3rd is the first link in that pipeline, upon which both the middle and high school links depend based on what children have learned during the first 6 years of education, as well as their engagement in that process. Each link builds on the preceding link; none can be successful without the previous ones.

PreK-3rd is not a silver bullet or a simple solution. It is an essential first link in a comprehensive, integrated transformed education system. Achieving that system is not easy.

BASIC ELEMENTS OF A PREK-3RD APPROACH

The basic elements of a PreK-3rd approach include 2 years of voluntary pre-K, starting at age 3, and full-day required kindergarten—both of which are well aligned in standards, an intensive literacy and well-rounded curriculum, and instruction informed by ongoing assessments from pre-K to Grade 3 (Shore, 2009a, 2009b). Especially where there are large numbers of children whose first language is not English, dual-language programs for all children from pre-K to Grade 3 are highly recommended. The engagement of parents in instruction, being knowledgeable about and focused on supporting what goes on in the classroom, is paramount.

Both district and school leadership should support joint professional development that includes all teachers and special staff from the pre-K levels or programs and K–3 grades, meeting on a regular basis, weekly or at least monthly (Shore, 2009a, 2009b). Teachers must be well prepared, with lead teachers qualified to teach any grade from pre-K to Grade 3. Classroom aides or assistant teachers should have associate's degrees in pre-K programs with 20 or more children (Shore, 2009a, 2009b). (For more information about what PreK-3rd approaches look like and what they cost on a state-by-state basis, visit http://www.fcd-us.org to view PreK-3rd Policy to Action briefs.)

PREK-3RD CAN BE EFFECTIVE

Research on PreK-3rd is just beginning. Most of the evidence is based on local efforts, such as Montgomery County, Maryland (Marietta, 2010); Bremerton, Washington (Sullivan-Dudzic, Gearns,

& Leavell, 2010); and South Shore School, Seattle; where these efforts have been independently evaluated, and where achievement gaps have narrowed for disadvantaged students. These studies do not meet the gold standard of randomized, controlled trials, but they provide some evidence that compared to similar children, students in PreK-3rd schools do make significant educational progress over comparable groups.

The negative evidence comes from pre-K programs which have an initial impact, but where the gains are not sustained when children attend low-resource or underfunded schools during the elementary school years. These findings are bolstered by other studies that indicate that when students have 2 or 3 years of good teachers, gains are more likely to be sustained, especially for low-income students, leading to the conclusion that every year counts.

Prospective longitudinal studies that track students from the pre-K years into elementary grades and beyond, based on PreK-3rd approaches, are likely in the coming years as more school districts try this approach. Meanwhile, secondary analysis of existing datasets such as Early Childhood Longitudinal Study-Kindergarten, while not designed to track the effects of PreK-3rd approaches, are supportive of the elements of the approach and its outcomes. The longitudinal evaluation of the Chicago Child-Parent Centers, funded by Title I, and supporting children from pre-K into the third grade, is also instructive (Reynolds, 2011).

LEARNING FROM EARLY EXPERIENCE

PreK-3rd is a work in progress. As more states and school districts take on this approach, it will be possible to learn from their experiences. Two excellent documentations of this approach can be found in *Leading for Equity: The Pursuit of Excellence in the Montgomery County Public Schools* (Childress, Doyle, & Thomas, 2009), and *In Plain Sight* about the Abbott districts in New Jersey (MacInnes, 2009). Another book written by educators, *Making a Difference for Children*, provides concrete guidance to educators based on 10 years of experience in the Bremerton, Washington, school district in connecting community-based centers to the school district (Sullivan-Dudzic et al., 2010).

These early pioneers played close attention to implementation and to results (Childress, Doyle, & Thomas, 2009; MacInnes, 2009). Thus the early lessons about what works can be summarized as follows:

- Districts that focus on literacy, use data to inform and adapt instruction, and align standards, curriculum, and assessments from pre-K to third grade can produce not only significant gains for disadvantaged children, but also narrow the achievement gap between them and more advantaged students.

- District leadership is critical to designing and implementing sound PreK-3rd learning experiences for students. Leadership by superintendents and elementary school principals are crucial for success.

- Joint professional development is required to implement a common curriculum and ambitious, responsive instruction. Teaching is a public and accountable act, where teachers work jointly on a common curriculum and on improving their teaching based on student data, as well as posting their students' outcomes for other staff and for parents (Raudenbush, 2009).

- A multiyear, intensive strategy with horizontal and vertical alignment of instruction takes place with each year building on what comes before and after (Sullivan-Dudzic et al., 2010).

- Feedback loops on student performance in K–3 provide information to pre-K programs about their children's progress (Sullivan-Dudzic et al., 2010).

- Parent and family engagement is focused on literacy and knowledge of children's performance during a school year.

- States and districts can build PreK-3rd linkages with both school and community-based pre-K programs, Head Start, and child care programs, but both leadership and systemic support are required for success.

- Making PreK-3rd connections is not for the fainthearted; the work is arduous and time consuming.

CREATING SUPPORTIVE POLICY STRUCTURES FOR PREK-3RD

Moving forward, both state, school district, and local policies must be in place to scale up and sustain PreK-3rd approaches. Policy makers should

- Address pre-K expansion as an essential part of an education reform agenda nationally and in the states
- Provide for PreK-3rd approaches in the reauthorization of the No Child Left Behind Act of 2001 (PL 107-110) as an evidence-based strategy to narrow the achievement gap and turn around failing schools
- Support the partnership of Head Start programs and local elementary schools to provide PreK-3rd approaches, based on evidence-based practice in Tulsa, Oklahoma's universal preschool program
- Support state education longitudinal data systems that start with children in pre-K to track children's experiences and progress as they move through a PreK-16 education system, including providing feedback to pre-K programs about student outcomes
- Support strong content and preparation in child development for all educators, including a PreK-3rd credential.
- Institute state and district structures that support PreK-3rd approaches, such as directors of early learning or PreK-3rd with responsibilities for pre-K through third grade. In larger primary schools, an assistant principal for PreK-3rd may be considered (Maeroff, 2006)

CONCLUSION

Educators and education policy makers agree that the United States has lost its edge in educational attainment, both in terms of the production of college graduates and the performance of its students on international tests of achievement. Today's children are less likely to graduate from high school than those in their parents' generation. The educational performance of African American, Latino/Hispanic, American Indian, and some Asian groups is unacceptable in a nation that aspires to equal opportunity, democratic governance, and international competitiveness.

PreK-3rd is a critical stage in the first 6 years of publicly supported education (3–8 years of age, spanning 2 years of pre-K programs, kindergarten, and Grades 1–3). Its promise is that, by providing a seamless learning continuum over those years, leaks in the education pipeline from pre-K to Grade 3 and beyond (which turn into gushers by the beginning of high school) will be lessened, and that most of our children will be well educated for a global society.

PreK-3 is not a silver bullet or the panacea for all our educational woes. It is just an important part of a lifelong educational experience that provides the fundamentals and fosters eagerness so that all children will continue to learn throughout their lifetimes. When children are well educated, they are healthier and more likely to live happier lives than those who are left behind in prisons and in poverty. They flourish. Our communities and the nation benefit.

CHAPTER 34

Redirecting Title I

Edward Zigler

Before his inauguration, President Barack Obama was signaling his plan to attack government waste and inefficiency. On *Meet the Press* in December 2008, he talked about "pork coming out of Congress," declaring, "those days are over" (Fischer, 2008). President Obama was clear and consistent in saying that he wants the federal government to stop funding programs that can produce little evidence they succeed.

In the spirit of these messages of change, I offer a recommendation about the federal role in education. It involves the nation's largest investment aimed at improving the educational trajectory of poor children: Title I of the Elementary and Secondary Education Act, which is known in its current incarnation as the No Child Left Behind Act of 2001 (PL 107-110).

Like the Head Start program, Title I was launched in 1965 by President Lyndon B. Johnson as part of a War on Poverty. But unlike Head Start, Title I has never been a specific program with agreed-on practices or standards. Rather, it is a stream of money bestowed on nearly all of the nation's school districts and many private schools. School administrators can mount any type of initiative they feel will be beneficial to the academic progress of poor children.

Thus, schools use the roughly $14 billion in annual Title I funding to support many undertakings: teachers and teacher training; whole-school programs; pull-out programs; after-school sessions; reading, math, and science instruction; and myriad other endeavors. Much of the money is spent on elementary school students, but some of it goes to preschool (about $300 million) and to secondary education. With such a laundry list of activities, one would be hard-pressed to explain to taxpayers exactly what they are purchasing.

The Title I funding stream represents precisely the type of pork President Obama was criticizing, yet little serious thought has been given to what schools are doing with all this money. Instead, the focus is on the formula that determines how much each state and district will receive, with legislators doing their best to optimize the amounts of money they can send back home (and then brag about to voters).

From its inception, the Head Start program has been monitored to assure accountability through a series of evaluation studies, culminating in the Clinton years with a national impact study. But because Title I is such a vast and heterogeneous effort, a similar demonstration of accountability is almost impossible. Indeed, when the U.S. Department of Education attempted a national impact study of Title I (Stullich, Eisner, & McCrary, 2007), it was difficult to adequately interpret the array of data involved. The information studied seemed to indicate that participating children had slight gains in some core competencies prescribed by the No Child Left Behind Act. But the investigators, as if to insert at least some scientific value to their findings, also conducted a study within a study (Torgesen et al., 2007), in which they tried various reading curricula and compared the results with those of students who received standard classroom instruction. It is hard to see how such a study would tell us anything about the efficacy of Title I because the curricula under investigation were not typical Title I fare.

There is a pressing need to reconceptualize Title I and turn it into a more uniform program that can easily be assessed for efficacy. The redesign should be based on sound scientific evidence of effective intervention practices—evidence that did not exist when Title I was originally adopted. As opposed to 1965, there now is a vast amount of literature available to inform planners and policy makers. The Nobel laureate James H. Heckman (2008) has studied this literature and concluded that program payoffs are much higher for young children than they are for interventions that occur at later ages. The national impact study of Title I supported this position, showing that younger students benefited more from reading instruction than older ones.

So it would seem that a key guide to effective programming is "the younger, the better." As one who believes strongly in the value of good, quality preschool education, I would certainly endorse the use of Title I money for more preschool programming for young poor children. But this would put Title I in competition with both Head Start and the programs in 38 states that offer public preschool for at-risk children. A better use of Title I funds would be to build on the benefits of preschool during children's early years of elementary school.

To its credit, Title I has never been tied to the inoculation model that pervaded the social sciences at the time it was launched. Everyone wanted to believe then that 1 or 2 years of preschool could serve as an inoculation against all the ravages of poverty that a child may experience long before starting and long after leaving a preschool intervention.

That hope has not faded. School boards continue to sell preschool as the ticket to later academic success, while doing little to improve the schools that children will attend 13 times longer than preschool. A more realistic developmental model should be used, in which the child is seen as moving from stage to stage in life, with each stage requiring appropriate environmental nutrients.

The nation has tried to move in this direction by fits and starts since the late 1960s, when Project Follow Through was mounted. I was on the planning committee for this program, and what we tried to do was create a dovetailed program from kindergarten through third grade that would continue to incorporate Head Start's bedrock principles of parent involvement and comprehensive services. These would be joined to appropriate curricula during these four foundational grades of primary school. Unfortunately, this design was never put into place because the huge costs of the Vietnam War depleted available funds. Instead of a school-age version of Head Start, Follow Through became a comparative assessment of various curricula during the early years of schooling (Bock, Stebbins, Proper, 1977).

There was another chance during the 1990s, when I worked with Senator Edward M. Kennedy of Massachusetts to conceptualize and mount the Head Start Transition Project, which was essentially the Follow Through program as envisioned by its planners. An evaluation of that effort mounted by Sharon and Craig Ramey was pretty much ignored by the field since the basic outcome was no significant difference between the treatment and control groups. Had scholars dug through the report to find what actually happened on the ground, however, they would have discovered very positive news: When personnel in the control schools saw what was going on in the experimental schools, they wanted to participate too, with some even raising outside funds for the extra services. The study thus was undermined by a huge diffusion effect, in which the benefits of the intervention were diffused to the control schools not intended to participate in the program but voluntarily adopting it.

Although there may have been no differences in the performance of the treatment and control groups, what was overlooked in the transition project of the 1990s was that both groups were functioning so well that they reached national norms. This is one of the rare times in my long experience where poor children attained and maintained national standards by the end of fourth grade.

Another extended intervention model is the Chicago Child-Parent Centers (Reynolds, 2000), which were funded through Title I. Like Head Start, that program emphasizes comprehensive services and parent participation, but it adds strong transition services. Arthur J. Reynolds, Director of the Chicago Longitudinal Study, found that children who had 2 years of preschool did better than those with only 1 year. Children did better still if the preschool program was followed by a dovetailed program in the early years of primary school. The benefits extended to adolescence in the form of better school and social adjustment.

The fact is that extended early childhood intervention has been proven to work. On the other hand, there is little to show for vast expenditures on Title I in its current form. I recommend that both the transition project and Title I's own Chicago Child-Parent Centers are used as models for a new Title I that would serve poor children from kindergarten through the third grade. Because it is well known that the child's school trajectory can pretty much be predicted by the end of third grade, these are appropriate years to target. This type of program would constructively deal with the empirical fact that some (not all) of the progress children make in preschool fades out during the early elementary grades.

The plan I am suggesting would enable Title I to evolve from a hodgepodge of efforts into a single program that could have performance standards to guide quality and make Title I more accountable. A designated portion of funding would be set aside for a rigorous longitudinal evaluation. Instead of pork, elected officials could then deliver to their constituents a promising way to close the recalcitrant achievement gap between poor and wealthier children.

PART III

What Next?

Lessons from the States

STUDY QUESTIONS

- What lessons can be learned from Oklahoma's program? New Jersey's program?

- What are some unique characteristics of both programs?

CHAPTER 35

Prekindergarten in Oklahoma

Elizabeth Rose

Which state leads the nation in providing preschool for its 4-year-olds? Many people outside the field are surprised to learn the answer: Oklahoma. In 2008, 71% of the state's 4-year-olds were enrolled in publicly funded preschool programs, taught by teachers certified in early childhood education. Both the scale and the quality standards of Oklahoma's 4-year-old program make it stand out among other state efforts to provide preschool. Furthermore, research studies in Tulsa (the state's largest school district) document higher cognitive gains for children who attend these preschool programs than have been found in studies of other public programs. Additional research also suggests positive—although more modest—effects on aspects of children's socioemotional development likely to influence success in later schooling. This chapter describes the development of Oklahoma's early childhood program and identifies some characteristics that have led to its success.

Over time and without much public fanfare, Oklahoma has essentially added prekindergarten (pre-K) as a grade to its public education system—albeit one that remains optional for both families and districts. Making pre-K part of Oklahoma's system of public education has made it universally available, while mandating high-quality standards. Pre-K developed within Oklahoma's existing school system in ways that did not seem possible in states like Georgia and New York, which also launched universal preschool programs during the 1990s (Rose, 2010). This was partly because the program was built up over time, starting as a small pilot in the 1980s, and because declining enrollment in some areas meant there was space available in school buildings as well as an incentive for school districts to launch programs. The 4-year-old program's integration into the system of public education in Oklahoma is evident from its funding through the state aid formula to its requirements for teachers. In a conservative state that struggles with poverty (51% of its K–12 students now qualify for free or reduced-price lunch), expanding preschool quietly through the schools has helped extend quality preschool opportunities on a scale that few imagined.

ORIGINS

Oklahoma's pre-K program started on a small scale in 1980 but with a broad vision of extending the benefits of the public education system to young children. Ramona Paul, a state education official and early childhood specialist, helped design a pilot program for 4-year-olds based in public schools and staffed by teachers certified in early childhood education. Starting on a small scale of about 10 classrooms for 4-year-olds around the state, the program grew as a part of the reform in Oklahoma's K–12 education system that state legislators demanded during a period of fiscal crisis in the late 1980s. Research on the long-term benefits of early childhood education helped to build support for expanding the program. A major school reform bill in 1990 incorporated funding for pre-K into the state education aid formula. The high standards that had been part of the initial pilot program continued to apply, including the requirement that preschool teachers be certified in early childhood education.

Like many other state pre-K programs created during this era, the 1990 legislation gave priority to children from low-income families. However, some legislators and education advocates wanted to expand it to serve a wider range of the state's children. For Democratic legislator Joe Eddins, a staffer explained, this was a natural step: "It did not seem logical to him to have restrictions on something that is in the public schools, [and] is supposed to be for all children" (M. Goff, personal communication, June 17, 2004). Statewide education groups also lobbied to make the program open to all children. Kay Floyd, the lobbyist for the Oklahoma State School Boards Association, remembered that the State Department of Education "was behind us on this; they felt that anything that was part of the public schools, funded through the state aid formula, should be for all children" (K. Floyd, personal communication, June 22, 2004; R. Raburn, personal communication, July 30, 2004).

Although Governor Frank Keating vetoed an initial attempt to expand eligibility for the program in 1996, two years later he approved it. Realizing that school districts were starting to enroll 4-year-olds in kindergarten classes, he agreed with legislators who preferred to put the 4-year-old program on more solid footing, while prohibiting the enrollment of underage children in kindergarten classes. In 1998, Oklahoma opened the program up to all 4-year-olds and increased its funding weight in the state's school aid formula.

With funding secure through the state aid formula and enrollment opened to all, the 4-year-old program became an integral part of the public schools in most Oklahoma districts. The 1998 legislation spurred a dramatic expansion in the number of 4-year-old programs across the state. Statewide preschool enrollment, which had already grown substantially during the mid-1990s, doubled in 1998. By 2003, Oklahoma was serving more 4-year-olds in state-funded pre-K than any state in the nation. By 2007, almost all of the state's 540 school districts were offering 4-year-old classes, reaching 68% of the state's 4-year-olds at a cost of about $118 million (Adams & Sandfort, 1994; Barnett et al., 2007; Schulman, Blank, & Ewen, 1999). Thousands of parents were clearly eager to enroll their children. For instance, when the district of Moore launched a preschool program in 1999, responding to continuous calls from the community, demand far outstripped supply when 300 children signed up for 160 slots. In 2003, officials decided they could no longer allow parents to camp out the night before pre-K enrollment to get their child a spot, citing security concerns raised by the local police (Anderson, 2003; Pagley, 1999). A teacher in one of the new pre-K programs in Tulsa said that parents "feel good it's being offered in a public school" (Dudley, 1998).

Creating universal pre-K was thus a quiet revolution, not the result of a highly visible campaign to build public support for early childhood education. Eddins explained, "Some states have made a big deal and the governor and the legislature say, 'Let's do something big.' That's not the way we did it here in Oklahoma" (Fuller, 2007, p. 102). Unlike Georgia's highly publicized education lottery, Oklahoma's funding of universal pre-K was nearly invisible and was not funded by any new source of revenue.

More than any other state, Oklahoma has provided universally accessible pre-K by working through the structure of the public schools. State education officials maintained high-quality standards in part by treating pre-K like other grades in the public education system: Districts had to hire teachers certified in early childhood education and compensate them at the same rate as their other teachers. Group size was limited to 20 children, and the adult-to-child ratio was kept to 1:10. There was no mandated curriculum (although the state did develop voluntary curriculum guidelines for pre-K programs and required use of a standard report card) and no extensive system for monitoring classrooms. Rather, the strategy was to hire well-trained teachers, give them some flexibility about meeting their goals, and make school leaders responsible for the success of the pre-K program. Although school districts are encouraged to collaborate with Head Start programs and child care centers in offering programs, the majority of 4-year-olds are served in school-based classrooms.

RESEARCH

Evidence for the effectiveness of Oklahoma's approach came from a series of studies conducted in Tulsa (the state's largest school district) by Georgetown University researchers in 2002–2003. Using a research design that reduced the problem of selection bias, the researchers found that the test scores of children who had completed pre-K were significantly higher than those of children who did not attend the program, especially in prereading and prewriting skills. The size of the effects—0.79 of standard deviation for prereading skills, 0.64 for prewriting, and 0.38 for premath—was much larger than the overall effect sizes for preschool participation found in the national Early Childhood Longitudinal Study-Kindergarten data (0.19 for reading and 0.17 for math; Gormley et al., 2005). Moreover, children from different backgrounds all benefited from the program, although benefits were greater for children from poorer and minority families (Gormley et al., 2005).

Of particular interest is the fact that Tulsa's pre-K program has managed to attract a large number of Hispanic students, despite the fact that Hispanic families nationwide are less likely to enroll their children in preschool. Looking more closely at the results for Hispanic children, Gormley found substantial improvements in prereading, prewriting, and premath skills (especially for students who were born in Mexico or whose parents speak Spanish at home), and he hypothesized that Tulsa's "strong academically focused pre-K program offers linguistic and cognitive benefits that their parents are less able to provide" (2008, p. 934). Moreover, the Tulsa program achieved these effects despite having very few Hispanic or bilingual teachers.

Tulsa's pre-K program also has some impact on children's socioemotional development, especially on aspects relevant to children's later success in school. Children in both school-based pre-K and in Head Start classrooms were found to enter kindergarten with greater capacities to pay attention, lower levels of timidity, and (in the school district classrooms) lower levels of apathy. Teachers rated these students' interactions with teachers as more positive than those students who did not attend pre-K, meaning they were more likely to be involved in class activities, to talk appropriately with the teacher, and to help with classroom jobs. The effect sizes (from .10 to .22) were modest but consistent with other research on socioemotional outcomes of preschool. Significantly, no evidence of greater aggressiveness and externalizing behavior was found in this group, as other studies have found for formal group care. The researchers hypothesized that higher levels of emotional and instructional support in Tulsa classrooms were responsible (Gormley, Philips, Newmark, & Perper, 2009).

Researchers are still seeking to explain why the pre-K program in Tulsa has shown stronger effects on children's cognitive development than have other state pre-K programs. Part of the answer is surely connected to the fact that Tulsa teachers seemed to be providing higher quality classrooms compared with pre-K classrooms studied in 11 other states. Tulsa teachers were rated significantly higher on observational measures of instructional support and classroom organization. They also devoted significantly more time to academic activities (especially literacy and math), while still providing the same level of emotional support to children. But it is not clear what aspects of Oklahoma's program led to this higher quality, as there was no clear connection between these measures of instructional quality and teachers' academic backgrounds, length of teaching experience, or curriculum used (Phillips, Gormley, & Lowenstein, 2009).

Two elements of Tulsa's program—teacher compensation and the role of the school district—deserve more attention. Like several other states, Oklahoma sets a fairly high standard for pre-K teachers, requiring that they have a bachelor's degree with a certification in early childhood education. Unlike most other states, however, Oklahoma requires that pre-K teachers be paid at the same rate as K–12 teachers, regardless of whether their classroom is located in a school building or a community site (e.g., child care center, church preschool). Furthermore, Tulsa County Head Start has chosen to pay its teachers of 4-year-olds at the same rate as the school district in order to compete for highly qualified staff. This is an important distinction, given that teacher salaries are one of the most robust predictors of the overall quality of the classroom learning environment, even after controlling for teacher education and training, staff-to-child ratio, and group size (Zigler et al., 2006a). The leading role that the school district plays in Tulsa's pre-K program may be another factor in explaining its greater instructional emphasis. The overwhelming majority of Tulsa's pre-K classrooms are sponsored by the school district, and the Head Start classrooms for 4-year-olds are collaborations between the school district and the Head Start program that meet the school district's quality standards. Tulsa's school superintendent explained the alignment between Head Start and district-sponsored classrooms: "I expect them to use our curriculum; they are right in step with us" (Fuller, 2007, p. 118). Phillips, Gormley, and Lowenstein noted that "perhaps the most policy-relevant conclusion from this study is a demonstration that a mixed-delivery system for pre-K *that brings all programs under the same umbrella of high-quality standards* can promote positive experiences for children across program auspices" (2009, p. 226; italics added). It may be that Oklahoma's reliance on the public schools to deliver pre-K has provided a means for promoting a consistent instructional emphasis going beyond that of other states offering universal pre-K.

Several characteristics of Oklahoma's program suggest lessons from which policy makers and advocates could learn. First, pre-K is fully integrated into the system of K–12 education and administered by public school districts. Districts may collaborate with Head Start and child care centers in order to serve more children, but most classrooms are school based. Of the states that currently enroll a large number of children in universal pre-K, Oklahoma is unique in relying primarily on the public schools. This school-based approach in Oklahoma was possible partly because of the way the program grew over time, from a small pilot program to an accepted part of the state's school aid formula. Pre-K was associated with K–12 education reform and included in the state's major school reform bill in 1990. Declining enrollments in some parts of the state played a role, creating both available space in some school buildings and incentives for school districts to start pre-K programs. Consistent leadership from the State Department of Education over a period of many years also enabled the program for 4-year-olds to become an integral part of Oklahoma's education system while maintaining high-quality standards.

Second, Oklahoma's approach to pre-K evolved over time from serving the neediest children to accepting all 4-year-olds whose parents wished to enroll them. Rather than making the cause of universal pre-K a public campaign or the signature issue of a political leader, opening up the existing program to all children was an incremental, quiet revolution undertaken by state legislators and education leaders.

Finally, as it expanded, the program maintained its high-quality standards, including requiring that teachers have bachelor's degrees and certification in early childhood education, that they be paid equally with other teachers, and that adult-to-child ratios be no more than 1:10. These quality standards were maintained in collaborations between schools, Head Start programs, and community child care providers, helping to ensure overall program quality.

Some of these characteristics reflect the particular history and context in which pre-K took root in Oklahoma. Nevertheless, other policy makers would do well to examine the reasons behind Oklahoma's success in offering a high-quality preschool program to all its 4-year-olds, which is making a difference in young children's learning. These include starting off with high program standards, addressing teacher compensation as well as degree requirements, expanding eligibility incrementally, and integrating early education with K–12 education as fully as possible.

CHAPTER 36

New Jersey's Abbott Prekindergarten Program
A Model for the Nation

Ellen C. Frede and W. Steven Barnett

In 1998, New Jersey's Supreme Court ordered a remarkable set of education reforms that included universal, well-planned, high-quality preschool education for 3- and 4-year-olds in 31 school districts. The ruling is part of the landmark *Abbott v. Burke* (1985) that has accumulated 20 state Supreme Court rulings through 2009. The districts involved serve about one quarter of the state's children, and the court ruling created a remarkable experiment that has allowed researchers to study the consequences of one of the most significant changes in early childhood policy anywhere in the United States.

The New Jersey Supreme Court set out only a few basic standards for the preschool education that it ordered: a certified teacher and an assistant for each class, maximum class size of 15 students, developmentally appropriate curriculum, adequate facilities, and transportation, health, and other related services as needed. The court mandated only a half-day school-year program because of concerns that the schools might be overburdened given their other urgent responsibilities, and the court permitted services to be provided through public school, Head Start, or community child care programs. School districts and the state were assigned the responsibility of ensuring that preschool programs met the court's standards and provided a high-quality education regardless of program auspice.

Subsequently, the state developed a full-day, full-year program that was initially available at no cost for 10 hours per day, 245 days a year. The Abbott prekindergarten (pre-K) program combines a 6-hour State of New Jersey Department of Education (DOE) program for at least 180 school days with a State of New Jersey Department of Human Services wraparound program of daily before- and aftercare, and up to 65 days of school holiday and summer care. Currently, low-income families continue to receive the wraparound services at no cost, but other families pay for that service. The state implemented incentive programs and deadlines for teachers to acquire bachelor's degrees and a P–3 certification (a new certification created in response to the court order). However, full implementation of the court's orders with respect to quality and the funding to meet quality standards did not begin until Governor James McGreevy took office in 2002. To ensure quality, the state created a system for continuous improvement. This chapter describes that system and the evidence that it raised the quality of children's early education with positive consequences for children's learning and school success.

THE NEW JERSEY CONTINUOUS IMPROVEMENT SYSTEM

The establishment of basic goals and stipulation of key program features and agency responsibilities are the key steps in the development of an effective preschool education system. Another key step is the provision of adequate funding. Funding for the DOE component is about $12,000 per year. To put this into perspective, New Jersey's public schools spend about $16,000 per child in K–12 (including the costs of special education). Yet, these steps are not sufficient to ensure that this or another preschool program achieves its goals. For that purpose, the DOE created a continuous improvement system. Creation of the system began with the development of uniform standards for program operation, learning, and teaching. This formed the foundation for a set of continuous improvement cycles at the state, district, and teacher levels, each requiring the collection of data linked to the standards that are then used to plan improvements (often through professional development). The state, school districts, and teachers each have responsibilities in the system and work together to improve policies, regulations, procedures, and practices (Frede, 2005).

State Standards

In 2002, the Early Childhood Education Work Group was formed consisting of representatives of school districts, private child care centers, Head Start, advocacy groups, community groups, higher education, teacher unions, early childhood professional organizations, and state agencies. Subcommittees developed recommendations for guidelines across relevant program component areas. These recommendations were revised and edited by the Department of Education and published as the *Abbott Preschool Program Implementation Guidelines* (revised for the entire state and summarized in State of New Jersey Department of Education, Division of Early Childhood, 2010a). The guidelines are derived from research and expert opinion. Developed as recommendations—not mandates—to accommodate local contexts and needs, many of the provisions were subsequently incorporated into state regulations as it became clear they were universally applicable.

Expectations for learning and teaching were first created in 2000 and then revised in 2002. Work groups were formed with representatives of many of the same groups who contributed to the program implementation guidelines, but with a strong emphasis on experts in each of eight domains of learning. Guidelines for learning outcomes were coupled with guidelines for teaching practices to ensure that the press to achieve learning goals did not lead to inappropriate teaching methods. The resulting document, *Preschool Teaching and Learning Expectations: Standards of Quality*, was adopted by the state board in 2004 but was used for professional development since its completion in 2002 and was subsequently revised (State of New Jersey Department of Education, Division of Early Childhood, 2009). Abbott districts are required to plan or adopt curriculum and teaching practices that will result in children meeting the expectations. The DOE provided intensive professional development to support the expectations and requires that districts adopt one of five curriculum models aligned with the expectations (districts may adopt an alternative under certain conditions). As described in the following section, assessment systems were developed at child, classroom, program, and state levels based on the expectations and guidelines.

The State's Role

The DOE developed statewide systems for accountability and program improvement that makes extensive use of samples of classrooms, children, and program financial data. Accountability requires some basic information on every child, classroom, program, and district, but sampling permits the state to obtain highly detailed data at a feasible cost in terms of time and money. Information is used to plan rules, regulations, technical assistance, and professional development. To help with this process, the DOE formed a partnership with higher education, the Early Learning Improvement Consortium (ELIC) in 2002. The ELIC has collected and reported data annually on program quality and children's learning for random samples of classrooms and children. Standardized measures of teaching and the classroom environment are collected by ELIC observers who have been trained for reliability and provide an external check on quality in each district. Each fall, kindergartners' abilities in language, literacy, and mathematics were assessed by ELIC staff trained to reliably administer individual standardized tests that have been widely used in early childhood research.

The ELIC conducted classroom observations using three instruments: the Early Childhood Environment Rating Scale–Revised (ECERS-R; Harms et al., 1998), the Support for Early Literacy Assessment (SELA; Smith, Davidson, & Weisenfeld, 2001), and the Preschool Classroom Mathematics Inventory (PCMI; Frede, Dessewffy, Hornbeck, & Worth, 2003). The ECERS-R provides a comprehensive look at classroom quality and allows the state to compare New Jersey's scores to programs in the research literature and in other states. The SELA provides more specific information on practices that support children's early language and literacy skills. The PCMI focuses on the materials and methods used in preschool classrooms to support and enhance children's math skills. The SELA and PCMI are considered important additions to the ECERS-R because they are designed to more directly assess teaching strategies that relate to academic learning. Teachers and their mentors readily understand the results of the SELA and PCMI and can easily translate them into professional development and program improvement plans. The criteria in both the SELA and PCMI are closely related to the teaching practices delineated in the state's *Preschool Teaching and Learning Expectations* (State of New Jersey Department of Education, 2009).

Four child assessments have been employed. Children are assessed in English or, if appropriate, Spanish. Language development is assessed using the Peabody Picture Vocabulary Test–III (PPVT-3; Dunn & Dunn, 1997) and, for Spanish speakers, the Test de Vocabulario en Imágenes Peabody (Dunn, Lugo, Padilla, & Dunn, 1986). Early literacy skills were measured with the Print Awareness subtest of the Preschool Comprehensive Test of Phonological and Print Processing (Lonigan, Wagner, Torgeson, & Rashotte, 2002). The Print Awareness subtest measures children's ability to distinguish words and letters from pictures; it also measures the extent to which children know that letters have distinct names, shapes, and sound associations. Mathematical skills were measured with the Woodcock-Johnson Tests of Achievement, Subtest 10, Applied Problems—and its Spanish language equivalent (Woodcock et al., 2001). It is recognized that this is far from a complete assessment of the extent to which the program's learning goals are achieved, but it is considered a reasonable way to monitor progress without imposing an excessive assessment burden.

The state also must ensure fiscal accountability. The transition from fee for service and the child care subsidy system to contracting with public schools posed challenges for private providers. The DOE instituted a number of fiscal accountability measures beginning with clear and specific budget guidance for private providers contracting with districts. In the first years of the program, every program budget was scrutinized at the classroom level. Expenditures were subject to quarterly review by district fiscal specialists and the state conducts district expenditure reviews. Finally, the state annually selected at random approximately 100 agencies from the more than 500 that contract to provide pre-K. Also, any reports of irregularities would lead to reviews and audits. Information obtained from reviews and audits was used to train fiscal specialists to provide technical assistance to private providers and to develop a training module on budgeting and fiscal accountability. Providers with gross negligence or actual malfeasance have lost their contracts.

The District's Role

The DOE developed the Self-Assessment Validation System (SAVS; Wilkins & Frede, 2005) to assist districts and the state in implementing the continuous improvement cycle as an annual process at the district level. The SAVS is designed to guide districts through systematic self-appraisal of their preschool programs as a basis for developing program improvement plans. The SAVS items and scoring criteria are derived from the *Abbott Preschool Program Implementation Guidelines* (State of New Jersey Department of Education, 2010a), providing an accountability measure linked to program standards. Each of the 45 items on the SAVS is rated on a 3-point scale, where 1 indicates *not met*, 2 indicates *in progress*, and 3 indicates *fully met*. The district then receives an overall SAVS score derived by averaging the item scores.

The SAVS process goes through two phases annually. In Phase I, district personnel, in collaboration with other relevant parties such as the local Early Childhood Advisory Council, assess their early childhood program. These initial ratings inform revisions to the operational plan and budget requests submitted to the DOE. Because the SAVS is a program improvement tool, districts are encouraged to look critically and honestly at their programs. In Phase I, districts conduct a self-assessment and plan for improvement. In Phase II, districts work with their DOE liaisons to rescore the SAVS with particular attention to growth and areas in need of development. Documentation must be provided to justify the SAVS scores. These results are then submitted to the DOE. Validation visits are made to approximately one third of the districts each year to verify the scores reported in the SAVS. In addition, districts combine the results of the SAVS with data from other sources to develop detailed professional development plans that are submitted to the DOE.

Since 2003, Abbott districts also have been required by regulation to conduct annual structured observations of all preschool classrooms and to use the information for program improvement. Preschool professional development coaches, called *master teachers*, conduct the observations in the beginning of each school year to help them tailor their classroom interventions and other professional development district wide. Typically, districts use the ECERS-R until most or all classrooms score above a 5. At that point, they switch to an observation instrument that either measures fidelity of implementation of their particular curriculum or that looks at more specific teaching practices.

Districts are required to set a low-end cutoff score for contracting classrooms. Any classroom that does not meet that cutoff must have a classroom improvement plan with a timeline for improvement. The district early childhood education supervisor and the master teacher assigned to that classroom meet with the center director and the teacher to develop the plan. The district is required to offer intensive assistance. If adequate progress is not made, an outside, trained, and reliable observer repeats the observation and a center may lose the contract. Although they are trained by the state in the observation instruments, not all master teachers have established reliability on the instruments. Therefore, the state does not collect this data and outside observers are required to corroborate the district findings before a contract is terminated.

Abbott districts provide one master teacher for every 17–20 pre-K teachers. They engage teachers in a cycle of reflective evaluation structured by planning, observation, and postobservation review (Costa & Garmston, 2002). The master teacher works together with each teacher to set goals for that teacher and classroom. The master teacher observes and collects objective data relating to the achievement of those goals, and then analyzes the data from the observations, together with the teacher, to plan future teaching practices, including the use of performance assessment to monitor child progress and inform teaching. Master teachers also work with teachers to plan professional development activities in addition to the coaching they provide, and they work with other administrators on broader supports for learning and teaching in pre-K.

The Teacher's Role

Teachers use ongoing child assessment systems to help improve their teaching. In 2003, the DOE, with the help of the ELIC, created a performance-based assessment of children's language and literacy development. The Early Learning Assessment System (ELAS; State of New Jersey Department of Education, Division of Early Childhood, 2010b) uses teacher observation and portfolio documentation to assess children's emerging oral language and literacy skills as delineated on the *Preschool Teaching and Learning Expectations* and the kindergarten *Core Curriculum Content Standards*. Originally, the ELAS was to be developed into a broader measure of learning and development covering multiple domains with sufficient validity established to allow aggregation at the classroom, district, and state levels. The DOE subsequently decided to require districts to adopt one of several existing performance-based assessments for use by teachers. The information from these performance-based assessments is used to adapt and individualize interactions for specific children and to adjust activities for the entire classroom as well. Unfortunately, use of multiple instruments precludes aggregation of data across districts.

RESULTS OF THE ABBOTT PRE-K PROGRAM

Prior to the Abbott pre-K program, nearly 80% of 4-year-olds and more than 40% of 3-year-olds in New Jersey's Abbott districts attended a public or private center-based program (Barnett, Tarr, Esposito-Lamy, & Frede, 2001). A quarter of each age group was served in private child care centers. About 30% of 4-year-olds and 5% of 3-year-olds were served by the public schools. Head Start served 22% of 4-year-olds and 11% of 3-year-olds. Nevertheless, most children were ill-prepared to succeed in school, and the quality of many of the preschool programs children attended was poor (Barnett et al., 2001). These were the problems that the Abbott pre-K program was supposed to resolve. How did the program perform as it increased enrollment from a small fraction of the population to nearly all children?

Program Quality

ELIC data provide a description of change in program quality from the beginning of the Abbott pre-K program to the 2008–2009 school year. In 1999–2000, structured observations of preschool programs in the Abbott districts yielded the following information. On the ECERS-R, the average score was 3.9, above the *minimal* level (3.0), but below *good* (5.0). Public school districts and Head Start–operated programs scored 4.4, whereas private programs scored 3.5. In addition, there was more variability among private providers. By 2008–2009, the average ECERS-R score had increased to 5.2, and 64% of programs now scored in the good to excellent range. Moreover, there was no longer any difference in average score between public schools and contracted private providers in the Abbott districts.

Results on the SELA revealed substantial improvements over time in teaching practices relating to language and literacy, although data on this measure go back only to 2002–2003. The percentage of classrooms scoring in the lowest quality range (less than 2) dropped from 12% to none by 2008–2009, whereas the percentage of classrooms scoring in the top range (4 or higher) increased from 10% to 47% in 2005.

Classroom scores on the PCMI also improved but remain toward the lower end of the scale compared to scores on the ECERS-R and the SELA. This may reflect the lack of emphasis given to math in preschool education generally, or the PCMI may be more demanding with a higher top end. Nevertheless, the percentage of classrooms scoring in the lowest range (less than 2) dropped from 41% in 2002–2003 to 11% in 2008–2009, whereas the percentage of classrooms scoring in the top two categories (3 or higher) increased from 14% to 32% in 2008–2009.

Impacts on Learning

The effects of 1 year of Abbott pre-K on learning were estimated at kindergarten entry using a regression-discontinuity design, which mimics a randomized trial in eliminating differences between the treatment and control group. Statistically significant effects were found on vocabulary, print awareness, and mathematics (Frede et al., 2007). One year of pre-K was estimated to increase the growth in vocabulary an extra 4 months above gains for the control group, with an effect size of 0.28 standard deviation (SD). The estimated effect on math was to increase learning by more than 40% (0.36 SD). Children who attended 1 year of Abbott pre-K made almost twice as much progress in print awareness as those who did not (0.56 SD). To put these gains in perspective, the estimated effect sizes are considerably larger than those found for 1 year of Head Start on the same measures (U.S. Department of Health and Human Services, 2010b).

The regression discontinuity approach cannot be used to estimate either long-term effects or the effects of more than 1 year of pre-K. A more conventional comparison of children who did and did not attend pre-K with statistical controls for family background was used to estimate long-term effects. This more conventional approach appears to underestimate the effects, but despite this limitation there were statistically significant effects on multiple measures through the end of second grade, which was the most recently completed follow-up (Frede et al., 2009).

The Abbott pre-K program appears to be producing substantial lasting educational benefits. At the end of second grade, effects are apparent on grade retention, language, and mathematics. On most measures, the effects of 2 years of pre-K were twice as large as the effect of 1 year. Grade retention was reduced from 10.7% for those who did not attend Abbott pre-K to 7.2% for those who had 1 year of Abbott pre-K and 5.3% for those who had 2 years. Estimated standardized effects on language (PPVT-3) at the end of second grade were 0.22 SD for 1 year of pre-K and 0.40 SD for 2 years. Estimated standardized effects on math (applied problems) were 0.24 ($p < .05$) for 1 year and 0.44 ($p < .01$) for 2 years of pre-K. The 2-year effects are similar in size to effects of the Chicago Child-Parent Centers, which were estimated to have produced benefits far greater than their cost (Reynolds, 2000). It was no longer appropriate to examine effects on print awareness, as essentially all children had mastered this skill by kindergarten. However, a significant effect was found on reading comprehension, a more appropriate measure of literacy development at this age.

CONCLUSION

New Jersey's Abbott pre-K program is an ambitious endeavor ordered by the court to ensure that young children in low-income, urban districts enter kindergarten better prepared to succeed in school. The program has high standards and is well resourced with highly educated, adequately paid teachers and small classes. However, the most important innovation in the Abbott pre-K program may be the development of an extensive data-based system to inform decision making from the classroom to the capitol. A continuous improvement cycle has been established for teachers, district administrators, and state administrators working together in partnership with higher education.

Although the data generated are far from complete or perfect, the system has made remarkable strides toward improving teaching and learning. The preschool classrooms that children attend are vastly improved. Children are learning more and maintaining substantial educational advantages as they move through elementary school. We doubt that these outcomes would have been achieved without the high standards, funding, or continuous improvement cycle. None of these three elements alone is likely to have been sufficient for the transformation of preschool education and care that took place. It is noteworthy that New Jersey did not rely on standardized testing of every child to achieve its goals but applied a more nuanced, multilevel, multimethod approach to assessing teaching and learning. It is a model that other states and the federal government might do well to emulate.

STUDY QUESTIONS

- What are the short-term and long-term impacts of early childhood education programs?

- What are the characteristics of these programs that enhance positive short-term impacts?

CHAPTER 37

A Warning Against Exaggerating the Benefits of Preschool Education Programs

Edward Zigler

Early intervention programs like Head Start and the HighScope Perry preschool were the inspiration for today's preschool education movement. Although early intervention and preschool are not the same, the two types of program share many common elements and are often treated as indistinguishable in the public mind. Over the years, I have been witness to the advances and retreats, the positives and negatives, in how early intervention has been perceived by decision makers, scientists, and society. I see some of the more regretful events in this history being repeated as the momentum in preschool education gathers speed. The purpose of this chapter is to remind readers of these missteps so they can recognize the patterns before they again bedevil our efforts on behalf of young children.

The most valuable lesson advocates for preschool education can take from the early intervention field is not to oversell the potential benefits. Wild expectations for what Head Start could achieve began shortly after the program's debut. For example, President Lyndon Johnson confidently promised Americans that Head Start would soon put an end to poverty and enable the preschool graduates to avoid welfare dependency and crime and to grow to be model citizens. This was certainly a lot to expect from an untried program that enrolled children living in poverty for a mere 6–8 weeks during the summer before they began elementary school, which is how the program started.

Johnson's War on Poverty czar, Sargent Shriver, had actually created Head Start for the practical reason of preparing poor children for school entry. In another capacity, he had visited Susan Gray and Rupert Klaus's (1970) experimental project that appeared to increase the IQ scores of children at high risk for intellectual disabilities. Shriver was fascinated by these results and began to think Head Start could do the same for poor children of average intelligence. Although he only used this card when it was politically expedient to do so, the notion that Head Start could make children smarter was impossible to uproot once it was planted. Scientists obliged and conducted study after study showing that children's IQ scores did go up after their brief experience in Head Start or just about any other preschool intervention. Once this advantage was found to fade away over time, the Head Start program was put on the federal chopping block. In fact, one of my first assignments when I arrived in Washington was to phase the program out over the next 3 years. My superior, Elliot Richardson, saved Head Start by appealing directly to the White House.

Adapted from a December 7, 2007, address at the National Invitational Conference of the Early Childhood Research Collaborative and the subsequently published conference proceedings: From Reynolds, A.J., Rolnick, A.J., Englund, M.M., & Temple, J.A. (Eds.). (2010). *Childhood programs and practices in the first decade of life: A human capital integration*. New York: Cambridge University Press. Copyright © 2010 Cambridge University Press. Reprinted with the permission of Cambridge University Press.

It was known in the 1960s that growing up in poverty was a threat to a child's optimal development. Head Start was designed to address some of the conditions of poverty that cause poor children to be ill-prepared when they enter school. Certainly Head Start's planners never believed that a brief summer program would have much effect on a poor child's entire life course. They just did not do a good job convincing policy makers and the public. Once the momentum built, they could not extinguish the hopes that this one little program could eradicate the centuries-old problem of poverty and make children smarter to boot.

The story was repeated in the 1990s when studies using neurological imaging revealed that brain development in the earliest years of life could be tracked and potentially linked to environmental events. Suddenly there was a revival of the belief that enriched early experiences can accelerate cognitive development. No wonder Head Start did not boost intelligence: It was offered too late in the cycle of the developing brain. Efforts to extend Head Start to younger children had begun shortly after the program did, but the neurological research gave advocates the ammunition they needed to validate an expansion of Head Start services to infants and toddlers. While I believe with all my heart in the wisdom and value of Early Head Start, I fear it was advertised for the wrong reasons. Neurological science only gives a glimpse into how brain development works, not how to make it work faster or better. If Early Head Start is eventually shown to have no demonstrable effect on synaptic development—or for that matter if the Family and Medical Leave Act of 1993 (PL 103-3) cannot be shown to change the brain's architecture—support for these worthy efforts may decline. A hint that this is not an unfounded worry comes from the fact that the makers of the Baby Einstein videos, which were created at the height of the media blitz over early brain development, are offering to give parents refunds—"a tacit admission that they did not increase infant intellect" (Lewin, 2009, p. A1).

Although it should be known by now, the tendency to imbue Head Start with unreal expectations of what the program can achieve persists. For example, President George W. Bush criticized Head Start on the grounds that the at-risk children who attended did not attain the same degree of school readiness as more affluent children. Of course they don't. Head Start cannot single-handedly fix broken families, raise incomes, quell neighborhood violence, improve lifetime health care and nutrition, and provide the multitude of enriching experiences that middle-class children have before they set foot in preschool. In response to Bush's comments, Jeanne Brooks-Gunn (2003) wrote a report she titled *Do You Believe in Magic?* It is magical thinking indeed to expect a year or two of preschool to eliminate the persistent achievement gap between poor and wealthier children.

There has never been an inoculation against the injurious effects of poverty, even several years of a model intervention program. I have argued that to overcome the ravages of poverty on human development, three dovetailed efforts must be used: a home-visiting program from pregnancy to 3 years of age, followed by 2 years of high-quality preschool, and then coordinated programming from kindergarten through the third grade. I believe this is the intensity of effort required to offset the harmful developmental effects of poverty.

Today's most vocal preschool education advocates are economists, and they strike me as a mixed blessing. Their approach is to quantify early intervention's monetary benefits and to extrapolate their findings to preschool programs. Their cost–benefit analyses support their argument that early childhood programs are a good investment for taxpayers and will eventually raise the quality of the American work force and ensure the nation's productivity and competitiveness in global markets. The literature and the media are filled with their varying estimates that every dollar spent on early childhood programs saves $7, or $17, or provides an 18% return on investment, or some other tantalizing figure. It seems to me the economists have brought the field full circle to Head Start's beginnings when the program was hurt by promises that this little preschool gesture would end poverty in America. If the savings to society that the economists are promising do not materialize or cannot be precisely quantified, the concept of preschool education will likewise disappoint. State preschool programs—many of which were mounted on the hope of economic returns—will be threatened or deemed failures.

The economists make their predictions and build their cost–benefit analyses mainly based on three model programs—HighScope Perry preschool, the Abecedarian project, and the Chicago Child-Parent Centers. All were early intervention programs that contained a preschool education component but offered an array of other services to children and/or their families. Although I believe the HighScope and Abecedarian projects are theoretically of great importance, I think it is unwise to make predictions about future benefits based on these two small interventions, each done in a single location many years ago. One reason is that the children selected for these two programs were not representative of the poor population, so it cannot be generalized from these findings to poor children in general. In the early days of intervention, there were close ties between intervention efforts and the desire to reduce the prevalence of intellectual disabilities. Thus, both HighScope and Abecedarian projects recruited children who were lower in intelligence than most children who live in poverty, many of whom have superior intelligence.

Another problem is that these programs were mounted decades ago and the results might not be replicable today. The face of poverty has certainly changed, especially with the surge of single-parent, fatherless households. Furthermore, when these studies were done it was possible to compare the experimental group with controls who had no alternative program. Brooks-Gunn (2010) has also noted the effect of an intervention is determined by the enhanced performance of the experimentals and the poor performance of the controls. She noted that in studies in the 1960s to 1980s, children in the control group often had no preschool or out-of-home experience. She points out this was unlikely to be the case in studies conducted in the 1990s and 2000s. In the early studies, the differences between the groups reflected the poor performance of the controls as well as the higher performance of the children who experienced the intervention. Such controls no longer exist. Modern comparisons of treatment and control groups are essentially value-added studies attributed to the particular treatment. Today the HighScope control children would probably be attending Head Start or Michigan's state preschool program. The North Carolina children would be in Head Start or the state's Smart Start Centers.

Another issue is that in absolute terms, the performance of the treatment groups in both programs was well below that of more affluent populations. Although studies invariably show that intervention children do better than comparison children, they still are held back in grade and get arrested more frequently than their middle-class peers. With this in mind, researchers must be careful not to oversell how much preschool attendance can accomplish in closing the achievement gap between poor and more advantaged children.

The HighScope and Abecedarian programs are called models for a reason. They were thoughtfully designed and carefully monitored to assure that the services being delivered were true to the creators' intent. Rolling out interventions in the real world where uniform implementation and high quality have been hard to come by should not be justified on the basis of efficacy studies of model programs. The question is how well will the intervention travel and how will it fare when run by outsiders? There is no effectiveness evidence on either the HighScope or the Abecedarian projects. As a scholar, I admire the theoretical contribution of these studies, but as a one-time decision maker and a long-time advisor to decision makers, I would ignore them in setting policy. Not only did the creators conceptualize and implement their models, but they also evaluated them. One would like arms-length tests across many sites utilizing the model, which is what exists in the Head Start National Impact Study as well as the evaluation of Early Head Start.

I find myself in agreement with Greg Duncan, who told me the only program among the three famous models worthy of decision makers' attention is the Chicago Child-Parent Centers. The intervention was conducted with representative poor children across many sites for many years. I also think much more attention should be paid to the Oklahoma universal preschool program, a program of high quality that is being externally evaluated by Bill Gormley and his colleagues. The results to date have certainly been impressive (e.g., Gormley et al., 2008). The National Institute for Early Education Research and many others are currently providing the additional evidence that is needed to make a solid case for the benefits of preschool education.

I am not saying the legacy programs are no longer relevant. They alerted everyone to the potential of early intervention programs to impact a wide range of desirable outcomes. I just do not think they should be used as the sole basis for advancing the cause of early childhood intervention or universal preschool, which is what I see being done. Instead of relying on programs mounted decades ago, new research must be conducted on contemporary programs and populations that will provide current data for predictions and cost–benefit analyses. As more of these analyses are run on more typical and more modern programs, I believe economists will moderate their predictions of the future monetary benefits of preschool education. This is already beginning to be seen in the literature.

The point I am trying to convey is that there is no need to take undue risks by riding the coat-tails of the latest popular, scientific, or political fads to promote an agenda. When we promise higher IQ scores, an end of poverty, invigorated brain development, or tempting savings from investments in early childhood programming, we promise too much—or at least more than science can support. Although I approach the economic evidence skeptically, I remain a champion of the value of high-quality early intervention and preschool education programs as well as the concept of home visiting. My plea is that researchers use the evidence they have judiciously and conservatively. I remain opti-mistic that eventually a sound empirical base will be produced—one that is adequate to the task of informing policy makers about the best course of action to take to improve the life chances of children who live in poverty and the educational success of all America's children.

CHAPTER 38

Early Childhood Education
The Likelihood of Sustained Effects

Jeanne Brooks-Gunn

A summer or a part-time 1-year program of early childhood education (ECE), no matter the qual-ity, is unlikely to result in sustained effects down the road. Zigler (1979) used the concept of an inoculation for low-income youngsters (and those with other risk factors such as having parents who are young, are not well educated, reside in poor neighborhoods, are not employed, or cycle between relationships): His argument was that one dose of early education does not protect children from the ongoing life experiences of poverty nor alter their educational experiences in school (Brooks-Gunn, 2003). This chapter examines what is known about effects of ECE at the beginning and end of ele-mentary school, whereas other chapters have considered the longer term effects of ECE. Of particular interest are the likelihoods of moderate to large effects (or impacts) at the end of an early childhood program, of sustained impacts during the elementary school years, of certain program characteristics contributing to the impacts, and of certain elementary schools and programs enhancing ECE impacts.

This chapter is divided into three sections. The first describes the short-term impacts of ECE pro-grams, with a focus on those that have offered center-based care to at least some of the children (Early Head Start sites differ on whether they provide services through home visiting, a center, or some combination of both). Programs that are focused on home visiting alone are not reviewed; see Howard and Brooks-Gunn (2009) or Sweet and Applebaum (2004) for reviews of this literature. Although programs are discussed that begin in the first years of life as well as those that begin in the third or fourth year of life, special atten-tion is paid to the former, which include the Milwaukee Project, the Parent-Child Development Centers, the Abecedarian Program, the Infant Health and Development Program (IHDP), and the Early Head Start (EHS) Evaluation. The second section considers program characteristics that seem to enhance the probability of finding moderate to large impacts of ECE programs in the short term. Third, longer term impacts are considered in light of characteristics of ECE programs, the types of families served, experiences of the control group, and the subsequent school experiences of children.

The writing of Chapter 38 was supported by the Pew Charitable Trusts, the March of Dimes Foundation, the Eunice Kennedy Shriver National Institute of Child Health and Human Development, and the U.S. Department of Health and Human Services Child Care Bureau and Administration of Children and Families. I wish to thank Rachel McKinnon for her invaluable help in manuscript preparation.

SHORT-TERM IMPACTS OF EARLY CHILDHOOD EDUCATION PROGRAMS

How can the short-term impacts of early childhood programs be characterized? Following current convention, effect sizes are the coin of the realm. They essentially are based on mean differences between treatment and control groups divided by the standard deviation of the measure in question (often based only on the control group descriptive statistics). Sometimes these are weighted. Depending on the evaluation, they might be weighted by number of children per site, by whether children in the treatment group received the treatment (which is called *treatment on treated*), by stratification at random assignment, or by size and quality of program in meta-analyses.

Estimates of impacts at the end of programs have been divided into three broad groups—cognitive and language skills, social and behavioral skills, and school achievement (this last category can only be assessed for children who received services up to age 5). Several meta-analyses have been conducted to provide estimates across ECE evaluations. Meta-analyses by Camilli et al. (2010) examined more than 120 studies of ECE interventions; they included evaluations using both random-assignment and quasi-experimental designs since the 1960s. Their focus was on programs that had a center-based component. Overall, the effect size for cognitive and language outcomes was .231 (based on 306 effect sizes), with smaller effects being seen for social outcomes (.156, based on 113 effect sizes) and school outcomes (.137 based on 60 effect sizes). These included effects at the end of the ECE programs as well as later on. The size of the cognitive effects was influenced by when the assessment was conducted, such that a .24 decrease was seen per follow-up period. This estimate becomes important when examining sustained effects. Somewhat surprisingly, decreases over time were not seen in the social/behavioral or the school domains.

Other meta-analyses cover different time periods. For example, analyzing 35 studies from 1990 to 2000 (Gorey, 2001), an effect size of .70 was found for intelligence and academic achievement at the end of the program. (This effect size would be in the range of the Camilli et al. [2010] study if just immediate program effects had been estimated.) In general, effect sizes at the end of ECE programs are in the range of .40 to .70 for cognitive and language measures. Less information is available for social/behavior effects, although one sixth to one quarter of a standard deviation seems to be the approximate range. These meta-analyses include programs for younger preschool children (defined here as 3 years and younger) and older preschool children (defined here as 3- and 4-year-olds).

What about the interventions that focus exclusively on the younger children? Four of the five programs mentioned previously—the Milwaukee Project, IHDP, Abecedarian, and Parent-Child Development Centers—all reported cognitive effect sizes around three quarters of a standard deviation (Infant Health and Development Program Staff, 1990; McCarton et al., 1997). All were center-based programs (although home visiting was part of each as well). In contrast, the EHS Evaluation reported impacts for the cognitive and language measures of one fifth to one third of a standard deviation at the end of the program (Love et al., 2005). The IHDP and EHS Evaluation reported decreases in behavior problems at the end of the program (about one fifth to one quarter of a standard deviation) as well (Brooks-Gunn et al., 1994; Klebanov, Brooks-Gunn, & McCormick, 2001; Love et al., 2005); the other programs did not assess behavior problems.

Because programs for younger children focus more directly on parenting than programs for older children (typically considering at least three domains: enhanced literacy and stimulating activities in the home, responsive and sensitive parenting, and nonharsh and nonpunitive parenting), these effect sizes are important as well. In the IHDP and the EHS Evaluation, all three aspects of parenting were affected, with effect sizes ranging from one fifth to one third of a standard deviation (Love et al., 2005; Smith & Brooks-Gunn, 1997; Spiker, Ferguson, & Brooks-Gunn, 1993). The other three programs did not assess mother–child interactions or harsh parenting as outcomes.

Another set of outcomes of interest to the programs for the younger children has to do with maternal health and employment. Maternal employment was enhanced in the IHDP and EHS Evaluation, as was maternal mental health at the end of the program (Brooks-Gunn, McCormick, Shapiro, Benasich, & Black, 1994; Klebanov et al., 2001; Love et al., 2005; Martin et al., 2008). It is believed that if a program influences parents, then sustained effects are more likely to occur. Also, when program staff are asked about what goals they have, enhanced parenting and parental mental health are almost always mentioned when younger children are the target of services (Administration for Children and Families, 2002).

EARLY CHILDHOOD EDUCATION
PROGRAM CHARACTERISTICS AND IMPACTS

Several characteristics of programs are discussed here. They are length of program, intensity of program, type of program, and quality of program.

Length and Intensity of Program

Are effect sizes larger for programs that last more years? Because evaluations have not compared by random assignment the children who received intervention (e.g., 1 year or 2 years), it is difficult to answer this question. With respect to the programs for children under 3, the two programs that used the same curricula and approach—the Abecedarian and the IHDP—had similar effect sizes at age 3. The Abecedarian Program, which offered center-based education until age 5, had somewhat larger effects at that age than did the IHDP, which ended at year 3 (although effect sizes were similar across the two programs at age 8). The meta-analyses suggest that programs that last longer have larger effect sizes (Camilli et al., 2010; Gorey, 2001; Nelson et al., 2003).

A related issue has to do with the intensity of services received within a given time period. Typically, intensity would be measured by the number of days that an individual child attended a center as well as the number of hours that a center was open. Weekly attendance records can provide these data. Surprisingly, of the programs for younger preschool children, only the IHDP collected such information. Using a propensity matching procedure, effect sizes for the heavier low birth weight children in IHDP were over one standard deviation for those children who went to the center more than 300 days in the 2-year period (Hill, Brooks-Gunn, & Waldfogel, 2003). It is likely that transportation in part accounts for the relatively large numbers of children going to the center 100 or 150 days per year.

It is important to note that all of these analyses are not based on random assignment and are subject to selection bias. However, propensity scoring matching procedures try to equate groups on dozens and dozens of covariates, which is thought to reduce but not eliminate selection bias (Hill, Waldfogel, Brooks-Gunn, & Han, 2005; Rubin, 1997).

Type and Quality of Program

In evaluations of programs for older preschoolers, virtually all of them focus on education provided in centers. For the younger preschoolers, some programs offered home visiting only and some a combination of home visiting and center-based care. The EHS sites differed on their approaches, with some home visiting, some mixed approach (both center and home visiting, although not all children got both), and some center based (children in these sites did receive home visits, but at a low level by design). Comparisons between approaches are difficult, as only one investigative team directly compared home visits only to home visits plus center care via random assignment (Abecedarian and Project CARE [Carolina Approach to Responsive Education]). In their analyses, significant impacts on cognitive and language skills were found in the home visit plus center-based condition but not in the home visiting only condition (Wasik, Ramey, Bryant, & Sparling, 1990).

EHS has been able to compare effect sizes within each of their three types of programs (although random assignment into different treatment groups within sites was not carried out by design). At the end of the program, larger and more consistent effects were seen in the mixed-approach sites than the home visiting or center-based sites (Love et al., 2005). This was true in the cognitive and language domains as well as in other domains.

Quality of programs has not been subjected to random assignment, given ethical and logistical concerns. The evaluations do differ, however, on whether specific curricula were used and detailed training was implemented. The Abecedarian and IHDP used a well-developed and easy-to-use curriculum (LearningGames; Sparling & Lewis, 2007) in both home visits and in the centers. Training was extensive. In addition, close monitoring was done, so it is possible to chart which activities children received in any given home visit or in any given week at the center (Sparling & Lewis, 1985).

In contrast, the EHS programs, although they followed the Head Start Performance Standards, did not seem to use a specific curriculum. Sites sometimes used portions of curricula but did not implement anything like LearningGames. In addition, it is not clear what training was provided or how frequently staff were observed and monitored for fidelity to a specific approach. Such aspects of a program are not tapped by commonly used observational systems. The evaluation was able to divide the sites into three groups based on their implementation of the Head Start Performance Standards—early implementers, later implementers, and not implemented.

SUBSEQUENT EXPERIENCES AND LONGER TERM IMPACTS

The size of sustained impacts will depend on the characteristics of preschool programs themselves, possibility characteristics of the families enrolled in the program, and the experiences of those in the control group. In addition, the experiences of subsequent school and after-school programs are expected to matter.

Characteristics of Preschool Programs and Families

Sustained effects of preschool programs have been reported in the meta-analyses as well. However, the size of the effects is lower during elementary school than earlier, at least for cognitive and language skills. As stated previously, a .24 decline in impacts was found over each follow-up (Camilli et al., 2010). Thus, if effect sizes in the .60s and .70s were found at the end of an intervention program, they are likely to drop to the .40s several years after an intervention ended. If effect sizes in the .40s were reported, sustained effects will probably be in the .20s. Initial effect sizes in the .20s would probably not be sustained (or be significant). The younger preschool children's programs in general follow these metrics (although in some cases, the declines were a bit higher). So, the Abecedarian and the IHDP had significant impacts on cognition and achievement in late elementary school (one quarter to one third of a standard deviation), whereas the Early Head Start evaluation did not have average impacts in these domains at the start of elementary school (remember that the effect sizes at the end of the program were in the .20s; Love, Cohen, Raikes, & Brooks-Gunn, 2011).

The brief review in the preceding section points to some possible characteristics of programs that might make sustained effects more likely to occur. First, the intensity of services is likely to make a difference (Camilli et al., 2010; Gorey, 2001). In the IHDP, for example, sustained effects in cognitive skills and in elementary school achievement were most pronounced for those children who went to the center more than 300 days; these effect sizes were, in some cases, three quarters of a standard deviation at age 8 for the highest dosage group, compared to about one third of a standard deviation for the entire group (Hill et al., 2003). Second, it is possible that more sustained effects will be seen when programs provide services in both the younger and older preschool periods (Love et al., 2011). However, estimates of such an effect are not available at this time. Third, the specificity of a curriculum might make a difference, although again direct comparisons in the younger preschool group are not possible. Fourth, the EHS results suggest that earlier and better implementation of programs are linked to larger effects of programs for younger preschoolers (Love et al., 2005). Fifth, although it is believed that combining center-based and home-based approaches is more effective than center-based approaches alone, at least for younger preschool children, evidence does not exist one way or the other. Whether home visiting programs alone for younger children yield cognitive or achievement impacts is vigorously debated. Effects in the social/behavioral and in the parenting domains are often seen for home visiting programs into the early elementary school years and sometimes beyond (Howard & Brooks-Gunn, 2009) but effects typically are not seen in the cognitive domains.

Thus far, characteristics of families have not been discussed. Programs that have large enough sample sizes are often able to do subgroup analyses, to see whether a set of services is more effective for one group than another. A notable example is taken from the EHS Evaluation, in which sustained impacts were more likely to be seen across a variety of measures for the African American families than for the Hispanic American or European American families (Love et al., 2011). The former's control group had lower scores on a variety of measures compared to controls in the latter two groups, suggesting that African American children were more disadvantaged than the other two groups (Brooks-Gunn & Markman, 2005). Even within poor populations, African American children are more disadvantaged than other groups (Brooks-Gunn, Klebanov, & Duncan, 1996). In addition, cognitive scores were higher for Spanish-speaking Hispanic treatment than control group children at follow-up in the EHS, perhaps speaking to the importance of such services for children of immigrants.

Experiences of the Control Group

Another important consideration for assessing sustained effects has to do with what the control group has experienced. In studies conducted in the 1960s to 1980s, children in the control group often had no preschool or out-of-home experiences. In the 1990s and 2000s, this was less likely to be the case, at least for the older preschoolers. Given that well over half of all 4-year-olds are in a formal preschool program, it becomes difficult to estimate effects of treatment over no treatment. Instead, comparisons are between a specified treatment (e.g., Head Start for the experimental group) and an amalgam of treatments in the control group (e.g., prekindergarten [pre-K] classes, for-profit centers, community centers, family child care). Therefore, the comparisons become a bit more like the treatment-to-treatment trials, which in general have not shown impacts compared to treatment–control comparisons (Camilli et al., 2010). This is one of the likely explanations for the lack of sustained effects in the Head Start Impact Study, assuming that the quality of the centers attended by those in the control group is of relatively high quality (which seemed to be the case in the Head Start Impact Study, at least for the 4-year-olds). In this study, short-term impacts were seen for the 3-year-olds, and for this age group, many fewer control group children were receiving intervention services (Puma et al., 2005).

In terms of the programs for the younger preschool children, control group experiences are also important, even though proportionately fewer children are receiving center-based education in the first 3 years of life. Also, the quality of programs overall is lower in community programs for the younger than the older preschool children at the present time. Still, control group experiences may influence impacts. In the IHDP, a comparison of cognitive scores at age 8 was made based on what the treatment group might have received if they had not been assigned to the treatment group (a sort of reverse propensity score matching technique; Hill, Waldfogel, & Brooks-Gunn, 2002). The treatment–control differences were much less pronounced in the comparisons between control group children who received center-based care and comparable treatment group children, with larger sustained effects for the maternal care and the family care groups. If the proportion of children in maternal care is low given maternal employment and increased supply of centers, then sustained effects would be less likely to appear today than in previous decades. Indeed, one policy recommendation is to increase the availability of ECE for children in underserved groups, such as Hispanic families (Magnuson & Waldfogel, 2005) because the impacts of ECE are likely to be larger for such groups (e.g., those who are receiving overall much less ECE). The EHS findings that Spanish-speaking children had sustained impacts on language might be such an example. Thus, studies today are perhaps better thought of as value-added studies rather than actual effects of a program compared to no program or treatment at all.

In nonexperimental analyses, comparisons among groups of preschoolers who have received different types of education and care are being made, using large data sets and sophisticated data analytic techniques to control, in part, for selection bias. In the Early Childhood Longitudinal Study, Kindergarten (ECLS-K; National Center for Education Statistics, 2009), children who received preschool education the year preceding kindergarten have higher early achievement scores (as well as higher aggressive behavior scores) than children who did not; these findings hold up when many covariates are entered into equations to control for preexisting differences between groups (Magnuson, Ruhm, & Waldfogel, 2007a). Using the Fragile Families data set (a 20-city birth cohort with an oversample of unmarried parents at the time of the birth; Reichman, Teitler, Garfinkel, & McLanahan, 2001) and comparing children who received Head Start, pre-K, other preschool, family child care, and mother care, scholars were able to use propensity score matching as well as control for age 3 child outcomes (no age 3 data were collected in the ECLS-K). Children in all of the preschool groups had better cognitive scores than those in the family child care and mother care groups; in addition, those in Head Start and pre-K did better than those in other preschools (Zhai, Brooks-Gunn, & Waldfogel, 2011). Differences favoring those children in Head Start and pre-K classes were also seen for enhanced attention and lower behavior problems.

These nonexperimental findings raise an interesting issue: In general, receiving preschool at age 4 is associated with doing better in kindergarten (in terms of academic achievement). How much does the type of preschool matter? Are the outcomes of Head Start and pre-K comparable? Will either be more likely to produce sustained effects? Unless one-to-one comparisons are made experimentally, it is difficult to say that one is superior to the other.

Subsequent School Experiences

The final issue has to do with the role of subsequent school experiences in either enhancing or devaluing the preschool experiences. Scholars have argued that, in the case of poor children, most attend neighborhood schools that spend less per pupil, have larger classrooms, have more inexperienced teachers, and have more poor children than do middle-class children (Lee, Loeb, & Lubeck, 1998). Does the type of school attended after preschool make a difference in terms of sustained effects? Two analyses using the ECLS-K are relevant. In one, Magnuson, Ruhm, and Waldfogel (2007b) looked at the quality of classroom interaction in kindergarten (based on teacher reports) to see if preschool effects were more likely to be sustained in higher quality classrooms. The answer was yes. In another, Holod, Gardner, and Brooks-Gunn (2011) examined the sustained effects of preschool education for poor, near-poor, and middle-class students as a function of the poverty of the elementary school that the students attended. Although sustained effects of preschool were seen through third grade, effects were most pronounced for poor children who attended more affluent schools (e.g., fewer children eligible for free or reduced lunch). In both analyses, proxies for quality (teacher reports of activities of children, proportion of students receiving free or reduced lunch) were associated with higher sustained effects.

After-school programs might be another avenue for maintaining impacts of preschool into the late elementary school years. No analyses have directly addressed this issue. However, some scholars have estimated that regular attendance at an after-school program with an academic component for 2 years might influence achievement test scores by one sixth of a standard deviation (Gardner, Roth, & Brooks-Gunn, 2009; Roth & Brooks-Gunn, 2003; Roth, Brooks-Gunn, Murray, & Foster, 1998). Whether preschool attendance would boost this effect is unknown.

CONCLUSION

Preschool educational programs do result in higher cognitive and achievement test scores at the end of the program. In addition, most programs have sustained impacts, albeit at a lower level than the initial impacts, through elementary school (the notable exception is the Head Start Impact Study). What factors lead to greater sustained impacts of ECE? Program curricula and staff training as well as the quality and intensity of the programs themselves all seem to play a role. In addition, the experiences of those children in the control group are important to understand, especially given the large numbers of 4-year-olds nationwide who are receiving some sort of preschool education. In addition, nonexperimental findings suggesting that children who received EHS followed by Head Start were doing better may indicate that service receipt in the younger and older preschool years will yield more sustained effects than in either period alone (Love et al., 2011). Finally, the experiences during elementary school may enhance the effects of ECE.

PART IV

Summary and Synthesis

Summary and Synthesis

STUDY QUESTIONS

- For whom and by whom should pre-K be provided?

- When and where should early childhood services be provided and for how long?

- What should the focus of instruction be, and how should pre-K programs be structured?

- What are the future considerations to take into account?

CHAPTER 39

The Prekindergarten Debates
Contrasting Perspectives, Integrative Possibilities, and Potential for Deepening the Debates

Martha Zaslow

This book presents a virtual decision tree regarding for whom, by whom, when, where, with what focus, and how prekindergarten (pre-K) should be expanded and fully implemented. A noteworthy question that is absent from this listing of *wh* questions is *whether*. It is a very important starting premise of this book that pre-K should be extended. The key questions for policy makers, practitioners, and researchers alike posed in this book focus on the parameters of expansion, not whether it should occur. The book starts from underlying agreement that young children, especially those at risk, will benefit from high-quality and educationally focused programs prior to kindergarten entry.

The contrasting perspectives presented in this book by respected leaders in the early childhood field are an extremely valuable resource to those thinking through the allocation of resources for well-planned and effective pre-K expansion. Interestingly, although contrasting possibilities are presented for each key decision involved in fully implementing pre-K, the chapters of this book also point the way toward some integrative positions and resolutions to the debates. The chapters also suggest ways in which future research and dialogue can and should deepen the debates. This concluding chapter summarizes the book's key contrasting positions, integrative resolutions, and further issues that might be examined in order to deepen the debates.

THE DEBATES ABOUT THE CENTRAL QUESTIONS

This chapter is structured around the key *wh* questions that will need to be addressed for further pre-K implementation: for whom (targeted versus universal), by whom (staff qualifications), where (in what settings), when (focusing on what age groups), what (curricular focus), and how (instructional approach and comprehensiveness). The book concludes by going beyond this framework of *wh* questions, noting further issues that decision makers will need to focus on in making pre-K not only available but maximally effective to young children in this country.

Chapter 39 provides a summary of Zigler, E., Gilliam, W.S., & Barnett, W.S. (Eds.). (2011). *The pre-k debates: Current controversies and issues.* Baltimore: Paul H. Brookes Publishing Co.

For Whom Should Pre-K Be Provided?

What Are the Contrasting Perspectives?   A first fundamental debate laid out in the chapters of this book is whether pre-K should be targeted (i.e., funded for children who meet specified criteria in terms of family income or other risk factors) or universal. Those taking the position that pre-K should be targeted note that the evidence of positive effects of high-quality early care and education is strongest for children from low-income families. They also note that because of limited resources, pre-K should go to those most in need (see Chapter 4). Those reviewing the economic evidence also argue that the cost–benefit analysis is most favorable and the returns for society are the greatest for low-income children participating in high-quality early care and education, with more limited benefits for society from participation by children from higher income families (see Chapter 3). Furthermore, there is the possibility that a universal program would involve unnecessary expenditures because of public provision of educational experiences that more affluent families would pay for on their own (see Chapter 1). Proponents of targeted pre-K note that such an approach parallels the provision of college scholarships, for which there is good public support; thus they anticipate broad public backing (see Chapter 3).

Arguments for publicly funded universal pre-K in this debate include the perspective that universal pre-K will actually be more effective at enrolling low-income children than targeted programs, in part because stigma will be removed and in part because programs will be widely known and in readily accessible community-based locations (see Chapter 5). They note that not only low-income children but a wider socioeconomic range, including middle-class children, have been shown to benefit from high-quality early care and education (see Chapters 5 and Chapter 27). A particular concern is the quality of care that low-income children just above the poverty level currently receive and the extent that they also stand to benefit from programs for which they might not otherwise be eligible if programs are targeted (see Chapter 7). A universal approach has a better likelihood of having low-income children participate in mixed-income rather than income-segregated classes, for which there is evidence of positive implications (see Chapters 7 and 25). A universal approach is more closely aligned with universal public school education, affirming that this is a downward extension in age for public education (see Chapter 35), a factor considered in this perspective to be important to gaining public support (see Chapter 6). A review of the economic data by those taking this perspective suggests greater overall economic benefits from including the full range of socioeconomic groups (see Chapter 5). Those holding that pre-K should be universal also note the costliness and possibility of errors in making the determinations for a targeted program, that such determinations need to be made with some periodicity, and they are open to challenge (see Chapter 5).

Is an Integrative Perspective Suggested by the Chapters in This Book?   Several chapters suggest that policy makers do not face an either–or decision in addressing the *for whom question.* They note that a universal program but with sliding fees would preclude the allocation of scarce resources for those who could already afford to pay for pre-K, yet protect the advantages of a program available in all neighborhoods and to all families and children (see Chapter 7). A universal system with a sliding fee scale could still involve active outreach and targeting of services to those most at risk (see Chapter 2). Thus, a possibility exists that would resolve this particular debate, integrating the potential benefits of each of the contrasting perspectives.

How Do the Chapters Suggest that the Debate Needs to Be Deepened?   The chapters in this book suggest that if pre-K programs are targeted, they may need a more nuanced approach to targeting than simply identifying families who meet an income criterion in order to reach those in most need of such a program. Demographic data suggest, for example, that middle-income Latino families are among those with low rates of participation in pre-K (see Chapter 4). Others note that income is a poor proxy for underlying risk in terms of children's school readiness and suggest that limited time, sensitivity, and stimulation in parenting behavior is the key risk factor or scarce resource (see Chapter 1). Yet, targeting on the basis of this underlying risk factor would require more intensive screening efforts. Deepening the debate here would require careful consideration of feasible strategies for targeting (or in a universal approach, for active outreach to enroll children) that would help to ensure the participation of those most in need of such a program.

This book highlights the presence of families at particularly heightened risk because of such factors as domestic violence, severe parental depression, or substance use. For families with such risk factors, it may be necessary to provide a program of greater comprehensiveness and duration than is currently available in age-limited pre-K programs. Furthermore, outreach to such families may be needed in order to gain and also maintain engagement. Those with extensive experience with families at moderate and high risk note that special efforts are needed to assure that child- and family-focused programs do not serve as a source of additional pressure and demands for such families, but rather as a source of support (see Chapter 30). Deepening the debate on "for whom" should also involve thoughtful consideration of efforts to include those most in need who might be less likely to enroll or maintain enrollment because of serious risk factors.

By Whom Should Pre-K Be Provided?

What Are the Contrasting Perspectives?   It is important to note that the debate about who should provide pre-K is often seen as focused solely on and framed around educational attainment of teachers—more specifically, whether or not lead teachers should be required to have a bachelor's degree and appropriate certification (e.g., certification to teach pre-K through Grade 3). A careful reading of this book, however, indicates that the underlying issue here is not just educational attainment but the combination of educational attainment and wages.

Those taking the perspective of stringent professional standards argue that pre-K teachers should have both qualifications and wages similar to those of K–12 teachers; they should be on the same professional ladder and have the same stature (see Chapters 8 and 9). Researchers holding this perspective note a body of research pointing to an association between educational attainment of lead teachers and quality in early childhood settings. They also note that stable and higher wages are related to less turnover and greater continuity of staff both for children and for institutions. They underscore that a combination of professional requirements and pay signals that pre-K teachers are part of a respected professional group. Other chapters take the position supporting stringent professional requirements, noting that the programs showing the strongest effects of pre-K on children had highly qualified teachers (see Chapters 26 and 27). They argue that if pre-K is to be taken seriously as a form of education, then the complexity of the task of educating young children must be fully acknowledged and teachers with more advanced qualifications must be provided (see Chapter 8). Such teachers will also be most able to benefit from professional development to support such practices as use of information from individualized assessments to guide instructional practices for children (see Chapter 18).

Those questioning the value of setting a high bar in terms of professional qualifications note that the evidence on the association between educational attainment, classroom quality, and children's academic progress is weak or mixed (see Chapters 4 and 11). Some point to a difference in research findings on the implications of teacher educational attainment by decade (see Chapter 13). Although earlier research showed an association between lead teacher's educational attainment or certification and quality, more recent studies do not show this association with any regularity. Several possible explanations are provided. In one, it is noted that the professional trajectories of early educators have changed over time, with more mobility for those with a bachelor's degree now because educational and certification credentials make it easier to move from child care into Head Start or pre-K, and from pre-K into higher elementary school grades. The greater mobility may mean that now (but not reflected in the data from earlier studies) less skilled teachers with bachelor's degrees and certification may remain in grades with younger children. In another possible explanation, the quality of higher education programs for early educators may be under stress due to the rapid expansion of pre-K programs. Some chapters in this book argue for professional development in which the criteria is not degree attainment but confirmation that specific practices are understood and are actually being carried out in the classroom (see Chapters 11 and 12), or for alternative pathways to professional stature, involving either educational attainment or ongoing professional development in an accredited program that involves multiple contextual supports for high quality (see Chapter 14).

Is an Integrative Perspective Suggested by the Chapters in This Book?   Two criteria are suggested by the chapters of this book for this debate. The first is that early childhood teachers should have qualifications and incomes that identify them clearly as respected professionals. The second criterion is that the professional requirements should be clearly and strongly related to observed quality in early childhood classrooms and to children's academic progress. There is little disagreement across the chapters of this book that specified professional requirements and wages on the same scale as for K–12 teachers would help to convey respect and professionalism to early educators and that this is essential to a transition toward viewing early care and education as an extension of public education. The disagreement largely focuses on the second criterion, of whether higher educational attainment is in fact associated with higher quality and greater academic gains for children. An integrative perspective sees the potential for improving the quality of higher education teacher preparation programs so that a bachelor's degree indeed serves as a marker of practices that support stronger gains for children in academic achievement and behavioral adjustment.

How Do the Chapters Suggest that the Debate Needs to Be Deepened?   The chapters of this book argue for standards of quality in higher education programs. At the same time, they suggest that the key issue is not only preservice training but also what types of supports early educators need once they are in the classroom in order to continue to improve in quality and maintain high quality (see Chapter 14). Deepening the debate here will require research that identifies effective professional development approaches, as well as identification of ways to build them into both higher education programs and in-service training (see Chapter 11). An emerging favorite candidate for such professional development is onsite and individualized coaching. An important caution here is that some but not all onsite individualized professional development approaches have evidence of effects in improving quality and strengthening child outcomes. It will be critical to begin to differentiate among such approaches and not make a blanket assumption of effectiveness (Zaslow, Tout, Halle, & Starr, 2010).

When Should Early Childhood Services Be Provided and for How Long?

What Are the Contrasting Perspectives?   This book presents not two contrasting perspectives but multiple perspectives on the issue of when early education should be provided. Although some chapters report on pre-K provided for 4-year-olds and turn to evidence of positive effects of such programs (see Chapter 35), others cite the evidence for greater effectiveness of pre-K programs that include both 3- and 4-year-olds (see Chapters 7, 25, 26, 27, 32, and 36). A key issue is whether a brief dose of pre-K, such as 9 months of part-time participation, suffices to result in effects that are of sufficient magnitude to endure into the elementary school years, when multiple studies show that effects of early childhood programs can be expected to diminish when children reach school if intervention is not continued (see Chapters 25, 34, 37, and 38). It is an important contribution of this book that multiple chapters provide evidence of stronger effects within programs according to how many years or days children participated (see Chapter 28 for the Infant Health and Development Program, Chapter 27 for the Chicago Child-Parent Centers, and Chapter 17 for *école maternelle* in France).

Still further chapters point to evidence of particularly strong effects when early childhood programs start in infancy and extend through the fifth year (see Chapters 1, 25, 29, 32, and 37), noting the particular importance of very early development for affecting brain development, strengthening infants' expectations for responsive caregiving relationships, and engaging them in verbal interaction. Two approaches are identified as showing promising evidence of positive effects: either the provision of high-quality center-based early care and education throughout the birth-to-5 period (e.g., see Chapter 26 for the Abecedarian program and Chapter 30 for Educare) or a combination of home visitation during the infancy and toddlerhood period followed by high-quality pre-K for 3- and 4-year-olds (see Chapters 25, 30, and 31). Although the effects of Early Head Start were strongest right after graduation for the program model in which there was a combination of home-based and center-based services, at later ages, the strongest effects were found when home-based services were offered in the early years and were followed by center-based care at ages 3 and 4 (see Chapter 30).

Further extending the question of "when," other chapters emphasize what follows rather than precedes pre-K. Authors point to the importance of focusing on transitions from pre-K to kindergarten, as well as aligning both educational expectations and professional development so that what is learned in pre-K builds systematically and consistently toward expectations for kindergarten through third grade (see Chapters 21, 22, and 33).

Is an Integrative Perspective Suggested by the Chapters in This Book?   If resources are constrained, one possibility suggested by the chapters in this book is to focus services for those from birth through age 3 on those at greatest risk. A finding noted from the Early Head Start evaluation is that the highest risk families (as noted previously, those facing issues such as parental depression, substance use, and/or domestic violence) appear to have benefited over the long term from a sequencing of services, with Early Head Start followed by Head Start. Such high-risk families did not show effects immediately after graduating from Early Head Start but rather started to show positive effects after sustained exposure to a comprehensive program (see Chapter 30).

How Do the Chapters Suggest that the Debate Needs to Be Deepened?   Chapter 38 cautions that one needs to think carefully about the available evidence from the perspective of what approaches to early education yield effects that are strong enough to persist into the elementary school grades despite a clear pattern of effect sizes diminishing over time across follow-up assessments in longitudinal studies as children proceed through elementary school. Dosage is an issue of great importance to consider from the perspective of sustained effects, with some available evidence, as summarized in this book, pointing to greater likelihood of sustained effects when children are exposed to high quality early education for multiple years rather than 1 year. Yet many examinations of this issue to date are subject to the concern that families have self-selected into more years of participation and may have differed to begin with (e.g., in the emphasis they placed on education for their children).

The Quality Features, Dosage and Thresholds and Child Outcomes study (U.S. Department of Health and Human Services, 2009b) was planned to provide a systematic examination of the issue of dosage, first reviewing the existing literature, and then using rigorous statistical techniques with data from existing early childhood datasets to more fully isolate the role of dosage of exposure to high-quality early care and education from selection effects (Zaslow, Anderson, et al., 2010). A systematic examination of dosage through experimental evaluations of 1 versus 2 (or multiple) years of participation in high-quality early childhood programs would be an important further addition. Raikes and colleagues (Chapter 30) note that the follow-up study of Early Head Start considering the sequencing of home visitation and Head Start services is promising but involves nonexperimental correlational analyses (see also the summary of findings on sequencing of program approaches in Chapter 25). The expansion of home visitation approaches with health care reform provides a very important opportunity for systematic and rigorous study of a sequencing of services in infancy and toddlerhood into the preschool years.

Where Should Pre-K Be Provided?

What Are the Contrasting Perspectives?   Multiple chapters of this book present the rationale for using public schools as the base or hub for pre-K (see Chapters 21–23 and 33). A fundamental issue identified is the benefit of building pre-K into a broader infrastructure, with supports such as the access to curricular experts, guidance counselors, and early intervention specialists, as well as ongoing professional development for teachers. Another core issue identified is having a stable and well-established funding stream that permits teachers to have wages comparable to that of elementary school teachers. If pre-K is built into a public school framework, it is much easier to support coordination of curricular approaches with later grades, transition practices, and common professional development approaches. In addition, in this approach, young children and parents become familiar with the school context and culture prior to entering kindergarten. Gilliam provides statistics in Chapter 22, noting that 68% of classes in state-funded pre-K programs are already located in schools, so this is a strong starting point for using schools as the location for pre-K. Findings from a number of evaluations point to strong effects of some school-based pre-K programs, such as the programs in Tulsa, Oklahoma, and Chicago (see Chapters 27 and 35).

Others, however, support a diverse delivery system that includes school-based pre-K, Head Start within and outside of public schools, and private child care (see Chapter 2). One chapter in the book notes that there is no systematic evidence that children fare better when they experience early education in a school as opposed to other early care and education settings and that there is actually a risk in school-based programs of using developmentally inappropriate didactic instructional approaches from upper grades when pre-K is provided through public schools (see Chapter 4). The concern is expressed that incorporating pre-K into school settings rather than the full range of early childhood settings in communities is less likely to reflect the diversity of families in communities in terms of cultural practices and backgrounds of educators (see Chapter 1). One chapter presents the position that having a diverse and choice-based system more appropriately reflects a democratic society and supports educational diversity rather than forced uniformity (see Chapter 24).

Is an Integrative Perspective Suggested by the Chapters in This Book? Even the chapters that argue for using schools as the framework for early care and education often acknowledge that school districts can serve as the hub of a diverse delivery system that includes Head Start and child care (see Chapters 5, 35, and 36). As an example, while pre-K in Oklahoma is under the jurisdiction of the school districts, it includes Head Start and private child care centers that meet program requirements. Research on the Abbott pre-K program indicates that participation by private child care in a pre-K program with clearly articulated standards and substantial supports can be an impetus for quality improvement (see Chapter 36). In an integrative perspective, pre-K is offered through a diverse delivery system but with a department of education or other agency providing coordination and leadership.

How Do the Chapters Suggest that the Debate Needs to Be Deepened? More detailed consideration of early childhood collaborations suggests the need for a more complex conceptualization of collaborations than whether one particular agency consistently provides leadership or coordination, irrespective of the facet of coordination involved. For example, in some states, although local education districts may provide oversight for staff selection and selection of curricula in pre-K programs irrespective of whether they are offered through public schools, in Head Start, or in private child care, another agency may provide oversight for the use of funding in collaborations, while yet a further (independent) entity may provide ongoing monitoring of classroom quality (see description of the roles of multiple agencies and organizations participating in such collaborations in New Jersey's Abbott pre-K programs in Chapter 36). A broader understanding of how collaborations are actually functioning is needed, one that acknowledges more complex structures for collaboration and includes an awareness of the challenges and strengths in differing collaborative structures.

There is also a need for evidence directly examining whether there are differing outcomes for children who participate in pre-K programs structured in different ways. Contrasting hypotheses need to be directly examined: that as long as a child participates in a program documented through observational measures to be of high quality, the broader context does not matter, versus the possibility that critical resources become available to teachers and children when pre-K is embedded in a broader structure such as a public school system, and as a result children consistently benefit. Such analyses should assess and weigh the cost of these additional resources.

What Should the Focus of Instruction Be?

What Are the Contrasting Perspectives? Although some of the chapters of this book urge a specific focus of instruction on cognitive skills (see Chapter 16), others present the perspective that a multifaceted curriculum that also includes a focus on social and emotional development is essential (see Chapters 17–19).

Researchers supporting a focus on cognitive skills note, for example, that evidence from analyses of data from multiple longitudinal studies indicates that early mathematics, language and literacy skills, and attention are the strongest predictors of later academic achievement (see Chapter 16). Gaps by both socioeconomic status and race/ethnicity emerge early in cognitive skills. Their importance is further underscored by the fact that they are the focus of later assessments of proficiency.

Those supporting a broader curricular focus emphasize the close interrelations of different domains of development and the need to support development in the whole child (see Chapters 15 and 25). Pedagogical practices in classrooms may support achievement but unintentionally diminish motivation and engagement (which are critical to staying in school and graduating) when they focus on direct instruction and emphasize performance (see Chapter 18). In low-income communities, high stress levels in the children's homes and communities can mean that in any one class, there may be multiple children with more severe behavioral challenges that require attention from the teacher and distract from instruction for the whole class (see Chapter 19). Economic analyses suggest the importance of noncognitive as well as cognitive skills, such as the ability to cooperate and pursue a common goal with a group, for both academic and eventual work outcomes (see Chapter 1).

Is an Integrative Perspective Suggested by the Chapters in This Book? There is no disagreement across the chapters in this book that supporting young children's language and literacy, early math skills, and attentional focus are important. Indeed, multiple chapter authors call for a multifaceted curriculum with strength in such areas as language and literacy development (see Chapters 17 and 33). An integrative perspective holds that helping children to become more competent in the social and behavioral domains will actually permit more focus at both the individual and classroom level on instructional content aimed at cognitive academic skills (see Chapter 19).

How Do the Chapters Suggest that the Debate Needs to Be Deepened? Although there are studies of specific curricular approaches in early childhood settings, such as the Preschool Curriculum Evaluation Studies (U.S. Department of Education, 2008a), a body of work that provides a systematic contrast of comprehensive versus cognitively focused curricula does not yet exist. Hirsch, in describing the approach taken in France's *école maternelle* in Chapter 17, goes one step further to discuss the way in which the curriculum implemented in these early childhood settings is not only comprehensive but also integrated (e.g., with the intentional introduction of vocabulary to support both language development and social and emotional development) as well as cumulative (so that later learning goals build intentionally on earlier ones). The pre-K debates would be deepened through consideration of whether comprehensive curricula support developmental outcomes in multiple domains better than implementing multiple domain-specific curricula, and whether development is fostered when curricula build in sequential and cumulative learning goals.

How Should Pre-K Programs Be Structured?

What Are the Contrasting Perspectives? One key question regarding how early education is provided concerns whether learning goals should be addressed through direct instruction versus learning through play. A clearly integrative perspective is presented in this book, with authors noting that a stark contrast of learning through play versus learning through direct instruction is outdated (see Chapter 20). Rather, it is now widely understood that teacher input during play can augment play and provide opportunities for learning; that teachers can structure the play environment to direct attention to specific content; and that instructional content can be introduced through learning games (see Chapters 20 and 26).

Although the chapter authors have moved beyond a stark dichotomy of learning through play versus direct instruction, observational studies suggest that the dichotomy still exists in practice, with some early childhood programs spending a substantial proportion of time in free play with limited teacher input and others prioritizing time for direct instruction and providing limited time for play (Chien et al., 2010).

A *second* key question regarding *how* early childhood instruction is provided focuses on breadth of services. Although some authors underscore the need for a strong and focused emphasis on narrowing the achievement gap in cognitive areas, others emphasize the importance of breadth of services, including a strong emphasis on the provision of health services and supports for family engagement along with an educational focus (see Chapters 15 and 25). Particularly for low-income children, health issues that are left untreated are seen as having the potential to lead to absenteeism and difficulty focusing on classroom activities.

Is an Integrative Perspective Suggested by the Chapters in This Book? As noted, a perspective that integrates direct instruction with play is presented repeatedly in the chapters of this book. It is presented, however, with the concern that providing guided learning through play requires a skilled and well-trained work force that is able especially to identify the level of understanding and needs for scaffolding of individual children.

The Chicago Child-Parent Center program is an important example of a comprehensive approach that includes both a strong educational focus within the classroom and an additional program emphasis on parent engagement (see Chapter 27). It is important to note that this more comprehensive approach was feasible to implement at scale within a public school setting. The authors hypothesize that evaluation results, pointing to stronger effects of this program relative to others (albeit evaluated without a randomized control trial), are in part due to an approach that addressed multiple pathways of influence on the children's development simultaneously (see Chapter 32).

How Do the Chapters Suggest that the Debate Needs to Be Deepened?   The debate here would be furthered through planned variation studies explicitly contrasting not only the immediate effects but also the costs and longer term benefits of programs that are more narrowly focused versus comprehensive. The feasibility and effectiveness of professional development approaches that intentionally prepare teachers for a more complex integration of direct instruction and learning through play would also be an important contribution.

EXTENDING THE DEBATES

The chapters of this book raise the possibility that some further branches on the decision tree may be needed in order to have a complete guidance document for those seeking to fully implement pre-K.

Infrastructure for Ongoing Support and Monitoring

One such further issue that the chapters point to is the infrastructure for ongoing support and monitoring of quality. The outlines of a debate can be anticipated in the chapters of this book, yet contrasting perspectives are not fully articulated. The experiences of one state, New Jersey, suggest the importance of a thoughtfully structured system for independent monitoring of quality and assessment of children's development, coupled with ongoing professional development supports occurring within classrooms (see Chapters 28 and 36). Yet another state, Oklahoma, with strong evidence of positive effects of its pre-K program, at least in the short term, has no such system for ongoing monitoring and support (see Chapter 35). The pre-K debates should include the question of what infrastructure, if any, should surround pre-K programs to help them attain and then maintain quality.

Taking the Diversity of the Early Childhood Population into Account

In several places, this book calls attention to the growing diversity of the early childhood population (see Chapters 4 and 24). This diversity includes substantial numbers of children who are dual-language learners. An issue that is touched on briefly and yet not fully debated in the book is whether early childhood classrooms should encourage young children to focus on mastering English alone or on maintaining and continuing to develop in a home language while also acquiring English.

Not all early care and education programs have an explicit policy on supports for dual-language learning. Yet, to some extent, the rough outlines of a debate can be seen emerging here as well. The Head Start Program Performance Standards explicitly call for supporting children's home language as well as English language acquisition. For example, these standards call for creating an environment of acceptances that conveys respect for home language and culture; communication with families in their preferred or primary language, or through an interpreter; and hiring of at least one staff member who speaks the home language of children when a majority speak a particular language other than English (Plutro, 2005). In contrast, in selected (although not all) states, the policy regarding language use in public school classrooms for K–12 students is English only. Although pre-K classrooms may not be explicitly included in the state K–12 educational policies regarding language, such policies may trickle down—or be assumed to apply to—pre-K classrooms when these are located in public schools. The potential exists for direct conflict in policies when Head Start programs are housed within public schools with English-only policies. This emerging debate therefore pertains to and extends the summary of the debate provided previously regarding where pre-K should be provided.

The Center for Early Care and Education Research: Dual-Language Learners (http://cecerdll. fpg.unc.edu), which is funded by the U.S. Department of Health and Human Services, is conducting critical reviews of the evidence on the language, cognitive, and social-emotional development of young dual-language learners in the United States, as well as reviews of developmental assessments and program quality measures for classrooms serving young dual-language learners. The work of the Center will include reviews of the evidence from intervention evaluations in which dual-language learners' English language acquisition and other developmental outcomes are studied in light of variation in whether and how instruction in children's home language is integrated into pre-K classrooms.

It will be critical for the pre-K debates to be extended so that the issue of policies regarding support for the home language in dual-language learners is explicitly and thoughtfully addressed. In addition to language of instruction, consideration should be given to how best to prepare teachers for working with dual-language learners and their families, including specific instructional approaches, family engagement, and classroom practices that incorporate awareness of and respect for children's cultures.

Approaches for Supporting Inclusion of Children with Special Needs

Finally, the issue of how best to support the development of children with special needs is mentioned but not drawn out as a separate focus in this book. Perhaps researchers are beyond the point of debating inclusion in pre-K programs for children with special needs. Yet more-nuanced questions beyond whether or not children with special needs should be included in pre-K programs still need to be addressed and debated.

For example, there is some evidence of variation in the behavioral outcomes of typically developing children in high-quality Head Start classrooms according to the percentage of children in the classroom who have special needs (Gallagher & Lambert, 2006). This suggests the need for careful consideration of classroom composition and staffing patterns in order to support the development of both typically developing children and children with special needs in pre-K classrooms. In addition, there have been important recent developments in approaches for ongoing assessments of how children with special needs are responding to early intervention approaches (Snow & Van Hemmel, 2008). There is a need for consideration of how best to integrate these assessment approaches into pre-K classrooms and prepare teachers for their use.

CONCLUSION

This book makes an invaluable contribution in laying out the key decisions that will need to be made as pre-K becomes available to more young children in the United States. The decision tree, which is elegantly and clearly drawn by the chapters in this book, needs just a few more branches to be complete.

In addition, there are important areas in which the knowledge base for pre-K decision making is limited. Among the multiple issues identified as needing follow-up through further research, issues of particularly high priority include the following:

Understanding the pre-K enrollment patterns of key population subgroups: Researchers need to understand better the enrollment policies (targeted versus universal, specific outreach approaches) and also program features (e.g., dual-language instruction, culturally sensitive family engagement, mental health supports) that may be associated with enrollment, as well as positive developmental outcomes for children from such key population subgroups as middle- and lower income Latino families, low-income families with incomes above the poverty line, and families facing multiple stressors.

Examining the sequencing and dosage of early childhood services for children and families across the birth-to-5 age range: Health care reform provides an important opportunity to consider how home visitation can contribute to young children's development and school readiness, both alone and when it is intentionally sequenced with pre-K participation at ages 3–5. It would be extremely valuable to use rigorous evaluation designs to study access to services during the full birth-to-5 age range, systematically varying which services are provided and at what portions of this age range. In addition, rigorous evaluations are needed to examine dosage of participation in pre-K programs within the 3-to-5 age range. What are the effects on children, both initially and over time, when they have access to and actually participate in 1 versus 2 years of high-quality pre-K programming?

Considering the effects on program quality when higher education degree-granting programs and ongoing professional development involve direct observation of specific classroom practices: Researchers are beginning to question whether higher education degrees should be seen as acceptable proxies for early educators' mastery of specific classroom practices. Systematic study is needed of the effects on classroom quality when higher education degree-granting programs have requirements for early educators to demonstrate specific practices before conferring degrees, as well as when pre-K programs systematically incorporate ongoing (in-service) professional development that involves a combination of monitoring and supports for specified classroom practices. Before it will be possible to embark on evaluations of such approaches, however, pre-K decision makers will need to engage in the critical step of articulating and agreeing on which classroom practices are essential.

Going beyond separate domain-specific curricula to consideration of coordinated curricula: Researchers are currently building a knowledge base on whether and how specific curricular approaches, as well as professional development to implement them, can strengthen children's development in separate domains, such as early language and literacy development, early mathematical skills, and social and emotional development. There are relatively few rigorous evaluations of curricula that focus simultaneously on multiple domains of development (Zaslow, Tout, Halle, Whittaker, & Lavelle, 2010). Study of curricula that intentionally build in coordinated goals across domains of development would be a valuable contribution. Planned variation studies looking at outcomes for children in classes with such coordinated curricula, in contrast with the implementation of multiple separate curricula or curricula only in one area, would help in understanding how children's development can best be supported through curricular approaches and professional development for their implementation.

Understanding the effects of differing instructional approaches and teacher preparation for those working with dual-language learners. It will be critical to continue to build the body of knowledge on how best to support the development of young children who are dual-language learners in pre-K programs. Such research should include consideration of the effects of differing approaches to teacher preparation and classroom instruction not only for children's language development but across multiple developmental domains. Research is also needed to inform practices on family engagement, cultural sensitivity, and classroom quality for dual-language learners.

References

Abbott v. Burke, 100 N.J. 269, 495 A.2d 376 (1985).

Abramovitz, M. (2000). *Under attack, fighting back: Women and welfare in the United States.* New York: Monthly Review Press.

Acevedo-Polakovich, I.D., Reynaga-Abiko, G., Garriot, P.O., Derefinko, K.J., Wimsatt, M.K., Gudonis, L.C., et al. (2007). Beyond instrument selection: Cultural considerations in the psychological assessment of U.S. Latina/os. *Professional Psychology: Research and Practice, 38,* 375–384.

Achenbach, T.M., & Rescorla, L.A. (2001). *Manual for the ASEBA school-age forms and profiles.* Burlington: University of Vermont Research Center for Children, Youth, & Families.

Ackerman, D.J. (2006). The costs of being a child care teacher: Revisiting the problem of low wages. *Educational Policy, 20,* 85–112.

Ackerman, D.J., & Barnett, W.S. (2006). *Increasing the effectiveness of preschool.* New Brunswick, NJ: National Institute for Early Education Research.

Ackerman, D.J., Barnett, W.S., Hawkinson, L.E., Brown, K., & McGonigle, E.A. (2009). Providing preschool education for all 4-year-olds: Lessons from six state journeys. In E.C. Frede & W.S. Barnett (Eds.), *Preschool policy briefs.* New Brunswick, NJ: National Institute for Early Education Research.

Ackerman, D.J., & Sansanelli, R. (2008). *Assessing the capacity of child care and Head Start centers to participate in New Jersey's preschool expansion initiative: Phase I.* New Brunswick, NJ: National Institute for Early Education Research.

Adams, G., & Sandfort, J. (1994). *First steps, promising futures: State prekindergarten initiatives in the early 1990s.* Washington, DC: Children's Defense Fund.

Administration for Children and Families. (2002). *Pathways to quality and full implementation in Early Head Start programs.* Washington, DC: U.S. Department of Health and Human Services.

Administration for Children and Families. (2003). *Head Start FACES 2000: A whole-child perspective on program performance. Fourth progress report.* Washington, DC: U.S. Department of Health and Human Services.

Administration for Children and Families. (2005). *Biennial report to Congress: The status of children in Head Start programs.* Washington, DC: U.S. Department of Health and Human Services.

Administration for Children and Families. (2007). *Head Start program fact sheet.* Retrieved March 25, 2008, from http://www.acf.hhs.gov/programs/hsb/about/fy2007.html

Administration for Children and Families. (2010). *Head Start program performance standards* (45 CFR Ch. XIII § 1306.32(a)). Retrieved February 21, 2011, from edocket.access.gpo.gov/cfr_2007/octqtr/pdf/45cfr1306.32.pdf

Alishahi, A., Fazly, A., & Stevenson, S. (2008). Fast mapping in word learning: What probabilities tell us. In *Proceedings of the Twelfth Conference on Computational Natural Language Learning* (pp. 57–64). Morristown, NJ: Association for Computational Linguistics.

American Academy of Pediatrics, Council on Child and Adolescent Health. (1998). The role of home-visitation programs in improving health outcomes for children and families. *Pediatrics, 10*(3), 486–489.

American Recovery and Reinvestment Act of 2009, PL 111-5, 26 U.S.C. §§ 1 *et seq.*

Ammerman, R., Putnam, F., Altaye, M., Chen, L., Holleb, L., Stevens, J., et al. (2009). Changes in depressive symptoms in first time mothers in home visitation. *Child Abuse and Neglect, 33,* 127–138.

Anderson, B. (2003, May 3). Enrollment campouts halted for Moore pre-K. *The Oklahoman.*

Andres-Hyman, R.C., Ortiz, J., Anez, L.M., Paris, M., & Davidson, L. (2006). Culture and clinical practice: Recommendations for working with Puerto Ricans and other Latina/os in the United States. *Professional Psychology: Research and Practice, 37,* 694–701.

Andrews, S.P., & Slate, J.R. (2001). Prekindergarten programs: A review of the literature. *Current Issues in Education, 4*(5). Retrieved January 16, 2011, from http://cie.asu.edu/volume4/number5/

Anisfeld, E., Sandy, J., & Guterman, N. (2004) *Best beginnings: A randomized controlled trial of a paraprofessional home visiting program.* Retrieved January 22, 2011, from http://www.healthyfamiliesamerica.org/downloads/eval_NY_bb_2004.pdf

Annie E. Casey Foundation. (2008). *Children under age 6 with all available parents in the labor force - data across states - KIDS COUNT data center.* Retrieved November 29, 2009, from http://datacenter.kidscount.org/data/acrossstates/Rankings.aspx?ind=62

Aos, S., Lieb, R., Mayfield, J., Miller, M., & Pennucci, A. (2004). *Benefits and costs of prevention and early intervention programs for youth.* Olympia: Washington State Institute for Public Policy.

Aos, S., Miller, M., & Mayfield, J. (2007). *Benefits and costs of K–12 education policies: Evidence-based effects of class size reductions and full-day kindergarten.* Olympia: Washington State Institute for Public Policy.

Applewhite, E., & Hirsch, L. (2003). *The Abbott preschool program: Fifth year report on enrollment and budget.* Newark, NJ: Education Law Center.

Arias, J., Azuara, O., Bernal, P., Heckman, J.J., & Villarreal, C. (2009, October 19). *Policies to promote growth and economic efficiency in Mexico.* Presented at the Challenges and Strategies for Promoting Economic Growth conference, Banco de Mexico, Mexico City, Mexico.

Arnold, D.H., Brown, S.A., Meagher, S., Baker, C.N., Dobbs, J., & Doctoroff, G.L. (2006). Preschool-based programs for externalizing problems. *Education and Treatment of Children, 29,* 311–339.

Arnold, D., Fisher, P., Doctoroff, G., & Dobbs, J. (2002). Accelerating math development in Head Start classrooms. *Journal of Educational Psychology, 94,* 762–770.

August, G.J., Realmuto, G.M., Hektner, J.M., & Bloomquist, M.L. (2001). An integrated components preventive intervention for aggressive elementary school children: The Early Risers program. *Journal of Consulting and Clinical Psychology, 69,* 614–626.

Avruch, S., & Cackley, A.P. (1995). Savings achieved by giving WIC benefits to women prenatally. *Public Health Reports, 110,* 27–34.

Baker, P.C., Keck, C.K., Mott, F.L., & Quilan, S.V. (1993). *NLSY child handbook: A guide to the 1986–1990 NLSY child data* (Rev. ed.). Columbus: The Ohio State University, Center for Human Resource Research.

Barnett, W.S. (1993). *Does Head Start fade out?* Retrieved February 27, 2010, from http://nieer.org/resources/research/BattleHeadStart.pdf

Barnett, W.S. (1996). *Lives in the balance: Age-27 benefit–cost analysis of the High/Scope Perry Preschool Program.* Ypsilanti, MI: The High/Scope Press.

Barnett, W.S. (2004). *Better teachers, better preschools: Student achievement linked to teacher qualifications.* New Brunswick, NJ: National Institute for Early Education Research.

Barnett, W.S. (2006). *A review of the Reason Foundation's report on preschool and kindergarten.* New Brunswick, NJ: National Institute for Early Education Research. Retrieved February 27, 2009, from http://nieer.org/docs/?DocID=150

Barnett, W.S. (2007). Benefits and costs of quality early childhood education. *The Children's Legal Rights Journal, 27,* 7–23.

Barnett, W.S. (2008). *Preschool education and its lasting effects: Research and policy implications.* New Brunswick, NJ: National Institute for Early Education Research.

Barnett, W.S., Brown, K., & Shore, R. (2004). *The universal vs. targeted debate: Should the United States have preschool for all?* Retrieved January 3, 2011, from http://nieer.org/resources/policybriefs/6.pdf

Barnett, W.S., Epstein, D.J., Friedman, A.H., Boyd, J.S., & Hustedt, J.T. (2008). *The state of preschool 2008: State preschool yearbook.* New Brunswick, NJ: National Institute for Early Education Research.

Barnett, W.S., Epstein, D.J., Friedman, A.H., Sansanelli, R., & Hustedt, J.T. (2009). *The state of preschool: 2009 state preschool yearbook.* New Brunswick, NJ: National Institute for Early Education Research.

Barnett, W.S., Frede, E., Mobasher, H., & Mohr, P. (1988). The efficacy of public preschool programs and the relationship of program quality to efficacy. *Educational Evaluation and Policy Analysis, 12,* 169–181.

Barnett, W.S., Friedman, A., Hustedt, J., & Stevenson-Boyd, J. (2009). An overview of prekindergarten policy in the United States: Program governance, eligibility, standards, and finance. In R. Pianta & C. Howes (Eds.), *The promise of pre-K* (pp. 3–30). Baltimore: Paul H. Brookes Publishing Co.

Barnett, W.S., Howes, C., & Jung, K. (2008). *California's state preschool program: Quality and effects on children's cognitive abilities at kindergarten entry.* New Brunswick, NJ: National Institute for Early Education Research.

Barnett, W.S., Hustedt, J.T., Friedman, A.H., Boyd, J.S., & Ainsworth, P. (2007). *The state of preschool 2007: State preschool yearbook.* New Brunswick, NJ: National Institute for Early Education Research.

Barnett, W.S., Hustedt, J.T., Robin, K.B., & Schulman, K.L. (2004). *The state of preschool: 2004 state preschool yearbook.* New Brunswick, NJ: National Institute for Early Education Research.

Barnett, W.S., Hustedt, J.T., Robin, K.B., & Schulman, K.L. (2005). *The state of preschool: 2005 state preschool yearbook.* New Brunswick, NJ: The National Institute for Early Education Research.

Barnett, W.S., Jung, K., Yarosz, D.J., Thomas, J., Hornbeck, A., Stechuk, R., et al. (2008). Educational effects of the Tools of the Mind curriculum: A randomized trial. *Early Childhood Research Quarterly, 23,* 299–313.

Barnett, W.S., Lamy, C., & Jung, K. (2005). *The effects of state prekindergarten programs on young children's school readiness in five states.* New Brunswick, NJ: National Institute for Early Education Research. Retrieved January 3, 2011, from http://nieer.org/resources/research/multistate/fullreport.pdf

Barnett, W.S., & Masse, L.N. (2007). Early childhood program design and economic returns: Comparative benefit–cost analysis of the Abecedarian program and policy implications. *Economics of Education Review, 26*(1), 113–125.

Barnett, W.S., Robin, K.B., Hustedt, J.T., & Schulman, K.L. (2003). *The state of preschool: 2003 state preschool yearbook.* New Brunswick, NJ: National Institute for Early Education Research.

Barnett, W.S., Tarr, J., Esposito-Lamy, C. & Frede, E. (2001). *Fragile lives, shattered dreams: A report on implementation of preschool education in New Jersey's Abbott districts.* New Brunswick, NJ: Rutgers University.

Baroody, A.J., & Dowker, A. (2003). The development of arithmetic concepts and skills: Constructing adaptive expertise. In A. Schoenfeld (Ed.), *Studies on mathematics thinking and learning.* Mahwah, NJ: Lawrence Erlbaum Associates.

Barratt, W. (2005). *The Barratt Simplified Measure of Social Status (BSMSS): Measuring SES.* Terre Haute: Indiana State University, Department of Educational Leadership, Administration, and Foundations.

Basham, P., Merrifield, J., & Hepburn, C.R. (2007). *Home schooling: From the extreme to the mainstream* (2nd ed.). Toronto: Fraser Institute.

Bassok, D. (2009). *Three essays on early childhood education policy.* Unpublished doctoral dissertation. Retrieved March 12, 2011, from http://gradworks.umi.com/33/64/3364495.html

Bassok, D. (2010). Do black and Hispanic children benefit more from preschool? Understanding differences in preschool effects across racial groups. *Child Development, 81,* 1828–1845.

Bassok, D., French, D., Fuller, B., & Kagan, S. (2008). Do child care centers benefit poor children after school entry? *Journal of Early Childhood Research, 6,* 211–231.

Bayley, N. (1993). *Bayley Scales of Infant Development—Second Edition.* New York: The Psychological Corporation.

Bazelon, E. (2008, July 20). The next kind of integration. *New York Times Magazine,* pp. 38–43.

Beatty, B. (1995). *Preschool education in America.* New Haven, CT: Yale University Press.

Becker, G.S. (1964). *Human capital.* New York: Columbia University Press.

Becker, W.C., & Gersten, R. (1982). A follow-up of Follow Through: The later effects of the direct instruction model on children in fifth and sixth grades. *American Educational Research Journal, 19,* 75–92.

Belfield, C.R. (2004). *Investing in early childhood education in Ohio: An economic appraisal.* Retrieved November 30, 2009, from http://www.clevelandfed.org/research/conferences/2004/november/belfield_paper.pdf

Belfield, C.R., Nores, M., Barnett, S., & Schweinhart, L. (2006). The High/Scope Perry Preschool program: Cost-benefit analysis using data from the age-40 follow-up. *Journal of Human Resources, 41,* 162–190.

Bell, D.M., Gleiber, D.W., Mercer A.A., Phifer, R., Guinter, R.H., Cohen, A.J., et al. (1989). Illness associated with child day care: A study of incidence and cost. *American Journal of Public Health, 79*(4), 479–484.

Belsky, J., & Cassidy, J. (1994). Attachment: Theory and evidence. In M. Rutter & D. Hay (Eds.), *Development through life* (pp. 373–402). Oxford, England: Blackwell.

Belsky, J., Spritz, B., & Crnic, K. (1994). Infant attachment security and affective-cognitive information processing at age 3. *Psychological Science, 7*(2), 111–114.

Bergen, D., & Mauer, D. (2000). Symbolic play, phonological awareness, and literacy skills at three age levels. In K.A. Roskos & J.F. Christie (Eds.), *Play and literacy in early childhood: Research from multiple perspectives* (pp. 45–62). Mahwah, NJ: Lawrence Erlbaum Associates.

Berger, K. (2008). *The developing person through childhood and adolescence* (8th ed.). New York: Worth Publishers.

Berk, L.E. (2001). *Awakening children's minds: How parents and teachers can make a difference.* New York: Oxford University Press.

Berryhill, J.C., & Prinz, R.J. (2003). Environmental interventions to enhance student adjustment: Implications for prevention. *Prevention Science, 4,* 65–87.

Besharov, C.J., & Call, D.M. (2008, Autumn). The new kindergarten: The case for universal pre-K isn't as strong as it seems. *The Wilson Quarterly, 28–35.*

Betts, J., Zau, A., & Rice, L. (2003). *Determinants of student achievement: New evidence from San Diego.* San Francisco: Public Policy Institute of California.

Bevilacqua, L. (2008). *What your preschooler needs to know: Read-alouds to get ready for kindergarten.* New York: Bantam Dell.

Biedinger, N., Becker, B., & Rohling, I. (2008). Early ethnic educational inequality: The influence of duration of preschool attendance and social composition. *European Sociological Review, 24*(2), 243–256.

Bierman, K.L., Domitrovich, C.E., Nix, R., Gest, S., Welsh, J.A., Greenberg, M.T., et al. (2008). Promoting academic and social-emotional school readiness: The Head Start REDI program. *Child Development, 79,* 1802–1817.

Blair, C. (2002). School readiness: Integrating cognition and emotion in a neurobiological conceptualization of child functioning at school entry. *American Psychologist, 57,* 111–127.

Blatchford, P., Goldstein, H., Martin, C., & Brown, W. (2002). A study of class size effects in English school reception year classes. *British Educational Research Journal, 28,* 169–185.

Blau, D. (2000). The production of quality in child care centers: Another look. *Applied Developmental Science, 4,* 136–148.

Bloom, B.S. (1964). *Stability and change in human characteristics.* New York: Wiley.

Bock, G., Stebbins, L., & Proper, E. (1977). *Education as experimentation: A planned variation model.* Washington, DC: ABT Associates.

Bodrova, E., & Leong, D.J. (2003). Chopsticks and counting chips: Do play and foundational skills need to compete for the teacher's attention in an early childhood classroom? *Young Children, 58,* 10–17.

Bodrova, E., Leong, D.J., Norford, J.S., & Paynter, D.E. (2003). It only looks like child's play. *Journal of Staff Development, 24,* 47–51.

Bogard, K., & Takanishi, R. (2005). *PK–3: An aligned and coordinated approach to education for children 3- to 8-years-old.* Retrieved January 15, 2011, from http://www.srcd.org/index.php?option=com_docman&task=doc_download&gid=107

Bogard, K., Traylor, F., & Takanishi, R. (2008). Teacher education and PK outcomes: Are we asking the right questions? *Early Childhood Research Quarterly, 23,* 1–6.

Borghans, L., Duckworth, A.L., Heckman, J.J., & ter Weel, B. (2008). The economics and psychology of personality traits. *Journal of Human Resources, 43*(4), 972–1059.

Bowman, B.T. (1999). *Dialogue on early childhood science, mathematics and technology education a context for learning: Policy implications for math, science, and technology in early childhood education.* Retrieved on November 30, 2009, from http://www.project2061.org/publications/earlychild/online/context/bowman.htm

Bowman, B.T., Donovan, M.S., & Burns, M.S. (2001). *Eager to learn: Educating our preschoolers.* Washington, DC: National Academies Press.

Boyce, C.A., & Fuligni, A.J. (2007). Issues for developmental research among racial/ethnic minority and immigrant families. *Research in Human Development, 4,* 1–17.

Brandon, K. (2002, October 20). Kindergarten less playful as pressure to achieve grows. *Chicago Tribune,* p. 1.

Bransford, J.D., Brown, A.L., & Cocking, R.R. (Eds.). (2000). *How people learn.* Washington, DC: National Academies Press.

Brauner, J., Gordic, B., & Zigler, E. (2004). Putting the child back into child care: Combining care and education for children ages 3-5. *SRCD Social Policy Report, 18*(3).

Bredekamp, S. (1987). *Developmentally appropriate practice.* Washington, DC: National Association for the Education of Young Children.

Bredekamp, S. (2004). Play and school readiness. In E.F. Zigler, D.G. Singer, & S.J. Bishop-Josef (Eds.), *Children's play: The roots of reading* (pp. 159–174). Washington, DC: ZERO TO THREE.

Bredekamp, S., & Copple, C. (2008). *Developmentally appropriate practice in early childhood programs serving children birth through age eight* (3rd ed.). Washington, DC: National Association for the Education of Young Children.

Bronfenbrenner, U. (1975). Is early intervention effective? In M. Guttentag & E. Struening (Eds.), *Handbook of evaluation research* (Vol 2., pp. 519–603). Thousand Oaks, CA: Sage Publications.

Bronfenbrenner, U. (1979). *The ecology of human development: Experiments by nature and design.* Cambridge, MA: Harvard University Press.

Bronfenbrenner, U. (1989). Ecological systems theory. *Annals of Child Development, 6,* 187–249.

Bronfenbrenner, U., & Morris, P. (1998). Ecological processes of development. In W. Damon (Ed.), *Handbook of child psychology: Theoretical issues* (Vol. 1, pp. 993–1028). New York: Wiley.

Brooks-Gunn, J. (2003). Do you believe in magic? What we can expect from early childhood intervention programs. *SRCD Social Policy Report, 17,* 3–14.

Brooks-Gunn, J. (2010). *Early childhood education: The likelihood of sustained effects.* Manuscript in preparation.

Brooks-Gunn, J., Klebanov, P.K., & Duncan, G.J. (1996). Ethnic differences in children's intelligence test scores: Role of economic deprivation, home environment, and maternal characteristics. *Child Development, 67,* 396–408.

Brooks-Gunn, J., Klebanov, P., Liaw, F., & Spiker, D. (1993). Enhancing the development of low-birthweight premature infants: Changes in cognition and behavior over the first three years. *Child Development, 64,* 736–753.

Brooks-Gunn, J., & Markman, L. (2005). The contribution of parenting to ethnic and racial gaps in school readiness. *The Future of Children, 15*(1), 138–167.

Brooks-Gunn, J., McCarton, C., Casey, P., McCormick, M., Bauer, C., Bernbaum, J., et al. (1994). Early intervention in low-birth-weight, premature infants: Results through age 5 years from the Infant Health and Development Program. *Journal of the American Medical Association, 272,* 1257–1262.

Brooks-Gunn, J., McCormick, M., Shapiro, S., Benasich, A.A., & Black, G. (1994). The effects of early education intervention on maternal employment, public assistance, and health insurance: The Infant Health and Development Program. *American Journal of Public Health, 84,* 924–931.

Brown, E. (2009, November 21). The playtime's the thing: A debate over the value of make-believe and other games in preschool classes is deepening as more states fund programs. *Washington Post,* p. B01.

Burchinal, M., Cryer, D., Clifford, R., & Howes, C. (2002). Caregiver training and classroom quality in child care centers. *Applied Developmental Science, 6,* 2–11.

Burchinal, M., Howes, C., & Kontos, S. (2002). Structural predictors of child care quality in child care homes. *Early Childhood Research Quarterly, 17,* 87–105.

Burchinal, M., Howes, C., Pianta, R., Bryant, D., Early, D., Clifford, R., et al. (2008). Predicting child outcomes at the end of kindergarten from the quality of prekindergarten teacher–child interactions and instruction. *Applied Developmental Science, 12,* 140–153.

Burchinal, M., Hyson, M., & Zaslow, M. (2008). Competencies and credentials for early childhood educators: What do we know and what do we need to know? *NHSA Dialog, 11*(1), 1–7.

Burchinal, M.R., Roberts, J.E., Riggins, R., Zeisel, S.A., Neebe, E., & Bryant, D. (2000). Relating quality of center-based child care to early cognitive and language development longitudinally. *Child Development, 71*(2), 339–357.

Burger, K. (2010). How does early childhood care and education affect cognitive development? An international review of the effects of early interventions for children from different social backgrounds. *Early Childhood Research Quarterly, 25,* 140–165.

Burton, A., Whitebook, M., Young, M., Bellm, D., Wayne, C., Brandon, R.N., et al. (2002). *Estimating the size and components of the U.S. child care workforce and caregiving population.* Retrieved December 9, 2009, from http://www.ccw.org/storage/ccworkforce/documents/publications/workforceestimatereport.pdf

Burts, D.C., Hart, C.H., Charlesworth, R., & DeWolf, M. (1993). Developmental appropriateness of kindergarten programs and academic outcomes in first grade. *Journal of Research in Childhood Education, 8,* 23–31.

Burts, D., Hart, C., Charlesworth, R., Fleege, P., Mosley, J., & Thomasson, R. (1992). Observed activities and stress behaviors of children in developmentally appropriate and inappropriate kindergarten classrooms. *Early Childhood Research Quarterly, 7,* 297–318.

Burts, D., Hart, C., Charlesworth, R., & Kirk, L. (1990). A comparison of frequencies of stress behaviors observed in kindergarten children in classrooms with developmentally appropriate versus developmentally inappropriate instructional practices. *Early Childhood Research Quarterly, 5,* 407–423.

Bush, G.W. (2003, January 8). *Remarks by the president on the first anniversary of the No Child Left Behind Act.* Retrieved September 10, 2003, from http://www.whitehouse.gov/news/releases/2003/01/20030108-4.html

Bushaw, W., & McNee, J. (2009). The 41st annual Phi Delta Kappa/Gallup poll of the public's attitudes toward the public schools. *Phi Delta Kappan, 91*(1), 8–23.

Bushouse, B.K. (2009). *Universal preschool: Policy change, stability, and the Pew Charitable Trusts.* Albany: State University of New York Press.

Buysse, V., & Wesley, P. (2005). *Consultation in early childhood settings*. Baltimore: Paul H. Brookes Publishing Co.

Buysse, V., Winton, P., & Rous, B. (2009). Reaching consensus on a definition of professional development for the early childhood field. *Topics in Early Childhood Special Education, 28*(4), 235–243.

Caldera, Y.M., McDonald Culp, A., Truglio, R.T., Alvarez, M., & Huston, A.C. (1999). Children's play preferences, construction play with blocks, and visual-spatial skills: Are they related? *International Journal of Behavioral Development, 23,* 855–872.

Caldwell, B.M. (1986). Day care and the public schools: Natural allies, natural enemies. *Educational Leadership, 43*(5), 34.

Calfee, R. (1997). Language and literacy, home and school. *Early Child Development and Care, 127,* 75–98.

Cameron, S.V., & Heckman, J.J. (2001). The dynamics of educational attainment for black, Hispanic, and white males. *Journal of Political Economy, 109*(3), 455–499.

Camilli, G., Vargas, S., Ryan, S., & Barnett, W.S. (2010). Meta-analysis of the effects of early education interventions on cognitive and social development. *Teachers College Record, 112*(3), 579–620.

Campbell, D.E. (2008). The civic side of school choice: An empirical analysis of civic education in public and private schools. *Brigham Young University Law Review, 2,* 487–524.

Campbell, D.T. (1987a). *Assessing the impact of planned social change.* Hanover, NH: The Public Affairs Center, Dartmouth College.

Campbell, D.T. (1987b). Problems facing the experimenting society in the interface between evaluation and service providers. In S.L. Kagan, D.R. Powell, B. Weissbourd, & E. Zigler (Eds.), *America's family support programs* (pp. 345–351). New Haven, CT: Yale University Press.

Campbell, D.T. (1991). Methods for an experimenting society. *American Journal of Evaluation, 12,* 223–260.

Campbell, D.T., & Boruch, R.F. (1975). Making the case for randomized assignment to treatments by considering the alternatives: Six ways in which quasi-experimental evaluations in compensatory education tend to underestimate effects. In C.A. Bennet & A.A. Lumsdaine (Eds.), *Evaluation and Experiment* (pp. 195–296). San Diego, CA: Academic Press.

Campbell, F.A., Pungello, E.P., Miller-Johnson, S., Burchinal, M., & Ramey, C.T. (2001). The development of cognitive and academic abilities: Growth curves from an early childhood education experiment. *Developmental Psychology, 37,* 231–242.

Campbell, F.A., & Ramey, C.T. (1995). Cognitive and school outcomes for high-risk African-American students at middle adolescence: Positive effects of early intervention. *American Educational Research Journal, 32,* 743–772.

Campbell, F.A., Ramey, C.T., Pungello, E., Sparling, J., & Miller-Johnson, S. (2002). Early childhood education: Young adult outcomes from the Abecedarian project. *Applied Developmental Science, 6*(1), 42–57.

Capizzano, J., Adams, G., & Ost, J. (2007). *Caring for children of color: The child care patterns of White, Black and Hispanic children under 5. Executive summary.* Washington, DC: The Urban Institute.

Carneiro, P., & Heckman, J.J. (2003). Human capital policy. In J.J. Heckman, A.B. Krueger, & B.M. Friedman (Eds.), *Inequality in America: What role for human capital policies?* (pp. 77–239). Cambridge, MA: The MIT Press.

Carter, A.S., Briggs-Gowan, M.J., Jones, S.M., & Little, T.D. (2003). The Infant-Toddler Social and Emotional Assessment (ITSEA): Factor structure, reliability, and validity. *Journal of Abnormal Child Psychology, 31,* 495–514.

Ceci, S.J., & Papierno, P.B. (2005). The rhetoric and reality of gap closing: When the "have-nots" gain but the "haves" gain even more. *American Psychologist, 60*(2), 149–160.

Center for Family Policy and Research. (2009). *The state of early childhood programs: 2009.* Columbia, MO: Center for Family and Policy Research. Retrieved December 21, 2009, from http://cfpr.missouri.edu/stateprograms09.pdf

Center for Law and Social Policy. (2006). *Early Head Start participants, programs, families, and staff in 2006.* Retrieved February 20, 2010, from http://www.clasp.org/admin/site/publications/files/0417.pdf

Center for Law and Social Policy. (2011). *CLASP DataFinder.* Retrieved January 5, 2011, from http://www.clasp.org/data

Chaffin, M. (2004). Is it time to rethink Healthy Start/Healthy Families? *Child Abuse and Neglect, 28,* 589–595.

Chang, H. (2006). *Getting ready for quality: The critical importance of developing and supporting a skilled, ethnically and linguistically diverse early childhood workforce.* Oakland, CA: California Tomorrow.

Chicago Fact Book Consortium. (1995). *Local community fact book: Chicago metropolitan area, 1990.* Chicago: Board of Trustees, University of Illinois.

Chicago Longitudinal Study. (2005). *Chicago Longitudinal Study user's guide* (Vol. 7). Madison: University of Wisconsin.

Chien, N.C., Howes, C., Burchinal, M., Pianta, R., Ritchie, S., Bryant, D.M., et al. (2010). Children's classroom engagement and school readiness gains in prekindergarten. *Child Development, 81,* 1534–1549.

Child Care Services Association. (2005). *Early childhood systems study.* Chapel Hill, NC: Child Care Services Association.

Child Care Services Association. (2008). *The early childhood workforce: Making the case for compensation.* Chapel Hill, NC: Child Care Services Association.

Childress, S.M., Doyle, D.P., & Thomas, D.A. (2009). *Leading for equity: The pursuit of excellence in the Montgomery County public schools.* Cambridge, MA: Harvard Education Press.

Christie, J.F. (1998). Play as a medium for literacy development. In E.P. Fromberg & D. Bergen (Eds.), *Play from birth to twelve and beyond: Contexts, perspectives, and meaning* (pp. 50–55). New York: Garland.

Christie, J.F., & Enz, B. (1992). The effects of literacy play interventions on preschoolers' play patterns and literacy development. *Early Education and Development, 3,* 205–220.

Christie, J., & Johnsen, E. (1983). The role of play in social-intellectual development. *Review of Educational Research, 53,* 93–115.

Christie, J., & Roskos, K. (2006). Standards, science and the role of play in early literacy education. In D. Singer, R.M. Golinkoff, & K. Hirsh-Pasek (Eds.), *Play = learning: How play motivates and enhances children's cognitive and social-emotional growth.* New York: Oxford University Press.

Cicirelli, V.G. (1969). *The impact of Head Start: An evaluation of the effects of Head Start on children's cognitive and affective development.* Athens: Ohio University.

Cimpian, A., Arce, H., Markman, E., & Dweck, C. (2007). Subtle linguistic cues affect children's motivation. *Psychological Science, 18,* 314–316.

Clarke-Stewart, A., & Allhusen, V. (2005). *What we know about child care.* Cambridge, MA: Harvard University Press.

Clarke-Stewart, K.A., Vandell, D.L., Burchinal, M., O'Brien, M., & McCartney, K. (2002). Do regulable features of child-care homes affect children's development? *Early Childhood Research Quarterly, 17*(1), 52–86.

Clements, D.H., & Sarama, J. (2007). Effects of a preschool mathematics curriculum: Summative research on the Building Blocks project. *Journal for Research in Mathematics Education, 38*(2), 136–163.

Clifford, D., & Maxwell, K. (2002). *The need for highly qualified prekindergarten teachers: Preparing highly qualified prekindergarten teachers symposium.* Chapel Hill: University of North Carolina, Frank Porter Graham Child Development Institute.

Coalition for Evidence-Based Policy. (2009). *Early childhood home visitation program models: An objective summary of the evidence about which are effective.* Washington, DC: Author.

Coleman, J.S. (1966). *Equality of educational opportunity.* Washington, DC: U.S. Government Printing Office.

Commonwealth of Australia. (2009). *Investing in the early years—A national early childhood development strategy: An initiative of the council of Australian governments.* Retrieved January 3, 2011, from http://www.coag.gov.au/coag_meeting_outcomes/2009-07-02/docs/national_ECD_strategy.pdf

Conduct Problems Prevention Research Group. (1999). Initial impact of the fast track prevention trial for conduct problems: II. Classroom effects. *Journal of Consulting and Clinical Psychology, 67,* 648–657.

Conduct Problems Prevention Research Group. (2002). Evaluation of the first three years of the Fast Track prevention trial with children at high risk for adolescent conduct problems. *Journal of Abnormal Child Psychology, 30,* 19–35.

Connor, C.M., Morrison, F.J., Fishman, B.J., Schatschneider, C., & Underwood, P. (2007). The early years: Algorithm-guided individualized reading instruction. *Science, 315,* 464–465.

Cook, D. (2000). Voice practice: Social and mathematical talk in imaginative play. *Early Child Development and Care, 162,* 51–63.

Cook, T.D. (2008). Waiting for life to arrive: A history of the regression-discontinuity design in psychology, statistics, and economics. *Journal of Econometrics, 142,* 636–654.

Copple, C., & Bredekamp, S. (2009). *Developmentally appropriate practice in early childhood programs serving children from birth through age 8* (3rd ed.). Washington, DC: National Association for the Education of Young Children.

Cost, Quality, and Outcomes Study Team. (1995). *Cost, quality, and child outcomes in child care centers.* Denver: University of Colorado at Denver.

Costa, A.L., & Garmston, R.J. (2002). *Cognitive coaching: A foundation for Renaissance schools* (2nd ed.). Norwood, MA: Christopher-Gordon.

Coulter, P., & Vandal, B. (2007). *Community colleges and teacher preparation: Roles, issues and opportunities.* Denver, CO: Education Commission of the States.

Council of Chief State School Officers. (2010). *Common core state standards initiative.* Retrieved January 30, 2010, from http://www.corestandards.org/

Cunha, F., & Heckman, J.J. (2007). The technology of skill formation. *American Economic Review, 97*(2), 31–47.

Cunha, F., & Heckman, J.J. (2008). Formulating, identifying and estimating the technology of cognitive and noncognitive skill formation. *Journal of Human Resources, 43*(4), 738–782.

Cunha, F., & Heckman, J.J. (2009). The economics and psychology of inequality and human development. *Journal of the European Economic Association, 7*(2–3), 320–364.

Cunha, F., Heckman, J.J., Lochner, L.J., & Masterov, D.V. (2006). Interpreting the evidence on life cycle skill formation. In E.A. Hanushek & F. Welch (Eds.), *Handbook of the economics of education* (pp. 697–812). Amsterdam: North-Holland.

Cunha, F., Heckman, J.J., & Schennach, S.M. (2010). Estimating the technology of cognitive and noncognitive skill formation. *Econometrica, 78*(3), 883–931.

Cunningham, A.E., Zibulsky, J., & Callahan, M.D. (2009). Starting small: Building preschool teacher knowledge that supports early literacy development. *Reading and Writing: An Interdisciplinary Journal, 22,* 487–510.

Currie, J. (2001). Early childhood education programs. *Journal of Economic Perspectives, 15,* 213–238.

Currie, J. (2004). *The take-up of social benefits, Working Paper 10488.* Cambridge, MA: National Bureau of Economic Research.

Currie, J., & Duncan, T. (2009). *Stalking the wild taboo: Does Head Start make a difference?* Retrieved February 22, 2011, from http://www.lrainc.com/swtaboo/taboos/headst01.html

Currie, J., & Neidel, M. (2007). Getting inside the black box of Head Start quality: What matters and what doesn't. *Economics of Education Review, 26,* 83–99.

D'Agostino, J.V., & Murphy, J.A. (2004). A meta-analysis of Reading Recovery in United States schools. *Educational Evaluation and Policy Analysis, 26,* 23–38.

Dalli, C. (1999, September). *Starting childcare: What young children learn about relating to adults in the first weeks of settling into a childcare centre.* Paper presented at the Early Childhood Convention, Nelson, New Zealand.

Darling-Hammond, L. (2010). *Performance counts: Assessment systems that support high-quality learning.* Washington, DC: Council of Chief State School Officers.

Darling-Hammond, L., & Bransford, J. (2007). *Preparing teachers for a changing world: What teachers should learn and be able to do.* San Francisco: Jossey-Bass.

Daro, D. (2000). Child abuse prevention: New directions and challenges. Nebraska Symposium on Motivation. *Journal on Motivation, 46,* 161–219.

Daro, D. (2006). *Home visitation: Assessing progress, managing expectations.* Chicago: Chapin Hall Center for Children and the Ounce of Prevention Fund.

Daro, D. (2009). The history of science and child abuse prevention: A reciprocal relationship. In K. Dodge & D. Coleman (Eds.), *Community-based prevention of child maltreatment* (pp. 9–25). New York: Guilford Press.

Daro, D., & Harding, K. (1999). Healthy Families America: Using research to enhance practice. *Future of Children, 9,* 152–176.

Daro, D., & McCurdy, K. (2006). Interventions to prevent child maltreatment. In L. Doll, J. Mercy, R. Hammond, D. Sleet, & S. Bonzo (Eds.), *Handbook on injury and violence prevention interventions.* New York: Kluwer Academic/Plenum Publishers.

Datta, L.E., McHalle, C., & Mitchell, S. (1976). *The effects of the Head Start classroom experience on some aspects of child development: A summary report of national evaluations, 1966–1969.* Washington, DC: Office of Child Development.

Davidson, J.I.F. (1998). Language and play: Natural partners. In E.P. Fromberg & D. Bergen (Eds.), *Play from birth to twelve and beyond: Contexts, perspectives, and meaning* (pp. 175–183). New York: Garland.

Davis, J., Smith, T., Hodge, R., Nakao, K., & Treas, J. (1991). *Occupational prestige ratings from the 1989 general survey.* Ann Arbor, MI: Interuniversity Consortium for Political and Social Research.

Decker, P.T., Mayer, D.P., & Glazerman, S. (2004). *The effects of Teach for America on students: Findings from a national evaluation.* Princeton, NJ: Mathematica Policy Research.

de Kruif, R.E.L., McWilliam, R.A., Ridley, S.M., & Wakely, M.B. (2000). Classification of teachers' interaction behaviors in early childhood classrooms. *Early Childhood Research Quarterly, 15*(2), 247–268.

Delaney, P., & Smith, S. (2000). *Study finds Asian countries are best in math, science: Newest TIMSS data indicates little progress for U.S. 8th graders.* Retrieved January 17, 2011, from http://www.bc.edu/bc_org/rvp/pubaf/chronicle/v9/d14/timss.html

DePanfilis, D., & Dubowitz, H. (2005). Family Connections: A program for preventing child neglect. *Child Maltreatment, 10*(2), 108–123.

Deutsch, M., Deutsch, C.P., Jordan, T.J., & Grallo, R. (1983). The IDS program: An experiment in early and sustained enrichment. In The Consortium for Longitudinal Studies (Ed.), *As the twig is bent…Lasting effects of preschool programs* (pp. 377–410). Mahwah, NJ: Lawrence Erlbaum Associates.

Devaney, B. (in press). WIC turns 35: Effectiveness and future directions. In A. Reynolds (Ed.), *Childhood programs and practices in the first decade of life: A human capital integration.* New York: Cambridge University Press.

Diamond, A., Barnett, W.S., Thomas, J., & Munro, S. (2007). Preschool program improves cognitive control. *Science, 318*(5855), 1387–1388.

Dickinson, D.K., & Brady, J.P. (2005). Toward effective support for language and literacy through professional development. In M. Zaslow and I. Martinez-Beck (Eds.), *Critical issues in early childhood professional development* (pp. 141–170). Baltimore: Paul H. Brookes Publishing Co.

Dickinson, D.K., & Caswell, L.C. (2007). Building support for language and early literacy in preschool classrooms through in-service professional development: Effects of the Literacy Environment Enrichment Program (LEEP). *Early Childhood Research Quarterly, 22*(2), 243–260.

Dickinson, D.K., Cote, L.R., & Smith, M.W. (1993). Learning vocabulary in preschool: Social and discourse contexts affecting vocabulary growth. In W. Damon & C. Daiute, *New directions in child development: The development of literacy through social interaction* (Vol. 61, pp. 67–78). San Francisco: Jossey-Bass.

Dickinson, D., & Freiberg, J. (in press). Environmental factors affecting language acquisition from birth–five: Implications for literacy development and intervention efforts. In National Research Council (Eds.), *The role of language in school learning.* Washington, DC: National Academies Press.

Dickinson, D., & Moreton, J. (1991, April). *Predicting specific kindergarten literacy skills from 3-year-olds' preschool experiences.* Paper presented at the biennial meeting of the Society for Research in Child Development, Seattle, WA.

Dickinson, D.K., & Tabors, P.O. (Eds.). (2001). *Beginning literacy with language: Young children learning at home and school.* Baltimore: Paul H. Brookes Publishing Co.

Dodge, K.A., Pettit, G.S., & Bates, J.E. (1994). Socialization mediators of the relation between socioeconomic status and child conduct problems. *Child Development, 65,* 649–665.

Doherty, K.M. (2002, January 10). Early learning. *Education Week, 17*(21), 54–56.

Dolan, L., Kellam, S., Brown, C., Werthamer-Larsson, L., Rebok, G., Mayer, L., et al. (1993). The short-term impacts of two classroom-based preventive interventions on aggressive and shy behaviors and poor achievement. *Journal of Applied Developmental Psychology, 14,* 317–345.

Donahue, P., Falk, B., & Provet, A.G. (2000). *Mental health consultation in early childhood.* Baltimore: Paul H. Brookes Publishing Co.

Dore, R. (1976). *The diploma disease.* Berkeley: University of California Press.

Dotterer, A.M., Burchinal, M., Bryant, D.M., Early, D.M., & Pianta, R.C. (2009). Comparing universal and targeted prekindergarten programs. In R.C. Pianta & C. Howes (Eds.), *The promise of pre-K* (pp. 65–76). Baltimore: Paul H. Brookes Publishing Co.

Dudley, K. (1998, August 19). Tulsa joins the push for early education. *Tulsa World.*

DuMont, K., Mitchell-Herzfeld, S., Greene, R., Lee, E., Lowenfels, A., Rodriguez, M., et al. (2008). Healthy Families New York (HFNY) randomized trial: Effects on early child abuse and neglect. *Child Abuse and Neglect, 32,* 295–315.

Duncan, A. (2009, November 19). *The early learning challenge: Raising the bar.* Presented at the National Association for the Education of Young Children Annual Conference.

Duncan, G., Dowsett, C., Claessens, A., Magnuson, K., Huston, A., Klebanov, P., et al. (2007). School readiness and later achievement. *Developmental Psychology, 43,* 1428–1446.

Duncan, G., Ludwig, J., & Magnuson, K. (2009). *Reducing poverty through early childhood interventions.* Retrieved February 21, 2011, from http://www.futureofchildren.org

Duncan, G., & Magnuson, K. (2009, November 19–20). *The nature and impact of early skills, attention, and behavior.* Presented at the Russell Sage Foundation conference on Social Inequality and Educational Outcomes.

Dunn, L.M., & Dunn, L.M. (1997). *Peabody Picture Vocabulary Test–Third Edition.* Circle Pines, MN: American Guidance Service.

Dunn, L., Lugo, D., Padilla, E., & Dunn, L. (1986). *Test de Vocabulario en Imagenes Peabody.* Circle Pines, MN: American Guidance Service.

Dutcher, B. (2007). *Let's help early childhood educators by offering a tax break.* Retrieved January 17, 2011, from http://www.edmondsun.com/opinion/local_story_323122303.html

Duthoit, M. (1988). L'enfant et l'ecole: Aspects synthetiques du suivi d'un echantillon de vingt mille eleves des ecoles. *Education et Formations, 16,* 3–13.

Early, D.M., Bryant, D., Pianta, R., Clifford, R., Burchinal, M., Ritchie, S., et al. (2006). Are teachers' education, major, and credentials related to classroom quality and children's academic gains in pre-kindergarten? *Early Childhood Research Quarterly, 21,* 174–195.

Early, D., Iruka, I., Ritchie, S., Barbarin, O., Winn, D., & Crawford, G. (2010). How do pre-kindergarteners spend their time? Gender, ethnicity, and income as predictors of experiences in pre-kindergarten classrooms. *Early Childhood Research Quarterly, 25,* 177–193.

Early, D.M., Maxwell, K.L., Burchinal, M., Alva, S., Bender, R.H., Bryant, D., et al. (2007). Teachers' education, classroom quality, and young children's academic skills: Results from seven studies of preschool programs. *Child Development, 78*(2), 558–580.

Early, D.M., & Winton, P.J. (2001). Preparing the workforce: Early childhood teacher preparation at 2- and 4-year institutions of higher education. *Early Childhood Research Quarterly, 16,* 285–306.

Edwards, C.P., & Raikes, H. (2002). Extending the dance: Relationship-based approaches to infant/ toddler care and education. *Young Children, 57*(4), 10–17.

Ehrenberg, R.G., Brewer, D.J., Gamoran, A., & Willms, J.D. (2001). Class size and student achievement. *Psychological Science in the Public Interest, 2,* 1–30.

Einarsdottir, J. (2005). We can decide what to play! Children's perception of quality in an Icelandic playschool. *Early Education and Development, 16,* 469–488.

Elementary and Secondary Education Act of 1965, PL 89-10, 20 U.S.C. §§ 241 *et seq.*

Elkind, D. (1981). *The hurried child: Growing up too fast, too soon.* Reading, MA: Addison-Wesley.

Elkind, D. (1987). *Miseducation: Preschoolers at risk.* New York: Knopf.

Elkind, D. (1988). The resistance to developmentally appropriate educational practice with young children: The real issue. In C. Warger (Ed.), *A resource guide to public school early childhood programs* (pp. 53–62). Alexandria, VA: Association for Supervision and Curriculum Development.

Elkind, D. (2001). Young Einsteins: Much too early. *Education Matters, 1*(2), 9–15.

Elkind, D. (2008). Can we play? *Greater Good, 4,* 14–17.

Engelmann, S., & Engelmann, T. (1966). *Give your child a superior mind: A program for the preschool child.* New York: Simon & Schuster.

Entwisle, D.R., Alexander, K.L., & Olson, L.S. (2007). Early schooling: The handicap of being poor and male. *Sociology of Education, 80,* 114–138.

Epstein, A.S., Schweinhart, L.J., & McAdoo, L. (1996). *Models of early childhood education.* Ypsilanti, MI: HighScope Press.

Espinosa, L.M. (2010). Assessment of young English language learners. In E. Garcia & E. Frede (Eds.), *Developing the research agenda for young English language learners* (pp. 119–142). New York: Teachers College Press.

Family and Medical Leave Act of 1993, PL 103-3, 5 U.S.C. §§ 6381 *et seq.,* 29 U.S.C. §§ 2601 *et seq.*

Fan, X., & Chen, M. (2001). Parental involvement and students' academic achievement: A meta-analysis. *Educational Psychology Review, 13,* 1–22.

Fantuzzo, J., Bulotsky-Shearer, R., McDermott, P.A., McWayne, C., Frye, D., & Perlman, S. (2007). Investigation of dimensions of social-emotional classroom behavior and school readiness for low-income urban preschool children. *School Psychology Review, 36,* 44–62.

Fantuzzo, J., Perry, M., & McDermott, P. (2004). Preschool approaches to learning and their relationship to other relevant classroom competencies for low-income children. *School Psychology Quarterly, 19,* 212–230.

Fantuzzo, J., Stoltzfus, J., Lutz, M.N., Hamlet, H., Balraj, V., Turner, C., et al. (1999). An evaluation of the special needs referral process for low-income preschool children with emotional and behavioral problems. *Early Childhood Research Quarterly, 14,* 465–482.

Fantuzzo, J.W., Sutton-Smith, B., Coolahan, K.C., Manz, P.H., Canning, S., & Debnam, D. (1995). Assessment of preschool play interaction behaviors in young low-income children: Penn Interactive Peer Play Scale. *Early Childhood Research Quarterly, 10,* 105–120.

Fein, G., & Rivkin, M. (1986). *The young child at play: Reviews of research.* Washington, DC: National Association for the Education of Young Children.

Fergusson, D., Grant, H., Horwood, J.L., & Ridder, E. (2005). Randomized trial of the Early Start Program of home visitation. *Pediatrics, 11*(6), 803–809.

Finn, C. (2009). The preschool picture. *Education Next, 9*(4), 13–19.

Finn, J.D., & Achilles, C.M. (1999). Tennessee's class size study: Findings, implications and misconceptions. *Educational Evaluation and Policy Analysis, 20,* 95–113.

Finn, J.D., Gerber, S.B., & Boyd-Zaharias, J. (2005). Small classes in the early grades: Academic achievement and graduation from high school. *Journal of Educational Psychology, 97,* 214–223.

Finn-Stevenson, M., & Zigler, E.F. (1999). *Schools of the 21st Century: Linking child care and education.* Boulder, CO: Westview Press.

Fischer, B. (Executive Producer). (2008, December 7). *Meet the Press.* New York: NBC.

Fisher, C.B., Hoagwood, K., Boyce, C., Duster, T., Frank, D.A., Grisso, T., et al. (2002). Research ethics for mental health science involving ethnic minority children and youths. *American Psychologist, 57,* 1024–1040.

Fisher, K.R. (2009). *ABC's and 1..2..3: Exploring informal learning in early childhood.* Unpublished manuscript, Temple University.

Foundation for Child Development. (2005). *Early education for all: Six strategies to build a movement for universal early education. FCD Policy Brief No. A-1: Organizing for PK–3.* New York: Author.

Foundation for Child Development. (2008). *America's vanishing potential: The case for preK-3rd education.* New York: Author.

Frede, E.C. (1998). Preschool program quality in programs for children in poverty. In W.S. Barnett & S.S. Boocock (Eds.), *Early care and education for children in poverty* (pp. 77–98). Albany, NY: SUNY Press.

Frede, E. (2005). *Assessment in a continuous improvement cycle: New Jersey's Abbott Preschool Program.* Retrieved March 5, 2010, from http://nieer.org/resources/research/NJAccountability.pdf

Frede, E., & Barnett, W.S. (1992). Developmentally appropriate public school preschool: A study of implementation of the High/Scope curriculum and its effects on disadvantaged children's skills at first grade. *Early Childhood Research Quarterly, 7*(4), 483–499.

Frede, E., Dessewffy, M., Hornbeck, A., & Worth, A. (2003). *Preschool classroom mathematics inventory.* New Brunswick, NJ: National Institute for Early Education Research.

Frede, E., Jung, K., Barnett, W.S., & Figueras, A. (2009). *The APPLES blossom: Abbott Preschool Program Longitudinal Effects Study (APPLES) preliminary results through 2nd grade interim report.* New Brunswick, NJ: National Institute for Early Education Research. Retrieved January 3, 2011, from http://nieer.org/pdf/apples_second_grade_results.pdf

Frede, E., Jung, K., Barnett, W.S., Lamy, C., & Figueras, A. (2007). *The Abbott Preschool Program Longitudinal Effects Study (APPLES). Report to the New Jersey Department of Education.* New Brunswick, NJ: National Institute for Early Education Research.

Froebel, F. (1897). *Pedagogics of the kindergarten.* (J. Jarvis, Trans.). London: Appleton.

Fry, R., & Passel, J. (2009). *Latino children: A majority are U.S.-born offspring of immigrants.* Washington, DC: Pew Hispanic Center.

Fryer, R.G., & Levitt, S.D. (2004). Understanding the black-white test score gap in the first two years of school. *The Review of Economics and Statistics, 86*(2), 447–464.

Fuchs, T., & Wossmann, L. (2006). *Governance and primary school performance: International evidence.* Munich, Germany: University of Munich.

Fukkink, R., & Lont, A. (2007). Does training matter? A meta-analysis and review of caregiver training studies. *Early Childhood Research Quarterly, 22*(1), 294–311.

Fuller, B. (1999). *Government confronts culture.* New York: Taylor & Francis.

Fuller, B. (2007). *Standardized childhood: The political and cultural struggle over early education.* Palo Alto, CA: Stanford University Press.

Fuller, B., Holloway, S., Rambaud, M., & Eggers-Piérola, C. (1996). How do mothers choose child care? Alternative cultural models in poor neighborhoods. *Sociology of Education, 69,* 83–104.

Fuller, B., & Huang, D. (2003). *Targeting investments for universal preschool: Which families to serve first? Who will respond?* Berkeley, CA: Policy Analysis for California Education.

Fuller, B., Kagan, S., Loeb, S., & Chang,Y. (2004). Child care quality: Centers and home settings that serve poor families. *Early Childhood Research Quarterly, 19,* 505–527.

Fuller, B., & Livas, A. (2006). *Proposition 82—California's "Preschool for All" initiative.* Berkeley, CA: Policy Analysis for California Education.

Fuller, B., & Strath, A. (2001). The child care and preschool workforce: Demographics, earnings, and unequal distribution. *Educational Evaluation and Policy Analysis, 23,* 37–55.

Gabrieli, C., & Goldstein, W. (2008). *Time to learn: How a new school schedule is making smarter kids, happier parents, and safer neighborhoods.* San Francisco, CA: Jossey-Bass.

Galinsky, E. (2006). *The economic benefits of high quality early childhood programs: What makes the difference? Report for the Committee on Economic Development.* New York: Family and Work Institute.

Gallagher, P.A., & Lambert, R.G. (2006). Classroom quality, concentration of children with special needs, and child outcomes in Head Start. *Exceptional Children, 73*(1), 31–52.

Garces, E., Thomas, D., & Currie, J. (2002). Longer-term effects of Head Start. *American Economic Review, 92,* 999–1012.

Garcia, E., Arias, M.B., Harris Murri, N.J., & Serna, C. (2010). Developing responsive teachers: A challenge for a demographic reality. *Journal of Teacher Education, 61*(1–2), 132–142.

Gardenhire, D. (2007). *New parental tax credit makes Oklahoma a national leader.* Retrieved January 17, 2011, from http://www.okhouse.gov/okhousemedia/pressroom.aspx?NewsID=1208

Gardner, M., Roth, J.L., & Brooks-Gunn, J. (2009). *Can after-school programs help level the academic playing field for disadvantaged youth?* New York: Teachers College, Columbia University.

Garfinkel, I. (1996). Economic security for children: From means testing and bifurcation to universality. In I. Garfinkel (Ed.), *Social policies for children* (pp. 33–82). Washington, DC: Brookings Publications.

Garvey, C. (1977). *Play.* Cambridge, MA: Harvard University Press.

Gayl, C., Young, M., & Patterson, K. (2009). *New beginnings: Using federal Title I funds to support local pre-K efforts.* Washington, DC: Pew Center on the States. Retrieved January 3, 2011, from http://www.preknow.org/documents/titleI_Sep2009.pdf

Gayl, C., Young, M., & Patterson, K. (2010). *Tapping Title I: What every school administrator should know about Title I, pre-K and school reform.* Washington, DC: Pew Center on the States. Retrieved January 3, 2011, from http://www.preknow.org/documents/TitleI_PartII_Jan2010.pdf

Gaylor, E., Spiker, D., & Hebbeler, K. (2009). *Evaluation of the Saint Paul early childhood scholarship program. Issue brief 2: Implementation in year 2.* Menlo Park, CA: SRI International.

Geeraert, L., Van den Noortgate, W., Grietens, H., & Onghena, P. (2004). The effects of early prevention programs for families with young children at risk for physical child abuse and neglect: A meta-analysis. *Child Maltreatment, 9*(3), 277–291.

Gelbach, J., & Pritchett, L. (2002). Is more for the poor less for the poor? The politics of means-tested targeting. *Topics in Economic Analysis and Policy, 2*(1), Article 26.

Gershater-Molko, R., Lutzker, J., & Wesch, D. (2003). Project SafeCare: Improving health, safety, and parenting skills in families reported for and at-risk of child maltreatment. *Journal of Family Violence, 18*(6), 377–386.

Gilliam, W.S. (2000, December). *The School Readiness Initiative in South-Central Connecticut: Classroom quality, teacher training, and service provision. Report of findings for fiscal year 1999.* New Haven, CT: Yale University Child Study Center.

Gilliam, W. (2005, May). *Prekindergarteners left behind: Expulsion rates in state prekindergarten programs. FCD Policy Brief Series No. 3.* Retrieved January 18, 2011, from http://www.fcd-us.org/sites/default/files/ExpulsionCompleteReport.pdf

Gilliam, W.S. (2006, June). *Partnerships and collaboration: Head Start, child care, and prekindergarten.* Keynote plenary presented at Head Start's Eighth National Research Conference, Washington, DC.

Gilliam, W.S. (2008). Head Start, public school prekindergarten, and a collaborative potential. *Infants and Young Children, 21,* 30–44.

Gilliam, W.S., & Leiter, V. (2003). Evaluating early childhood programs: Improving quality and informing policy. *Zero to Three, 23*(6), 6–13.

Gilliam, W.S., & Ripple, C.H. (2004). What can be learned from state-funded preschool initiatives? A data-based approach to the Head Start devolution debate. In E. Zigler & S.J. Styfco (Eds.), *The Head Start debates* (pp. 477–497). Baltimore: Paul H. Brookes Publishing Co.

Gilliam, W.S. Ripple, C.H., Zigler, E.F., & Leiter, V. (2000). Evaluating child and family demonstration programs: Lessons from the Comprehensive Child Development Program. *Early Childhood Research Quarterly, 15,* 5–39.

Gilliam, W.S., & Stahl, S. (2008). *The Connecticut School Readiness Program: Comparative strengths and challenges in relation to state prekindergarten systems across the nation.* New Haven, CT: Yale University School of Medicine, The Edward Zigler Center for Child Development and Social Policy.

Gilliam, W.S., & Zigler, E.F. (2001). A critical meta-analysis of all evaluations of state-funded preschool from 1977 to 1998: Implications for policy, service delivery and program evaluation. *Early Childhood Research Quarterly, 15,* 441–473.

Gilliam, W.S., & Zigler, E.F. (2004). *State efforts to evaluate the effects of prekindergarten, 1977-2003.* New Brunswick, NJ: National Institute for Early Education Research.

Ginicola, M., Finn-Stevenson, M., & Zigler, E. (2008). *The added value of the School of the 21st Century when combined with a statewide preschool program.* Manuscript submitted for publication.

Ginsburg, H.P. (2008). *Early Mathematics Assessment System (EMAS).* New York: Author.

Ginsburg, H.P., Kaplan, R.G., Cannon, J., Cordero, M.I., Eisenband, J.G., Galanter, M., et al. (2006). Helping early childhood educators to teach mathematics. In M. Zaslow & I. Martinez-Beck (Eds.), *Critical issues in early childhood professional development* (pp. 171–202). Baltimore: Paul H. Brookes Publishing Co.

Ginsburg, H., Lee, J.S., & Boyd, J. (2008). *Mathematics education for young children: What it is and how to promote it.* Retrieved January 15, 2011, from http://www.srcd.org/index.php?option=com_docman&task=doc_download&gid=85

Ginsburg, H., Pappas, S., & Seo, K. (2001). Everyday mathematical knowledge: Asking young children what is developmentally appropriate. In S.L. Golbeck (Ed.), *Psychological perspectives on early childhood education: Reframing dilemmas in research and practice* (pp.181–219). Mahwah, NJ: Lawrence Erlbaum Associates.

Glaser, D. (2000). Child abuse and neglect and the brain: A review. *Journal of Child Psychology and Psychiatry, 41,* 97–118.

Glazner, J., Bondy, J., Luckey, D., & Olds, D. (2004). *Effects of the Nurse Family Partnership on government expenditures for vulnerable first-time mothers and their children in Elmira, New York, Memphis, Tennessee, and Denver, Colorado.* Washington, DC: U.S. Department of Health and Human Services.

Goffin, S.G., & Washington, V. (2007). *Ready or not: Leadership choices in early care and education.* New York: Teachers College Press.

Goldhaber, D.D., & Brewer, D.J. (2000). Does teacher certification matter? High school teacher certification status and student achievement. *Educational Evaluation and Policy Analysis, 22*(2), 129–145.

Goldstein, L.S. (1997). Between a rock and a hard place in the primary grades: The challenge of providing developmentally appropriate early childhood education in an elementary school setting. *Early Childhood Research Quarterly, 12*(1), 3–27.

Gomby, D. (2005). *Home visitation in 2005: Outcomes for children and parents.* Retrieved January 22, 2011, from http://www.partnershipforsuccess.org/docs/ivk/report_ivk_gomby_2005.pdf

Gonzales, N.A., Knight, G.P., Birman, D., & Sirolli, A.A. (2003). Acculturation and enculturation among Latino youth. In K.I. Maton, C.J. Schellenback, B.J. Leadbeater, & A.L. Solarz (Eds.), *Investing in children, youth, families, and communities: Strengths-based research and policy* (pp. 285–302). Washington, DC: American Psychological Association.

Gopnik, A. (2009, August 16). Your baby is smarter than you think. *The New York Times,* p. WK10.

Gopnik, A., Meltzoff, A.N., & Kuhl, P.K. (1999). *The scientist in the crib: Minds, brains, and how children learn.* Fairfield, NJ: William Morrow.

Gorey, K.M. (2001). Early childhood education: A meta-analytic affirmation of the short- and long-term benefits of educational opportunity. *School Psychology Quarterly, 16,* 9–30.

Gorman-Smith, D., Beidel, D., Brown, T.A., Lochman, J., & Haaga, A.F. (2003). Effects of teacher training and consultation on teacher behavior towards students at high risk for aggression. *Behavior Therapy, 34,* 437–452.

Gorman-Smith, D., Tolan, P.H., Henry, D.B., Leventhal, A., Schoeny, M., Lutovsky, K., et al. (2002). Predictors of participation in a family-focused preventive intervention for substance use. *Psychology of Addictive Behaviors, 16,* 55–64.

Gormley, W.T. (2005). The universal pre-K bandwagon. *Phi Delta Kappan, 87*(3), 246–249.

Gormley, W.T. (2007). Early childhood care and education: Lessons and puzzles. *Journal of Policy Analysis and Management, 26*(3), 633–671.

Gormley, W. (2008). The effects of Oklahoma's pre-K program on Hispanic children. *Social Science Quarterly, 89*(4), 916–936.

Gormley, W., & Gayer, T. (2005). Promoting school readiness in Oklahoma: An evaluation of Tulsa's pre-k program. *Journal of Human Resources, 40,* 533–558.

Gormley, W., Gayer, T., Phillips, D., & Dawson, B. (2005). The effects of universal pre-K on cognitive development. *Developmental Psychology, 41,* 872–884.

Gormley, W., & Phillips, D. (2005). The effects of universal pre-K in Oklahoma: Research highlights and policy implications. *Policy Studies Journal, 33,* 65–82.

Gormley, W.T., Jr., & Phillips, D. (2009). *The effects of pre-K on child development: Lessons from Oklahoma.* Washington, DC: National Summit on Early Childhood Education, Georgetown University.

Gormley, W.T., Phillips, D., & Gayer, T. (2008). Preschool programs can boost school readiness. *Science, 320,* 1723–1724.

Gormley, W., Philips, D., Newmark, K., & Perper, K. (2009, April 3). *Socio-emotional effects of early childhood education programs in Tulsa.* Presented at the meeting of the Society for Research in Child Development, Denver, CO.

Graue, E., Clements, M.A. Reynolds, A.J., & Niles, M.D. (2004). More than teacher directed or child initiated: Preschool curriculum type, parent involvement, and children's outcomes in the Child-Parent Centers. *Education Policy Analysis Archives, 12*(72).

Gray, S.W., & Klaus, R.A. (1970). The Early Training Project: A seventh-year report. *Child Development, 41,* 909–924.

Greenfield, D.B., Dominguez, M.X., Fuccillo, J.M., Maier, M.F., & Greenberg, A.C. (2009, April). *Development of an IRT-based direct assessment of preschool science.* Presented at the biennial meeting of the Society for Research in Child Development, Denver, CO.

Greenspan, S.I. (1990). Emotional development in infants and toddlers. In J.R. Lally (Ed.), *Infant/toddler caregiving: A guide to social-emotional growth and socialization* (pp. 15–18). Sacramento: California Department of Education.

Greenwald, R., Hedges, L.V., & Laine, R.D. (1996). The effect of school resources on student achievement. *Review of Educational Research, 66,* 361–396.

Griffin, S.A., & Case, R. (1996). Evaluating the breadth and depth of training effects, when central conceptual structures are taught. In R. Case & Y. Okamoto (Eds.), *The role of central conceptual structures in the development of children's thought. Monographs of the Society for Research in Child Development, 61,* 83–102.

Griffin, S.A., Case, R., & Siegler, R.S. (1994). Rightstart: Providing the central conceptual prerequisites for first formal learning of arithmetic to students at risk for school failure. In K. McGilly (Ed.), *Classroom lessons: Integrating cognitive theory and classroom practice* (pp. 25–49). Cambridge, MA: The MIT Press.

Grindle, M., & Thomas, J.W. (1991). *Public choices and policy change: The political economy of reform in developing countries.* Baltimore: Johns Hopkins University Press.

Gromley, W.T. (2007). *Small miracles in Tulsa: The effects of universal pre-K on cognitive development.* Retrieved January 3, 2011, from http://www.humancapitalrc.org/events/2007/hcconf_ecd/gormley-slides.pdf

Gross, D., Fogg, L., Webster-Stratton, C., Garvey, C., Julion, W., & Grady, J. (2003). Parent training with multi-ethnic families of toddlers in day care in low-income urban neighborhoods. *Journal of Consulting and Clinical Psychology, 71,* 261–278.

Grossman, P., Compton, C., Igra, D., Ronfeldt, M., Shahan, E., & Williamson, P. (2009). Teaching practice: A cross-professional perspective. *Teachers College Record, 111*(9), 2055–2100.

Grunewald, R., & Rolnick, A.J. (2006). *A proposal for achieving high returns on early childhood development.* Retrieved January 3, 2011, from http://www.minneapolisfed.org/publications_papers/studies/earlychild/highreturn.pdf

Gullo, D. (2000). The long term educational effects of half-day vs. full-day kindergarten, *Early Child Development and Care, 160,* 17–24.

Guterman, N. (2001). *Stopping child maltreatment before it starts: Emerging horizons in early home visitation services.* Thousand Oaks, CA: Sage Publications.

Guthrow, K. (2007). *Memo: Final legislative session wrapup.* Austin: Texas Early Childhood Education Coalition.

Hagedorn, M., Brock Roth, A., O'Donnell, K., Smith, S., & Mulligan, G. (2008). *National Household Education Surveys program of 2007: Data file user's manual: Vol. 1. Study overview and methodology.* Retrieved February 28, 2011, from http://nces.ed.gov/nhes/pdf/userman/NHES_2007_Vol_I.pdf

Hahn, R., Bilukha, O., Crosby, A., Fullilove, M., Liberman, A., Moscicki, E., et al. (2003). First reports evaluating the effectiveness of strategies for preventing violence: Early childhood home visitation. Findings from the Task Force on Community Prevention Services. *Morbidity and Mortality Weekly Report, 52*(RR-14), 1–9.

Hamre, B.K., Pianta, R.C., Burchinal, M., & Downer, J.T. (2010, March). *A course on supporting early language and literacy development through effective teacher–child interactions: Effects on teacher beliefs, knowledge and practice.* Paper presented at the annual meeting of the Society for Research on Educational Effectiveness, Washington, DC.

Harms, T., Clifford, R.M., & Cryer, D. (1998). *Early Childhood Environment Rating Scale* (Rev. ed.). New York: Teachers College Press.

Harris, I. (1994). *Should public policy be concerned with early childhood development?* Chicago: University of Chicago, Harris Graduate School of Public Policy Studies.

Hart, B., & Risley, T.R. (1995). *Meaningful differences in the everyday experience of young American children.* Baltimore: Paul H. Brooks Publishing Co.

Hart, K., & Schumacher, R. (2005). *Making the case: Improving Head Start teacher qualifications requires increased investment.* Washington, DC: Center for Law and Social Policy.

Haskins, R. (2006). *Work over welfare: The inside story of the 1996 welfare reform law.* Washington, DC: Brookings.

Haskins, R., & Barnett, W.S. (Eds.). (2010). *Investing in young children: New directions in federal preschool and early childhood policy.* Washington, DC: Center on Children and Families at Brookings and the National Institute for Early Education Research.

Haskins, R., Paxson, C., & Brooks-Gunn, J. (2009). *Social science rising: A tale of evidence shaping public policy.* Retrieved January 22, 2011, from http://www.princeton.edu/futureofchildren/publications/docs/19_02_PolicyBrief.pdf

Hawkins, J.D., Catalano, R.F., Kosterman, R., Abbott, R., & Hill, K.G. (1999). Preventing adolescent health-risk behaviors by strengthening protection during childhood. *Archives of Pediatrics and Adolescent Medicine, 153,* 226–234.

Head Start Bureau. (1999). *Head Start program regulations (45 CFR, Parts 1301-1311).* Retrieved August 16, 2000, from www2.acf.dhhs.gov/programs/hsb/regs/regs/rg_index.htm

Healthy Families America. (2005). *Starting early starting smart: Final report.* Great Falls, VA: Author.

Healthy Families Arizona. (2005). *Healthy Families Arizona: Evaluation report 2005.* Tucson, AZ: Author.

Healthy Families Florida. (2005) *Health Families Florida: Evaluation report January 1999–December 2003.* Miami, FL: Author.

Heckman, J. (2000a). *Invest in the very young.* Chicago: University of Chicago.

Heckman, J. (2000b). Policies to foster human capital. *Research in Economics, 54,* 3–56.

Heckman, J. (2003). Human capital policy. In J. Heckman & A. Krueger (Eds.), *Inequality in America: What role for human capital policy?* Cambridge, MA: The MIT Press.

Heckman, J. (2006, January 10). Catch 'em young. *Wall Street Journal,* p. A14.

Heckman, J.J. (2007). The economics, technology and neuroscience of human capability formation. *Proceedings of the National Academy of Sciences, 104*(3), 13250–13255.

Heckman, J.J. (2008). Schools, skills and synapses. *Economic Inquiry, 46*(3), 289–324.

Heckman, J.J., Grunewald, R., & Reynolds, A.J. (2006). The dollars and cents of investing early: Cost–benefit analysis in early care and education. *Zero to Three, 26*(6), 10–17.

Heckman, J.J., Humphries, J.E., & Mader, N. (2011). *Hard Evidence on Soft Skills.* Chicago: University of Chicago Press.

Heckman, J.J., & LaFontaine, P.A. (2010). The American high school graduation rate: Trends and levels. *Review of Economics and Statistics, 92*(2), 244–262.

Heckman, J.J., Malofeeva, L., Pinto, R., & Savelyev, P.A. (2011). Understanding the mechanisms through which an influential early childhood program boosted adult outcomes. *American Economic Review.*

Heckman, J.J., & Masterov, D.V. (2007). The productivity argument for investing in young children. *Review of Agricultural Economics, 29*(3), 446–493.

Heckman, J.J., Moon, S.H., Pinto, R., Savelyev, P.A., & Yavitz, A.Q. (2010a). Reanalysis of the Perry Preschool Program: Multiple-hypothesis and permutation tests applied to a quasi-randomized experiment, *Quantitative Economics, 1,* 1–49.

Heckman, J.J., Moon, S.H., Pinto, R., Savelyev, P.A., & Yavitz, A.Q. (2010b). The rate of return to the HighScope Perry preschool program. *Journal of Public Economics, 94*(1–2), 114–128.

Heckman, J.J., Stixrud, J., & Urzua, S. (2006). The effects of cognitive and noncognitive abilities on labor market outcomes and social behavior. *Journal of Labor Economics, 24*(3), 411–482.

Heinicke, C., Fineman, N., Rodning, C., Ruth, G., Recchia, S., & Guthrie, D., (2001). Relationship-based intervention with at-risk mothers: Outcomes in the first year of life. *Infant Mental Health Journal, 20*(4), 349–374.

Henrich, C., & Blackman-Jones, R. (2006). Parent involvement in preschool. In E. Zigler, W. Gilliam, & S.M. Jones, *A vision for universal preschool education* (pp. 149–168). New York: Cambridge University Press.

Henry, G., & Gordon, C. (2006). Competition in the sandbox: A test of the effects of preschool competition on educational outcomes. *Journal of Policy Analysis and Management, 25,* 97–127.

Henry, G.T., Gordon, C.S., & Rickman, D.K. (2006). Early education policy alternatives: Comparing quality and outcomes of Head Start and state prekindergarten. *Educational Evaluation and Policy Analysis, 28*(1), 77–99.

Henry, G., Ponder, B., Rickman, D., Mashburn, A., Henderson, L., & Gordon, C. (2004). *An evaluation of the implementation of Georgia's pre-K program, 2002-2003.* Atlanta: Georgia State University, Andrew Young School of Policy Studies.

Henry, G.T., & Rickman, D.K. (2007). Do peers influence children's skill development in preschool? *Economics of Education Review, 26*(1), 100–112.

Herzenberg, S., Price, M., & Bradley, D. (2005). *Losing ground in early childhood education: Declining workforce qualifications in an expanding industry, 1979–2004.* Washington, DC: Economic Policy Institute.

Hess, R., & Shipman, V. (1965). Early experience and the socialization of cognitive modes in children. *Child Development, 36,* 869–886.

Higher Education Opportunity Act of 2008, PL 110-315, 22 Stat. 3078–3508.

Hill, J., Brooks-Gunn, J., & Waldfogel, J. (2003). Sustained effects of high participation in an early intervention for low-birth-weight premature infants. *Developmental Psychology, 39,* 730–744.

Hill, J., Waldfogel, J., & Brooks-Gunn, J. (2002). Differential effects of high-quality child care. *Journal of Policy Analysis and Management, 21,* 601–627.

Hill, J.L., Waldfogel, J., Brooks-Gunn, J., & Han, W.J. (2005). Maternal employment and child development: A fresh look using newer methods. *Developmental Psychology, 41,* 833–850.

Hirsch, E.D., Jr. (n.d.). *Equity effects of very early schooling in France.* Retrieved March 17, 2011, from http://www.coreknowledge.org/mimik/mimik_uploads/documents/95/Equity%20Effects%20of%20Very%20Early%20Schooling%20in%20France.pdf

Hirsch, E.D., Jr. (2009). *The making of Americans: Democracy and our schools.* New Haven, CT: Yale University Press.

Hirsch, E.S. (1996). *The block book* (3rd ed.). Washington, DC: National Association for the Education of Young Children.

Hirsh-Pasek, K., & Golinkoff, R.M. (2003). *Einstein never used flashcards: How our children really learn and why they need to play more and memorize less.* Emmaus, PA: Rodale Press.

Hirsh-Pasek, K., Golinkoff, R.M., Berk, L., & Singer, D. (2009). *A mandate for playful learning in preschool: Presenting the evidence.* New York: Oxford University Press.

Hodgkinson, H.L. (2003). *Leaving too many children behind: A demographer's view on the neglect of America's youngest children.* Washington, DC: Institute for Education Leadership.

Holmes, S.L., Morrow, A.L., & Pickering, L.K. (1996). Childcare practices: Effects of social change on the epidemiology of infectious diseases and antibiotic resistance. *Epidemiologic Reviews 18*(1), 10–28.

Holod, A., Gardner, M., & Brooks-Gunn, J. (2011). *Elementary school poverty and the persistence of preschool cognitive benefits: A growth curve analysis.* Manuscript in preparation, Teachers College, Columbia University.

Honig, A.S. (1998, August). *Attachment and relationships: Beyond parenting.* Paper presented at the Head Start Quality Network Research Satellite Conference, East Lansing, MI.

Honig, A.S. (2002). *Secure relationships: Nurturing infant/toddler attachment in early care settings.* Washington, DC: National Association for the Education of Young Children.

Horan, D. (2009). *Teacher reports on vertical curriculum alignment reflecting the organizational culture of community-based preschool and public school kindergarten programs.* Retrieved January 16, 2011, from http://gradworks.umi.com/3355170.pdf

Hough, R.L., Landverk, J.A., Karno, M., Burman, A., Timbers, D.M., Escobar, J.L., et al. (1987). Utilization of health and mental health services by Los Angeles Mexican Americans and non-Hispanic whites. *Archives of General Psychiatry, 44,* 702–709.

Howard, K., & Brooks-Gunn, J. (2009). The role of home-visiting programs in preventing child abuse and neglect. *Future of Children, 19*(2), 119–146.

Howes, C. (1997). Children's experiences in center-based child care as a function of teacher background and adult-child ratio. *Merrill-Palmer Quarterly, 43,* 404–425.

Howes, C., Burchinal, M., Pianta, R., Bryant, D., Early, D., Clifford, R.M., et al. (2008). Ready to learn? Children's preacademic achievement in pre-kindergarten programs. *Early Childhood Research Quarterly, 23*(1), 27–50.

Howes, C., James, J., & Ritchie, S. (2003). Pathways to effective teaching. *Early Childhood Research Quarterly, 18,* 104–120.

Howes, C., Phillips, D., & Whitebook, M. (1992). Thresholds of quality: Implications for the social development of children. *Child Development, 63,* 449–460.

Howes, C., Whitebook, M., & Phillips, D. (1992). Teacher characteristics and effective teaching in child care: Findings from the National Child Care Staffing Study. *Child & Youth Care Forum. Special Issue: Meeting the child care needs of the 1990s: Perspectives on day care: II, 21,* 399–414.

Howse, R., Calkins, S., Anastopoulos, A., Keane, S., & Shelton, T. (2003). Regulatory contributions to children's kindergarten achievement. *Early Education & Development, 14,* 101–119.

Humphrey, D.C., Weschler, M.E., & Hough, H.J. (2008). Characteristics of effective alternative certification programs. *Teachers College Record, 110*(1), 1–63.

Hunt, J.M. (1961). *Intelligence and experience.* New York: Ronald Press.

Hyson, M. (2003a, April). Putting early academics in their place. *Educational Leadership,* 20–23.

Hyson, M. (2003b). *The emotional development of young children: Building an emotion-centered curriculum.* New York: Teachers College Press.

Hyson, M., Tomlinson, H.B., & Morris, C. (2008). *Does quality of early childhood teacher preparation moderate the relationship between teacher education and children's outcomes?* Paper presented at the annual meeting of the American Educational Research Association, New York.

Ialongo, N.S., Werthamer, L., Kellam, S.G., Brown, C.H., Wang, S., & Lin, Y. (1999). Proximal impact of two first-grade preventive interventions on the early risk behaviors for later substance abuse, depression, and antisocial behavior. *American Journal of Community Psychology, 27,* 599–641.

Iceland, J. (2003). *Dynamics of economic well-being, poverty 1996-1999.* Retrieved June 30, 2009, from http://www.census2010.gov/hhes/www/poverty/sipp96/sipp96.html

Imbens, G.W., & Angrist, J.D. (1994). Identification and estimation of local average treatment effects. *Econometrica: Journal of the Econometric Society, 62*(2), 467–475.

Improving Head Start for School Readiness Act of 2007, PL 110-134, 42 U.S.C. 9801 *et seq.*

Infant Health and Development Program Staff. (1990). Enhancing the outcomes of low birth weight, premature infants: A multi-site randomized trial. *Journal of the American Medical Association, 263,* 3035–3042.

Institute of Government Studies, University of California, Berkeley. (n.d.). *Election results update (June 6, 2006 statewide primary election).* Retrieved February 25, 2011, from http://igs.berkeley.edu/library/research/quickhelp/elections/2006primary/htUniversalPreschool.html

Interagency Consortium on School Readiness. (2003). *Effectiveness of early childhood programs, curricula, and interventions in promoting school readiness* (ACF 2002–2003). Washington, DC: Administration for Children and Families Office of Planning, Research and Evaluation.

Isaacs, J.B. (2009). *The effects of the recession on child poverty.* Washington, DC: The Brookings Institution.

Isaacs, J., & Roessel, E. (2008). *Impacts of early childhood programs.* Retrieved January 17, 2011, from http://www.firstfocus.net/sites/default/files/r.2008-9.8.isaacs3.pdf

Jarousse, J.P., Mingat, A., & Richard, M. (1992). *La scolarisation maternelle a deux ans: Effets pedagogiques et sociaux in Education et Formations.* Paris: Ministere de l'Education Nationale.

Jester, R.E., & Guinagh, B.J. (1983). The Gordon Parent Education Infant and Toddler Program. In Consortium for Longitudinal Studies (Ed.), *As the twig is bent: Lasting effects of preschool programs* (pp. 103–132). Mahwah, NJ: Lawrence Erlbaum Associates.

Johnson, D.L., & Blumenthal, J.B. (1985). A ten year follow-up. *Child Development, 56,* 376–391.

Johnson, H., & Thomas, A. (2004). Professional capacity and organizational change as measures of educational effectiveness: Assessing the impact of postgraduate education in development policy and management. *Compare: A Journal of Comparative Education, 34,* 301–314.

Johnson, K. (2009). *State-based home visiting: Strengthening programs through state leadership.* New York: National Center for Children in Poverty, Columbia University.

Johnson, L., Pai, S., & Bridges, M. (2004). *Advancing the early childhood workforce: Implementation of training and retention initiatives in the Bay Area.* Berkeley: University of California, Policy Analysis for California Education.

Johnson, N., Oliff, P., & Williams, E. (2009). *An update on state budget cuts.* Washington, DC: Center on Budget and Policy Priorities.

Johnson, Z., Howell, F., & Molloy, B. (1993). Community mothers' programme: Randomised controlled trial on non-professional intervention in parenting. *British Medical Journal, 306,* 1449–1452.

Jones, S.M., Brown, J.L., & Aber, J.L. (2008). Classroom settings as targets of intervention and research. In M. Shinn & H. Yoshikawa (Eds.), *The power of social settings: Transforming schools and community organizations to enhance youth development* (pp. 58–77). New York: Oxford University Press.

Jones, S.M., & Zigler, E. (2002). The Mozart effect: Not learning from history. *Journal of Applied Developmental Psychology, 23,* 355–372.

Jung, Y., Howes, C., & Pianta, R. (2009). Emerging issues in prekindergarten programs. In R. Pianta & C. Howes (Eds.), *The promise of pre-K* (pp. 169–176). Baltimore: Paul H. Brookes Publishing Co.

Justice, L., Cottone, E., Mashburn, A., & Rimm-Kauffman, S. (2008). Relationships between teachers and preschoolers who are at-risk: Contribution of children's language skills, temperamentally based attributes, and gender. *Early Education and Development, 19*(4), 600–621.

Kagan, S.L. (1993). Entitlement in early care and education: A tale of two rights. In M. Jensen & S. Goffin (Eds.), *Visions of entitlement: The care and education of young children* (pp. 3–30). Albany, NY: SUNY Press.

Kagan, S.L., Kauerz, K., & Tarrant, K. (2008). *Early care and education teaching workforce at the fulcrum: An agenda for reform.* New York: Teachers College Press.

Kagan, S.L., & Lowenstein, A.E. (2004). School readiness and children's play: Contemporary oxymoron or compatible option? In E.F. Zigler, D.G. Singer, & S.J. Bishop-Josef (Eds.), *Children's play: The roots of reading* (pp. 59–76). Washington, DC: ZERO TO THREE.

Kagan, S.L., Moore, E., & Bredekamp, S. (Eds.). (1995). *Reconsidering children's early development and learning: Toward common views and vocabulary.* Washington, DC: U.S. Government Printing Office.

Kagan, S.L., & Neuman, M.J. (1998). Lessons from three decades of transition research. *Elementary School Journal, 98,* 365–379.

Kamins, M., & Dweck, C. (1999). Person versus process praise and criticism: Implications for contingent self-worth and coping. *Developmental Psychology, 35,* 835–847.

Karoly, L.A., & Bigelow, J.H. (2005). *The economics of investing in universal preschool education in California.* Santa Monica, CA: RAND Corporation.

Karoly, L.A., Ghosh-Dastidar, B., Zellman, G., Perlman, M., & Fernyhough, L. (2008). *Nature and quality of early care and education for California's preschool-age children: Results from the California Preschool Study.* Santa Monica, CA: Rand Corporation.

Karoly, L.A., Greenwood, P.W., Everingham, S.S., Hoube, J., Kilburn, M.R., et al. (1998). *Investing in our children: What we know and don't know about the costs and benefits of early childhood interventions.* Santa Monica, CA: RAND Corporation.

Karoly, L., Kilburn, R., & Cannon, J. (2005). *Early childhood interventions: Proven results, future promise.* Santa Monica, CA: RAND Corporation.

Karoly, L.A., Zellman, G.L., and Li, J. (2009). *Promoting effective preschool policy.* Santa Monica, CA: RAND Corporation.

Kauerz, K. (2006). *Ladders of learning: Fighting fade-out by advancing PK-3 alignment.* Washington, DC: New America Foundation.

Kavanaugh, R.D., & Engel, S. (1998). The development of pretense and narrative in early childhood. In O.N. Saracho & B. Spodek (Eds.), *Multiple perspectives on play in early childhood education* (pp. 80–99). Albany, NY: SUNY Press.

Keats, E.J. (1976). *The snowy day.* New York: Puffin.

Keels, M., & Raver, C.C. (2009). Early learning experiences and outcomes for children of U.S. immigrant families: Introduction to the special issue. *Early Childhood Research Quarterly, 24*(4), 363–366.

Kellam, S.G., & Langevin, D.J. (2003). A framework for understanding evidence in prevention research and programs. *Prevention Science, 3,* 137–153.

Kellam, S.G., & Van Horn, Y.V. (1997). Life course development, community epidemiology, and preventive trials: A scientific structure for prevention research. *American Journal of Community Psychology, 25,* 177–188.

Kelley, P., & Camilli, G. (2007). *The impact of teacher education on outcomes in center-based early childhood education programs: A meta-analysis.* New Brunswick, NJ: National Institute for Early Education Research.

Kingdon, J.W. (1995). *Agendas, alternatives, and public policies.* New York: Addison-Wesley.

Kirp, D.L. (2007). *The sandbox investment: The preschool movement and kids-first politics.* Cambridge, MA: Harvard University Press.

Kisker, E., Raikes, H., Chazan-Cohen, R., Carta, J., & Puma, J. (2009, March). *Assessing program impacts on the highest risk families in Early Head Start.* Presented at the meeting of the Society for Research in Child Development biennial meeting, Denver, CO.

Kitzman, H. Olds, D., Henderson, C.R., Hanks, C., Cole, R., Tatelbaum, R., et al. (1997). Effect of prenatal and infancy home visitation by nurses on pregnancy outcomes, childhood injuries and repeated childbearing: A randomized controlled trial. *JAMA, 278,* 644–752.

Klebanov, P.K., Brooks-Gunn, J., & McCormick, M.C. (2001). Maternal coping strategies and emotional distress: Results of an early intervention program for low birth weight young children. *Developmental Psychology, 37,* 654–667.

Knight, G.P., & Hill, N.E. (1998). Measurement equivalence in research involving minority adolescents. In V.C. McLoyd & L. Steinberg (Eds.), *Studying minority adolescents: Conceptual, methodological, and theoretical issues* (pp. 183–210). Mahwah, NJ: Lawrence Erlbaum Associates.

Knudsen, E.I., Heckman, J.J., Cameron, J., & Shonkoff, J.P. (2006). Economic, neurobiological, and behavioral perspectives on building America's future workforce. *Proceedings of the National Academy of Sciences, 103*(27), 10155–10162.

Koh, S., & Neuman, S. (2009). The impact of professional development in family child care: A practice-based approach. *Early Education and Development, 20,* 537–562.

Kokko, K., Tremblay, R.E., LaCourse, E., Nagin, D., & Vitaro, F. (2006). Trajectories of prosocial behavior and physical aggression in middle childhood: Links to adolescent school dropout and physical violence. *Journal of Research on Adolescence, 16*(3), 404–428.

Kontos, S., & Wilcox-Herzog, A. (2001). How do education and experience affect teachers of young children? *Young Children, 52,* 4–12.

Kreader, L., Ferguson, D., & Lawrence, S. (2006). *Impact of training and education for caregivers of infants and toddlers.* Washington, DC: Child Care and Early Education Research Connections.

Krueger, A.B. (2003). Economic considerations and class size. *Economic Journal, 113,* F34–F63.

Laird, E. (2009, May). *Connecting the dots: Making longitudinal data work for young children.* Data Quality Campaign. Retrieved February 10, 2010, from http://www.dataquality-campaign.org/resources/details/478

Landauer, T.K., & Dumais, S.T. (1997). A solution to Plato's problem: The Latent Semantic Analysis theory of the acquisition, induction, and representation of knowledge. *Psychological Review, 104,* 211–240.

Landry, S.H., Swank, P.R., Smith, K.E., Assel, M.A., & Gunnewig, S.B. (2006). Enhancing early literacy skills for preschool children: Bringing a professional development model to scale. *Journal of Learning Disabilities, 39,* 306–324.

La Paro, K.M., Pianta, R.C., & Stuhlman, M. (2004). The classroom assessment scoring system: Findings from the prekindergarten year. *Elementary School Journal, 104,* 409–426.

Larsen, J.M., Hite, S.J., & Hart, C.H. (1983). The effects of preschool on educationally advantaged children: First phases of a longitudinal study. *Intelligence, 7,* 345–352.

Larsen, J.M., & Robinson, C.C. (1989). Later effects of preschool on low-risk children. *Early Childhood Research Quarterly, 4,* 133–144.

Lazar, I. (1970). *National survey of the parent child center programs.* Washington, DC: Office of Child Development.

Lazar, I., & Darlington, R. (1982). Lasting effects of early education: A report from the Consortium for Longitudinal Studies. *Monographs of the Society for Research in Child Development, 47*(2–3).

Lee, V.E., Loeb, S., & Lubeck, S., (1998). Contextual effects of prekindergarten classrooms for disadvantaged children on cognitive development: The case of Chapter 1. *Child Development, 69,* 479–494.

LeMoine, S. (2008). *Workforce designs: A policy blueprint for state professional development systems.* Washington, DC: National Association for the Education of Young Children.

Levenstein, P., Kochman, A., & Roth, H. (1973). From laboratory to real world: Service delivery of the Mother–Child Home Program. *American Journal of Orthopsychiatry, 43,* 72–78.

Levenstein, P., Levenstein, S., & Oliver, D. (2002). First grade school readiness of former child participants in a South Carolina replication of Parent–Child Home Program. *Journal of Applied Developmental Psychology, 23,* 331–353.

Levenstein, P., O'Hara, J., & Madden, J. (1983). The Mother-Child Home Program of the Verbal Interaction Project. In Consortium for Longitudinal Studies (Ed.), *As the twig is bent:*

Lasting effects of preschool programs. Mahwah, NJ: Lawrence Erlbaum Associates.

Levin, H.M., & McEwan, P.J. (2001). *Cost-effectiveness analysis: Methods and applications* (2nd ed.). Thousand Oaks, CA: Sage Publications.

Lewin, T. (2009, October 24). No Einstein in your crib? Get a refund. *New York Times*, p. A1.

Lewis, M.D., & Todd, R.M. (2007). The self-regulating brain: Cortical-subcortical feedback and the development of intelligent action. *Cognitive Development, 22*(4), 406–430.

Liang, X., Fuller, B., & Singer, J. (2002). Ethnic differences in child care selection. *Early Childhood Research Quarterly, 15,* 357–384.

Li-Grining, C., Raver, C.C., Champion, K., Sardin, L., Metzger, M.W., & Jones, S.M. (2010). Understanding and improving classroom emotional climate in the "real world": The role of teachers' psychosocial stressors. *Early Education and Development, 21*(1), 65–94.

Lillard, A., & Else-Quest, N. (2006). Evaluating Montessori education. *Science, 313,* 1893–1894.

Lochman, J.E., & Wells, K.C. (2003). Effectiveness of the Coping Power program and of classroom intervention with aggressive children: Outcomes at a 1-year follow-up. *Behavior Therapy, 34,* 493–515.

Loeb, S., Bridges, M., Bassok, D., Fuller, B., & Rumberger, R. (2007). How much is too much? The influence of preschool centers on children's social and cognitive development. *Economics of Education Review, 26,* 52–66.

Loeb, S., Fuller, B., Kagan, S., & Carroll, B. (2004). Child care in poor communities: Early learning effects of type, quality, and stability. *Child Development, 75,* 47–65.

Lonigan, C., Wagner, R., Torgeson, J., & Rashotte, C. (2002). *Preschool Comprehensive Test of Phonological & Print Processing (Pre-CTOPPP).* Tallahassee: Florida State University.

Lonigan, C.J., & Whitehurst, G.J. (1998). Relative efficacy of parent and teacher involvement in a shared-reading intervention for preschool children from low-income backgrounds. *Early Childhood Research Quarterly, 13*(2), 263–290.

Love, J. (2009, April 2). *The Early Head Start Evaluation: Impacts at the end of the program, two years later, and the context for ongoing research.* Poster prepared for the biennial meeting of the Society for Research in Child Development, Denver, CO.

Love, J.M., Cohen, R.C., Raikes, H., & Brooks-Gunn, J. (2011). *What makes a difference: Early Head Start Evaluation findings in a longitudinal context.* Manuscript submitted for publication.

Love, J.M., Kisker, E.E., Ross, C.M., Raikes, H.H., Constantine, J.M., Boller, K., et al. (2005). The effectiveness of Early Head Start for 3-year-old children and their parents: Lessons for policy and programs. *Developmental Psychology, 41,* 885–901.

Lubeck, S. (1989). Four-year-olds and public schooling: Framing the question. *Theory into Practice, 28*(1), 3–10.

Lubienski, C., & Weitzel, P. (2008). The effects of vouchers and private schools in improving academic achievement: A critique of advocacy research. *Brigham Young University Law Review, 2,* 447–486.

Luthar, S., & Latendresse, S. (2005). Children of the affluent. *Current Directions in Psychological Science, 14,* 49–53.

Lutton, A. (2009). NAEYC Early childhood professional preparation standards: A vision for tomorrow's early childhood teachers. In A. Gibbons & C. Gibbs (Eds.), *Conversations on early childhood teacher education: Voices from the working forum for teacher educators.* Redmond, WA: World Forum Foundation and New Zealand Tertiary College.

Lynch, R.G. (2007). *Enriching children, enriching the nation: Public investment in high-quality prekindergarten.* Washington, DC: Economic Policy Institute.

Lyttelton, K. (1899). *Jouvert: A selection from his thoughts.* New York: Dodd, Mead and Co.

MacInnes, G. (2009). *In plain sight: Simple, difficult lessons from New Jersey's expensive effort to close the achievement gap.* New York: Century Foundation Press.

Maeroff, G.I. (2006). *Building blocks—Making children successful in the early years of school.* New York: Palgrave MacMillan.

Magnuson, K., Duncan, Metzger, M., & Lee, Y. (2009). *School adjustment and high school dropout.* Paper presented at the Society for Research in Child Development.

Magnuson, K.A., Ruhm, C., & Waldfogel, J. (2004). Inequality in preschool education and school readiness. *American Educational Research Journal, 41,* 115–157.

Magnuson, K.A., Ruhm, C., & Waldfogel, J. (2007a). Does prekindergarten improve school preparation and performance? *Economics of Education Review, 26,* 33–51.

Magnuson, K.A, Ruhm, C., & Waldfogel, J. (2007b). The persistence of preschool effects: Do subsequent classroom experiences matter? *Early Childhood Research Quarterly, 22,* 18–38.

Magnuson, K.A., & Waldfogel, J. (2005). Early childhood care and education: Effects on ethnic and racial gaps in school readiness. *Future of Children, 15,* 169–196.

Manning, M., Homel, R., & Smith, C. (2010). A meta-analysis of the effects of early developmental prevention programs in at-risk populations on non-health outcomes in adolescence. *Children and Youth Services Review, 32,* 506–519.

Marcon, R. (1993). Socioemotional versus academic emphasis: Impact on kindergartners' development and achievement. *Early Child Development and Care, 96,* 81–91.

Marcon, R. (1999). Differential impact of preschool models on development and early learning of inner-city children: A three cohort study. *Developmental Psychology, 35,* 358–375.

Marcon, R. (2002). Moving up the grades: Relationships between preschool model and later school success. *Early Childhood Research and Practice, 4,* 517–530.

Marietta, G. (2010). *Lesson for PreK-3rd from Montgomery County Public Schools. An FCD case study.* New York: Foundation for Child Development.

Martin, A., Brooks-Gunn, J., Klebanov, P., Buka, S.L., & McCormick, M.C. (2008). Long-term maternal effects of early childhood intervention: Findings from the Infant Health and Development Program (IHDP). *Journal of Applied Developmental Psychology, 29*(2), 101–117.

Mashburn, A.J., Justice, L., Downer, J.T., & Pianta, R.C. (2009). Peer effects on children's language achievement during prekindergarten. *Child Development, 80*(3), 686–702.

Mashburn, A.J., Pianta, R.C., Hamre, B.K., Downer, J.T., Barbarin, O.A., Bryant, D., et al. (2008). Measures of classroom quality in prekindergarten and children's development of academic, language, and social skills. *Child Development, 79*(3), 732–749.

Masse, L.N., & Barnett, W.S. (2002). *A benefit–cost analysis of the Abecedarian early childhood intervention.* New Brunswick, NJ: National Institute for Early Education Research.

Matthews, H., & Lim, T. (2009). *Infants and toddlers in CCDBG: 2009 Update.* Retrieved February 13, 2010, from http://www.clasp.org/admin/site/publications/files/ccdbg-participation_2009babies.pdf

Maxwell, K.L., & Clifford, R.M. (2006). Professional development issues in universal prekindergarten. In E. Zigler, W.S. Gilliam, & S.M. Jones (Eds.), *A vision for universal preschool education.* New York: Cambridge University Press.

Maxwell, K.L., Field, C.C., & Clifford, R.M. (2006). Defining and measuring professional development in early childhood research. In M. Zaslow & I. Martinez-Beck (Eds.), *Critical issues in early childhood professional development* (pp. 21–48). Baltimore: Paul H. Brookes Publishing Co.

McCabe, J. (1995). *A program evaluation: Does the Center Project effectively reduce parental stress?* Unpublished doctoral dissertation, University of Colorado at Denver.

McCall, R.B. (2009). *Evidence-based programming in the context of practice and policy.* Retrieved January 20, 2011, from http://www.srcd.org/index.php?option=com_docman&task=doc_download&Itemid=&gid=654

McCarton, C., Brooks-Gunn, J., Wallace, I., Bauer, C., Bennett, F., Bernbaum, J., et al. (1997). Results at 8 years of intervention for low birth weight premature infants: The Infant Health Development Program. *Journal of the American Medical Association, 227,* 126–132.

McDermott, P.A., Leigh, N.M., & Perry, M.A. (2002). Development and validation of the Preschool Learning Behaviors Scale. *Psychology in the Schools, 39,* 353–365.

McLanahan, S. (2004). Diverging destinies: How children are faring under the second demographic transition. *Demography, 41*(4), 607–627.

McWilliam, R., Scarborough, A., & Kim, H. (2003). Adult interactions and child engagement. *Early Education & Development, 14,* 7–27.

Meaney, M.J. (2001). Maternal care, gene expression, and the transmission of individual differences in stress reactivity across generations. *Annual Reviews in Neuroscience, 24,* 1161–1192.

Mehana, M., & Reynolds, A.J. (2004). School mobility and achievement: A meta-analysis. *Children and Youth Services Review, 26,* 93–119.

Meisels, S.J. (1999). Assessing readiness. In R.C. Pianta & M. Cox (Eds.), *The transition to kindergarten* (pp. 39–66). Baltimore: Paul H. Brookes Publishing Co.

Meisels, S.J. (2007). Accountability in early childhood: No easy answers. In R.C. Pianta, M.J. Cox, & K. Snow (Eds.), *School readiness, early learning, and the transition to kindergarten.* Baltimore: Paul H. Brookes Publishing Co.

Mero, P.T., & Sutherland Institute. (2007). *Vouchers, vows, and vexations: The historic dilemma over Utah's education identity.* Retrieved January 17, 2011, from http://www.sutherlandinstitute.org/uploads/vouchersvows.pdf

Milfort, R., & Greenfield, D.B. (2002). Teacher and observer ratings of Head Start children's social skills. *Early Childhood Research Quarterly, 17,* 581–595.

Miller, E., & Almon, J. (2009). *Crisis in the kindergarten: Why children need to play in school.* College Park, MD: Alliance for Childhood.

Ministere de l'Education Nationale. (2011). *Les guides des parents.* Retrieved January 10, 2011, from http://www.education.gouv.fr/pid23398/guide-pratique-des-parents-votre-enfant-ecole.html#/maternelle/

Minnesota Center for Professional Development. (2009). *Relationship-based professional development.* Retrieved December 21, 2009, from http://mncpd.org/rbpd.html

Minnesota Early Learning Foundation. (2009). *Annual report: Fiscal year 2008.* Retrieved December 1, 2009, from http://www.melf.us

Moon, S.H. (2010). *Multi-dimensional human skill formation with multi-dimensional parental investment.* Unpublished manuscript, University of Chicago.

Moore, E.K., & Phillips, C. (1989). Early public schooling: Is one solution right for all children? *Theory into Practice, 28*(1), 58–63.

Nation, M., Crusto, C., Wandersman, A., Kumpfer, K.L., Seybolt, D., Morrisey-Kane, E., et al. (2003). What works in prevention: Principles of effective prevention programs. *American Psychologist, 58,* 449–456.

National Academies. (2008). *Early childhood assessment: Why, what and how.* Washington, DC: National Academies Press.

National Association for Nursery Education. (1929). *Minimum essentials for nursery education.* Chicago, IL: Author.

National Association for the Education of Young Children. (1998). *Accreditation criteria and procedures of the National Academy of Early Childhood Programs.* Washington, DC: Author.

National Association for the Education of Young Children. (2001). *NAEYC standards for early childhood professional preparation initial licensure programs.* Retrieved January 6, 2011, from http://www.naeyc.org/ncate/standards

National Association for the Education of Young Children. (2003). *Early childhood curriculum, child assessment and program evaluation: Building an accountable and effective system for children birth through age eight. A joint position statement of NAEYC and NAECS/SDE.* Washington, DC: Author.

National Association for the Education of Young Children. (2005). *NAEYC early childhood program standards and accreditation criteria: The mark of quality in early childhood education.* Washington, DC: Author.

National Association for the Education of Young Children. (2009a). *Developmentally appropriate practice in early childhood programs serving children from birth to age 8: A position statement.* Retrieved June 5, 2009, from http://naeyc.org/about/positions/pdf/PSDAP.pdf

National Association for the Education of Young Children. (2009b). *NAEYC standards for early childhood professional preparation programs.* Washington, DC: Author.

National Association of Child Care Resource and Referral Agencies. (2008). *Parents' perceptions of child care in the United States.* Retrieved September 6, 2009, from http://www.naccrra.org/publications/naccrra-publications/parents-perceptions-of-child-care

National Association of Child Care Resource and Referral Agencies. (2009a). *Unequal opportunities for preschoolers: Differing standards for licensed child care centers and state-funded prekindergarten programs.* Washington, DC: Author.

National Association of Child Care Resource and Referral Agencies. (2009b). *We CAN do better: 2009 update: NACCRRA's ranking of state child care center regulation and oversight.* Retrieved December 9, 2009, from http://issuu.com/naccrra/docs/we-can-do-better-2009-update

National Association of Early Childhood Specialists in State Departments of Education. (2000). *STILL unacceptable trends in kindergarten entry and placement: A position statement developed by the National Association of Early Childhood Specialists in State Departments of Education.* Washington, DC: Author.

National Black Child Development Institute. (1985). *Child care in the public schools: Incubator for inequality?* Washington, DC: Author.

National Board for Professional Teaching Standards. (2001). *NBPTS early childhood generalist standards.* Retrieved January 6, 2011, from http://www.nbpts.org/userfiles/File/ec_gen_standards.pdf

National Center for Education Statistics. (2007). *Status and trends in the education of racial and ethnic minorities.* Retrieved January 3, 2011, from http://nces.ed.gov/pubs2007/minoritytrends/

National Center for Education Statistics. (2009). *Early Childhood Longitudinal Study–Kindergarten Class of 1998–99 (ECLS–K): Eighth grade methodology report.* Washington DC: Author.

National Center for Fair and Open Testing. (2007). *The case against high stakes testing.* Retrieved May 25, 2010, from http://www.fairtest.org/organizations-and-experts-opposed-high-stakes-test

National Child Care Information Center. (2007). *Child Care Bulletin, 32.* Retrieved February 16, 2011, from http://stage.nccic.org/files/resources/issue32.pdf

National Child Care Information Center. (2009). *Early childhood professional development systems toolkit.* Washington, DC: Child Care Bureau, Administration for Children and Families.

National Early Literacy Panel. (2009). *Developing early literacy.* Jessup, MD: C.J. Lonigan & T. Shanahan.

National Education Association. (2010). *Rankings and estimates: Rankings of the states 2009 and estimates of school statistics 2010.* Retrieved January 5, 2011, from http://www.nea.org/assets/docs/010rankings.pdf

National Institute of Child Health and Human Development, Early Child Care Research Network. (1996). Characteristics of infant child care: Factors contributing to positive care giving. *Early Childhood Research Quarterly, 11,* 269–306.

National Institute of Child Health and Human Development, Early Child Care Research Network. (1999). Child outcomes when child care center classes meet recommended standards of quality. *American Journal of Public Health, 89,* 1072–1077.

National Institute of Child Health and Human Development, Early Child Care Research Network. (2000). Characteristics and quality of child care for toddlers and preschoolers. *Applied Developmental Science, 4*(3), 116–135.

National Institute of Child Health and Human Development, Early Child Care Research Network. (2002a). Child-care structure, process, outcome: Direct and indirect effects of child-care quality on young children's development. *Psychological Science, 13*(2), 199–206.

National Institute of Child Health and Human Development, Early Care Research Network. (2002b). Early child care and children's development prior to school entry: Results from the NICHD Study of Early Child Care. *American Educational Research Journal, 39*(1), 133–164.

National Institute of Child Health and Human Development, Early Child Care Research Network. (2003). Does amount of time spent in child care predict socioemotional adjustment during the transition to kindergarten? *Child Development, 74*(4), 976–1005.

National Institute of Child Health and Human Development, Early Child Care Research Network. (2005a). *Childcare & child development: Results from the NICHD Study of Child Care and Youth Development.* New York: Guilford Press.

National Institute of Child Health and Human Development, Early Child Care Research Network (2005b). Early child care and children's development in the primary grades. *American Educational Research Journal, 42,* 537–570.

National Institute of Child Health and Human Development. (2005c). Pathways to reading: The role of oral language in the transition to reading. *Developmental Psychology, 41,* 428–442.

National Research Council. (2001). *Eager to learn: Educating our preschoolers.* Washington, DC: National Academies Press.

National Research Council. (2009). *Mathematics learning in early childhood: Paths toward excellence and equity.* Retrieved December 9, 2009, from http://www.nap.edu/openbook.php?record_id=12519&page=1

National Scientific Council on the Developing Child. (2008). *Mental health problems in early childhood can impair learning and behavior for life: Working paper #6.* Retrieved January 10, 2011, from http://developingchild.harvard.edu/library/reports_and_working_papers/working_papers/wp6/

National Scientific Council on the Developing Child. (2009). *Excessive stress disrupts the architecture of the developing brain.* Retrieved January 3, 2011, from http://developingchild.harvard.edu/index.php/library/reports_and_working_papers/working_papers/wp3/

Neidell, M., & Waldfogel, J. (2008). *Cognitive and non-cognitive peer effects in early education* (NBER Working Paper W14277). Cambridge, MA: National Bureau of Economic Research.

Nelson, G., Westhues, A., & MacLeod, J. (2003). A meta-analysis of longitudinal research on preschool prevention programs for children. *Prevention & Treatment, 6,* Article 31.

Nelson, K. (2007). Universalism versus targeting: The vulnerability of social insurance and means-tested minimum income protection in 18 countries, 1990–2002. *International Social Security Review, 60*(1), 33–58.

Neugebauer, R. (2003). *Update on child care in the public schools.* Redmond, WA: Exchange Press.

Neuman, S., & Roskos, K. (1992). Literacy objects as cultural tools: Effects on children's literacy behaviors during play. *Reading Research Quarterly, 27,* 203–223.

Newman, L.S. (1990). Intentional and unintentional memory in young children: Remembering vs. playing. *Journal of Experimental Child Psychology, 50,* 243–258.

Nichols, S.L., & Berliner, D.C. (2007). *Collateral damage: How high-stakes testing corrupts America's schools.* Cambridge, MA: Harvard Education Press.

Nicolopoulou, A., McDowell, J., & Brockmeyer, C. (2006). Narrative play and emergent literacy: Storytelling and story-acting meet journal writing. In D. Singer, R. Golinkoff, & K. Hirsh-Pasek (Eds.), *Play = learning: How play motivates and enhances children's cognitive and social-emotional growth* (pp. 124–144). New York: Oxford University Press.

No Child Left Behind Act of 2001, PL 107-110, 115 Stat. 1425, 20 U.S.C. §§ 6301 *et seq.*

Nores, M., Belfield, C.R., & Barnett, W.S. (2005). Updating the economic impacts of the High/Scope Perry Preschool Program. *Educational Evaluation and Policy Analysis, 27*(3), 245–261.

Nye, B., Konstantopoulos, S., & Hedges, L. (2004). How large are teacher effects? *Educational Evaluation and Policy Analysis, 26,* 237–257.

Obama, B. (2008). *Barack Obama: A champion for children.* Retrieved May 15, 2009, from www.barackobama.com/pdf/issues/FactSheetChildAdvocacy.pdf

Olds, D.L. (2002). Prenatal and infancy home visiting by nurses: From randomized trials to community replication. *Prevention Science, 3*(2), 153–172.

Olds, D., Eckenrode, J., Henderson, C.R., Jr., Kitzman, H., Powers, J., Cole, R., et al.. (1997). Long-term effects of nurse home visitation on maternal life course and child abuse and neglect: fifteen-year follow up of a randomized trial. *JAMA, 278,* 637–643.

Olds, D., Henderson, C., Kitzman, H., & Cole, R. (1995). Effects of prenatal and infancy nurse home visitation on surveillance of child maltreatment. *Pediatrics, 95,* 365–372.

Olds, D.L., Henderson, C.R., Phelps, C., Kitzman, H., & Hanks, C. (1993). Effects of prenatal and infancy nurse home visitation on government spending. *Medical Care, 31,* 155–174.

Olds, D.L., Kitzman, H., Cole, R., Robinson, J., Sidora, K., Luckey, D.W., et al. (2004). Effects of nurse home-visiting on maternal life course and child development: Age 6 follow-up results of a randomized trial. *Pediatrics, 114,* 1550–1559.

Olds, D., Robinson, J., O'Brien, R., Luckey, D.W., Pettitt, L.M., Henderson, C.R., et al. (2002). Home visiting by paraprofessionals and by nurses: A randomized, controlled trial. *Pediatrics, 110*(3), 486–496.

Olds, D.L., Sadler, L., & Kitzman, H. (2007). Programs for parents of infants and toddlers: Recent evidence from randomized trials. *Journal of Child Psychology and Psychiatry, 48,* 355–391.

Olsen, D., & Snell, L. (2006). *Assessing proposals for preschool and kindergarten: Essential information for parents, taxpayers and policymakers.* Los Angeles: The Reason Foundation.

Osborne, A.F., & Milbank, J.E. (1987). *The effects of early education: A report from the Child Health and Education Study.* Oxford: Clarendon Press.

Owocki, G. (1999). *Literacy through play.* Portsmouth, NH: Heinemann.

Pagley, C. (1999, July 26). Students getting younger. *The Oklahoman.*

Palardy, G., & Rumberger, R. (2008). Teacher effectiveness in first grade: The importance of background qualifications, attitudes, and instructional practices for student learning. *Educational Evaluation and Policy Analysis, 30,* 111–140.

Park, J. (2007). *Early Childhood Longitudinal Study, birth cohort: Longitudinal 9-month-preschool restricted-use data file and electronic codebook.* Washington, DC: National Center for Education Statistics.

Patton, M.Q. (2008). *Utilization-focused evaluation* (4th ed.). Thousand Oaks, CA: Sage Publications.

Peisner-Feinberg, E., Burchinal, M., Clifford, R., Culkin, M., Howes, C., Kagan, S., et al. (2001). The relation of preschool child-care quality to children's cognitive and social developmental trajectories through second grade. *Child Development, 72*(5), 1534–1553.

Peisner-Feinberg, E., Burchinal, M., Clifford, R., Yazejian, N., Culkin, M., Zelazo, J., et al. (1999). *The children of the Cost, Quality, and Outcomes Study go to school.* Chapel Hill: University of North Carolina, FPG Child Development Center.

Pellegrini, A. (2009). Research and policy on children's play. *Child Development Perspectives, 3,* 131–136.

Pellegrini, A.D., & Galda, L. (1990). Children's play, language, and early literacy. *Topics in Language Disorders, 10,* 76–88.

Pennsylvania Cross-Systems Technical Assistance Workgroup. (2007). *Cross systems technical assistance definitions.* Harrisburg, PA: Pennsylvania Early Learning Keys to Quality. Retrieved December 21, 2009, from http://www.pakeys.org/private/ta/ta_docs.asp?dtid=2

Perry, D.F., Dunne, M.C., McFadden, L., & Campbell, D. (2008). Reducing the risk for preschool expulsion: Mental health consultation for young children with challenging behaviors. *Journal of Child and Family Studies, 17,* 44–54.

Pew Center on the States. (2007). *Taking stock: Assessing and improving early childhood learning and program quality.* Retrieved January 3, 2011, from http://www.pewtrusts.org/our_work_report_detail.aspx?id=30962

Pew Center on the States. (2009). *Votes count: Legislative action on pre-K fiscal year 2010.* Retrieved January 3, 2011, from http://www.pewcenteronthestates.org/uploadedFiles/Votes_Count_2009.pdf

Pew Center on the States. (2010). *Leadership matters: Governors' pre-K proposals fiscal year 2010.* Retrieved January 3, 2011, from http://www.pewcenteronthestates.org/uploadedFiles/Leadership_Matters_Final.pdf

Phillips, D., Gormley, W., & Lowenstein, A. (2009). Inside the pre-kindergarten door: Classroom climate and instructional time in Tulsa's pre-K programs. *Early Childhood Research Quarterly, 24,* 213–228.

Phillips, D., Mekos, D., Scarr, S., McCartney, K., & Abbott-Shim, M. (2000). Within and beyond the classroom door: Assessing quality in child care centers. *Early Childhood Research Quarterly, 15*(4), 475–496.

Phillipsen, L., Burchinal, M., Howes, C., & Cryer, D. (1997). The prediction of process quality from structural features of child care. *Early Childhood Research Quarterly, 12,* 281–303.

Piaget, J. (1932). *Play, dreams, and imitation.* New York: Norton.

Piaget, J. (1970). *Science of education and the psychology of the child.* New York: Orion Press.

Pianta, R.C., Barnett, W.S., Burchinal, M., & Thornburg, K.R. (2009). The effects of preschool education: How public policy is or is not aligned with the evidence base, and what we need to know. *Psychological Science in the Public Interest, 10*(2), 49–88.

Pianta, R.C., & Cox, M.J. (Eds.). (1999). *The transition to kindergarten.* Baltimore: Paul H. Brookes Publishing Co.

Pianta, R.C., & Howes, C. (Eds.) (2009). *The promise of pre-K.* Baltimore: Paul H. Brookes Publishing Co.

Pianta, R.C., Howes, C., Burchinal, M., Bryant, D., Clifford, R., Early, C., et al. (2005). Features of pre-kindergarten programs, classrooms, and teachers: Do they predict observed classroom quality and child–teacher interactions? *Applied Developmental Science, 9,* 144–159.

Pianta, R.C., & Kraft-Sayre, M. (2003). *Successful kindergarten transition: Your guide to connecting children, families, and schools.* Baltimore: Paul H. Brookes Publishing Co.

Pianta, R.C., La Paro, K.M., & Hamre, B.K. (2008). *Classroom Assessment Scoring System™ (CLASS™).* Baltimore: Paul H. Brookes Publishing Co.

Pianta, R., Mashburn, A., Downer, J., Hamre, B., & Justice, L. (2008). Effects of web-mediated professional development resources on teacher–child interactions in pre-kindergarten classrooms. *Early Childhood Research Quarterly, 23,* 431–451.

Pianta, R., & Stuhlman, M. (2004). Teacher–child relationships and children's success in the first years of school. *School Psychology Review, 33,* 444–458.

Plutro, M. (2005). *Program performance standards: Supporting home language and English acquisition. Head Start Bulletin #78: English language learners.* Washington, DC: U.S. Department of Health and Human Services.

Posner, M., & Rothbart, M. (2000). Developing mechanisms of self-regulation. *Development and Psychopathology, 12*(3), 427–442.

Powell, D.R., Diamond, K.E., Burchinal, M.R., & Koehler, M.J. (2010). Effects of an early literacy professional development intervention on Head Start teachers and children. *Journal of Educational Psychology, 102*(2), 299–312.

Pre-K Now. (2009). *Votes count: Legislative action on pre-k fiscal year 2010.* Washington, DC: Pew Center on the States.

Preschool Curriculum Evaluation Research Consortium. (2008). *Effects of preschool curriculum programs on school readiness* (NCER 2008–2009). Washington, DC: National Center for Education Research, Institute of Education Sciences.

Promising Practices Network. (2009). *Programs that work to make children ready for school.* Retrieved December 9, 2009, from http://www.promisingpractices.net/programs_outcome_area.asp?outcomeid=27

Puma, M., Bell, S., Cook, R., Heid, C., Lopez, M., Zill, N., et al. (2005). *Head Start impact study: First year findings.* Washington, DC: U.S. Department of Health and Human Services.

Puma, M., Bell, S., Cook, R., Heid, C., Shapiro, G., Broene, P., et al. (2010). *Head Start impact study: Final report.* Washington, DC: U.S. Department of Health and Human Services.

Quality Education Data. (2005). *HighScope early childhood curriculum final report.* Denver, CO: Author.

Raikes, H. (1993). Relationship duration in infant care: Time with a high-ability teacher and infant teacher attachment. *Early Childhood Research Quarterly, 8*(3), 309–325.

Raikes, H. (1996). A secure base for babies: Applying attachment concepts to the infant care settings. *Young Children, 51*(5), 59–67.

Raikes, H., & Pope Edwards, C. (2009). *Extending the dance in infant and toddler caregiving.* Baltimore: Paul H. Brookes Publishing Co.

Ramey, C.T., & Campbell, F.A. (1984). Preventive education for high-risk children: Cognitive consequences of the Carolina Abecedarian Project. *American Journal of Mental Deficiency, 88,* 515–523.

Ramey, C.T., Campbell, F.A., Burchinal, M., Skinner, M.L., Gardner, D.M., & Ramey, S.L. (2000). Persistent effects of early intervention on high-risk children and their mothers. *Applied Developmental Science, 4,* 2–14.

Ramey, C.T., & Ramey, S.L. (1998a). Early intervention and early experience. *American Psychologist, 53,* 109–120.

Ramey, C.T., & Ramey, S.L. (1998b). The transition to school: Opportunities and challenges for children, families, educators, and communities. *Elementary School Journal, 98,* 293–295.

Ramey, S.L., Ramey, C.T., & Lanzi, R.G. (2004). The transition to school: Building on preschool foundations and preparing for lifelong learning. In E. Zigler & S.J. Styfco (Eds.), *The Head Start debates* (pp. 397–413). Baltimore: Paul H. Brookes Publishing Co.

Ramey, S.L., Ramey, C.T., Phillips, M.M., Lanzi, R.G., Brezausek, C., Katholi, C.R., et al. (2000). *Head Start children's entry into public school: A report on the National Head Start/Public School Early Childhood Transition Demonstration Study.* Birmingham: University of Alabama.

Raudenbush, S.W. (2009). Fifth annual Brown Lecture in education research. The Brown legacy and the O'Connor challenge: Transforming schools in the images of children's potential. *Educational Researcher, 38*(3), 169–180.

Raver, C.C. (2002). Emotions matter: Making the case for the role of young children's emotional development for early school readiness. *Social Policy Report, 16*(3), 3–24.

Raver, C.C. (2003). Young children's emotional development and school readiness. *ERIC/EECE Clearinghouse on Elementary and Early Childhood Education, 15,* 11.

Raver, C.C. (2004). Child care as a work support, a child-focused intervention, and as a job. In A.C. Crouter & A. Booth (Eds.), *Work-family challenges for low-income parents and their children.* Mahwah, NJ: Lawrence Erlbaum Associates.

Raver, C.C., Gershoff, E.T., & Aber, J.L. (2007). Testing equivalence of mediating models of income, parenting, and school readiness for White, Black, and Hispanic children in a national sample. *Child Development, 78,* 96–115.

Raver, C.C., Jones, A.S., Li-Grining, C.P., Metzger, M., Smallwood, K., & Sardin, L. (2008). Improving preschool classroom processes: Preliminary findings from a randomized trial implemented in Head Start settings. *Early Childhood Research Quarterly, 23,* 10–26.

Raver, C.C., Jones, S.M., Li-Grining, C.P., Zhai, F., Metzger, M.W., & Solomon, B. (2009). Targeting children's behavior problems in preschool classrooms: A cluster-randomized controlled trial. *Journal of Consulting and Clinical Psychology, 77,* 302–316.

Raver, C.C., & Zigler, E.F. (1991). Three steps forward, two steps back: Head Start and the measurement of social competence. *Young Children, 46,* 3–8.

Raver, C.C., & Zigler, E.F. (2004). Public policy viewpoint. Another step back? Assessing readiness in Head Start. *Young Children, 59,* 58–63.

Ravitch, D., & Null, W. (Eds.) (2006). *Forgotten heroes of American education: The great tradition of teaching teachers.* Greenwich, CT: Information Age.

Ray, B.D. (2009). *Homeschooling across America: Academic achievement and demographic characteristics.* Retrieved January 17, 2011, from http://www.nheri.org/Latest/Homeschooling-Across-America-Academic-Achievement-and-Demographic-Characteristics.html

Reichman, N.E., Teitler, J.O., Garfinkel, I., & McLanahan, S.S. (2001). Fragile families: Sample and design. *Children and Youth Services Review, 23,* 303–326.

Resnick, L.B. (1999, June 16). Making America smarter. *Education Week,* pp. 38–40.

Reynolds, A.J. (2000). *Success in early intervention: The Chicago Child-Parent Centers.* Lincoln: University of Nebraska Press.

Reynolds, A.J. (2003). The added value of continuing early intervention into the primary grades. In A.J. Reynolds, M.C. Wang, & H.J. Walberg (Eds.), *Early childhood programs for a new century* (pp. 163–196). Washington, DC: CWLA Press.

Reynolds, A.J. (2011). Age 26 cost–benefit analysis of the Child-Parent Center early education program. *Child Development, 82*(1), 379–404.

Reynolds, A.J., Mathieson, L.C., & Topitzes, J.W. (2009). Can early childhood intervention prevent child maltreatment? A review of research. *Child Maltreatment, 14,* 182–206.

Reynolds, A., Ou, S., & Topitzes, J.W. (2004). Paths of effects of early childhood intervention on educational attainment and delinquency: A confirmatory analysis of the Chicago Child-Parent Centers. *Child Development, 75,* 1299–1328.

Reynolds, A.J., Rolnick, A.J., Englund, M.E., & Temple, J.A. (Eds.). (2010). *Childhood programs and practices in the first decade of life: A human capital integration.* New York: Cambridge University Press.

Reynolds, A.J., & Temple, J.A. (1998). Extended early childhood intervention and school achievement: Age 13 findings from the Chicago Longitudinal Study. *Child Development, 69,* 231–246.

Reynolds, A.J., & Temple, J.A. (2008). Cost-effective early childhood development programs from preschool to third grade. *Annual Review of Clinical Psychology, 4,* 109–139.

Reynolds, A.J., Temple, J.A., Ou, S., Robertson, D.L., Mersky, J.P., Topitzes, J.W., & Niles, M.D. (2007). Effects of a school-based, early childhood intervention on adult health and well being: A 19-year follow up of low-income families. *Archives of Pediatrics & Adolescent Medicine, 161*(8), 730–739.

Reynolds, A.J., Temple, J.A., Robertson, D.L., & Mann, E.A. (2001). Long-term effects of an early intervention on educational achievement and juvenile arrest: A 15-year follow-up of low-income children in public schools. *JAMA, 285*(18), 2339–2346.

Reynolds, A.J., Temple, J.A., Robertson, D.L., & Mann, E.A. (2002). Age 21 cost–benefit analysis of the Title I Chicago Child-Parent Centers. *Educational Evaluation and Policy Analysis, 4*(24), 267–303.

Reynolds, A.J., Temple, J.A., White, B.A., Ou, S., & Robertson, D. L. (2011). Age 26 cost–benefit analysis of the Child-Parent Center early education program. *Child Development, 82,* 379–404.

Reynolds, A.J., Wang, M.C., & Walberg, H.J. (Eds.). (2003). *Early childhood programs for a new century.* Washington, DC: CWLA Press.

Riley-Ayers, S., & Frede, E. (2009). *Establishing the psychometric properties of a standards-derived performance based assessment: Can it be used for accountability as well as informing instruction?* Poster presented at the annual meeting of the American Educational Research Association, San Diego, CA.

Riley-Ayers, S., Frede, E., Barnett, W.S., & Brenneman, K. (2011). *Improving early education programs through data base decision making.* Retrieved February 23, 2011, from http://nieer.org/pdf/Preschool_Research_Design.pdf

Rimm-Kaufman, S., Curby, T., Grimm, K., Nathanson, L., & Brock, L. (2009). The contribution of children's self-regulation and classroom quality to children's adaptive behaviors in the kindergarten classroom. *Developmental Psychology, 45,* 958–972.

Rimm-Kaufman, S.E., Fan, X., Chiu, Y.-J., & You, W. (2007). The contribution of the Responsive Classroom Approach on children's academic achievement: Results from a three year longitudinal study. *Journal of School Psychology, 45,* 401–421.

Rindermann, H., & Ceci, S.J. (2008). *Education policy and country outcomes in international cognitive competence studies.* Graz, Austria: Institute of Psychology, Karl-Franzens-University Graz.

Ripple, C.H., Gilliam, W.S., Chanana, N., & Zigler, E. (1999). Will fifty cooks spoil the broth? The debate over entrusting Head Start to the states. *American Psychologist, 54*(5), 327–343.

Ritchie, S., & Willer, B.A. (Eds.). (2005). *Standard 6: Teachers: A guide to the NAEYC early childhood program standards and related accreditation criteria.* Washington, DC: National Association for the Education of Young Children.

Rolnick, A., & Grunewald, R. (2003). *Early childhood development: Economic development with a high public return.* Retrieved January 3, 2011, http://www.minneapolisfed.org/publications_papers/pub_display.cfm?id=3832

Rose, E. (2007). Where does preschool belong? Preschool policy and public education, 1965–present. In C.F. Kaestle & A.E. Lodewick (Eds.), *To educate a nation: Federal and national strategies of school reform* (pp. 281–303). Lawrence: University of Kansas Press.

Rose, E. (2010). *The promise of preschool: From Head Start to universal pre-kindergarten.* New York: Oxford University Press.

Rosenbaum, D.T., & Ruhm, C.J. (2007). Family expenditures on child care. *The B.E. Journal of Economic Analysis & Policy, 7*(1), Article 34.

Roskos, K., & Christie, J.F. (Eds.). (2002). *Play and literacy in early childhood: Research from multiple perspectives.* Mahwah, NJ: Lawrence Erlbaum Associates.

Roskos, K., & Christie, J. (2004). Examining the play–literacy interface: A critical review and future directions. In E.F. Zigler, D.G. Singer, & S.J. Bishop-Josef (Eds.), *Children's play: Roots of reading* (pp. 95–123). Washington, DC: ZERO TO THREE.

Ross, C., Emily, M., Meagher, C., & Carlson, B. (2008). *The Chicago program evaluation project: A picture of early childhood programs, teachers, and preschool age children in Chicago.* Princeton, NJ: Mathematica Policy Research.

Roth, J.L., & Brooks-Gunn, J. (2003). Youth development programs: Risks, prevention and policy. *Journal of Adolescent Health, 32,* 170–182.

Roth, J.L., Brooks-Gunn, J., Murray, L., & Foster, W. (1998). Promoting healthy adolescents: Synthesis of youth development program evaluations. *Journal of Research on Adolescence, 8,* 423–459.

Rothstein, J. (2008). *Teacher quality in educational production: Tracking, decay, and student achievement.* Cambridge, MA: National Bureau of Economic Research.

Rothstein, J. (2009). Student sorting and bias in value-added estimation: Selection on observables and unobservables. *Education Finance and Policy, 4*(4), 537–571.

Royce, J., Darlington, R., & Murray, H. (1983). Pooled analyses: Findings across studies. In Consortium for Longitudinal Studies (Ed.), *As the twig is bent: Lasting effects of preschool programs* (pp. 411–459). Mahwah, NJ: Lawrence Erlbaum Associates.

Rubin, D.B. (1997). Estimating causal effects from large data sets using propensity scores. *Annals of Internal Medicine, 127,* 757–763.

Rudner, L.M. (1999). Scholastic achievement and demographic characteristics of home school students in 1998. *Education Policy Analysis Archives, 7,* 8–47.

Rusk, D. (2006). Housing policy is school policy. In N.F. Watt, C. Ayoub, R.H. Bradley, J.E. Puma, & W.A. LeBeouf (Eds.), *The crisis in youth mental health. Vol. 4: Early intervention programs and policies* (pp. 347–371). Westport, CT: Praeger.

Ryan, K., & Cooper, J.M. (1998). *Those who can, teach* (12th ed.). Boston: Wadsworth Cengage Learning.

Ryan, S., & Ackerman, D.J. (2005, March 30). *Using pressure and support to create a qualified workforce.* Retrieved February 24, 2010, from http://epaa.asu.edu/epaa/v13n23/

Saluja, G., Early, D.M., & Clifford, R.M. (2002). Demographic characteristics of early childhood teachers and structural elements of early care and education in the United States. *Early Childhood Research and Practice, 4*(1). Retrieved January 5, 2010, from http://ecrp.uiuc.edu/v4n1/saluja.html

San Antonio Independent School District v. Rodriguez, 411 U.S. 1, 34-37 (1973).

Sandberg, J., & Hofferth, S. (2001). Changes in children's time with parents: United States, 1981–19. *Demography, 38*(3), 423–436.

Saracho, O.N., & Spodek, B. (2006). Young children's literacy-related play. *Early Child Development and Care, 176,* 707–721.

Sarama, J., & Clements, D.H. (2009a). *Early childhood mathematics education research: Learning trajectories for young children.* New York: Routledge.

Sarama, J., & Clements, D.H. (2009b). Teaching math in the primary grades: The learning trajectories approach. *Young Children, 64,* 63–65.

Scarborough, H.S. (2001). Connecting early language and literacy to later reading (dis)abilities: Evidence, theory, and practice. In S.B. Neuman & D.K. Dickinson (Eds.), *Handbook of early literacy research* (pp. 97–110). New York: Guilford.

Scarr, S., Eisenberg, M., & Deater-Deckard, K. (1994). Measurement of quality in child care centers. *Early Childhood Research Quarterly, 9*(2), 131–151.

Schatschneider, C., Buck, J., Torgesen, J.K., Wagner, R.K., Hassler, L., Hecht, S., et al. (2004). *A multivariate study of* factors that contribute to individual differences in performance on the Florida Comprehensive Reading Assessment Test. Technical report #5. Tallahassee, FL: Florida Center for Reading Research.

Schechter, C., & Bye, B. (2007). Preliminary evidence for the impact of mixed-income preschool on low-income children's language growth. *Early Childhood Research Quarterly, 22,* 137–146.

Schmitz, M.F., & Velez, M. (2003). Latino cultural differences in maternal assessments of attention deficit/hyperactivity symptoms in children. *Hispanic Journal of Behavioral Sciences, 25,* 110–122.

Schore, A. (2001). The effects of a secure attachment relationship on right brain development, affect regulation, and infant mental health. *Infant Mental Health Journal, 22,* 7–66.

Schore, A. (2003). *Affect dysregulation and disorders of the self.* New York: WW Norton.

Schore, A. (2005). Attachment, affect regulation, and the developing right brain: Linking developmental neuroscience to pediatrics. *Pediatrics in Review, 26,* 6.

Schuerger, J.M., & Witt, A.C. (1989). The temporal stability of individually tested intelligence. *Journal of Clinical Psychology, 45*(2), 294–302.

Schulman, K., & Barnett, W.S. (2005). *The benefits of prekindergarten for middle-income children.* New Brunswick, NJ: National Institute for Early Education Research. Retrieved January 3, 2011, from http://nieer.org/resources/policyreports/report3.pdf

Schulman, K., Blank, H., & Ewen, D. (1999). *Seeds of success: State prekindergarten initiatives, 1998-1999.* Washington, DC: Children's Defense Fund.

Schultz, T., & Kagan, S.L. (2007). *Taking stock: Assessing and improving early childhood learning and program quality.* Retrieved January 20, 2011, from http://www.pewtrusts.org/our_work.aspx?category=102

Schumacher, R., Greenberg, M., & Mezey, J. (2003, June 2). *Head Start reauthorization: A preliminary analysis of H.R. 2210, the School Readiness Act of 2003.* Washington, DC: Center for Law and Social Policy.

Schutz, G., Ursprung, H.W., & Wossmann, L. (2008). Education policy and equality of opportunity. *Kyklos, 61,* 279–308.

Schweinhart, L. (2004). *The HighScope Perry preschool study through age 40.* Ypsilanti, MI: HighScope Educational Research Foundation.

Schweinhart, L., Barnes, H., & Weikart, D. (1993). *Significant benefits: The HighScope Perry pre-school study through age 27.* Ypsilanti, MI: HighScope Press.

Schweinhart, L.J., Montie, J., Xiang, Z., Barnett, W.S., Belfield, C.R., & Nores, M. (2005). *Lifetime effects: The HighScope Perry preschool study through age 40.* Ypsilanti, MI: HighScope Press.

Schweinhart, L.J., & Weikart, D.P. (1997). *Lasting differences: The HighScope Preschool Curriculum Comparison Study through age 23.* Ypsilanti, MI: HighScope Press.

Schweinhart, L.J., Weikart, D., & Larner, M.B. (1986). Consequences of three preschool curriculum models through age 15. *Early Childhood Research Quarterly, 1,* 15–45.

Seitz, V. (1990). Intervention programs for impoverished children: A comparison of educational and family support models. *Annals of Child Development, 7,* 73–104.

Seitz, V., Rosenbaum, L.K, & Apfel, N.H. (1985). Effect of family support interventions: A ten-year follow up. *Child Development, 56,* 376–391.

Shanahan, T., & Barr, R. (1995). Reading Recovery: An independent evaluation of the effects of an early instructional intervention for at-risk learners. *Reading Research Quarterly, 30,* 958–996.

Shanker, A. (1987). The case for public school sponsorship of early childhood education revisited. In S.L. Kagan & E. Zigler (Eds.), *Early schooling: The national debate* (pp. 45–64). New Haven, CT: Yale University Press.

Shaw, D.S., Dishion, T.J., Supplee, L., Gardner, F., & Arnds, K. (2006). Randomized trial of a family-centered approach to the prevention of early conduct problems: 2-year effects of the family checkup in early childhood. *Journal of Consulting and Clinical Psychology, 74,* 1–9.

Shonkoff, J.P., & Phillips, D. (2000). *From neurons to neighborhoods: The science of early childhood development.* Washington, DC: National Academies Press.

Shore, R. (1998). *Ready schools.* Washington, DC: National Education Goals Panel.

Shore, R. (2009a). *PreK–3rd: What is the price tag?* New York: Foundation for Child Development.

Shore, R. (2009b). *The case for investing in preK–3rd education: Challenging myths about school reform.* New York: Foundation for Child Development.

Shumow, L., & Miller, J.D. (2001). Parents' at-home and at-school academic involvement with young adolescents. *Journal of Early Adolescence, 21*(1), 68–91.

Siegler, R.S. (1996). *Emerging minds: The process of change in children's thinking.* New York: Oxford.

Singer, D.G., Golinkoff, R.M., & Hirsh-Pasek, K. (Eds.). (2006). *Play = learning: How play motivates and enhances children's cognitive and social-emotional growth.* New York: Oxford University Press.

Singer, D.G., Singer, J.L. Plaskon, S.L., & Schweder, A.E. (2003). A role for play in the preschool curriculum. In S. Olfman (Ed.), *All work and no play: How educational reforms are harming our preschoolers* (pp. 59–101). Westport, CT: Greenwood Publishing Group.

Singer, J.L. (2002). Cognitive and affective implications of imaginative play in childhood. In M. Lewis (Ed.), *Child and adolescent psychiatry: A comprehensive textbook* (3rd ed., pp. 252–263). Philadelphia: Lippincott Williams & Wilkins.

Skodak, M., & Skeels, H.M. (1945). A follow-up study of children in adoptive homes. *Journal of Genetic Psychology, 66,* 21–58.

Smith, J.R., & Brooks-Gunn, J. (1997). Correlates and consequences of harsh discipline for young children. *Archives of Pediatrics and Adolescent Medicine, 151,* 777–786.

Smith, S., Davidson, S., & Weisenfeld, G. (2001). *Support for Early Literacy Assessment (SELA).* New York: New York University.

Snow, C.E., & Van Hemel, S.B. (Eds.). (2008). *Early childhood assessment: Why, what and how. Report of the Committee on Developmental Outcomes and Assessments for Young Children.* Washington, DC: National Academies Press.

Solomon, D. (2007). *As states tackle poverty, preschool gets high marks.* Retrieved January 3, 2011, from http://online.wsj.com/article/SB118660878464892191.html

Sosinsky, L.S., & Gilliam, W.S. (in press). Assistant teachers in prekindergarten programs: What roles do lead teachers feel assistants play in classroom management and teaching? *Early Education and Development.*

Sparling, J., & Lewis, I. (1981). *Learning games for the first three years: A program for parent/center partnership.* New York: Walker.

Sparling, J.J., & Lewis, I.S. (1985). *Partners for learning.* Winston-Salem, NC: Kaplan.

Sparling, J., & Lewis, I. (2007). *The Creative Curriculum Learning Games 36–48 months.* Bethesda, MD: Teaching Strategies.

Spence, S., Shapiro, D., & Zaidel, E. (1996). The role of the right hemisphere in the physiological and cognitive components of emotional processing. *Psychophysiology, 33,* 112–122.

Spiker, D., Ferguson, J., & Brooks-Gunn, J. (1993). Enhancing maternal interactive behavior and child social competence in low birth weight, premature infants. *Child Development, 64,* 754–768.

Sroufe, L.A. (1996). *Emotional development.* Cambridge, UK: Cambridge University Press.

Stanovich, K.E. (1992). Speculations on the causes and consequences of individual differences in early reading acquisition. In P. Gough, L. Ehri, & R. Treiman (Eds.), *Reading acquisition* (pp. 307–342). Mahwah, NJ: Lawrence Erlbaum Associates.

State of New Jersey Department of Education, Division of Early Childhood. (2009). *Preschool teaching and learning standards.* Retrieved February 24, 2011, from http://www.state.nj.us/education/cccs/2009/PreSchool.doc

State of New Jersey Department of Education, Division of Early Childhood. (2010a). *Preschool program implementation guidelines.* Retrieved February 24, 2011, from http://www.state.nj.us/education/ece/guide/impguidelines.pdf

State of New Jersey Department of Education, Division of Early Childhood. (2010b). *Teachers' manual for the NJ Early*

Learning Assessment System. Retrieved January 28, 2011, from http://www.state.nj.us/education/ece/archives/curriculum/elas/manual.pdf

Stecher, B.M. (2002). Consequences of large-scale, high-stakes testing on school and classroom practice. In L.S. Hamilton, S.P. Klein, & B.M. Stecher (Eds.), *Making sense of test-based accountability in education* (p. 79). Santa Monica, CA: Rand Corporation.

Stevens, A.H., & Schaller, J. (2009). *Short-run effects of parental job loss on children's academic achievement.* Cambridge, MA: National Bureau of Economic Research.

Stewart, A.K. (2009). *State writing test shows racial, income gap.* Retrieved January 17, 2011, from http://www.deseretnews.com/article/705342752/State-writing-test-shows-racial-income-gap.html

Stipek, D. (2002). *Motivation to learn: Integrating theory and practice* (4th ed.). Boston: Allyn & Bacon.

Stipek, D. (2004). Teaching practices in kindergarten and first grade: Different strokes for different folks. *Early Childhood Research Quarterly, 19,* 548–568.

Stipek, D. (2006). Accountability comes to preschool: Can we make it work for young children? *Phi Delta Kappan, 87*(10), 740–747.

Stipek, D., & Daniels, D. (1988). Declining perceptions of competence: A consequence of changes in the child or in the educational environment? *Journal of Educational Psychology, 80,* 352–356.

Stipek, D., Daniels, D., Galluzzo, D., & Milburn, S. (1992). Characterizing early childhood education programs for poor and middle-class children. *Early Childhood Research Quarterly, 7,* 1–19.

Stipek, D., Feiler, R., Byler, P., Ryan, R., Milburn, S., & Salmon, J. (1998). Good beginnings: What difference does the program make in preparing young children for school? *Journal of Applied Developmental Psychology, 19,* 41–66.

Stipek, D., Feiler, R., Daniels, D., & Milburn, S. (1995). Effects of different instructional approaches on young children's achievement and motivation. *Child Development, 66,* 209–223.

Stipek, D., Salmon, J., Givvin, K., Kazemi, E., Saxe, G., & Mac-Gyvers, V. (1998). The value (and convergence) of practices suggested by motivation researchers and mathematics education reformers. *Journal for Research in Mathematics Education, 29,* 465–488.

Stone, S.J., & Christie, J.F. (1996). Collaborative literacy learning during socio-dramatic play in a multiage (K–2) primary classroom. *Journal of Research in Childhood Education, 10,* 123–133.

Storch, S.A., & Whitehurst, G.J. (2001). The role of family and home in the literacy development of children from low-income backgrounds. In P.R. Britto & J. Brooks-Gunn (Eds.), *The role of family literacy environments in promoting young children's emerging literacy skills* (pp. 53–71). San Francisco: Jossey-Bass.

Strauss, V. (2003, January 17). U.S. to review Head Start program: Bush plan to assess 4-year-olds' progress stirs criticism. *Washington Post,* p. A1.

Stuber, J., & Schlesinger, M. (2006). Sources of stigma for means-tested government programs. *Social Science and Medicine, 63*(4), 933–945.

Stullich, S., Eisner, E., & McCrary, J. (2007). *National assessment of Title I final report—Volume I: Implementation.* Washington, DC: U.S. Department of Education.

Sullivan, W., & Rosin, M. (2008). *A new agenda for higher education: Shaping the life of the mind for practice.* New York: The Carnegie Foundation for the Advancement of Teaching.

Sullivan-Dudzic, L., Gearns, D.K., & Leavell, K. (2010). *Making a difference: 10 essential steps to building a PreK-3 system.* Thousand Oaks, CA: Corwin.

Suomi, S.J. (2004). How gene-environment interactions can influence emotional development in Rhesus monkeys. In C.E.L. Bearer & R.M. Lerner (Eds.), *Nature and nurture: The complex interplay of genetic and environmental influences on human behaviour and development* (pp. 35–51). Mahwah, NJ: Lawrence Erlbaum Associates.

Sussman, C., & Gillman, A. (2007). *Building early childhood facilities: What states can do to create supply and promote quality.* New Brunswick, NJ: National Institute for Early Education Research.

Sweet, M.A., & Appelbaum, M.I. (2004). Is home visiting an effective strategy? A meta-analytic review of home visiting programs for families with young children. *Child Development, 75,* 1435–1456.

Sylva, K., Melhuish, E., Sammons, P., Siraj-Blatchford, I., & Taggart, B. (2004). *The final report: Effective pre-school education. Technical paper 12.* London: Institute of Education, University of London.

Sylva, K., Melhuish, E., Sammons, P., Siraj-Blatchford, I., & Taggart, B. (2008). *Final report from the primary phase: Pre-school, school and family influences on children's development during key stage 2.* Nottingham, UK: Department for Children, Schools and Families.

Takanishi, R. (2009). *A new primary education system beginning with preK–third grade: A paradigm shift for early education.* Manuscript submitted for publication.

Takanishi, R. (2010). PreK–third grade: A paradigm shift. In V. Washington & J.D. Andrews (Eds.), *Children of 2020: Creating a better tomorrow* (pp. 28–31). Washington, DC: Council for Professional Recognition & National Association for the Education of Young Children.

Takanishi, R., & Kauerz, K. (2008). PK inclusion: Getting serious about a P–16 education system. *Phi Delta Kappan, 89*(7), 480–488.

Tamis-LeMonda, C.S., Uzgiris, I.C., & Bornstein, M. (2002). Play in parent–child interactions. In M. Bornstein (Ed.), *Handbook of parenting: Practical issues in parenting* (pp. 221–242). Mahwah, NJ: Lawrence Erlbaum Associates.

Tarullo, L.B., Vogel, A.C., Aikens, N., Martin, E.S., Nogales, R., & Del Grosso, P. (2008, December). *Implementation of the Head Start National Reporting System: Spring 2007 final report.* Retrieved February 10, 2010, from http://www.mathematica-mpr.com/publications/PDFs/EarlyChildhood/headstart_nrs2007

Temple, J.A., & Reynolds, A.J. (1999). School mobility and achievement: Longitudinal findings from an urban cohort. *Journal of School Psychology, 37,* 355–377.

Temple, J.A., & Reynolds, A.J. (2007). Benefits and costs of investments in preschool education: Evidence from the Child-Parent Centers and related programs. *Economics of Education Review, 26*(1), 126–144.

Thompson, R. (2009). Doing what doesn't come naturally: The development of self regulation. *Zero to Three, 30*(2), 33–39.

Todd, P.E., & Wolpin, K.I. (2003). On the specification and estimation of the production function for cognitive achievement. *The Economic Journal, 113*(485), 3–33.

Todd, P.E., & Wolpin, K.I. (2007). The production of cognitive achievement in children: Home, school, and racial test score gaps. *Journal of Human Capital, 1*(1), 91–136.

Torgesen, J., Schirm, A., Castner, L., Vartivarian, S., Mansfield, W., Myers, D., et al. (2007). *National assessment of Title I final report—Volume II: Closing the reading gap: Findings from a randomized trial of four reading interventions for striving readers.* Washington, DC: U.S. Department of Education, Institute of Education Sciences.

Torquati, J.C., Raikes, H., & Huddleston-Cass, C.A. (2007). Teacher education, motivation, compensation, workplace support, and links to quality of center-based child care and teachers' intention to stay in the early childhood profession. *Early Childhood Research Quarterly, 22,* 261–275.

Tout, K., Zaslow, M., & Berry, D. (2005). Quality and qualifications: Links between professional development and quality in early care and education settings. In M. Zaslow & I. Martinez-Beck (Eds.), *Critical issues in early childhood professional development* (pp. 77–110). Baltimore: Paul H. Brookes Publishing Co.

Tremblay, R., Pagani-Kurtz, L., Mâsse, L., Vitaro, F., & Pihl, R. (1995). A bimodal preventive intervention for disruptive kindergarten boys: Its impact through mid-adolescence. *Journal of Consulting and Clinical Psychology, 63,* 560–568.

Trust for Early Education. (2004, Fall). *A policy primer: Quality pre-kindergarten.* Retrieved May 16, 2008, from www.trustforearlyed.org/docs/TEE-Primer4.pdf

Unrau, Y.A. (2001). Using client exit interviews to illuminate outcomes in program logic models: A case example. *Evaluation and Program Planning, 24,* 353–361.

U.S. Advisory Board on Child Abuse and Neglect. (1991). *Creating caring communities: Blueprint for an effective federal policy for child abuse and neglect.* Washington, DC: U.S. Department of Health and Human Services.

U.S. Bureau of Labor Statistics. (2009). *Occupational employment and wages, May 2008. 25-2011 Preschool teachers, except special education.* Retrieved December 9, 2009, from http://www.bls.gov/oes/current/oes252011.htm

U.S. Bureau of Labor Statistics. (2010). *Child day care services.* Retrieved March 2, 2010, from http://www.bls.gov/oco/cg/cgs032.htm#earnings

U.S. Census Bureau. (2006). *Hispanics in the United States.* Retrieved March 25, 2008, from http://www.census.gov/population/www/socdemo/hispanic/hispanic_pop_presentation.html

U.S. Census Bureau. (2008a). *Educational attainment—Current population survey data on educational attainment.* Retrieved February 28, 2011, from http://www.census.gov/hhes/socdemo/education/data/cps/index.html

U.S. Census Bureau. (2008b). *School enrollment—Social and economic characteristics of students: October 2008.* Retrieved April 19, 2010, from http://www.census.gov/population/www/socdemo/school/cps2008.html

U.S. Department of Education. (2007). *The condition of education.* Retrieved January 17, 2011, from http://nces.ed.gov/programs/coe/

U.S. Department of Education. (2008a). *Effects of preschool program curriculum programs and school readiness: Report from the preschool curriculum evaluation research initiative.* Washington, DC: Institute for Education Sciences, National Center for Education Evaluation and Regional Assistance.

U.S. Department of Education. (2008b). *Higher education—Legislation: Editor's picks.* Retrieved January 3, 2011, from http://www2.ed.gov/policy/highered/leg/edpicks.jhtml

U.S. Department of Education. (2009a). *Evaluation of the DC Opportunity Scholarship Program.* Retrieved October 30, 2009, from http://ies.ed.gov/ncee/pubs/20094050/pdf/20094051.pdf

U.S. Department of Education. (2009b). *Initiatives: The early learning challenge fund: Results-oriented, standards reform of state early learning programs.* Retrieved January 3, 2011, from http://www2.ed.gov/about/inits/ed/earlylearning/elcf-factsheet.html

U.S. Department of Education. (2010). *A blueprint for reform: The reauthorization of the Elementary and Secondary Education Act.* Washington, DC: Author.

U.S. Department of Health and Human Services. (1994). *The statement of the Advisory Committee on Services for Families with Infants and Toddlers.* Washington, DC: Author.

U.S. Department of Health and Human Services. (2000). *Head Start child outcomes framework.* Washington, DC: Author.

U.S. Department of Health and Human Services. (2001). *Building their Futures: How Early Head Start programs are enhancing the lives of infants and toddlers in low-income families. Summary report.* Washington, DC: U.S. Department of Health and Human Services.

U.S. Department of Health and Human Services. (2002). *Making a difference in the lives of infants and toddlers and their families: The impacts of Early Head Start.* Washington, DC: U.S. Department of Health and Human Services.

U.S. Department of Health and Human Services. (2005). *Head Start Impact Study: First year findings.* Retrieved December 9, 2009, from http://www.acf.hhs.gov/programs/opre/hs/impact_study/reports/first_yr_finds/first_yr_finds.pdf

U.S. Department of Health and Human Services. (2006). *Findings from the survey of Early Head Start programs: Communities, programs, and families.* Washington, DC: U.S. Department of Health and Human Services.

U.S. Department of Health and Human Services. (2008). *Statutory degree and credentialing requirements for Head Start teaching staff (ACF-IM-HS-08-12).* Retrieved November 6, 2009, from http://www.acf.hhs.gov/programs/ohs/policy/im2008/acfimhs_08_12.html

U.S. Department of Health and Human Services. (2009a). *2008-09 Head Start program information report.* Retrieved January 5, 2011, from http://eclkc.ohs.acf.hhs.gov/hslc/Program%20Design%20and%20Management/Head%20Start%20Requirements/Program%20Information%20Report/2008-2009%20PIR%20Survey%20Changes_070809.pdf

U.S. Department of Health and Human Services. (2009b). *Quality features, dosage and thresholds and child outcomes: Study design.* Retrieved January 28, 2011, from http://www.acf.hhs.gov/programs/opre/cc/q_dot/qdot_overview.html

U.S. Department of Health and Human Services. (2010a). *About the child care and development fund.* Retrieved January 3, 2011, from http://www.acf.hhs.gov/programs/ccb/ccdf/index.htm

U.S. Department of Health and Human Services. (2010b). *Head Start impact study. Final report.* Washington, DC: Author.

U.S. Department of Health and Human Services. (2011). *Annual update of the HHS poverty guidelines.* 76(13) Fed. Reg. 3637–3638.

Vail, K. (2003, November). Ready to learn. What the Head Start debate about early academics means for your schools. *American School Board Journal, 190*(11). Retrieved May 25, 2005, from www.asbj.com/2003/11/1103coverstory.html

Vandell, D. (2004). Early child care: The known and the unknown. *Merrill-Palmer Quarterly, 50,* 387–414.

van de Walle, D. (1998). Targeting revisited. *World Bank Research Observer, 13*(2), 231–248.

Vecchiotti, S. (2003). Kindergarten: An overlooked educational policy priority. *SRCD Social Policy Report, 17*(2), 1–19.

Vega, W.A., Kolody, B., Aguilar-Gaxiola, S., & Catalano, R. (1999). Gaps in service utilization by Mexican Americans with mental health problems. *American Journal of Psychiatry, 156,* 928–934.

Vu, J.A., Jeon, H.-J., & Howes, C. (2008). Formal education, credential, or both: Early childhood program classroom practices. *Early Education and Development, 19*(3), 479–504.

Vygotsky, L. (1978). Play and its role in the mental development of the child. In J.K. Gardner (Ed.), *Readings in developmental psychology* (pp. 130–139). Boston: Little Brown.

Vygotsky, L. (1986). *Thought and language.* (A. Kozulin, Trans.). Cambridge, MA: The MIT Press. (Original work published 1934)

Wagner, M., & Clayton, S. (1999). The Parents as Teachers program: Results from two demonstrations. *Future of Children, 9,* 91–115.

Wagner, M., & Spiker, D. (2001). *Multisite parents as teachers evaluation: Experience and outcomes for children and families.* Menlo Park, CA: SRI International.

Walberg, H.J. (2007). *School choice: The findings* (1st ed.). Washington, DC: Cato Institute.

Waldfogel, J. (2006). Early childhood policy: A comparative perspective. In K. McCartney & D. Phillips (Eds.), *Blackwell Handbook of Early Childhood Development* (pp. 576–594), Oxford, UK: Blackwell Publishing.

Waldfogel, J., & Zhai, F. (2008). Effects of public preschool expenditures on the test scores of fourth graders: Evidence from TIMMS. *Educational Research and Evaluation, 14*(1), 9–28.

Wargo, S. (2008). *Hail to the new chief: A guide to the 2008 presidential candidates' education agenda.* Retrieved January 3, 2011, http://www.edutopia.org/whats-next-2008-politicseducation

Warren, J.R. (2002). *Graduation rates for choice and public school students in Milwaukee 2003–2008.* Retrieved January 17, 2011, from http://www.schoolchoicewi.org/data/currdev_links/2010-Grad-Study-1-31-2010.pdf

Wasik, B.H., Ramey, C.T., Bryant, S.M., & Sparling, J.J. (1990). A longitudinal study of two early intervention strategies: Project CARE. *Child Development, 61,* 1682–1696.

Wat, A. (2007). *Dollars and sense: A review of economic analyses of pre-K.* Washington, DC: Pre-K Now.

Wat, A. (2010). *The case for pre-K in education reform: A summary of program evaluation findings.* Retrieved January 3, 2011, from http://www.preknow.org/documents/thecaseforprek_april2010.pdf

Watson, S. (2010). *The right policy at the right time: The pew pre-kindergarten campaign.* Washington, DC: Pew Center on the States.

Weber, R., & Trauten, M. (2008). *A review of the literature in the child care and early education profession: Effective investments.* Corvallis, OR: Oregon Child Care Research Partnership.

Webster-Stratton, C., Reid, M.J., & Hammond, M. (2001). Preventing conduct problems, promoting social competence: A parent and teacher training partnership in Head Start. *Journal of Clinical Child Psychology, 30,* 283–302.

Webster-Stratton, C., Reid, M.J., & Hammond, M. (2004). Treating children with early-onset conduct problems: Intervention outcomes for parent, child, and teacher training. *Journal of Clinical Child and Adolescent Psychology, 33,* 105–124.

Webster-Stratton, C., Reid, M.J., & Stoolmiller, M. (2008). Preventing conduct problems and improving school readiness: Evaluation of the Incredible Years Teacher and Child Training Programs in high-risk schools. *Journal of Child Psychology and Psychiatry, 49,* 469–470.

Wehlage, G., Smith, G., & Lipman, P. (1992). Restructuring urban schools: The new futures experience. *American Educational Research Journal, 29,* 51–93.

Weikart, D.P. (1998). Changing early childhood development through educational intervention. *Preventive Medicine, 27,* 233–237.

Wessel, D. (2009, October 8). Wider health-care access pays off. *Wall Street Journal,* p. A2.

Westheimer, M. (Ed.). (2003). *Parents making a difference: International research on the Home Instruction for Parents of Preschool Youngsters (HIPPY) Program.* Jerusalem: The Hebrew University Magnes Press.

White, B.A., Temple, J.A, & Reynolds, A.J. (2010). Predicting adult criminal behavior from juvenile delinquency: Ex-ante vs. ex-post benefits of early intervention. *Advances in Life Course Research, 15,* 161–170.

Whitebook, M. (2002). *Estimating the size and components of the U.S. child care workforce and caregiving population.* Seattle: University of Washington, Human Services Policy Center.

Whitebook, M. (2003a). *Bachelor's degrees are best: Higher qualifications for pre-kindergarten teachers lead to better learning environments for children.* Washington, DC: Trust for Early Education.

Whitebook, M. (2003b). *Early education quality: Higher teacher qualifications for better learning environments—A review of the literature.* Berkeley: University of California at Berkeley, Institute for Research on Labor and Employment, Center for the Study of Child Care Employment.

Whitebook, M., Gomby, D., Bellm, D., Sakai, L., &. Kipnis, F. (2009). *Preparing teachers of young children: The current state of knowledge, and a blueprint for the future.* Berkeley, CA: Center for the Study of Child Care Employment, Institute for Research on Labor and Employment.

Whitebook, M., Sakai, L., Kipnis, F., Almaraz, M., Suarez, E., & Bellm, D. (2008). *Learning together: A study of six B.A. completion cohort programs in early care and education. Year I report.* Berkeley: University of California at Berkeley, Institute for Research on Labor and Employment, Center for the Study of Child Care Employment.

Whitehurst, G.J. (2001). Young Einsteins: Much too late. *Education Matters, 1*(2), 16–19.

Whyte, J.C., & Bull, R. (2008). Number games, magnitude representation, and basic number skills in preschoolers. *Developmental Psychology, 44,* 588–596.

Wiggins, A.K. (Ed.). (2009). *Preschool sequence and teacher handbook.* Charlottesville, VA: Core Knowledge Foundation.

Wilkins, R., & Frede, E. (2005). *Self-Assessment Validation System (SAVS) 2004–2005: Preliminary report on statewide progress in Abbott Preschool Program implementation.* Trenton: New Jersey Department of Education.

Winsler, A., Tran, H., Hartman, S., Madigan, A., Manfra, L., & Bleiker, C. (2008). School readiness gains made by ethnically diverse children in poverty attending center-based childcare and public school pre-kindergarten programs. *Early Childhood Research Quarterly, 23*(3), 314–329.

Winter, M., & Rouse, J.M. (1991, September). Parents as Teachers: Nurturing literacy in the very young. *Zero to Three,* 80–83.

Witte, D.E. (1996). People v. Bennett: Analytic approaches to recognizing a fundamental parental right under the Ninth Amendment. *Brigham Young University Law Review, 1,* 183–280.

Witte, D.E. (2003). *Benjamin Franklin—Practical wise man.* Retrieved January 17, 2011, from http://www.quaqua.org/franklin.htm

Witte, D.E. (2009). *Massachusetts Bay Colony.* Retrieved January 17, 2011, from http://www.quaqua.org/pilgrim.htm

Witte, D.E. (2010a). *Fostering educational innovation in choice-based multi-venue and government single-venue settings.* Retrieved January 17, 2011, from http://sutherlandinstitute.org/uploads/Choice-based_Educational_Innovation.pdf

Witte, D.E. (2010b). *Fostering innovation in Utah schools: Common elements of educational success.* Retrieved January 17, 2011, from http://sutherlandinstitute.org/uploads/Fostering_Innovation_in_Utah_Schools.pdf

Witte, D.E., & Mero, P.T. (2008). Removing classrooms from the battlefield: Liberty, paternalism, and the redemptive promise of educational choice. *Brigham Young University Law Review, 2,* 377–414.

Wolf, P.J. (2008). School voucher programs: What the research says about parental school choice. *Brigham Young University Law Review, 2,* 415–446.

Wolf, P.J. (2009). *Lost opportunities: Lawmakers threaten D.C. scholarships despite evidence of benefits.* Retrieved January 17, 2011, from http://educationnext.org/files/ednext_20094_wolf_unabridged.pdf

Wolfgang, C.H., Stannard, L.L., & Jones, I. (2003). Advanced construction play with LEGOs among preschoolers as a predictor of later school achievement in mathematics. *Early Child Development and Care, 173,* 467–475.

Wong, V.C., Cook, T.D., Barnett, W.S., & Jung, K. (2008). An effectiveness-based evaluation of five state pre-kindergarten programs. *Journal of Policy Analysis and Management, 27*(1), 122–154.

Woodcock, R.W., McGrew, K.S., & Mather, N. (2001). *Woodcock-Johnson Tests of Achievement III (WJ III).* Rolling Meadows: IL: Riverside.

Yazejian, N., & Bryant, D.M. (2010). *Promising early returns: Educare implementation study data, January 2010.* Chapel Hill, NC: FPG Child Development Institute.

Yoshikawa, H., & Knitzer, J. (1997). *Lessons from the field: Head Start mental health strategies to meet changing needs.* New York: National Center for Children in Poverty.

Youcha, G. (1995). *Minding the children: Child care in America from colonial times to the present.* New York: Scribner.

Young, K.T., Marsland, K.W., & Zigler, E. (1997). Regulatory status of center-based infant and toddler child care. *American Journal of Orthopsychiatry, 67,* 535–544.

Zaslow, M. (1991). Variation in child care quality and its implications for children. *Journal of Social Issues, 47,* 125–134.

Zaslow, M., Anderson, R., Redd, Z., Wessel, J., Tarullo, L., & Burchinal, M. (2010). *Quality dosage, thresholds, and features in early childhood settings: Literature review tables. OPRE 2011-5a.* Washington, DC: U.S. Department of Health and Human Services. Retrieved February 25, 2011, from http://www.acf.hhs.gov/programs/opre/cc/q_dot/index.html

Zaslow, M., & Martinez-Beck, I. (Eds.). (2006). *Critical issues in early childhood professional development.* Baltimore: Paul H. Brookes Publishing Co.

Zaslow, M., Reidy, M., Moorehouse, M., Halle, T., Calkins, J., & Margie, N.G. (2003). Progress and prospects on the development of indicators of school readiness. In *Child and youth indicators: Accomplishments and future directions.* Bethesda, MD: National Institutes of Health.

Zaslow, M., Tout, K., Halle, T., & Starr, R. (2010). Professional development for early educators: Reviewing and revising conceptualizations. In S. Neuman & D. Dickinson (Eds.), *Handbook of early literacy research* (Vol. 3, pp. 425–434). New York: Guilford Press.

Zaslow, M., Tout, K., Halle, T., Whittaker, J.V., & Lavelle, B. (2010). *Towards the identification of features of effective professional development for early childhood educators.* Retrieved January 28, 2011, from http://www2.ed.gov/rschstat/eval/professional-development/literature-review.pdf

Zhai, F., Brooks-Gunn, J., & Waldfogel, J. (2011). Head Start and urban children's school readiness: A birth cohort study in 18 cities. *Developmental Psychology, 47,* 134–152.

Zhai, F., Raver, C.C., Jones, S.M., Li-Grining, C.P., Pressler, E., Gao, Q., et al. (in preparation). Dosage effects of classroom-based interventions on child school readiness: Evidence from a randomized experiment in Head Start settings. *Journal of Policy Analysis and Management.*

Zigler, E. (1970). The environmental mystique: Training the intellect versus development of the child. *Childhood Education, 46,* 402–412.

Zigler, E. (1979). Head Start: Not a program but an evolving concept. In E.F. Zigler & J. Valentine (Eds.), *Project Head Start: A legacy of the war on poverty* (pp. 367–378). New York: Free Press.

Zigler, E. (1984). Foreword. In B. Biber (Ed.), *Education and psychological development* (pp. ix–xi). New Haven, CT: Yale University Press.

Zigler, E.F. (1994). Foreword. In M. Hyson (Ed.), *The emotional development of young children: Building an emotion-centered curriculum* (pp. ix–x). New York: Teachers College Press.

Zigler, E.F. (2007). Giving intervention a head start: A conversation with Edward Zigler. *Educational Leadership, 65,* 8–14.

Zigler, E., & Berman, W. (1983). Discerning the future of early childhood intervention. *American Psychologist, 38,* 894–906.

Zigler, E., & Bishop-Josef, S. (2004). Play under siege: A historical overview. In E. Zigler, D.G. Singer, & S. Bishop-Josef (Eds.), *Children's play: The roots of reading* (pp. 1–13). Washington, DC: ZERO TO THREE.

Zigler, E.F., & Bishop-Josef, S.J. (2006). The cognitive child versus the whole child: Lessons from 40 years of Head Start. In D. Singer, R. Golinkoff, & K. Hirsh-Pasek (Eds.), *Play = learning: How play motivates and enhances children's cognitive and social-emotional growth* (pp. 15–35). New York: Oxford University Press.

Zigler, E., & Butterfield, E.C. (1968). Motivational aspects of changes in IQ test performance of culturally deprived nursery school children. *Child Development, 39,* 1–14.

Zigler, E., & Finn-Stevenson, M. (2007). From research to policy and practice: The school of the 21st century. *American Journal of Orthopsychiatry, 77*(2), 175–181.

Zigler, E., Gilliam, W.S., & Jones, S.M. (2006a). *A vision for universal preschool education.* New York: Cambridge University Press.

Zigler, E., Gilliam, W., & Jones, S.M. (2006b). What the School of the 21st Century can teach us about universal preschool. In E. Zigler, W. Gilliam, & S.M. Jones, *A vision for universal preschool education* (pp.194–215) . New York: Cambridge University Press.

Zigler, E., & Jones, S.M. (2002). Reflections—Where do we go from here? In B. Bowman (Ed.), *Love to read: Preparing African-American children for reading success* (pp. 83–93). Washington, DC: U.S. Department of Education, Office of Educational Research and Improvement.

Zigler, E., Marsland, K., & Lord, H. (2009). *The tragedy of child care in America.* New Haven, CT: Yale University.

Zigler, E., Pfannenstiel, J., & Seitz, V. (2008). The Parents as Teachers program and school success: A replication and extension. *Journal of Primary Prevention, 29,* 103–120.

Zigler, E.F., Singer, D.G., & Bishop-Josef, S.J. (Eds.) (2004). *Children's play: The roots of reading.* Washington, DC: ZERO TO THREE.

Zigler, E., & Styfco, S.J. (Eds.). (1993). *Head Start and beyond: A national plan for extended childhood intervention.* New Haven, CT: Yale University Press.

Zigler, E., & Styfco, S.J. (2004). *The Head Start debates.* Baltimore: Paul H. Brookes Publishing Co.

Zigler, E., & Trickett, P. (1978). IQ, social competence, and evaluation of early childhood intervention programs. *American Psychologist, 33,* 789–798.

Zill, N. (1990). *Behavior problem index based on parent report.* Washington, DC: Child Trends.

Zill, N. (2003). *Letter naming task.* Rockville, MD: Westat.

Zill, N., Resnick, G., Kim, K., O'Donnell, K., Sorongon, A., McKey, R.H., et al. (2003). *Head Start FACES (2000): A whole child perspective on program performance—Fourth progress report.* Retrieved December 9, 2009, from http://www.acf.hhs.gov/programs/opre/hs/faces/reports/faces00_4thprogress/faces00_4thprogress.pdf

Index

Page numbers followed by *f* indicate figures; those followed by *t* indicate tables.